'Incisive, academic, and witty, Jason Pack pulls no punches in his sharp critique of the so-called "international community". He demonstrates how, together with their Libyan allies, international actors perpetuated and, in some cases profited from, Libya's descent into chaos. *Libya and the Global Enduring Disorder* is a timely reminder of how aspects of today's era of global disorder exacerbate governmental dysfunction, encourage rampant corruption, and provide impunity for human rights abusers. In addition to accurately diagnosing Libya's problems, Pack provides some good recommendations on the way forward, particularly with regard to measures to improve the performance and transparency of Libya's economic and financial institutions.'

Stephanie Williams, Former Acting UN Envoy for Libya

'*Libya and the Global Enduring Disorder* is your authoritative guide through the dense complexity of post-Qadhafi Libya as well as the intricate, self-serving world of Libya policy in Washington. Harnessing his extensive business experience, deep historical knowledge, and personal familiarity with the protagonists inside and outside Libya, Jason Pack tells his story with flair, erudition, and occasional humour. His book is a must-read for anyone in western capitals serious about understanding Libya.'

Julian Borger, World Affairs Editor, *The Guardian*

'Candid, opinionated, by turns gossipy and scholarly, Jason Pack delivers a lively and provocative assessment of the state of the current global system through the lens of his deeply informed and instructive appraisal of post-Qadhafi Libya. Pack's acerbic assessment of the international system is not for the faint of heart. His portrayal of the consequences of today's global disorder on Libya is a powerful illustration of his argument—and a devastating indictment of the 'international community.''

Lisa Anderson, Past President American University of Cairo

'*Libya and the Global Enduring Disorder* employs a novel method in its investigation of recent events in Libya, examining the circumstances that drove the country's conflicts and crises in order to illustrate the broader breakdown in the international system. Jason Pack explains recent trends in international politics—including the lack of US leadership, divisions in Europe and heightened competition between regional powers. He illustrates that the failure of international collective action towards Libya is an excellent model for demonstrating the importance of reforming the United Nations and multilateral institutions more broadly. The book is essential reading, not only for scholars of the Middle East, but for all those who are interested in understanding today's changing international system.'

Peter Millett, former British ambassador to Libya (2015–2018)

'With his riveting new book, *Libya and the Global Enduring Disorder*, Jason Pack has strengthened his reputation as a leading writer on modern Libya. This revelatory work explodes some of the harmful myths about this poorly misunderstood Mediterranean country and its people. His exploration of the Enduring Disorder impact on post-Qadhafi Libya and the true motives of those who are profiteering from the lack of coherent international collective action may make uncomfortable reading for those who worked to liberate Libya in 2011. However, his penetrating analysis– based on meticulous research and personal experience—also provides a practical way forward to reintegrate Libya into the international community. This is a must-read book for anyone interested in understanding how global organizations have become paralysed in the 21st century.'

Rupert Wieloch, Senior British Military Commander in Libya
(2011 and 2012)

'*Libya and the Global Enduring Disorder* draws upon Jason Pack's deep knowledge of Libya's history and his personal participation in the country's contemporary politics to introduce a new paradigm to the broader field of international relations theory. He uses the Libyan microcosm to shed light on the main geopolitical dynamics in action in the contemporary world. The book's narration is brilliantly enriched by the author's reflections on his many direct experiences transacting business and undertaking research in key areas of the geopolitical chessboard–thus adding a high degree of originality, nuance, and readability.'

Karim Mezran, Director of the North Africa Initiative and Senior Fellow,
The Atlantic Council

'In *Libya and the Global Enduring Disorder*, Jason Pack makes an essential contribution to the literature on post-revolutionary Libya by diagnosing the underlying economic roots of the country's ongoing conflict. Pack's innovative assessments demonstrate how the institutions created in the Qadhafi era have acquired "semi-sovereignty" since 2011, dispelling the myth that modern Libya does not have institutions. He argues instead that it has the wrong ones, and that the current set of institutions are at the heart of Libya's problems.'

Tim Eaton, Senior Research Fellow, Chatham House

LIBYA AND THE GLOBAL ENDURING DISORDER

JASON PACK

Libya and the
Global Enduring Disorder

OXFORD
UNIVERSITY PRESS

Oxford University Press is a department of the
University of Oxford. It furthers the University's objective
of excellence in research, scholarship, and education
by publishing worldwide.

Oxford   New York
Auckland   Cape Town   Dar es Salaam   Hong Kong   Karachi
Kuala Lumpur   Madrid   Melbourne   Mexico City   Nairobi
New Delhi   Shanghai   Taipei   Toronto

With offices in
Argentina   Austria   Brazil   Chile   Czech Republic   France   Greece
Guatemala   Hungary   Italy   Japan   Poland   Portugal   Singapore
South Korea   Switzerland   Thailand   Turkey   Ukraine   Vietnam

Oxford is a registered trade mark of Oxford University Press
in the UK and certain other countries.

Published in the United States of America by
Oxford University Press
198 Madison Avenue, New York, NY 10016

Library of Congress Cataloging-in-Publication Data is available
Jason Pack.
Libya and the Global Enduring Disorder.
ISBN: 9780197631317

Printed in the United KIngdom on acid-free paper by
Bell and Bain Ltd, Glasgow

For Polybius, the first historian of the Global System, who more than twenty-one centuries ago wrote:

Now up to this time the world's history had been, so to speak, a series of disconnected transactions, as widely separated in their origin and results as in their localities. But from this time forth History becomes a connected whole: the affairs of Italy and Libya are involved with those of Asia and Greece, and the tendency of all is to unity.

Book 1, Chapter 3, Polybius of Megalopolis (200BC–c. 118BC),
The Histories, 1889 Translation of Evelyn Shuckburgh

Just as Fortune made almost all the affairs of the world incline in one direction, and forced them to converge upon one and the same point; so, it is my task as an historian to put before my readers a compendious view of the part played by Fortune in bringing about the general catastrophe... I thought it, therefore, distinctly my duty neither to pass by myself, nor allow anyone else to pass by, without full study, a characteristic specimen of the dealings of Fortune at once brilliant and instructive in the highest degree.... It is only by the combination and comparison of the separate parts of the whole ... that a man can obtain a view at once clear and complete; and thus secure both the profit and the delight of History.

Book 1, Chapter 4, Polybius, *The Histories*, Shuckburgh translation

CONTENTS

ABOUT THE AUTHOR

Born in 1980 in Manhattan and raised in New Jersey, Jason majored in Biology at Williams College. The shocking events of 11 September 2001 changed his life. Shortly thereafter, he abandoned his senior thesis involving implanting mice with blood pressure measuring telemeters, deciding instead to grow a beard and move to Beirut. Little did he know that nearly all Lebanese university students are clean shaven. He went on to study in Morocco, Jordan, and Egypt. In Autumn 2003, when he was ready to take the next leap forward with his Arabic, his parents forbade him from travelling to Yemen. He responded by going to Baghdad and Karbala.

Between 2004–5, he was a Fulbright Scholar in Syria focusing on French policy towards the Alawites. This focus continued into his first attempt at graduate work at Oxford, which he abandoned in the Autumn of 2008 to move to Libya to assist Western businesses in understanding the late Qadhafi-era reforms. After that consulting project went bust due to a backpayment issue, he became the Program Manager of the US-Libya Business Association under the tutelage of the Sage from West Virginia, where together they attempted to help other business with their backpayment issues. In Autumn 2010, he returned to Oxford to give graduate school another try. When the Arab Spring kicked off in 2011, Jason drew upon his recent experiences in Tripoli to advise Western policymakers and appear in the media. The timing was also propitious to create his own consulting company. These distractions notwithstanding, he just about managed to complete his M.St. in Global and Imperial History at St Antony's College, Oxford Univeristy. At the University of Cambridge, where he was a PhD student from 2011–2015, he would not be so lucky.

As the side businesses grew in complexity and the PhD became more protracted than one of General Haftar's attempts to 'liberate' a city against its will, it made sense to give academia a break for a while. In 2015, prior to ISIS's capture of Sirte, he founded a charity, Eye on ISIS, a NJ-registered 501(c)3, dedicated to calling attention to the jihadi threat by promulgating accurate real-time information about the activities of ISIS in Libya. In 2017–18, he returned to Washington, DC to serve as the Executive Director of the US-Libya Business Association.

A man who doesn't mind the fashion implications of wearing many hats on top of each other, he is currently the President of Libya-Analysis LLC, the Libya Analyst at CRCM North Africa, a Board Member at the American Chamber of Commerce in Libya, and a Senior Non-Resident Fellow at the Middle East Institute. In these various guises, Jason has worked with nearly every head of post-Qadhafi Libya's semi-sovereign institutions and almost every Fortune 500 company with business interests with those institutions. He has been personally invited by two different sitting Libyan Prime Ministers to organize a trade mission of U.S. companies to Libya. His commentary and analysis articles have appeared in *The New York Times*, *The Washington Post*, *The Wall Street Journal*, *The Guardian*, *The Financial Times*, *The Spectator*, *Newsweek*, *Foreign Policy*, and *Foreign Affairs*.

In addition to academic and policy writing focused on Libya, he publishes on U.S. politics, Brexit, Eastern Europe, wine tast-

ABOUT THE AUTHOR

ing, and ancient philosophy. He was the 2018 World Champion of Doubles Backgammon and is the CEO of Birthplace of Wine Experience. In 2020, Jason was awarded the UK Global Talent Visa after receiving the endorsement of the British Academy as a global leader in his subfield and an asset to the UK economy. He looks forward to calling London home.

ACKNOWLEDGEMENTS

Inspiration and motivation cannot be forced. Passion, dedication, and a glimmer of hope that the effort will make the world a better place are required to channel knowledge into output. After a futile decade trying to force myself to 'just finish up the PhD,' the following individuals have given me the support, guidance, insights, encouragement, comradery, and constructive criticism needed to bring this volume to fruition.

I must start by thanking Polybius—to whom this book is dedicated—for helping me muster the passion and the courage to attempt to write a universal history of our times by focusing on one primary conflict, and seeking to uncover through it, the causative dynamics playing out across the world system. Discovering his *Histories* at the start of the pandemic, his otherworldly prose effortlessly replaced human companionship: prompting trains of thought that resonated across the centuries with a 2017 suggestion from Michael Dwyer, the publisher at Hurst.

Over a glass of ancient style, Qvevri/Amphora-aged wine in my subterranean downtown DC apartment, Michael had suggested that I shelve my plans to organize wine tours to the Republic of Georgia, but instead write a book entitled, *Why Libya Matters?* He intended that such a book would address an

ACKNOWLEDGEMENTS

Anglo-American audience and explain why conflict in Libya (which many people think of as disconnected from broader geo-political developments and not as "important" as Syria, North Korea, or Israel-Palestine) was in fact causative of many of the core economic, demographic, and counterterrorism challenges facing the Western world. Michael's suggestion interacted with Polybius' broader perspective to mould this volume's primary concept: that Libya is central to the unique dynamics of our mid-21st century world and constitutes the ideal microcosm within which to examine them.

To investigate this bifocal thesis appropriately, I have had to brush up on many subfields: from International Relations theory, to the economics of Venezuela, to the geopolitics of Ukraine. Then on the Libya side, I have revisited my colleagues' work on jihadis, social media monitoring, militia mapping, investigative due diligence, and trend forecasting. In this feat, I have leaned hard on my team at Libya-Analysis LLC, as well as my friends, mentors, and colleagues. Nonetheless, this volume's controversial analyses and possible errors of foresight or hindsight are my responsibility alone.

* * *

Rhiannon Smith has been my partner at Libya-Analysis for seemingly two lifetimes. She is an incredibly talented researcher, editor, writer, and systematiser. Without her support, this book simply would not have been possible. The rest of the core Libya-Analysis Team—Sabina Henneberg, Mohamed Htewish, Verity Hubbard, and James Roslington—have all been instrumental in keeping me informed of developments on the ground, cross checking sources, proofreading drafts, and helping with the Russian, Arabic, French, and Ancient Greek source materials. That said it is critical to point out that this book is not a Libya-Analysis LLC product, and my teammates would have written it very differently if it were.

ACKNOWLEDGEMENTS

Karl Karim Zakhour has not only read every page of every draft, but his insights into the blind spots of Realist International Relations theory and the scholarship on neo-liberal economics have been most revelatory. Kerry McIntosh was a crucial support when the most challenging of the events described in Chapter 5 were unfolding, and since then she has been a rigorous editor and fellow traveller in the quest to compare the structures of post-Arab Spring and post-Soviet states. The retired American and British diplomats and officials who have lent their insights and feedback on the text are too numerous to list. A few need to be singled out, nonetheless. Former British Ambassadors to Libya Sir Vincent Fean, Peter Millett, and Richard Northern have been incredibly generous in sharing their friendship, perspectives, and interpretation of behind-the-scenes dynamics. On the Washington side of things, Ambassador David Mack and Nate Mason have provided much camaraderie and crucial insights on doing business with Libya. Although, there is not much of a New Jersey-based Libya expert community, Phillip Escaravage has compensated for that with truly Libyan levels of hospitality combined his with invaluable insights into the policy formation processes during the Trump years and deep background on intra-agency feuds over Libya.

It is impossible to be an expert of all fields at all times. I am grateful to those experts outside the Libya field who very generously helped me fill in gaps in my knowledge. Laura Cretney, Raul Gallegos, Joshua Landis, and various businessmen, economists, and diplomats who wish to remain anonymous were all particularly generous with their time and perspectives.

Over the years, my views about the Libyan economy's unique features have benefited from Abdul-Rahman al-Ageli, Husni Bey, Hamam Elfasi, Tim Eaton, Faisel Gergab, Ahmed Jehani, and Mustafa Sanalla's insights. I would also like to thank other Libyan colleagues who wish to remain anonymous, given the

ACKNOWLEDGEMENTS

sensitivity of many of the subjects dealt with in this volume, for their valuable contributions.

To the Sage from West Virginia: thank you for predicting the future, for pointing out that things can always get worse, and for helping me find both the humour and the tragedy in the patterns lurking behind the seeming chaos that is the U.S.-Libya commercial relationship. Speaking of which, only the rarest of individuals can fight against the flow of history and truly alter its course. Debbie Hirst, the Director of the American Chamber of Commerce in Libya, is one such titan. I admire you both greatly.

On all things publishing related, the insights and counsel of my St Antony's colleagues, Brian Klaas and Sasha Polakow-Suransky have been invaluable. Michael Athanson, deputy map librarian and geo-spatial data specialist at the Bodleian Library at Oxford University, produced the battle maps of the 2011 Libyan Uprisings and the territorial control maps relating to ISIS covering 2014–2017. On the Cambridge side of things, the late Professor Sir Christopher Bayly's perspectives on the British Empire, India, Africa, and Islam are all sorely missed. Professor Sir Christopher Clark's humour and insights into the Libya issue within 20th century European history will not be forgotten. Saul Kelly of Shrivenham and King's College London has been incredibly supportive, gracious, and patient with me over the years. Moreover, his scholarship has helped put Libya in its proper place within military history.

To those who have co-authored with me the various think tank reports, journal articles, and commentary pieces which form such an integral part of this volume, Alia Brahimi, Haley Cook-Simmons, Martin van Creveld, Mohamed Eljarh, Stefano Marcuzzi, Karim Mezran, Wolfgang Pusztai, Will Raynolds, James Roslington, Youssef Sawani, Brendan Simms, Rhiannon Smith, Lachlan Wilson, Anja Wollenberg, and Sami Zaptia: I believe scholarship is a team sport and I've been honoured to be

ACKNOWLEDGEMENTS

able to work together and learn from you. Special thanks are due to the *Atlantic Council*, *Istituto Affari Internazionali* (IAI Rome), *Istituto per gli studi di politica internazionale* (ISPI Milan), and the *Middle East Institute* (MEI) for graciously allowing the re-publication of my prior reports. To my colleagues at MEI, especially Jess Agostinelli, Emiliano Alessandri, Mietek Boduszyński, Rachel Dooley, Gerald Feierstein, Tamara Kalandiya, Colin Tait, and Alistair Taylor, it has been a pleasure to work together in keeping the Libya issue alive. My deepest gratitude is due to Ambassador Jonathan Winer for being a mentor, friend, and highly principled advocate for all policies which truly benefit both Libyans and Americans. His 'Afterword: How Global Competition Led to Chaos in Libya' is both a cogent summary of Libya's recent history and a *tour de force* explanation of why developments in Libya mirror global dynamics.

Lastly, my parents Fred and Sandy Pack have, through no fault of their own, been made to vicariously suffer the slings and arrows of outrageous fortune that life in the trenches of Libya policy has subjected me to. It has also been a pleasure to share the moments of joy that Libya occasionally provides. Thank you for being there to support me through those moments of struggle, betrayal, uncertainty, and coordination complexities. In this world of Enduring Disorder, you have remained reliable providers of order.

PREFACE

WELCOME TO THE ENDURING DISORDER

Today's international system is like a ship adrift during a pandemic. With the captain lost to the virus—and the most capable and conscientious members of the crew self-isolating in their cabins—the deck is now teeming with contagious megalomaniacs. Rather than collaborate, each thinks he knows how to steer the ship better than the admirals.

As the winds pick up, a fight breaks out among those scrambling to infiltrate the bridge. When the winners emerge from this melee and reach the captain's chair, some choose to deliberately steer into the choppiest waters—each clutching the steering wheel until a competitor bursts in behind them and ejects them from the hot seat. As the vessel craters from stem to stern, those with fainter constitutions or a greater respect for the competency hierarchy have simply chosen to retire to their cabins.

Will the crew eventually re-emerge from their quarters to put the technocrats back in charge? Might the most reckless passenger subjugate the others, lock the convalescent crew members in their quarters, and emerge as the new de facto captain? Or could some sort of self-sustaining equilibrium have been reached with the vessel zigging and zagging indefinitely, neither capsizing nor reaching port?

Questioning assumptions

From my vantage point watching US policy towards Libya veer this way and that over the years, the events of the spring and summer of 2019 stood out as a high watermark of chaos and contradiction with a multiplicity of relevant actors vying for prominence. They were also representative in microcosm of larger global trends. Witnessing them led me to question my assumptions about the West's future role in the world and the fundamental principles underpinning the international system. It was dawning on me that the contemporary ship of state had become permanently unmoored—careening back and forth due to contradictory decisions undertaken by ill-coordinated power centres.

Plato envisioned such a scenario in *The Republic*.[1] He warned that true democracy would lead to populism. Contempt for experts would ensue, eventually culminating in short-sighted and reversal-prone approaches to policy formation. He also warned that once this point was reached, it would be nearly impossible to put the genie back in the bottle.

Over the last few years, my day-to-day experience of the foreign policymaking process in Washington, London, and Tunis, and the resulting outcomes in Libya, seemed to be embodying Plato's forecasts. In keeping with this observation, this book proposes that the international system has exited the post-Cold War period with its well-established features and dynamics and entered a new historical epoch, termed 'The Enduring Disorder'. This new historical period, which remains under-researched, is characterized by its own structures, trends, and interactions. They are not scientific laws that can be definitively discovered through experimentation, but rather patterns and trendlines that need to be intuited from lived experience.

My main contentions about our historical moment are interrelated: (1) that the international system's interaction with Libya is an ideal arena to describe the key features of this new historical era, but that study of the Syrian, Yemeni, Venezuelan, or Ukrainian microcosms would likely work as well; and (2) that the Enduring Disorder will long outlast the specific sequence of events set in motion by former American President Donald Trump or any given Libyan warlord.

My analysis is that their emergence on the world stage was merely symptomatic of the Enduring Disorder, not its root cause. Actually, it is the Enduring Disorder that has given rise to Trump, Brexit, and the unique trajectories of state implosion that have befallen Libya, Yemen, and Syria.

A clandestine War on the Banks of the Potomac

On the ground in Libya in May 2019, the latest round of civil war had settled into an uneasy stalemate. Economic activity was stymied, the water and electricity grids were periodically shut down by the combatants, civilian casualties mounted, and international peace-making efforts had ground to a halt. The previously bustling southern suburbs of Tripoli were now crisscrossed by the ebb and flow of tanks and technicals.[2] A parallel war of manoeuvre was also unfolding on the banks of the Potomac. The allies of President Trump sought to outflank the permanent institutions of the US government in the tussle to shape American policy towards Libya's perpetual conflict.[3] This was yet another skirmish between familiar adversaries.

In the prior battles between Team Trump and the US institutions to set various aspects of Russia, Ukraine, and Middle East policy, each side had already demonstrated its unique strengths and weaknesses. This dynamic of Team Trump versus the institutions would become intimately familiar to all Americans during the tug-of-war to set the governmental response to the Covid pandemic.[4]

So what were the relative tactics of the adversaries? Trump's Twitter bravado was highly effective at manipulating the media but usually quite impotent at formally changing entrenched US governmental policies. Was the president actually trying to change American policy but exhibiting a lack of understanding of the tools open to the executive branch, or was he achieving his aim simply by strewing confusion, creating uncertainty, and preventing coherent coordination with America's traditional allies? Was the mere existence of the War on the Banks of the Potomac a victory for him, independent of the result of any of the skirmishes?

Conversely, American institutions such as the US Departments of State and Defense have robust procedures and deep bureaucratic inertia that help them stay the course, even when pressured by appointed partisans, but prevent them from using the media in a savvy way to communicate their official stances or call attention to internal malfeasance. Furthermore, Congress has the power to hold hearings, subpoena documents, withhold funds, and call for investigations, but it is only able to transcend its partisan divisions for relatively limited and uncomplicated objectives.

This internecine American fight over Libya has been mirrored by its allies' bureaucracies approach to the Libya file. In certain Italian administrations, such as that of Prime Minister Matteo Renzi, the Interior Ministry dominated Libya policy and quashed interagency rivals. In other Italian administrations, the portfolio was led by the Prime Minister's Office, as happened under Silvio Berlusconi, or the Foreign Ministry, as was the case under Paolo Gentiloni. In France, the President's Office and certain key individuals like Jean-Yves Le Drian have taken turns sidelining the permanent staff of the Quai d'Orsay in the formulation of Libya policy.[5]

To further increase the complexity, America's French and Italian allies were also constantly feuding with each other over Libya: each with their own specific business, migration, counterterror, and security interests. Conversely, the British, who traditionally attempted to harmonize otherwise divergent Western approaches towards the Middle East, had largely absented themselves from non-European foreign policy issues as Brexit negotiations sucked up most of their government capacity. At various times, certain American positions dovetailed with one of its top allies' stated goals, but at other times undermined them.

When is a phone call more than just a phone call?

On 7 April 2019, three days after the latest phase of the Libya war broke out in Tripoli on 4 April, Secretary of State Michael Pompeo broke the Trump Administration's silence by issuing an unusually stern condemnation of the aggressor, General Khalifa Haftar,[6] who had upended the UN peace process by attempting to conquer Tripoli just days before the flagship 'National Conference' scheduled for 14 April 2019. Haftar had even exhibited the unprecedented gall to launch his offensive by firing artillery shells into central Tripoli on the very day of UN Secretary General António Guterres's visit.[7] The symbolism was quite clear—Haftar was calling the international community's bluff. He might even have been acting on deep insights or intuitions about the prevailing international system. He certainly understood that at that precise moment the international arena was far too disunited to coordinate a coherent counterstroke against him, even in response to such brazen provocations.

Then, on 19 April, Trump made a surprise announcement that he had held a phone call with Haftar four days previously. The official call notes stated that the two men had discussed Haftar's role in global counterterrorism efforts.[8] Subsequent leaks concerning the call have provided evidence that they may also have discussed investments in beachfront real estate and the Virginia property market.[9]

Investigative reporting by *The New York Times* and *The Wall Street Journal* has since shown that the call was proximally occasioned by a request from Egyptian President Abdul Fateh al-Sisi during an in-person Oval Office meeting on 9 April.[10] At that same meeting, Trump rebuffed Sisi's one concrete policy demand concerning Libya, namely to 'recognize' Haftar as having some sort of official status as Libya's 'sovereign'. Trump conferred with his National Security Council (NSC) during a break in the meeting and then informed Sisi that that request would be impossible as US diplomatic practice concerning formal recognition of sovereign actors recognizes 'states', not governments or leaders, and as such did not allow President Trump to 'recognize' Haftar in the way that Sisi had requested.[11]

My discussions with various members of Trump's outer circle suggest that the NYT reporting[12] about the backstory to the call has uncovered most of the relevant chain of events, but that it could be wrong on one or two points. The NYT reporting suggested that prior to Sisi's request, National Security Advisor John Bolton had advocated for such a call. My own research[13] suggests that it was initiated solely by Trump, alongside possibly his son-in-law Jared Kushner, as a favour to Sisi (and *inter alia* the Saudis and Emiratis), in lieu of giving Sisi what he actually wanted—a formal change in US policy towards Haftar. American sources close to events corroborate that, as part of the extended follow up from the 9 April Trump–Sisi meeting, the president did not promise Sisi any specific future policy outcomes, merely that he would happily arrange to talk to Haftar.

Despite these conflicting reports from journalists and eyewitness observers, there are a few things that we can know for certain about the 15 April call. One is that no concrete policy proposals were in fact discussed and the call did not change official US policy in its formal support for—and legal recognition of—Haftar's opponents, the Tripoli-based UN-backed Government of National Accord (GNA). Despite this, the call did convincingly signal that the president 'might', at some indeterminate point in the future, be willing to covertly support Haftar, while formally adhering to American commitments to the GNA.[14]

Given this implication, the deliberate post-facto publicity about the call was consciously engineered by the White House to illustrate internationally that depending on changing battlefield conditions the US 'might' further support its Emirati and Egyptian allies by adopting a policy towards Haftar more akin to France's.[15] Those in the Middle East who would favour such a development became media cheerleaders for this interpretation of the call. For example, a commentator for the pro-Haftar outlet *Rai'i Al-Youm Libiyya* wrote: 'There is no explanation [for the phone call] between President Trump and Marshal Khalifa Haftar yesterday [other than] that [President Trump] approves of Haftar as the next Libyan president and [signals Trump's] complete support of the Egyptian, Saudi, and Emirati [positions towards Haftar].'[16] Despite this interpretation being pushed by cheerleading media, there could be no doubting that, if the flow of battle swung the other way, the United States might decisively revert to its established policy of backing the GNA and the UN peace process—an approach that is more in line with that of Britain, traditionally America's closest ally on Libya.

The publicity surrounding the call certainly reinforced the notion that Trump loves a winner. And hell, if General Haftar was gonna win, Trump would happily give him some tips about where to buy vacation properties in Virginia Beach. Trump's steering of the private 'confidence building' chit chat with General Haftar to real estate matters was not actually as ridiculous as it might seem.

PREFACE

For all those who think the former US president would give just any aspiring dictator tips about the greater DC holiday property market, I am sorry to disappoint. Trump was cleverly trying to find a point of common ground with Haftar, who he knew had spent more than two decades living in Virginia and whose family still owns various investment properties there.[17]

Just the tip of the iceberg

Presidential phones are about a lot more than what is or is not said on the line. The whole world was to witness this phenomenon in the Fall of 2019 with the release of the partial transcripts of the 25 July 2019 phone call between Presidents Trump and Volodymyr Zelensky of Ukraine. American presidential calls in which the executive appears to be sending different signals from official State Department policy or Congressional legislation are particularly problematic. To what extent are the president's innuendo or requests binding upon the rest of government? Do they constitute 'policy'?

Furthermore, each call generates its own optics. Given this, people in power might wish to submerge entirely, or selectively reveal, certain details about contentious presidential phone calls to control those optics. As such, the official notes on the phone calls represent merely the visible tip of the iceberg of longstanding interagency and international struggles to set and coordinate public policy. One contentious phrase from the president's mouth about 'a favour' or 'counterterrorism cooperation' represents an entire submerged iceberg of conflict on the banks of the Potomac. Such phrases may also be indicative of the geopolitical climate of the Enduring Disorder, where policy outcomes reflect the chaotic interplay of structural forces and personal incentives rather than well-coordinated attempts to maximize public utility.

PREFACE

The Zelensky and Haftar presidential phone calls mirrored an international situation and American foreign policy formation environment unlike anything seen in previous decades. The president was not setting a new, coherent whole-of-government approach towards contentious American foreign policy; he was deliberately confusing and attempting to undermine specific aspects about the existing direction. The president was not using the powers vested in his office to foster order in the world or even to clarify America's policy goals. He was mongering chaos and policy confusion. And his phone calls were just a symptom of larger developments in the global system writ-large, among them America's inability to coordinate with its allies to protect their shared interests in geostrategic hotspots like Ukraine or Libya.

The Libyan maze

From 2013 to 2019, the United States outwardly appeared to withdraw from the Libya file, ceding it to be vehemently contested among Italy, France, Russia, Egypt, Turkey, the Gulf states, and the UN. At times, American diplomats and soldiers have engaged to support the UN peace process, to host critical meetings in Tunisia on economic reform, or to provide reconnaissance assistance and training to certain Libyan militias that fight jihadi groups. But as those diplomatic and military cogs methodically churned behind the scenes, President Trump and his aides had incrementally sought to leverage American policy formation towards Libya to appease Russia, Egypt, Saudi Arabia, and the UAE, who each in their own ways supported nascent strongman Haftar in his attempts to overturn the GNA and become Libya's new dictator.

The key thing to appreciate here is that just like with the Haftar phone call, the Trump administration never formally changed American policy towards Libya. Trump himself did not undertake concrete actions that changed the formal basis of US policy towards Libya (treaties, ambassadorial appointments, and bilateral agreements) nor did he ever issue public statements or internal directives bringing American objectives formally into alignment with those of Russia, Egypt, Saudi Arabia, and the UAE. At the formal level, all the president did was to employ various statements and actions to cast doubt about American policy's future trajectory. At the level of shadow policy,[18] Trump may have also encouraged his personal allies like Blackwater founder and private military contractor Erik Prince to engage in some form of profiteering or shadow policy meant to help Trump's Gulfi friends while simultaneously undermining official State Department policy.[19] In the Libyan microcosm, as elsewhere, the president had simply acted as an agent of deliberative disorder—keeping America's traditional allies guessing while inviting adversaries and rogue actors to sway its policy responses from the inside.

Personally uninterested in what destination was reached, Trump was inviting the passengers on deck to take turns steering the vessel. Vis-à-vis Libya, as with other international conflict zones, the passengers he tended to encourage to exert the largest global role were Russia, the UAE, and Saudi Arabia—not America's traditional NATO allies. And those non-NATO countries, even when united on certain specific policy outcomes (such as, for example, their shared desire to see an anti-Islamist strongman in charge of Libya), lack the coordination forums or foreign policy traditions to genuinely compromise on specific national interests to achieve mutually beneficial outcomes.

While overtly directing American institutions to withdraw from certain official aspects of the Libya file, covertly the Trump inner circle has initiated illicit contact with rogue Libyan actors—frequently mediated through the UAE, right-wing DC think tanks, shady businessmen, and Trump's outer circle. On various occasions, I witnessed some of our diplomats and armed forces attempt to sideline these suspect engagements and minimize their policy fallout. In the spring of 2019, I observed the media and parts of our intelligence community get outflanked by Team Trump's tactics. The Haftar phone call episode was a huge tactical win for Team Trump. The State and Defense Departments were blindsided and uncertain of how to respond.[20] The media fell for the bait and assumed that where there was smoke there must have been fire.

As in other Western capitals, the fighting inside Washington to shape Libya policy is intense. There are billions to be made and lost; diplomats have their retirement gigs and legacies to think about; corporations, and the states in which they are headquartered, all wish to secure back payments on outstanding contracts and to be seen supporting the winning side when the dust settles. Libya matters.

I have witnessed this interagency and inter-governmental tug-of-war first hand due to my two decades of multi-faceted engagement with Libya as an academic, consultant, business owner, think tank scholar, government briefer, and the executive director of a trade association.[21] I've hosted Libya's most powerful officials—some of whom I have witnessed attempt to curry favour with American companies by dangling preferential business opportunities out of the mistaken belief that those companies' lobbyists could help them secure American diplomatic support. I've seen the Trump administration prevent top State Department officials from attending key international summits on Libya such as the Palermo Conference in November 2018 or business to government networking events, like the dinner that I hosted in honour of the Libyan prime minister on the margins of the 2017 UN General Assembly.

When the 'War for Tripoli' began in April 2019, a new wave of lobbyists from Libya's opposing factions descended on

Washington and other major capitals. The Libyan factions quickly learned to emulate their respective Emirati and Turkish patrons by throwing millions at K Street hoping to shape American policy from the inside.[22] One outcome of this flurry of influence peddling was that Libya's role as ISIS's most important base outside of Syria dropped off the agenda.[23]

Standing firm during this tussle, the US Department of State upheld its recognition of the GNA as Libya's sovereign and maintained its policy that the UN-mediated negotiations must take primacy over bilateral efforts—the same high-level policies adopted under the Obama administration. Stymied since 2017 from disrupting the straightjacket of official policy, the new round of violence allowed Team Trump a fresh opportunity to challenge this status quo by applying the disruptive tactics they had learned elsewhere: shutting down key intelligence investigations with national security implications and conducting a war of disinformation. They did so not with the aim of implementing an alternative policy but simply with the desire of strewing confusion and keeping lawmakers and the intelligence community in the dark about what US policies might be in the future or what its adversaries were really doing.

The world's most powerful ostrich

Months before General Haftar's April 2019 assault on Tripoli, an official from AFRICOM—the US Army's Stuttgart-based Africa Combatant Command—reached out to me. My initial hope was to advise on ways to counter the Islamic State in Libya and to monitor the movements of Libyan militias—topics in which my consulting company specializes, and about which I have long advised the British. After numerous phone calls on encrypted apps, in May 2019 we finally met in Manhattan.

Rather than talking about ISIS and militias as I had hoped, the official explained that he was in fact a mid-ranking officer with the Defense Intelligence Agency operating via a secondment to AFRICOM. He obliquely explained his real interest in the Libya file. We then discussed the sources and methods he hoped to use to study Russian actions and operatives inside Libya. During our meeting, he obliquely suggested that Trump's April phone call to Haftar—then only a few weeks old—had undermined his ability to persuade potential sources to help him conduct his investigation. He explained that he was, nonetheless, determined to press onwards, as understanding and countering Russia's reach inside Haftar's Libyan National Army (LNA) was a key priority for his agency and a prerequisite for the US to formulate a coherent policy, *no matter which side we wanted to back.*

Upon grasping his brief, I delivered an impromptu lecture on the historical background of Russian interests in Libya—detailing Stalin's attempts to prevent the independence of a unified Libyan monarchy after the Second World War, Brezhnev's opportunistic use of Qadhafi as a conduit to arm Third World liberationist movements, President Dmitry Medvedev's and Prime Minister Vladimir Putin's famous spat about how to approach the Libyan Arab Spring in 2011,[24] and Putin's subsequent desire to undermine post-Qadhafi governance structures to make a manifest failure out of what he saw as a surreptitious NATO regime change mission. I stressed how Russian governmental objectives combine the immediate geostrategic with longer-term calculations on behalf of Russian companies seeking to restart contracts and to collect back payments from the late Qadhafi period. I detailed how I had noticed that the Egyptian Army helps mediate Russian technical assistance and mechanical repairs for Haftar's forces, and that Putin refuses to pay for either that assistance or for the Russian mercenaries that serve on the Tripoli front lines. I explained that the Emiratis appear to have shell companies to fund both forms of Russian engagement.

Seemingly satisfied and seeking to cement our connection, he said that he would be working on this topic for the next three years and would like to phone me from time to time. A few weeks, and a few WhatsApp messages later, he emailed me in late May to inform me that: 'In this past week there has been a shift in focus from what we discussed and unfortunately, I will no longer be pursuing those topics of interest. This also means I will no longer be available for contact.' The agent's message was another slightly visible tip of a much larger iceberg of interagency conflict over Libya. My future attempts to email him bounced back, while my WhatsApp messages stayed with one grey check.

One does not need to be a foreign policy professional to imagine various scenarios possibly unfolding underneath the surface. The agent could have decided to block me because he felt he had already learned all he needed to know from my historical lesson; he could have been shifted to another case for standard bureaucratic reasons; yet, the most probable explanation appears to be that in the wake of Haftar's assault on Tripoli, and President Trump's publicly phoning the aggressor while spurning the internationally recognized Libyan prime minister's requests for a meeting, Trump appointees inside the Department of Defense pulled the plug on, or sought to obstruct, the American intelligence community's long-standing attempts to understand and counteract Russian meddling in Libya. This was a moment where there was an acting secretary of defense rather than one who had been Senate confirmed.[25] It could easily be that in an attempt to curry favour, the acting secretary or his underlings wanted to proactively make information that Team Trump might consider unfavourable simply disappear.

Such a move to shut down the gathering of factual intelligence and to block attempts at counterespionage would certainly not be unique to the Libyan theatre. The parallels with the Russia investigation into election meddling or into various issues pertaining to Ukraine are quite apparent. But why would actively seeking to 'not know' be a frequent policy choice of the world's greatest superpower with by far the most highly developed intelligence community?

Potentially, because if specific findings were set to paper, they would automatically occasion policy responses that were intended to restore order out of chaos. Or alternatively, because the Republican Party, in general, and the Trump administration, in particular, had come to adopt a 'post-policy' strategy in their approach to world affairs—that is, wishing to maintain complete policy flexibility so as to be able to change any given policy whenever doing so would suit their electoral or personal interests.[26]

If disorder was the goal, factual knowledge gathered by experts and placed on official letterhead is certainly the enemy. Many observers would analyse this and other episodes of deliberate disorder as deriving exclusively from the predilections of the Trump administration and not from systemic problems in American foreign policymaking or in the overall world order. Yet, it was the systemic forces at work in the Enduring Disorder that gave rise to Trump, and not Trump who gave rise to the Enduring Disorder. As such, this book argues that the Trump administration embraced an approach of cultivating disorder, misinformation, and deliberate ignorance. It did so because it aligned with Trump's personal inclinations and because the prevailing world situation incentivizes and rewards such an approach—and will continue to do so until key structural and ideological changes take place.

Misinformation, distraction, and deliberate disorder

This same battle to prevent the truth from being researched and disseminated had taken shape in Team Trump's manipulative approach to the media and desire to spin Trump's phone call with

Haftar as signalling a shift in American policy. This was just one of tens of thousands of instances where tweets and leaked phone calls disrupted the news-cycle and led to widespread speculation in the media. Years into the Trump presidency, most media outlets and even knowledgeable commentators continued to take the bait, failing to understand the distinction between Trump's pronouncements and the actual policies of the U.S. government enshrined in law and multilateral diplomacy.

Mietek Boduszyński, who served at the US embassy in Tripoli during the early post-Qadhafi years, wrote an article in *The Washington Post*'s 'Monkey Cage blog' on 3 May 2019 entitled 'Trump Changed U.S. Policy toward Libya'. Boduszyński wrote of a 'complete U-turn in US policy'. On 6 May, *The New York Times* published an article, 'On Muslim Brotherhood, Trump Weighs Siding with Autocrats and Roiling the Middle East', written by the world class journalists Eric Schmitt and David Kirkpatrick. The article reads, 'the White House also announced another reversal of American foreign policy: in a statement on 19 April, Mr. Trump publicly endorsed Khalifa Hifter'. On 12 May, *The Wall Street Journal* followed suit, publishing an article entitled 'Trump Backed Libyan Warlord after Saudi Arabia and Egypt Lobbied Him', alleging that Trump's phone call 'marked a significant shift in the American stance toward Gen. Haftar'.[27]

Savvy Arab commentators eager to know exactly which way US policy might shift did not fall into the same trap as their American counterparts. *Ain Libya* news magazine wrote on 20 April 2019:

> A military expert [informed us] that the call took place four days earlier and it was not announced in an official statement by the White House [at the time]. Haftar also did not announce it [right away] despite his need [for the beneficial optics it would provide] to support his military campaign. This [the call not being immediately

disclosed] means that the call's content was not in the interest of [Haftar] forces' attack on the capital.[28]

The rest of the article illustrates the *Ain Libya* reporter's correct deduction that the call did not represent a concrete change in official American policy away from supporting the GNA and towards supporting Haftar, but rather only Trump's attempt to simply appease the Emiratis and Egyptians by agreeing to have a private call with Haftar while also trying to stir up confusion about American policy.

In short, the articles in major Western publications postulated a formal change in policy where none had occurred, as informed Libyan commentators were able to determine. The NYT, WSJ, and *Washington Post* took President Trump at his word, assuming that it automatically reflected official American foreign policy, forgetting that Trump had been contradicting the Departments of State and Defense on Libya throughout his entire presidency and that he lacked the ability to singlehandedly reverse their policies by simply making a phone call in which no concrete policy proposals were discussed. When Trump met with then-Italian Prime Minister Gentiloni in the spring of 2017, he said that the US has 'no interests in Libya, other than counter-terrorism', exactly at the moment that the State Department was supporting major political engagements through the UN. Those engagements still went ahead.[29]

Furthermore, Trump neither endorsed Haftar in a 19 April White House press statement nor in his prior phone call with Haftar on 15 April. For the US government to officially 'endorse' or 'recognize' Haftar would have been a major formal action with permanent implications. It would have required the State Department to override its formal procedures. Trump showed neither President Sisi nor the interagency process any desire to engage in those challenging steps. Trump's 'post-policy' approach to foreign affairs illustrated the patterns and trends that characterized the new historic era of the Enduring Disorder and will likely continue for many US administrations to come. But when did these dynamics emerge?

When did we stop caring about order?

Ever since the Second World War, the United States has maintained strategic interests and strategic plans for all parts of the world simultaneously. A core objective of the American Departments of State, Commerce, Energy, and Defense was to deconflict those many interests and plans into one coherent vision for an ordered world. Total order was never achieved, but the apparatus intrinsically strove towards order and coordination.

Considering the brief snippet of events I have related from the spring of 2019, it is difficult to avoid the conclusion that the Trump administration's misinformation, misdirection, and inter-agency feuding reveals that the president was simply uninterested in changing official US policy on complex topics like Libya that he perceived to have no implications for issues of his electability or domestic popularity.

Trump did not see his mission as promoting global order or policy consistency. Instead, he tweeted about various policy-relevant items or 'leaked' old phone calls, knowing that the media would lap it up and the official policies and procedures of the US government would become confused in the public eye and to America's allies. This is what connects leaked phone calls to cancelled covert investigations. They both paint a picture of an administration unique in its lack of desire to coordinate policy with its allies or internally among the different branches of government. Numerous commentators[30] have analysed similar events as unique to Trump and his allies' particular ways of doing things. This book seeks to transcend that approach and paint the picture of the emergence of a novel historical era, the Enduring

Disorder, which incentivizes and gives rise to these behaviours and of which the Trump administration's actions were merely indicative symptoms. According to this line of thought, it is crucial not to confuse Trump's, Putin's, Viktor Orbán's, Xi Jinping's, or Jair Bolsonaro's actions for the underlying disease. These leaders are merely products of the Enduring Disorder, not its authors. According to this analysis, the dominant leaders of the non-democratic world have all embraced the logic of the Enduring Disorder and sought to profit from it.

Arguably, then, the defining feature of the Enduring Disorder is the systematic lack of coordination of collective action to achieve mutually beneficial aims. This lack of coordination is perceptible at nearly every level of analysis: domestic and international political institutions exhibit it, as do the private, public, and non-governmental sectors. A lack of trust pervades how citizens relate to their governments, how partisans deal with their political opponents, and how nationalists work with rival countries.

Some commentators perceive Putin as a master manipulator sitting atop an Axis of Evil.[31] Conversely, the Enduring Disorder paradigm sees Russia as incapable of leading an axis of coordinated allies; in fact, Putin is just as poor at coordinating with the leaderships in Belarus and Kazakhstan (two of his most geostrategically important client states) as the US has become at working with its traditional allies. Brian Whitmore, an expert on Russian foreign policy, described the Russian–Belarusian relationship in 2019 as progressively deteriorating and 'among the most dysfunctional partnerships in the former Soviet space', citing Belarusian President Lukashenko's resistance to establishing a new air base for Russian use and his continual refusal to allow Belarusian territory to be used by Putin to attack third party territory.[32] Similarly, after the 2014 annexation of Crimea, Kazakhstan became wary that a wave of Russian separatism might spread to its ethnically Russian northern regions. As a result, it has reduced its economic and foreign policy coordination with its powerful northern neighbour.[33]

Despite its global ascendancy, China is beset by similar problems. Most of its neighbours oppose its regional ambitions, other than weak, poor, and dependent North Korea and increasingly isolated Myanmar, which is suffering from waves of domestic upheaval. And rather than being able to count on North Korea as a subservient vassal state, the Chinese leadership are frequently caught off-guard by Kim Jong-un's missile launches and policy pronouncements. And although Myanmar requires Chinese support, it does not intimately coordinate major domestic and international initiatives with Beijing.

Fostering consensus and perfecting seamless coordination are not the current watchwords of global politics. Trump's exit from the White House has neither unified Americans' domestic ability to coordinate across partisan lines nor dramatically restored America's role as a coordinator of unified international responses to pressing collective challenges. Similarly, Putin's eventual ouster or death in Russia seems even less likely to turn Russia into a key bulwark for a consensus-based international system built on transparency, compromise, and international collaboration. In fact, as the media and academics continually subject the psychologies of Trump, Putin, Xi, Erdoğan, and others to immense scrutiny, analysts have been largely ignoring the hypothesis that their individual personalities have not really been driving events, and hence, their individual departures from the scene are likely to make little difference unless their replacements actively seek to reorder the world system.

Will the Biden administration inhibit the momentum towards the Enduring Disorder?

In the wake of Trump's departure, many fervently hoped that the world system would gradually return to the certitudes and alliance structures that characterized the early post-Cold War period. Even before Joe Biden began governing, there were many reasons to speculate that this could not happen. Highly respected centrist political pundits had been pointing out that Western states were no longer capable of efficient coordination and global leadership.[34] Trump and his actions were symptoms and consequences of the Enduring Disorder, not their root cause. Long before Trump, NATO allies no longer shared information the way they once did. Diplomats no longer committed their candid assessment to formal cables out of fear they would be leaked.

Study of the lack of coordination within the international system on the Libya file during the Trump years strikes me as indicative of many of the coordination failures we are likely to witness going forward in other policy domains and which will prevail into the Biden administration and beyond. Obscuring relevant information and blocking investigations are merely extremes within the larger pantheon of disorder.

Biden is an unlikely messiah

Seen in this light, it is unclear if the Biden administration's genuine commitment to multilateralism and a 'return to normalcy'[35] will prove capable of addressing any of the root causes of the Enduring Disorder or will turn out to be mere rhetorical flourish partially obscuring the continually deteriorating state of global coordination. No one doubts the Biden administration's genuine desire to reinforce multilateral approaches towards major global problems like climate change, counter-proliferation, fake news, tax havens, and global public health. Yet, such renewed focus on multilateralism is unlikely to be sufficient, as the current approach is based on treating the symptoms of the Enduring Disorder, not its causes.

It is no secret that the United Nations is no longer fit for purpose and that NATO is currently divided against itself. The

Biden administration merely proposed a return to normalcy. Establishment political figures in their late seventies are not usually the agents of messianic change. Given this, executive orders re-joining international agreements and announcements of enhanced cooperation with global institutions are unlikely to match the scale of the current challenges.[36] Seen from early 2021, it is these minor palliative measures that globalists and establishment centrists in America and Europe have on offer, while the neo-populist right and woke left are primarily proposing radical alterations to international affairs that would further undercut consensus-based international collaboration. Therefore, as a betting man, I feel comfortable wagering big that the Enduring Disorder seems here to stay. Smart forecasting indicates that neither the Biden administration nor subsequent leaderships of major governments from China, Russia, the EU, or US are likely to propose a radically new framework of multilateralism or the new alliance structures fit to address the mid-twenty-first-century challenges of climate change, pandemics, migration, demographic shift, cyberwarfare, or proxy wars and state implosion in geostrategically and economically important theatres like Libya.

To treat the root causes of mid-twenty-first-century global crises and cope with the scale of the coordination problems discussed in this book, the arena of international affairs and multilateral institutions would need to be fundamentally deconstructed and then thoroughly reconstructed. This is something that a centrist American administration is well positioned to mediate, but only as a 'total war'-style project fully leveraging the undivided support of the American populace, multinational corporations, international institutions, and major bilateral allies. As of 2021, there are no indications of such an eventuality in the short-to-medium term.

To my mind, it will take major socio-cultural change and a bottom-up movement to demand such consensus change to the global order. How this might unfold is something I return to in the conclusion. If it does not, the progressive deepening of the Enduring Disorder will usher in a period of interregnum, eventually followed by the rise of a new hegemon promoting its own form of order. When such a new force will arise, and the form it might take, is anyone's guess.

Enduring disorder not multipolarity

Policymaking has always been lived by participants as comprised of reversals, tug-of-wars, and competition among power centres. But post-2011 chaos on the international scene appears to differ not only in degree but in kind from what came before.

Not only is the international system unmoored due to a lack of American leadership, a development that predated and will long outlast the Trump administration, but also because major powers have failed to create suitable institutional coordination mechanisms to deal with the new kinds of 'collective action problems'[37] presented by the twenty-first century. This has led to a free-for-all.

This is not the multipolarity of previous eras of competition—like the interwar period, where each aspirant to power strove to order and expand its own sphere of influence—but a new era of deliberate disorder, where major international players actively undermine global order, eschew collaboration, and block knowledge accumulation.[38] Whatever the behind-the-scenes rationale for the DIA operative's behaviour, that episode—plus the two Presidential phone calls which chronologically framed it for me—starkly highlighted that America was no longer a global hegemon seeking to order the international sphere by working with traditional allies and against traditional adversaries. Various powers are muscling in on traditional American domains and perverting American information-gathering and the policy formation process from the inside. These actors may not be 'restoring a balance of power', as 'realist' International Relations (IR) theorists have postulated that lesser powers automatically do as a hegemon declines.[39] Furthermore, these ascending powers may not be concerned with an ordered or balanced international system.

Most of these medium and great powers are certainly competing to secure their own particular interests in Libya. Yet, none of these other international actors are willing to effectively impose order on the country or sufficiently collaborate with their allies to even contain its disorder. The world seems to have gone directly from a hegemonic US-led international system to an interregnum in global order. The traditional phase of multipolarity—or a restoration of the balance of power, or even a struggle among rival systems of order has been skipped.[40] Welcome to the Enduring Disorder.

The modern route: from global hegemony to multipolarity

Global hegemons seeking to project their preferred order on to a truly global system are relatively new. For most of human history, a sphere of global, rather than regional, politics simply could not exist due to the shortcomings of the prevailing communications technology. Yet when politics verged on the global, it was due to the expansive tendencies of hegemonic powers. From Cyrus, to Alexander, to the Romans, Arabs, Mongols, Spanish Habsburgs, and even Napoleon, regional hegemons usually pursued further expansion until they were checked. Global conquest eluded even the best and the brightest, partly because prevailing communications technologies were not up to the task of permitting worldwide coordination.

Due to technological and administrative progress, the British imperial system from the late eighteenth to early twentieth century gradually established and then upheld the first truly global world order, even though much of the world was outside its ambit of direct control.[41] After a century or so of relative ascent, from 1880 onwards, Britain's relative power was in decline. British hegemony was gradually challenged by rising powers like Germany, America, and Japan, as well as established lesser imperial powers like Russia and France. This incipient multipolarity brought the Pax Britannica to an end. It also led to the First World War. It prevailed during the chaotic interwar period and was only resolved by the outcome of the Second World War, in which America emerged as the dominant power, able to set new global rules of engagement.[42]

As this most recent example of a transition from one global hegemony to another illustrates, a 'normal' state of affairs is the gradual or abrupt decline of one hegemon leading to a period of multipolarity, or in the realists' phrase, 'restoration of the balance of power'. For classical realist IR theorists, the multipolar competition can only resolve with either the emergence of a new global hegemon or an ordered balance of power—the latter being conceived as a self-perpetuating system, in which every action or disturbance will cause an opposite reaction, whereby the system will tend to order.[43]

Pax Britannica led to Pax Americana, albeit with a brief interlude of multipolar global conflict and uncertainty in between. What happens if while one hegemon is declining, other powers are not striving to—or not capable of—developing the capabilities to fill the vacuum or are not concerned with providing order? In short, this book's conception of our entering a novel historical period, as illustrated by international policy towards Libya, is offered as a corrective to prevailing assumptions in mainstream scholarship about international politics. To unpick how novel these developments are, we must briefly investigate other historical instances of the collapse of order.

The older route: from hegemony to interregnum

At other points in world history, such as with the collapse of the Roman Empire or the weakening of the Habsburgs throughout the seventeenth century, rather than one hegemonic order gradually giving way to another via a period of multipolarity, there was a lengthy interregnum between two totally different systems of order. These interregnums did not necessarily feature competing poles of order or a balance of powers but were sometimes characterized by a lack of global and regional order. Most of those interregnums were characterized by ongoing strife, declining standards of living and life expectancy, and disintegration of the sinews of civilization, such as trade and travel.

This contrast begs the question: are we in a period of incipient multipolarity at the tail end of the American-led order or are we entering a period of interregnum? Scholars have explained the post-Cold War period as commencing with unfettered American hegemony or hyperpower (circa 1989–2003) and progressively acquiring attributes of multipolarity in the wake of the American invasion of Iraq (2003–present), the 2008 financial crisis, the rise of China, the Arab Spring, America's gradual retreat from the world, and the Covid pandemic.[44] Other diplomatic historians and realist IR theorists examine the nature of Britain's decline to postulate that our current trajectory indicates that an era of multipolarity and conflict is on the horizon.[45] For these realists, the extreme concentration of American might (now) or British power (then) threatened lesser powers and inherently caused coalition-building to oppose the overstretched hegemon and restore the balance of power. For them, America's ascent (from around 1865 to 2003) and now descent (2003–present) roughly mirrors the similar progression from British imperial hegemony (1815–1913) to full-blown multipolarity during the Great War, the interwar period, and Second World War—what Charles de Gaulle termed the Second Thirty Years War (1914–45).[46]

Yet, that analysis sees state power (military, diplomatic, and soft) as still able to shape the main dynamics of the international arena as it did in the nineteenth and twentieth centuries. Following Robert Kaplan, Martin Van Creveld, Sean McFate, and Richard Haass, there are reasons to view the reach of the Western state in the twenty-first century as significantly diminished. Van Creveld was more than prescient when he wrote in the 1990s that the power of the state in the Western World was in decline.

The return of populist nationalism to democracies around the world over the last decade has not heralded the return of state power. In fact, it has illustrated the opposite: try as their new leaders might to 'put America [or Britain or Italy] first', they still fail to improve the relative power of their nations. In fact, in today's world there appears no surer a recipe for decline than a deliberate policy of isolation or unilateralism because global non-state forces, particularly those emanating from technology, climate, migration, and pathogens, are not able to be effectively countered by a single state's power. Irony of ironies, the goals of today's hyper-nationalist populists can only be dealt with effectively by acting in concert with other powers.

Seen in this light, America is only very partially losing its hegemonic power via a direct competition with China and Russia, the way that the British Empire primarily lost its power to Germany, America, and the USSR. Today, American power is being eviscerated by many non-state actors, decentralizing technologies, corporate behemoths, superbugs, and stateless capital.[47] The American empire is not being challenged by an alternative order per se, but by an alternative disorder, and American leaders (including establishment centrists like McCain, Romney, Obama and Biden) were not able to propose new forms of multilateral institutions and alliances to confront these challenges. These indicators, and the lack of viable proposals for a new format of international order, point to an interregnum rather than a multipolar contest among states, which may shortly resolve itself with a victor.

During periods of multipolarity, the different poles compete to spread their own form of order. That was the global pattern in the late nineteenth and early twentieth century and during the interwar period. The British and French empires, Wilhelmine and later Nazi Germany, a rising Japanese Empire, and the United States cultivated spheres of influence in which they imposed and policed order. This is dissimilar to the pattern we see today. Seen from 2021, America, Russia, the EU, and China do not necessarily represent alternative poles of order or international standards, each competing to expand its sphere of influence and rules. Nor have they meaningfully collaborated with their allies on major challenges like global warming, public health, and arms proliferation. In fact, coordination seems to be coming undone (as one would imagine in an interregnum) rather than being reconfigured (as one would imagine in a period of multipolarity) or restored (as one would imagine if the balance of power was reasserting itself after a period of lopsided American hegemony).

Is China rising to global leadership or promoting Enduring Disorder?

Much ink has been spilled about the rise of China and the inevitable transition from an American-led to a Chinese-led world order. It would seem that the prevailing paradigm within realist approaches to IR theory, and that which underpins most governmental scenario planning, is that we are in a period of increasing multipolarity with an inevitable contestation for global dominance looming between the United States and China, with China rapidly wresting soft and hard power from the US.[48] This tale of 'China Rising' is many realist IR theorists' big picture perspective of how to analyse world events in the early to mid-twenty-first century.[49] The idea of the primary dynamic in the international system consisting of a new struggle for hegemony between the US and China has even become a popular media narrative, especially in response to the geopolitical and economic shifts deriving from the Covid pandemic.[50]

This book will not investigate this 'China Rising' paradigm substantively, as it has been examined comprehensively elsewhere and, to my mind, it sheds little light on dynamics unfolding in the Middle East in general, and in Libya, specifically. Not only does it seem to be based on outdated conceptions about the international system 'tending towards order' or nature abhorring a vacuum and hence facilitating a competition for hegemonic order, but it also fails to help explain 'the big questions' like why neo-populism[51] has spread like wildfire across the Western world or why international coordination on issues like climate change, Middle Eastern civil wars, and public health is so weak. The 'China Rising' thesis would suggest that China would be coordinating an ordered response to these challenges—either in its sphere of influence or globally. And yet, China is largely absent from coordinating consensus solutions for nearly all the most important questions that cry out for global collective action.

Or worse, China may actively seek to prevent global coordination. This book therefore analyses China as deliberately stoking the Enduring Disorder and seeking to exploit it. There is much concrete evidence to suggest that Chinese leaders have learned to emulate their Russian counterparts. Both see their nations as wronged by the West and believe that they will benefit from events that induce disorder in their democratic rivals. It also seems quite clear that the Chinese Communist Party have had a 'good pandemic.' The very nature of a highly contagious respiratory disease afforded them perfect cover to increase their surveillance over their citizenry. It also helped the CCP forbid protests on the home front, quell dissent in Hong Kong, and keep their mass incarceration of the Uighurs largely concealed.[52]

It has long been established that the Chinese government wilfully held back information about the virus's progression in its early days and has undercut attempts to buttress global health coordination.[53] A world with less global coordination, in which future pandemics can run rampant, appears to be a world that the CCP feels is safer for itself and gives it a comparative advantage. Such a world may be one in which China can more easily dominate the fields of the future like 5G, biotech, and surveillance capitalism.[54]

Rather than the widespread engagement with the multipolarity or 'China Rising' theses, very little scholarship has considered whether China is an agent of deliberate global disorder that simultaneously seeks to create a hegemonic regional order in its near abroad. If so, China is aided and abetted in both endeavours by new technologies and ideologies. Overall, this state of affairs could mean that we are moving to a post-hegemonic system: a semi-permanent interregnum of global order characterized by the absence of enforceable global rules and norms.

Of course, history is lived forwards but written backwards. Hence, there is no way to know at present if the events of America's relative decline and China's relative ascent since 2003 will culminate in a decisive transfer of the sceptre and the dawn of a Chinese-led, rules-based world order. Contextualizing the current period as not multipolar but as a semi-permanent interregnum does not make that the reality. I am putting forth one hypothesis, one potential framing of our historical moment, as an attempt to understand the causation and structures underlying the myriad developments we are witnessing. Consider this contextualization as a contingent thought experiment: if various data fit the model—or better yet, if the model proves to be predicative—then it can help us conceptualize the interplay between regional conflicts and global collective action problems.

* * *

Libya: posterchild of the Enduring Disorder

As stated, this book postulates that we have already entered an interregnum of global order—characterized by the decline of American hegemony, China's failure to take on global leadership, and the lack of genuine competition among viable alternative poles of order. We have left the post-Cold War period and entered this new historical period, which I term the 'Enduring Disorder'. Through investigation of Libya as a case study, this book presents various historical events that suggest that we are in fact exiting an era of one hegemon's system of order without entering that of another. The ongoing Libya conflict—slightly more than even the civil wars in Yemen, Syria, Venezuela, and Eastern Ukraine—may in fact provide the most powerful demonstration of the prior collapse of the post-Cold War order. Furthermore, it also highlights the self-reinforcing nature of these developments. Libya's ongoing implosion gives rise to contagion, which incrementally reinforces further implosions of order at the global level. If the previous theories of the international system were that 'order begat order' and 'imbalance led to a restoration of balance', what if the reverse is true and local disorder can beget regional disorder, which, in today's globalized world, can foster Enduring Disorder?

If this interregnum is self-perpetuating, who knows how long it may endure. Theoretically, it could rapidly culminate in a Chinese-led world order or new challenges could lead to novel forms of global collaboration within a decade or so. Conversely, it may be that this new disorder deepens as it persists for generations to come.

Developments in Libya present an interesting arena in which to investigate these questions. As Libya has imploded and Russia has undermined Western-led attempts to foster order, have the Chinese stepped in to provide an alternative vision of order for Libya? They have not.[55] Furthermore, they have barely lifted a finger in Yemen, Syria/Iraq, Venezuela, Ukraine, or Libya[56]—the world's five most geostragically important active civil wars. Conversely, in the long-standing international disputes surrounding Iran and North Korea, the Chinese are major players, yet they tacitly preserve, and seek to benefit from, the very situation that has given rise to the conflict rather than proposing a new order. They seem to prefer the status quo of an interregnum in global order rather than having to embrace the burden of formulating a wholly new global order.

In Libya, many actors compete to secure rival commercial and geostrategic interests, but none of the major powers seeks to invest sufficient political capital to forge a durable order. Rather, regional powers like Turkey, Egypt, and the UAE seek to project power into Libya to tip the regional balance of power in their favour. This fight to set a new regional order does nothing to create a global order, as neither America, nor the EU, nor China are integrating the various regional actors' visions into a larger global system. While the Chinese have emerged as significant buyers of resources across Africa, they have not shown a willingness to invest political capital. Rather, in resource-rich or geostragically important danger zones such as Somalia or Libya, the Chinese have remained aloof; they have not emerged as order builders like the expanding empires of old.

IR theorists writing around 2000 envisioned the Chinese buying into, and then upholding, the rules-based, free trading order established by Britain and America over the last 200 years. They envisioned the Chinese eventually picking up where the Anglo-Saxons had left off, after incrementally taking on the burden of policing global politics. Some spoke of 'Confucian capitalism' as a new global system. Others pontificated that the Chinese would inevitably have to reinforce the prevailing liberal order as part of their global ascent.[57] Seen from the vantage point of 2021, there are no indications that would corroborate such optimistic forecasting. China's economic and military rise has not corresponded to commensurate burden-sharing or the creation of Chinese-led multilateral global order-building institutions.[58] The reasons for this may well be a sharp calculus on behalf of the CCP that they wish to live in an ordered East Asian region, surrounded by various forms of global disorder from which they can benefit. Both Xi and Putin are firmly committed to the nation-state and the charismatic supreme leader as the loci of power, not multilateral global-ordering institutions.

Given this Russian and Chinese approach, what if this current suboptimal lack of order contains self-reinforcing mechanisms making it likely to endure until prevailing conditions fundamentally shift? If so, this will be a period of human history with different rules, different conflicts, and different arenas of contestation from any that came before it.

There is little we can forecast about such a period other than to remember Heraclitus' dictum 'that the only constant is change'. However, amid this uncertainty, we may be able to elucidate some of the prevailing trends by investigating and depicting those very few case studies that represent the cutting edge of geopolitics—arenas where newer forms of power relationships are already playing out.

The world is currently characterized by ungoverned spaces that suck in outside actors and emit threats to global stability. These microcosms of Enduring Disorder—Libya foremost among them—allow us to imagine how this new historical period might unfold elsewhere as the conditions that propagate the Enduring Disorder spread: creating new power vacuums and new flows of migrants, hot money, and cyberwarriors.

Despite many Westerners who pin their hopes on Joseph Robinette Biden Jr. to heal the fissures that divide America and restore its position as global order provider, it now seems wiser to envision a period of disorder that will get worse before it gets better. This conclusion is reinforced by lessons drawn from the Libyan microcosm. Until the diplomacy surrounding the conflict in Libya is integrated into a settling of larger global diplomatic issues and it is tethered to an aspiring or existing global player's sphere of influence, it will be impossible to adjudicate among the conflicting visions for the country held by various regional, domestic, and international actors.

Seen in this light, solving the collective action problem on the Libya file appears as far off as fixing climate change. In fact, it is difficult to imagine this happening in the 2020s, even if America's foreign policy orientation fully returns to its traditional approach vis-à-vis its NATO allies or if the rifts in the American–Chinese global relationship were significantly healed. It is simply too difficult to envision a consensus-based global order emerging given the centrifugal forces at play.

Always at the cutting edge

Looking to Libya to explain new phenomena in the international system is not as original an approach as you might imagine. From time immemorial, Libya has been acknowledged as the birthplace of novel phenomena. In the fourth century BCE, Aristotle wrote in his *Historia Animalium* that 'Libya always brings forth something new.'[59] Over its skies, the world's first extraterritorial drone war began in April 2019.[60] Libyans did not pilot the drones or typically choose the targets, nor did they pay for the drones' acquisition and upkeep. Tragically, the only thing Libyan about this drone war was the nationality of most of the casualties and displaced persons.

In this new kind of war, the UAE and Turkey provided and piloted the drones. The mercenaries for whom the drones provided air support hailed from Syria, Russia, Chad, Sudan, and elsewhere. Libyan militias of every stripe were engaged in their own internecine struggles; these foreign actors rarely fully coordinated with them. The EU and NATO were largely absent on the ground, but France and Italy lent critical diplomatic support to opposite sides of the conflict. Due to their willingness to flout international norms and violate the UN arms embargo, medium powers like Turkey, the UAE, and Russia have far more ability to project power into Libya than the economic juggernauts: the US, EU, and China. Neither China nor the US perceives its own interests as threatened enough to try to order the international system in a way that could lead to a resolution in Libya (or similar conflict zones). Conversely, the EU perceives its core interests as fundamentally threatened by developments in Libya but is unable to coordinate its internal disagreements sufficiently to formulate a coherent response. Possibly more than any other territory on earth, even Syria, the conflict in Libya reveals the absence of global order and the failure of global organizations to provide it.

In this regard, the spread of Covid in early to mid-2020 merely heightened the existing global trendlines at play in Libya and elsewhere. Allied and neighbouring countries frequently exhibited divergent and haphazard governmental responses towards the pandemic. As the outbreak worsened, countries looked inward. In the blink of an eye, many of the institutions of the global community's ability to coordinate an international response to any geopolitical crisis were shown to be dysfunctional. Then, even more bizarrely, as the pandemic continued, coordination and burden-sharing among allied nations became further eviscerated—the exact opposite to what happened during the First and Second World Wars, which began with poor coordination and burden-sharing among the allies' general staffs but rapidly improved as the fighting progressed. A stark illustration of this is to contrast Trump's decision to defund the World Health Organization in mid-April 2020 at exactly the moment that New York City had become the global epicentre of the pandemic,[61] as opposed to the increased Commonwealth recruitment to the Entente cause in the wake of the Gallipoli fiasco or the decision of FDR to increase Lend Lease to Britain and the USSR after the Fall of France in June 1940.

In fact, in many ways the international system during the pandemic exhibited many of the hallmark characteristics of the start of a world war or of the beginning of an interregnum of global order—borders closing, expatriates fleeing to their home countries, global supply chains breaking down, and nations pointing fingers at other nations. Even one of the best examples of an institution that pools sovereignty, the EU, proved unable to effectively share healthcare resources among its core member states. Instead of rallying together as the Western allies had done when confronted by major challenges in the twentieth century, the world powers responded to the largest acute global crisis of the twenty-first century by going their own separate ways. Rather than rising to the challenge as Aristotle's, Hegel's, or Peter Turchin's[62] conceptions of the inexorable forward progress of human coordination would have predicted, the pandemic broke the back of the globe's coordinating institutions without replacing them with anything. As the world economy slowly recovers from the pandemic but with global collective action in shambles, the possibility of enforcing the UN arms embargo on Libya or meaningfully pushing forward the political or economic mediation tracks established at the January 2020 Berlin Conference on Libya seems about as unlikely as the creation of a binding global compact to allocate all doses of the Covid vaccine via an equitable and mutually beneficial international sharing scheme.

Libya has illustrated in microcosm that no matter how big the potential win, nor how achievable the desired result, major powers are simply unable to coordinate to maximize shared global utility during the Enduring Disorder. Consider how global coronavirus stimulus spending has been nearly entirely uncoordinated. Over twenty trillion US dollars have been spent globally, with many countries simply competing for the same supplies and driving up their price. If, however, one-hundredth of this spending had been used on peace-making and reconstruction in Syria and Yemen (the twenty-first century's two longest civil wars and gravest humanitarian crises), both wars could likely have been stopped, the countries' infrastructures and economies rebuilt, and the next generation of jihadis prevented from emerging. If a quarter of the global coronavirus stimulus spending had been used to create green technologies and then incentivize their use, many experts believe that 2-degree centigrade warming could have been prevented.[63]

Could Libya's very uniqueness be representative?

How did we get here? When did the global institutions become broken? How can studying Libya provide the answers? Many people have forgotten that before the conflicting blocs in the international system became mired in post-Qadhafi Libya, its Arab Spring transition began surprisingly well. Qadhafi's ouster was actively supported by most major world powers and was not overtly opposed by any, not even Russia. During the 2011 Libyan Uprisings, nary a medium power lent military support to the Qadhafi regime or its post-ouster remnants. The regime's removal initially led to economic growth, burgeoning civic engagement, free and fair elections (won by a non-Islamist majority, unlike in Tunisia and Egypt), and a proliferation of citizen-controlled media outlets. Then, the dysfunctional economic inheritance of the Qadhafi period, the Libyan leadership vacuum, and the start of a new phase of global geopolitics began to overwhelm the positive domestic trends initially unleashed by the Uprisings.

In the wake of Qadhafi's death at the hands of the Libyan Uprisings in October 2011, the erstwhile international allies staked out competing alliances with rival Libyan factions in the ensuing struggle for the post-Qadhafi future. In 2012–13, these tensions remained latent as oil production mostly recovered and attempts at a transition to constitutional governance proceeded by fits and starts. Yet, both the economy and the political transition conclusively stalled in 2014. Since then, Libya has been mired in two distinct rounds of civil war, known as the Wars for Post-Qadhafi Succession, with various Libyan factions serving as proxies for regional and international players, each trying to secure its own interests.[64] The first war (2014–15) pitted Operation Dawn, an assortment of Tripolitanian militias opposed to the results of the June 2014 elections, against the warlord Khalifa Haftar's Operation Dignity, which sought to abolish civilian control of Libya under the guise of fighting terrorism. The most recent round of civil war (2019–20) took the form of an all-out battle for control of Tripoli. It was sparked by Haftar's April 2019 assault on the Libyan capital being opposed by an ad hoc coalition of militias loosely aligned to Libya's internationally recognized government. During the second civil war, the extent and nature of foreign intervention morphed—as the introduction of mercenaries and the development of novel forms of extra-territorial aerial combat illustrate.[65] Despite a resounding Turkish victory in the defense of Tripoli in the spring of 2020,[66] the broad adherence of the ensuing Sirte–Jufra ceasefire line from June 2020 onwards, and the widespread acceptance across the political spectrum of the need to hold elections in December 2021, the UN-led mediation process still culminated in a new transitional government marred by allegations of bribery, illegality, and illegitimacy.[67] Yes, this Government of National Unity made some remarkable headway in its first months in office, consolidating power from both eastern and western institutions and getting its cabinet list approved by the Tobruk-based House of Representatives. This progress is certainly to be applauded.

Yet, no genuine longer-term stability has appeared possible for Libya without a new global order emerging to nurture it. Without such an order, the interfering powers have shown themselves unwilling to compromise on their various interests in Libya or to unite behind a consensual, Libyan-led political process and then uphold any ensuing mutual compromises for the good of all.

Libya, then, is the epitome of the type of geopolitical outcome that our current historic era of Enduring Disorder appears poised to produce.[68] And if Libya is allowed to continue in this seemingly never-ending cycle of violence, corruption, and penetration by outside actors, it will emit migrants, jihadis, corrupt financial gains, polarized rhetoric, cyberwarriors, disinformation experts, warlords, and large-scale regional conflicts, all of which further deepen the very foundations of the Enduring Disorder.

Jason Pack
Metuchen, New Jersey
April 2021

INTRODUCTION

THE GREAT UNRAVELLING

PART I
SOLVING COLLECTIVE ACTION PROBLEMS IS THE PRIMARY
FUNCTION OF THE INTERNATIONAL SYSTEM

Libya as a product of the Global Enduring Disorder

As Trump's phone calls and Haftar's assaults illustrated in the Preface, the ongoing struggle for Libya's post-Qadhafi future provides a privileged lens into a wholly new period of international relations—one that is essentially devoid of modern historical parallels. In fact, examining Libya's ongoing civil war demonstrates that the current world system is not multipolar or even tending towards multipolarity—because its major powers do not seek to impose their system of order on to strategically located arenas of disorder.[1] Rather, it is characterized by competition among a wide range of actors: from the legacy colonial powers, to rising regional powers, to transnational non-state actors like multinational corporations and the Islamic State. None of these actors necessarily intend to foster a comprehensive world order or even a coherent regional order within their sphere of influence. This is in stark contrast to the Cold War period, in which no

1

location was unimportant enough for America or the USSR to cede ground by letting its opponent export its system of order there unrivalled.[2]

Many foreign actors have interfered militarily and diplomatically in Libya's post-Qadhafi wars, but none of the major powers have sought to resolve these wars by comprehensively absorbing Libya into their sphere of influence. The interested parties' goals do not include a twenty-first-century version of colonization to contain the inherent disorder that a wealthy and geostrategically-important ungoverned space like Libya inherently emits.

None of the major powers are willing to invest sufficient political capital to bring about stability—in Libya or globally—in the short or medium term. In this new global system, instead of using their power to foster order, neo-populist leaders like Donald Trump, Vladimir Putin, Recep Tayyip Erdoğan, Xi Jinping, and Mohammed bin Salman deliberately promote disorder. Like the imaginary megalomaniac passengers on the ship adrift during the pandemic, these leaders may feel that they benefit from a certain form of disorder prevailing internationally if it helps them stay in power domestically. As will be shown, Libya was the first theatre (with Syria a close second) in which major features of this new type of international relations have played out.

Libya as a catalyst for the Global Enduring Disorder

Libya's deepening disorder, like Syria's and Ukraine's, has already had profound effects elsewhere, including on such major geopolitical issues as Brexit, Trump's election, the rise of Italy's Five Star Movement, conflicts among EU member states, Russian stoking of anti-EU parties, and Russia's increased ties to the UAE and Egypt. Libya has both borne the consequences of neo-populist forces and reinforced them.

For example, Libya's implosion post-2011, combined with Syria's civil war, led to these two countries becoming prime movers of the migration crisis that has in turn moved previously marginal neo-populist politics into the mainstream centre-right and allowed anti-globalist and pro-Russian sentiment to gain ground throughout Europe.[3] Similarly, neo-populists like Congressman Trey Gowdy and Trump were able to capitalize on the murder of American Ambassador Chris Stevens at the US Special Mission in Benghazi on 12 September 2012 and the related scandal surrounding Hillary Clinton's emails in their partisan attacks against the Democrats, whereas Establishment Republicans like Jeb Bush or John Kasich would not stoop so low as to blame Secretary Clinton for the Ambassador's death or to have their rallies chant 'Lock her up'.

Just as Nigel Farage rose to prominence by sparking irrational fear of hordes of migrants arriving at Calais and then promising that the corrupt establishment sought to increase migrant inflows, Trump and other populists used the Clinton email scandal[4] as one of the central ways of discrediting her as part of the 'corrupt establishment'. Most Brits and Americans are familiar with the neo-populist tropes of 'hordes of Turkish migrants' and 'Crooked Hillary' yet are not conscious that those tropes succeed largely because they are the tail end of long processes that began in Libya and Syria with collective action failures to adopt a consensus approach among the Western allies towards those conflicts.[5]

This type of indirect causation is typical of the Enduring Disorder and illustrates the positive feedback loop connecting state implosion in geostrategic hotspots with the spread of the Enduring Disorder more broadly. These causation chains suggest that the Enduring Disorder's defining feature and root cause is the failure among allied nations or political factions within a specific country to solve collective action problems in a way that leads to real world outcomes with maximal shared utility.[6]

LIBYA AND THE GLOBAL ENDURING DISORDER

Collective action problems are thornier than military interventions

Like most major foreign policy challenges unfolding during the Enduring Disorder, the most difficult aspect of the post-2011 Libya crisis is the collective action problem. This makes solving it more like coordinating a coherent international approach to global warming or the Covid pandemic, and less like the military failures of the Iraq or Vietnam Wars. In fact, it is the re-emergence of the paramountcy of collective action problems (rather than the realist or constructivist IR paradigm's emphasis on the struggle between competing interests) that is the very hallmark of the Enduring Disorder.

Western policymaking towards the conflicts, pandemics, and climate crises of this new era may ultimately end in failure—even if they have the right local networks, a workable plan, and a coherent exit strategy—due to the challenge of aligning enough countries and institutions together to reach decisions and carry them out in a coherent, integrated fashion. In fact, it seems unlikely that there will be any coherent 'Western' approach towards these issues at all—until a new historical era emerges.

Since 2000, the G7 nations' policies have been progressively diverging in each nation's approach to financial, public health, climate, and geostrategic issues. In short, there is ample evidence to support the belief that getting allied governments on the same page to tackle a straightforward, solvable shared problem like tax havens[7] is far more difficult than for a single government to formulate coherent solutions to intellectually challenging problems like post-conflict reconstruction plans in war-torn countries lacking institutions and possessing sectarian cleavages.

Furthermore, collective action problems differ not just in magnitude but in kind from the 'normal' institutional rivalries within a given country's bureaucracy. When 'normal' institutional rivalries lead to a tug of war to set national policy, a coherent chain of command or delineation of spheres of authority and competence exists, whereas with multinational collective action problems, it does not. Study of the implications of this uncontroversial observation constitutes a large lacuna in the realist school of IR theory and the field of political science more generally.

On the one hand, there is a lot of political science scholarship about what happens when hegemony crumbles, as has clearly been happening to America's ability to order the global system. Quite overlooked is the issue of institutional coherency among allies in the wake of the hegemon's departure. On the other hand, there is the assumption among realists that a hegemon wants to expand its power and dominance, while middle powers inherently oppose that and try to push back until a balance of power is reached.[8] These dynamics do not seem to apply to the mid-twenty-first-century world.

Imperial powers from Rome to Great Britain to the United States during the Cold War have frequently contended with institutional tug of wars among their different component institutions, with each scrambling to set national policy. During their hegemonic heyday, the greatest competitor to Whitehall's policymaking towards a given part of the globe was usually not the French Third Republic or tsarist Russia but other centres of authority within the British imperial bureaucracy, like the Colonial or India Offices. In areas in which they traditionally held sway, the British imperial authorities were remarkably skilled at keeping the tsar and the French at bay, even as interoffice rivalries led to many a suboptimal policy outcome.

But in such circumstances, no matter how hard the India Office tried to undermine the Cairo Bureau of the Foreign Office's policy goals—as infamously happened in the Arabian Peninsula during the First World War when it supported Ibn Saud and opposed the Hashemites, while the Cairo Bureau did the opposite[9]—there were limits to such struggles and a certain

5

civility inherent in them. The rival institutions were both seeking to forward their vision of the national interest. Each could ultimately be made to answer to the national chain of command but only if national leadership brought sufficient political capital to bear on sorting out the mess.

President George W. Bush famously favoured the Pentagon over the State Department in the formulation of his post-conflict reconstruction policy in Iraq—effectively forcing his diplomats to defer to his generals.[10] Was that the right decision? Probably not, but it was the president's decision—and it was duly implemented within the bureaucracy. If he had reversed it a few months into the conflict, the Pentagon would have likely stood down and State Department plans would have been implemented.

Multinational collective action problems are different. When Italy and France have opposing policies towards post-Qadhafi Libya, the EU lacks a mechanism to force the French to adopt the Italians' preferred policy or vice versa. The EU does not even have the right to demand that efforts be undertaken to formulate, let alone implement, a compromise policy. In fact, as rival sovereign national actors, there exists no decision-making hierarchy to adjudicate between them. As a result, in the absence of binding mechanisms to adjudicate collective action complexities among their members, international institutions like the EU, UN, and NATO become venues for feuding national powers to attempt to capture those institutions' policymaking capacities. They may also become venues for proponents of disorder to erect institutional roadblocks to stymie the gears of collaboration or to promote suboptimal multilateral collaboration. This latter approach defines much of Russian diplomacy in the UN over the last decade.

Global governance is a myth: The nation-state still reigns sovereign

The international organizations that arose in the wake of the Second World War simply enshrined the Westphalian logic that

6

national sovereignty is absolute and constitutes the immutable building block of all international political life. Those institutions were built to prevent states from violating other states' sovereign rights.[11] According to a maximalist interpretation, frequently put forth by China and Russia, the logic of the Westphalian and postcolonial order of sovereign nation-states entails that all states intrinsically have the right to adopt any domestic policies they wish—such as to pollute, adopt discriminatory legislation, and to incarcerate, re-educate, or kill those they deem criminals.[12] This view is upheld by certain classical IR theorists who perceive this as the necessary corollary of a Westphalian world.

Conversely, the post-Second World War period has seen some facets of national sovereignty delegated to a range of transnational governance institutions like the International Monetary Fund, the World Bank, IAEA (International Atomic Energy Agency), UNDP (United Nations Development Programme), UNHCR (United Nations High Commissioner for Refugees), WHO (World Health Organization), and ICC (International Criminal Court), as well as curtailed by treaties on climate change, human rights, anti-terrorism, and anti-corruption. However, according to many non-European powers and classical IR scholars like Richard Haass, these delegations of sovereignty can only be done voluntarily by states and as such uphold the principle of immutable Westphalian national sovereignty on which modern international relations and the post-1945 global institutions are based.

This principle of absolute national sovereignty, which is not contested in most schools of international law, inherently enshrines collective action problems among nations, unless like-minded nations voluntarily work together, defer to more powerful allies/transnational bodies, or are compelled to abide by rules of engagement set by a hegemon. Given this, the EU seeks to get around this conundrum by pooling some aspects of sovereignty. Nonetheless, it still cannot compel even Malta (its smallest member state) to follow EU guidelines as they pertain to Libya.[13] The UN has even less leverage over its members, especially when the five permanent members of the UN Security Council are divided, as they are on the Libya file, and therefore unwilling to work together to enforce UN Security Resolutions against specific members of the General Assembly.[14]

Despite these widely known facts, there remains a widespread misconception about the major post-war international organizations, namely that they exist to provide global governance but are just doing a bad job of it.[15] Paradoxically, this canard is promoted both by advocates of global governance on the centre-left and its opponents on the anti-globalization right.

In fact, the famous post-war international organizations listed above do nothing to forward genuine global governance and were not created to do so. They are built upon the bulwark of the supremacy of national sovereignty, which they deliberately reinforce. As such, international institutions do not alleviate the collective action problems that the system of sovereign nation-states and international competition engender. According to this perspective, no amount of reform or strengthening of international institutions will allow them to engage in the functions of mediating collective action problems among their members.

In our current international system, the only thing that does is hegemonic power. This has been the main contention of a large subfield of realist IR scholars like Hans J. Morgenthau, Kenneth Waltz, and others. Another group of historians—we can term them civilizationalists—have analysed five millennia of written human history to demonstrate that peace, prosperity, and coordination among nations are more likely to reign when a single power rules the seas, sets the terms of trade, and imposes, polices, and funds its own version of world order.[16] Given this state of affairs, it should surprise no one that since 2011 new forms of global disorder have arisen as American hegemony has receded.

That bygone era when men were men, allies were loyal, and America ruled the roost

The Libya context provides every indication that Western policy incoherence will worsen as American hegemony fades and transatlantic cooperation recedes. In fact, the Libyan microcosm reveals quite clearly the weakness of international institutions and the inability of the EU, UN, or NATO to serve as an appropriate venue to coordinate differing Western interests. Those bodies still function effectively as coordinating vehicles when states share interests and are aligned on policy outcomes. But what happens when states have slightly different interests and are unwilling to compromise for the sake of the greater good? These institutions and our current system of international relations are insufficient to bridge the gap between recalcitrant sovereign actors divided on fundamental policy goals.

It is not a question of reforming those institutions or giving them more money or expanding their remits. These institutions are not fit for purpose to face the challenges posed by the era of the Enduring Disorder. As explained, they were created to protect states against violations of their own sovereignty and to buttress the basic 'values-based' tenets[17] of an American-led Cold War world order—already characterized by a great degree of voluntary Western cooperation in the economic, military, and foreign policy spheres.

During the entire Cold War period and the two decades after it,[18] nearly all major Western military interventions and post-conflict reconstruction attempts were led by the United States. Those that did not have American approval, like the Anglo-French Suez Campaign of 1956, ended in ignominy.[19] It was understood in the corridors of power that Western military responses to global problems were, perforce, to be American-led. Hence inconsistencies between conception and execution could clearly be traced to the interplay among various US political institutions like Congress, the civilian cabinet-level departments (State, Treasury, Commerce, etc.), and the plethora of intelligence and military agencies that also sit under the executive branch.

In each of the famous cases of early post-Cold War 'American leadership'—the Balkans, Afghanistan, and Iraq—military actions might have been undertaken for the wrong reasons or the exit strategy poorly thought out, but they were 'coherently' conceived and executed by a US-led coalition. The role of the UN or NATO was one of providing a rubber stamp (or not) in the case of the former and a coordination mechanism (or not) in the case of the latter. NATO and the UN did not independently create the political will or draft the action plans that undergirded decision-making or its execution. International organizations are not governments, they have no direct electoral legitimacy, and hence cannot generate political will independently from their member states. The EU is slightly different as it has directly elected officials and is theoretically able to generate crosscutting political will directly from its constituents rather than mediated via national leaderships, but there are few, if any, examples of it successfully imposing its will on recalcitrant member states.

International organizations like those already discussed, as well as the IMF, World Bank, and the regional associations like the Gulf Cooperation Council (GCC) and Association of Southeast Asian Nations (ASEAN), fulfil the role for which those bodies were designed: coordinating mechanisms to undergird pre-existing cooperation, consensus-building, coordination, information-sharing, and deconfliction among nations states. They were not originally conceived, nor given the structures, budgets, and staffs, to replace national-level decision-making, to devise and orchestrate longer-term strategic planning, or to adjudicate entrenched disputes among members.[20]

In short, we do not, and have never, lived in a world with effective global or regional governance institutions able to forge compromises among divergent sovereign actors. Human history is characterized by periods of disorder punctuated by those of occasional hegemonic order, usually deriving from control of the Eurasian heartland. The last bout of American hegemony differed from previous empires in that: (1) it did not arise from the Eurasian heartland, and (2) it spawned a range of permeant bureaucratic coordinating forums, rather than the ad hoc ones that characterized previous empires like the British, Habsburg, and Roman.[21]

The Cold War (1947–89) and early post-Cold-War periods (1991–2003) could, therefore, be characterized in the military sphere by the 'American-led, global institution-mediated, coalition of the willing' approach. Its drawbacks were legion, but that model had one clear strength that has not attracted enough scholarly attention: an identifiable and enforceable hierarchy of decision-making. The 'adults in the room' may have been misguided, as during the Iraq War, or they may have chosen the wrong local partners, as in Afghanistan, but in both cases high-level strategy was set in Washington and diligently implemented in the field. Washington's policy was not undermined or scuttled in the field by American troops, diplomats, or its allies. Policy blunders like de-baathification were chosen by Undersecretary of Defense Douglas Feith, cleared through the interagency process, received the imprimatur of the President, and were then delegated to the Head of the Coalition Provisional Authority Ambassador Paul Bremer to implement in Baghdad.[22]

The buck stopped at the top of the legible hierarchy of command linking the president, secretary of state, National Security Council, the Armed Services, and the intelligence community.

Even so, coordinating the ever-expanding behemoth that is the US government proved difficult enough. On many occasions the State Department, intelligence community, and the Pentagon had different approaches to a given conflict, giving rise to one of the aforementioned tug-of-war of forces.

This phenomenon was on clear display in the months after the toppling of Saddam Hussein in 2003. The State Department had elaborate plans concerning an invasion of Iraq left over from 1991. These were not consulted by the Pentagon, where officials kept their colleagues at other departments in the dark.[23] However, even as the Pentagon was undermining the State Department's objectives, America's British, Polish, Georgian, and other allies were in the field diligently carrying out the responsibilities that the US Central Command (CENTCOM) had assigned to them. Behind closed doors, those allies might forcefully disagree with the action plan chosen—and in their public diplomatic pronouncements, they might articulate slightly different policy goals from their American partners—but they never deliberately undermined American objectives, either covertly or overtly.

Scuttling US initiatives was simply not how allies treated the US during the Cold War and early post-Cold War periods. Even dissenting allies like the Germans and French during the Second Iraq War stayed away from overtly or even covertly undermining American objectives. They simply sat the campaigns out. The same had happened in Vietnam.[24] US allies did not pursue divergent or opposing policies aimed at facilitating American military failures.

As a result, there was no multinational tug of war to set Western policy towards Iraq or Afghanistan. America ran the show, chose wisely or poorly, and its allies either chose to be involved or respectfully sat on the side lines. Yes, American enemies like Russia, Iran, and Syria pursued policies meant to undermine American objectives, but they did not subvert

Western policy formation from the inside. That was simply not how the game was played during the Cold War and early post-Cold War periods.[25]

It would be difficult to overestimate how much things have changed in about a decade's time.

PART II
A COLLECTIVE MALFUNCTION

Presidents and prime ministers tend to fight the last war

As complex and dysfunctional as the forces that shaped American-led military policy towards Iraq in 2003–9 might seem, Western policy towards Libya from 2011 to the present involved yet another new layer of complexity. The contrasts between foreign policymaking towards Iraq as opposed to Libya vividly highlight the collective action challenges that Western efforts to solve foreign policy problems will almost certainly encounter as we move further into the era of the Enduring Disorder.

How did America's will to lead, and the willingness of its allies to follow, dissipate so quickly? It was not primarily caused by a shift in relative economic muscle, as America's proportion of the global economy and percentage of global military spending only gradually declined as its hegemony waned—and both figures were far higher than the British Empire ever enjoyed, even during the peak of its global hegemony.[26] The ballooning American national debt over the course of the early twenty-first century is also unlikely to have played a role, as its growth did not curb American military, diplomatic, or foreign aid spending—nor has it deterred the massive globalization of American venture capital or the competitiveness of American firms. One major component of the answer is that the quagmire in Iraq gave rise to imperial fatigue in the American electorate. Conversely, in major allied capitals it furthered the desire to develop separate military and foreign policies able to counterbalance those of the US.[27]

In the wake of the Iraq quagmire, President Obama promised that America would no longer pursue unilateral solutions to foreign policy problems, while Prime Minister David Cameron and President Nicolas Sarkozy also moved in the opposite direction from their predecessors, promising more robust British and French actions separately from the 'misguided Americans'.

All three leaders came into office vowing to do the opposite of what their predecessors had done in Iraq. Bush cast a particularly long shadow over Obama. Obama did not want to make any foreign policy decisions that could be perceived as 'American unilateralism', instead aiming to deploy the military primarily for humanitarian objectives rather than to secure 'hard' geostrategic interests.[28] Cameron, on the other hand, wished to lead 'authentically British' foreign policy responses. He did not want to emulate Tony Blair as an enabler and apologist of American intervention. Somewhat paradoxically, Sarkozy opted for both increased Atlanticism combined with a neo-Gaullism in protection of 'uniquely French' interests. He did not wish to emulate Jacques Chirac's perceived passivity in the face of French interests being harmed by American-led misadventures, yet he also wanted to strengthen the Franco-American ties that his predecessor had frayed.

Ironically, the three leaders were profoundly disunited by their shared desires to make the opposite choices of their predecessors—all of whom 'happened' to be from the opposite political parties. Therefore, heading into the Arab Spring uprisings, the geopolitical stage could not have been more perfectly set for the main players to make the exact opposite mistakes to what their predecessors had done vis-à-vis the Iraq intervention.

The Arab Spring was also the first major foreign policy challenge to test this new constellation of leaders, as well as the inner workings of a less hegemonic global order. As events kicked off in December 2010, Sarkozy was seen as too slow to remove his support from Ben Ali in Tunisia. When Ben Ali was toppled, protests then erupted 3,000 kilometres away in Egypt on 25 January 2011. As street demonstrations around Cairo's Tahrir Square grew larger and occasioned counterreactions from regime thugs, Obama sought to maintain a cautious approach, preferring to await developments even as the crisis was profoundly affecting American alliances in the region.[29] Obama truly found himself in an impossible position. Any statements he would make or actions he might undertake would be attacked by one side or another. Even cautious non-action risked angering key allies. His perceived passivity upset the United States' Saudi and Emirati allies who wanted the Americans to help keep Egyptian President Hosni Mubarak in power. Conversely, Egyptian civil society groups that America had nurtured felt that the US had abandoned them and failed to come to the aid of democracy-loving protestors while allowing the regime to crack down with impunity.[30]

Shortly after Mubarak was ousted on 11 February by an alliance of convenience between the Army top brass and the protestors, Libyans began organizing their own 'Day of Rage', explicitly scheduled for the 17 February anniversary of protests against the Danish cartoons satirizing the prophet Muhammad. When these protests developed a life of their own and erupted in Libya two days ahead of schedule, Qadhafi's brutal repression quickly transformed them into an armed insurrection. The possibility of an ensuing humanitarian crisis galvanized the international community to study and formulate a possible reaction in a way that events in Tunisia and Egypt had not.

Each power wished to engage in Libya for slightly different reasons, with the US overtly seeking to transfer its traditional leadership/coordination burden. Yet, no other nation or coalition was ready or able to adopt the task. Since the Iraq war had played out as an unprovoked American-led intervention followed by an imposed nation-building exercise that occasioned massive opposition globally to any future Western military interventions in the Middle East, the West was slow to offer the Libyan protestors concrete military support, even when requested by the rebel administration and the Arab League. The major Western powers only provided a light-touch aerial support mission, and then left before offering or imposing the requisite capacity-building assistance.[31]

Obama was truly a man of his word. Prior American presidents had sought to recalibrate America's role abroad, but then in the throes of a crisis, defaulted to traditional patterns of hegemonic leadership, which manifested themselves anew as if they were encoded in the American military and diplomatic establishment's DNA. Yet, Obama was able to oppose the bureaucracy's inclinations. As early as the campaign trail, he knew his own mind about America's new place in the world. Once in office, when push came to shove, he remained wedded to a novel style of global leadership: consultative, hands-off, rigorously within the bounds of international law.

And yet, as a gentleman and a legal scholar, he had read his Hobbes. He knew that in moments of crisis, like wars and pandemics, humans tend to prefer efficient tyrannical governments to no government at all. Yet, he did not extend this thinking to the game of nations.

The 2011 Uprisings in Libya as the opening act of the Enduring Disorder

When peaceful protests began in Benghazi on 15 February 2011, the Qadhafi regime cracked down in a far more brutal way than the Tunisian or Egyptian regimes had responded to their own

Arab Spring demonstrations a few weeks earlier. Rather than the old logic of an abrupt massacre quelling dissent, images of brutality went viral and drove more protestors outside. The damage was compounded when Qadhafi's reformist son and heir apparent, Saif al-Islam, doubled down on the regime's message that the protestors needed to be quashed.

Saif was the head of the *Libya al-Ghad* project that was touted as creating a reformed, transparent, and free media landscape supposedly fostering open political dialogue to address Libyans' justified grievances. He was also the figurehead for the post-2005 economic restructuring at the hands of the Anglo-American consultancy Monitor Group and the re-opening of Libya to Western companies. Many had therefore hoped that he would bridge the gap between regime hardliners and the protesters by promising meaningful reforms and pointing to the legitimacy of certain popular grievances.[32] Instead, he made incendiary speeches and used his vast media empire to echo his father's line about the protestors being Islamists, rats, and enemies of the people. The *Qurina* newspaper, for example, known to be controlled by Saif al-Islam, behaved like a Soviet-style propaganda organ and not an outlet of open political dialogue as Saif had promised.[33]

In the wake of a united Qadhafi family approach of old school propaganda and senseless repression, what had started as civil society activists and lawyers protesting peacefully outside the Benghazi courthouse quickly metastasized into a full-fledged rebel movement with defectors from the Qadhafian bureaucracy, army, and diplomatic core creating the nascent institutions of a new sovereign authority in waiting. Simultaneously, they claimed to speak on behalf of those who had taken up arms, the *thuwwar* or rebels.[34]

As the anti-Qadhafi movement quickly gained control of much of eastern Libya and then pushed westward across the oil crescent region of central Libya, these successes sparked copycat movements deep inside Qadhafi-held territory. What had started as a leaderless uprising also developed a kind of 'institutionality' via the formation of the National Transitional Council (NTC)[35] and various military coordination mechanisms.

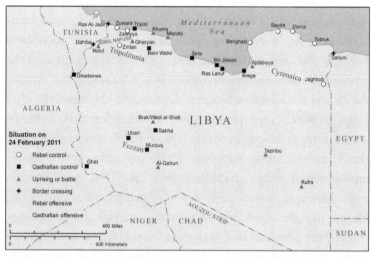

Map 1: February 2011—Disconnected Uprisings Sweep across Libya

As his forces were haemorrhaging territory in late February, Qadhafi gave his infamous '*shibr shibr, beit beit, zenga zenga*' speech in Arabic, humorously calling for a genocide.[36] He followed this up days later with an address in broken English containing the memorable lines: 'No demonstrations in the streets, no demonstrations at all. They love me all my beoble [*sic*], they love me all, they will die to protect me.'[37] Taken together, these speeches simultaneously proclaimed two mutually contradictory claims: (1) that all the Libyan people loved Qadhafi, would die to protect him, and that there were no protests; and (2) that Qadhafi would personally oversee the hunting down of the protestors house by house, street by street, alley by alley, and massacre them. Even more paradoxically, it was these two perverse speeches, more than any of the regime's military actions, which occasioned both viral YouTube spoofs and the international diplomatic conferences that led to the regime's downfall. The two phenomena (the YouTube parody of Qadhafi's speech set by an Israeli musician to a backdrop of a mirrored image of a scantily clad blond dancing to disco music[38] and the calls for the no-fly zone) were not as unconnected as they might seem.[39] This was an early example of the efficacy of social media-friendly strategic communications during the Enduring Disorder—a historical epoch where popular attention could easily be captured by click baiting memes. As a result, political leaders careened between inaction to genuine threats and overreaction to sensationalized developments, which happened to be capturing their constituents' attention at any given moment.[40]

Given the success of the Arab Spring movements in Egypt and Tunisia over the previous three months, certain Western countries' foreign ministries and military establishments considered overtly supporting the rebel movement in the third week of February, but ultimately didn't want to take the plunge, while the outcome of the military conflict hung in the balance and it seemed quite likely that the Qadhafi regime would emerge victorious. During this wait and see period, the UN passed UNSCR 1970 on 26 February 2011, launching an international commission of inquiry into Qadhafi's response to the Uprisings, along with sanctions and an arms embargo.[41] At the time, the swiftness and unanimity of the international community allowed pundits to hail these moves as 'a triumph of multilateralism'.[42] But behind the façade of effective unified actions at the UN, these first steps attempting to tip the balance in favour of the *thuwwar* were ineffective.

In the wake of Resolution 1970, the tide of battle reversed against the *thuwwar* in early March. Only at this point was serious international action to tip the scales being contemplated. The French and Qataris were the first to advocate for a proactive international community-led military response: Western aerial support imposing a 'humanitarian' no-fly zone coupled with diplomatic recognition of the rebel movement. As the British, Emiratis, Turks, and Scandinavians joined the fray, they did not see themselves as following the French lead but as independently shaping the international community's policy towards Libya. Was this the 'triumph of multilateralism' hailed in governmental speeches or a disorderly leaderless scramble to formulate policy?

By 6 March, the rebel movement was in full-scale retreat eastward across the oil crescent towards Benghazi. It had already faced major military reversals and the loss of most of the territory that it initially acquired via defections of whole garrisons in the first twenty days of the Uprisings.[43]

On 12 March, the Arab League tossed its hat in the ring when it called for a no-fly zone to be enforced over Libyan skies. This was the first time in the institution's sixty-five-year history that it had called for non-Arab powers to undertake military actions inside an Arab state. The Arab diplomats who had voted for such bold action sought to portray a united Arab front, even papering over Syria's and Algeria's opposition as 'non-representative'.[44]

Armed with this propaganda victory courtesy of the Arab League, the NTC declared itself the sovereign government of Libya and invited foreign powers to enforce a no-fly zone over what it deemed its sovereign air space. The French echoed these proposals as a means to overcome a potential Russian or Chinese veto at the UN.[45] And Bernard-Henri Lévy, the Franco-Jewish philosopher with North African roots, vouched for the credentials of the rebel leadership and warned that a 'real genocide' might ensue if no Western support was offered.[46] He was joined by other philosophers and various international legal scholars who presented the case for invoking the legal principle of the

'Responsibility to Protect'. In response to these developments, a triumvirate of senior Obama foreign policy officials—Susan Rice, Samantha Power, and Hillary Clinton—progressively nudged the Obama administration off the fence, foregrounding humanitarian and PR concerns rather than geostrategic imperatives.[47]

Obama Doctrine

The US administration had been slow to react to developments in Tunisia and Egypt. It was unclear if this was because changing entrenched policies in the American ship of state was like attempting to steer the *Titanic* once the iceberg was spotted or because the top brass were absorbed with their contemplations of what Colin Powell termed the Pottery Barn Rule: 'You break it. You own it'. With Mubarak's fall, Obama's caution had made it seem to some as though the US sought to prop up the North African *ancien régimes* as long as that remained possible, but also wished to switch sides once the protestors were clearly on the verge of toppling the incumbent power structure. Scarred by their personal experiences in Iraq, many American diplomats sought to avoid dictating to America's allies the overarching goals of any international action or the necessary structures of coordination.

It has since come to light that secret conversations were held on the margins of the UN General Assembly about regime change and nation-building, as opposed to merely massacre prevention, but that these were led by the French and the British.[48] These discussions were spurred forward by the Qadhafi regime's seemingly relentless counterattack: first eastward across the oil crescent in the first week of March and then northward from Ajdabiya towards Benghazi from 14 to 18 March.

In its policy towards the Libyan crisis, the US was balancing a need for better optics with a desire to implement a wholly new kind of foreign policy strategy: striving to appear to be on the

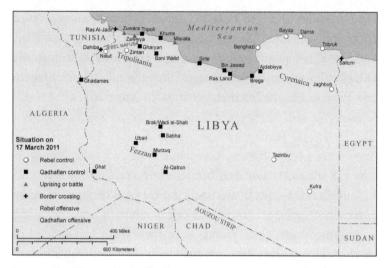

Map 2: March 2011—Qadhafi's Imminent Attack on Benghazi Prompts the No-Fly Zone

side of the protestors (unlike in Egypt) while also waiting for a consensus to arise among the other major international actors so as not to seem to be unduly influencing the trajectory of the response. Therefore, despite the significant risk that further delay might allow for the complete destruction of the rebel army or portrayals of America as unwilling to stand up for democratic protestors when the regime they were opposing had restarted major oil production sharing arrangements with American companies, the Obama administration resisted defaulting to traditional patterns of hegemonic leadership.

As stated above, this was genuinely remarkable. Obama followed through on his campaign trail promise. The 'America leads and a coalition of the willing follows' approach, which had characterized American crisis leadership for seven decades, was now a thing of the past. Even when faced with dissenters in his cabinet, Obama was wedded to his new style of global leadership: inclusive, hesitant, and consultative. He was genuinely committed to going with the flow of our allies' wishes, even when American interests and lives were imperilled.

There was a new sheriff in town and his formative experience was as a Chicago community organizer and son of an anthropology professor rather than as a Texas oilman and son of a billionaire former president. Obama and his secretaries of state sought to avoid leading the old fashioned American cowboy way. They were genuinely committed to the noble goal of reversing the wrong-headed unilateralism of the Bush years without ever fully acknowledging the collective action problems that such an approach entailed for the international system as a whole.

The American ship of state had careened from the chauvinistic Bush-era 'you are either with us or against us' to the scholarly 'we should further study the matter and don't want to get out in front of our allies, let's wait until they convene a committee'. The assertive approach of old—that 'the world needs a leader and the accidents of history have anointed us', to which America's best statesmen from Marshall, to Kennan, to Kissinger, to Scowcroft had subscribed—was now a thing of the remote past.

During the 2011 Libyan Uprisings, the novel 'Obama Doctrine' was much praised on the left and centre of the American political spectrum. Yet, less than a decade later, as a result of his subsequent inaction in Syria and Crimea, Obama's legacy is now widely perceived as chequered.[49] It could be said that in many realms, domestic and international, his moderation and careful circumspection inadvertently aided and abetted the opposite political forces of those he meant to support. This illustrates another paradox at the heart of the Enduring Disorder. The Western left's focus on equality, rule of law, identity politics, and personal choice may end up undermining each of those lofty goals by engendering policymaking paralysis by empowering exactly those civil society voices who prefer to contend with one another rather than take direction from policy elites.[50]

LIBYA AND THE GLOBAL ENDURING DISORDER

The genie was never going to go back in the bottle

Some American foreign policy experts mistook Obama's new wait-and-see-what-our-allies-do approach towards Libya as stemming from a lack of US interests in the country and an ambivalence to how the war would turn out. Richard Haass claimed at the time and since[51] that the lacklustre American response was occasioned by Libya's lack of direct importance for American geostrategic interests. Haass argued that, win or lose, Qadhafi did not pose a large threat to, nor his replacement a major opportunity for, the United States. The corollary to his thesis was that when supposedly 'more significant American interests' were threatened, then the Obama administration would employ more assertive and unilateral leadership styles.

Contrary to Haass's expectations, no matter how big the geostrategic implications at stake, Obama never defaulted to hegemonic leadership. The 2014 Ukraine crisis touched the most essential conceivable US interests as defined by Haass himself,[52] and still the Obama administration did not hegemonically spearhead a unified Western response.

Rather, American delegation to its allies or outright inaction was the same over Ukraine as over Syria, where US interests were distinctly more peripheral. Yet in all these cases, both those of profound geostrategic and economic import (Ukraine and to a slightly lesser extent Libya) and those of more humanitarian and demographic importance (Syria and Yemen), the Obama administration did not coordinate a robust international response nor did the Europeans step into the void, even though these crises were all in their proverbial backyard and risked unleashing truly existential threats for the European Union.[53]

What was happening vis-à-vis the coordination of the Western response to the Libyan Uprisings had nothing to do with the size of the geopolitical or financial interests at stake, but with new types of difficulties regarding collective action.[54] As events were unfolding, I argued the opposite of Haass, namely that Libya was far 'too big to fail'[55] and that its continued stability, wealth, and pro-NATO orientation was a *sine qua non* for Western security, energy, counterterror, and economic interests being upheld throughout the Middle East, Africa, and Southern Europe.[56]

Moreover, abandoning the *thuwwar* after they had requested Western assistance and the Arab League had called for it would have weakened American soft power throughout the region. It would likely have been only a slightly worse media relations disaster than the Second Iraq War. It is quite possible that it would have led to a proxy civil war as brutal as Syria's.[57] The Qadhafi regime had opened up diplomatically and financially to the West during the détente period of 2003–10.[58] However, it had made clear since the Uprisings began that it saw the West as complicit in the rebel movement. Qadhafi proclaimed that the West had put LSD in the water to turn the innocent Libyan youth against him. He made amply clear that if he emerged 'victorious' in reasserting control, he would be forced to adopt a neo-rogue posture—returning to the bad old days of the 1980s: working with the Russians, and supporting so-called liberation movements and terrorists across the entire developing world.[59]

A failure to counter Qadhafi's threats against the civilian population of Benghazi and moves to reimpose his dictatorship across Libya would have damaged Western influence in the country and throughout Africa and the Middle East. It would have been especially humiliating for the United States given its previous rhetoric about human rights and the responsibility to protect. It would also have had costs. American firms had billions of dollars in back payments to collect and tens of billions worth of signed projects to administer or build. A neo-rogue Qadhafi— who had reoccupied and 'cleansed' Benghazi—was not going to allow Halliburton to fix the pipeline network, Hill International to finish building new Libyan university campuses, Merck to deliver diabetes medicines, or ConocoPhillips to reap the benefits of upgrading the storage tankers at Sidra. Western inaction over Libya's skies leading to a neo-rogue Qadhafi fighting an ongoing civil war against his own people would also have been a highly welcome outcome for Putin.[60] Either Qadhafi would find himself bogged down in years of a brutal Syria-style civil war and would need to become a direct Russian client to eventually prevail, or if he miraculously defeated his challengers and reverted to hardline totalitarianism, Putin would be able to become allies with a neo-rogue Qadhafi ensconced at the very centre of the Mediterranean, sitting on 400 billion dollars in sovereign wealth and over three trillion dollars worth of proven crude reserves.[61] In short, the genie was out of the bottle, it could never be put back, and the only people who would benefit from a Qadhafi victory lived in places like Moscow, Tehran, Caracas, and Pyongyang.

Leading from behind

Despite the profound geostrategic implications that hung in the balance, the Obama administration neither pushed for urgent action over Libya's skies nor sought to define the goals of the international mission that might arise. In the shadow of this existential threat to Western interests in the very heart of the Mediterranean, the language of the Security Council resolutions was largely provided by Britain, amended by France, and quickly hammered out among all Security Council members permanent and non-permanent to assure zero no votes and abstentions from only Russia, China, Germany, Brazil, and India.[62]

UNSCR 1973, passed on 18 March 2011, called for a no-fly zone to prevent harm to civilians—it also indirectly served as legal cover to provide international aerial support to the Libyan rebels. To legitimate this violation of Libyan sovereign air space, it invoked the international legal principle of Responsibility to Protect or R2P. Yet, those who advocated for this course of action were primarily concerned with geostrategic interests.[63] Rather than being the world's first successful R2P operation, it should be seen as the first act of Western military policy to be formulated according to the new zeitgeist of the Enduring Disorder. Many actors and institutions vied to set the Western response, the final outcome was not the intention of any individual actor, US leadership was largely absent, and even in the early stages, as Russia and China sat on the sidelines, Western nations were not in agreement among themselves. As the no-fly zone took shape, supporters of the president christened his masterful handling of the crisis as laying out a new 'Obama Doctrine'. His opponents referred to his performance derogatorily as 'leading from behind'.[64]

In this opening act of the Enduring Disorder, part of the reasons for the Western powers' course of action was coordination failures between different actors, with each simply trying not to appear flat-footed. The whole episode occurred during a rare moment when the US–Russia 'reset' was working and the Russians were amenable to 'allowing' Western support for the Libyan protestors as a show of their goodwill towards Western interests. The Medvedev government condoned its implicit violation of the Russian interpretation of the immutable principle of state sovereignty by not vetoing Resolution 1973.[65] As the ambit of the no-fly zone was widened as 2011 progressed, the Russians felt betrayed by the West and vowed to block UN-sanctioned actions against the Assad regime's crackdown against its own people.[66] In fact, Russian disappointment over Libya was one of the key issues that led to Putin pulling the foreign affairs portfolio from then President Medvedev and the restart of neo-Cold War dynamics.[67]

Syria was then the second act of the Enduring Disorder— inevitably linked to Libya, yet with the roles of the Russians and the West essentially reversed. In the words of Richard Northern, British ambassador to Libya at the time the Uprisings broke out:

> A perverse consequence of the [diplomatic] success of [the international community to gain legal approval to act] in Libya was repeated Russian and Chinese obstruction of a coordinated international response to the situation in Syria in early to mid-2012. Never again would Putin succumb to humanitarian or popular pressure to grant UN-sanction to a Western-led attempt to remove a Russian ally.[68]

Let the fireworks begin

With the resolution in hand, the bombing began. Despite the novel collective action complexities posed by the multipolar Western policy formation process, the military enforcement of the no-fly zone was coordinated quite effectively. Nonetheless, the French made sure to get a few sorties in prior to the UN resolution officially coming into force—likely to compensate for their delayed action in Tunisia and to showcase domestically Sarkozy's swashbuckling persona and defence of long-term French interests prior to an upcoming election.[69]

The first few official days of sorties brought with it the need for American in-air refuelling capacity. This necessitated that American targeting procedures be followed. Immediately after Qadhafian command and control structures were obliterated and the immediate existential threat to the rebel movement was obviated, NATO was appointed as the coordinating body for the no-fly zone—even though some NATO members like Germany sat the operation out, and non-NATO members like Jordan, the Emirates, and Qatar all flew sorties.[70] At this stage, policy was merely being implemented and deconflicted, rather than formulated *de novo*. As such, NATO mechanisms were tailormade for the mission and functioned remarkably effectively.

Due to superior technology than that employed in the Iraq War, there were surprisingly few civilian casualties from NATO airstrikes. Precision munitions hit Qadhafi-regime power centres, the Qadhafian air force was wiped out in a matter of hours, and most tanks and armed personnel carriers (APCs) threatening rebel civilian population centres were obliterated as soon as they drove towards their targets. By mid-April, the rebels had regained the territory that they had lost in early March. Then the war bogged down over the summer as Qadhafian forces altered their tactics, trading in their easy to spot and destroy tanks and APCs for crude imitations of the camouflaged pickup trucks and 'technicals' (4x4s with mounted machine guns)[71] used by the rebel forces.[72]

Amid this new way of war, centrifugal tendencies were at work. Each militia fought Qadhafi's forces separately. Most towns gave rise to multiple militias with very loose command and control linkages. The French, British, Americans, and Emiratis each developed special ties with different militia elements in Zintan. The British, Turks, and Italians built on pre-existing linkages with Misrata, while the Qataris and Turks cast themselves as the patrons of those Tripoli-based militias who derived their military expertise from returnees from the Afghan jihad.

During nearly three months of stalemate, the different social segments that had risen up against Qadhafi began to squabble among themselves. The NTC's generalissimo Abdul-Fateh Younis was killed on 28 July under mysterious circumstances. Some blamed the Islamists, others the hardline revolutionaries who refused to be led by a defector from the Qadhafi regime. The implications were far-reaching—Younis's eastern 'Obeidat tribe was permanently alienated from the NTC's and later the General National Congress's (GNC) power centres for their failure to bring the killers to justice. More critically, circumstances were never again as conducive for the emergence of a professionalized army with a single leader answerable to legitimate civilian authorities and tasked with incorporating the militias.

Younis's death was the original sin of the anti-Qadhafi Uprisings. The revolution had eaten its own, and it had developed a taste for such cannibalism. Nonetheless, with their command and control structures in increasing disarray, the rebels broke through, capturing Tripoli on 20 August. Qadhafian defences evaporated as key defenders switched sides.[73] A scramble ensued. It was the culmination of a long competition among militias backed by Qatar,[74] Italy, the UK, and Turkey and those backed by France, the Emirates,[75] and the United States. Each grouping wanted to seize the capital first and control key strategic locations like the airport, banks, hospitals, and ministries.

Our man in Tripoli

No sooner had Tripoli fallen than alternative Western plans were put forth for its stabilization. In theory, the UN Stabilization Team headquartered in Abu Dhabi was the coordinating body through which these plans were to flow, but in reality, a policy vacuum appeared on the ground as no coherent plans existed. Despite the six months of war, the inhabitants of Tripoli had not directly joined the Uprisings and hence were liberated by 'outsiders', whom many perceived as a new occupying force. To make matters worse, Tripoli had fallen too abruptly and without any coherent leadership emerging on either the military or the political wings of the anti-Qadhafi coalition. Neighbourhood councils and militias sprouted up everywhere to protect their constituents. In short, no one knew who was now in charge. Yes, the key NTC players who claimed to be in charge—Mahmoud Jibril, Mustafa Abdul Jalil, and Ali Tarhouni—were widely known in Libyanist circles, but the powerbrokers on the ground with guns were mostly unknown, untested entities.[76]

At this critical juncture, what was most urgently needed was the immediate imposition of civilian control by the NTC over

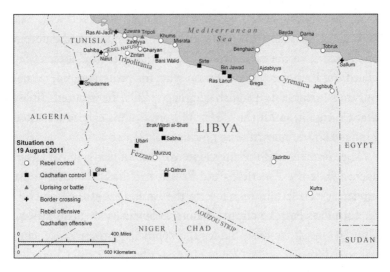

Map 3: August 2011—The Rebel Assault on Tripoli

the mopping up and stabilization activities of the victorious militias in concert with international peacekeepers and capacity-builders.[77] Yet, within the evolving NTC power structure, the Americans, British, and French had each cultivated their own preferred interlocutors, while the NTC was wary of not only international peacekeepers but even of Western capacity-building assistance. The new NTC leaders were becoming addicted to their first taste of power, something they had never really experienced even as senior public servants under the Qadhafi regime.

Abdul-Jalil was a former Qadhafian justice minister who had occasionally stood up for innocent civilians against the Qadhafi regime. Long considered a Muslim Brotherhood sympathizer, he had cultivated an image of saintly piety and preferred ties with Turkey and Qatar. Jibril was known to drink wine and have a high opinion of himself. Armed with his PhD from Pittsburgh, he had been appointed the head of the Economic Development Board in 2007, which was set up by the Monitor Group consultancy to implement the neo-liberal reforms associated with Saif al-Islam. Like many other reformist technocrats, he had defected to the rebels in the early days of the Uprisings. After successfully charming both Lévy and Clinton with his professorial demeanour and formidable English-language skills, he secured diplomatic recognition for the NTC. As a reward, his colleagues chose him as Libya's interim prime minister.[78]

The Germans and Italians suspected Jibril of being an American agent, while the Americans and British felt that his anti-Islamist tendencies made him too close to the Emiratis and the French.[79] In a similar vein, American advisors to Secretary of State Hillary Clinton—most famously Sidney Blumenthal, an investigative journalist and former senior White House staffer under Bill Clinton—were afraid that any peacekeepers/capacity-builders would be European-led. Blumenthal anticipated that British and French capacity-building efforts would create new Libyan institutions in such a way as to favour those nations' commercial interests, especially in the fields of oil and construction.[80]

Hegemonic corruption is the cleanest kind

It is worth digressing a bit from the narration of the exciting kinetic events of the 2011 Libyan Uprisings to investigate how distinctly novel Blumenthal's concern was.[81] America, in its role as global hegemon, had long been accused of taking more than its fair share of the global spoils and doing so in less than meritocratic ways—funnelling contracts in Iraq to Halliburton, for example.[82] But there was never any suspicion that British units in Basra or Helmand chose specific strategies that would favour British commercial interests in the wake of the fighting, or even more absurdly, that the small Polish or Georgian contingents in Iraq or Afghanistan would somehow cultivate linkages with the warlords that would help the commercial interests of those nations. At worst, the British, Poles, and Georgians could be accused of sending their youth to die in order to derive geopolitical and economic favours from the American hegemon, not from specific Iraqi or Afghan factions.

Like the Cold War period before it, the early post-Cold War period witnessed 'normal' hegemonic corruption and overreach—in which those at the top of the heap of the dominant country's power structure feathered their own nests once in a while. This amounted to something akin to collecting a tax for providing global policing services. This type of corruption was commonplace in the Roman, Habsburg, British, and other hegemonic empires. But lesser powers did not step out of line inside the hegemon's sphere of influence.

Therefore, even Blumenthal's rumours—picked up by WikiLeaks email dumps and again in Clinton's email scandal[83]— indicate that the decision matrices undergirding actions in Libya during the 2011 Uprisings were orders of magnitudes more complex than the old system of 'clean hegemonic corruption'. Rather than acting in concert—or disagreeing in the open—as they had previously, senior American officials suspected their French and British counterparts of secret plans. In the wake of Qadhafi's ouster, there was simply no consensus about which factions to back, which leaders to anoint, what development and reconstruction policies to pursue, or how the populace should be treated by their militia conquerors.

As would come to define post-conflict situations during the Enduring Disorder, events on the ground became catch-as-catch-can, rather than driven by any overarching policy promulgated by a dominant power. Exactly two months after the fall of Tripoli, the Misratans conquered the last Qadhafian strongholds in Sirte. A son of that city shot and captured Qadhafi before hauling his corpse off to a meat locker back in his hometown.[84] The Zintanis sought to push Qadhafi's allies among the Tuareg out of the south-west of the country and usurp their valuable smuggling networks.[85] In so doing, they captured Qadhafi's son Saif who was attempting to flee to Niger dressed as a Tuareg. Until the present, the Misratans and their international backers (at various times headed by the British, Qataris, Italians, Americans, and Turks) exert a sphere of expanding and contracting influence stretching from Tripoli to the western edge of the Sirte Basin. Conversely, the Zintanis' control over the southern Tripoli suburbs, Jabal Nafusa, and the Fezzan has ebbed and flowed. So too have their American, Emirati, and French allies' reach into those areas.

Like Blumenthal's fears about America's allies, each Libyan power base accused its sister militias and their backers of secret corrupt practices. Just as the Libyans forged a coalition of the willing that fell apart when the shared enemy disappeared, neither the French, British, Americans, Italians, EU, or UN could stake a claim to be *primus inter pares* among the relevant deci-

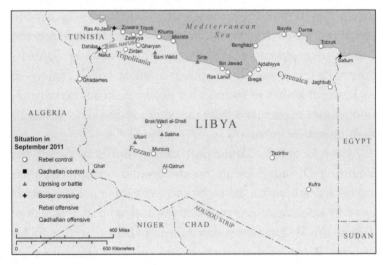

Map 4: September 2011—The Rebels Lay Siege to the Last Qadhafian Strongholds

sion-making organizations. The more time elapsed from Qadhafi's death, the more the different rebel power bases and their international power backers diverged from whatever coordination mechanisms had been in place to unify their actions during the no-fly zone.

Me against my brother, my brother and I against my cousin

Given the lack of coordination at the international level during the Enduring Disorder, no single coherent policy was pursued, nor any single coalition of Libyan leadership cultivated. In theory, the UN Support Mission in Libya (UNSMIL) was to be the sole coordinating body for all international policy towards Libya—stipulating that the top Western powers would primarily exert their influence through it. Reality did not play out accordingly, however. Each country's intelligence agencies, humanitarian aid agency, foreign ministry, and outsourced contractors conducted that nation's policy alone. National resources were not necessarily lent to the UN or other international organizations.

The true absurdity of this situation can be highlighted in the sphere of humanitarian development—the domain that one would imagine to be the least conflictual. Western countries poured development funding into an already wealthy Libya but with minimal results in terms of democracy promotion, women's rights, or constitutional awareness as a payoff. Donor meetings were organized in Tripoli in 2012–13, and later in Tunis from 2014 to the present, and much of the efforts of outfits like USAID, GIZ, and DFID were exerted on deconfliction of their aid priorities. Libyan civil society groups were jealously guarded by their international patrons, to avoid their preferred clients working with other donors or receiving training offered by NGOs of a rival nationality or agenda.[86]

The development sphere mirrored what was transpiring more covertly in the realm of policy. I still vividly recall a meeting I had with the EU ambassador to Libya, Nataliya Apostolova, in mid-2013. The ambassador invited me to her luxurious private residence in the Palm City residential complex on the outskirts of Tripoli, overlooking the southern Mediterranean's craggy shoreline. Her top policy aide was an affable Irishman who had convinced her that she needed to meet with the Misratans to try to get them on board with then-Prime Minister Ali Zeidan's policies.

She asked me who she should get in touch with in Misrata. I mentioned the obvious names of prominent individuals with respected international reputations: Abdurrahman al-Sweihli, grandson of the famous anti-colonial political leader Ramadan al-Sweihli and future head of the Higher State Council from 2015 to 2017; Fathi Bashaagha, a key leader in the Misratan Military Council, then an HoR parliamentarian, and later the interior minister from 2018 to 2021; and the then-Interior Minister Fawzi Abdul-Aal. Apostolova and her aide wrote these names down, even though these were among the most prominent figures in the country, names that the average journalist or European graduate student studying North Africa would have known. The ambassador then asked me if I had al-Sweihli's phone number. I replied that I did not, but that he was one of the leading political personalities in the country. She asked me if I could get his number for her. I told her that I knew the British embassy would have it, as Ambassador Michael Aron was famous for his close relations to both al-Sweihli and Bashaagha. Without a hint of irony, she informed me that the British embassy would definitely not share that kind of 'intelligence' with her.

I had a brainwave. I suggested that surely the political section chiefs of the French and the Italian embassies could arrange a joint briefing for her on the major Misratan personalities and then put her in touch with any politicians, businessmen, or notables she was particularly keen to meet. Perhaps she could even undertake a joint diplomatic field trip to Misrata with either of the French or Italian ambassadors.

My brainwave turned out to be a gaffe. I had incorrectly assumed that those continental powers must surely coordinate with the EU Commission's ambassador more than their supposedly Eurosceptic British counterparts. My remarks had clearly irked the ambassador: she cut the discussion off by saying she would have her aide phone Brussels the next day to request that the EU Commission make formal introductions.

The upshot was clear: the EU ambassador to Libya lacked the rolodex of any of the embassies of the EU member states. The Finnish, Swedish, and Slovenian embassies each likely had more robust contact networks in Libya than the EU ambassador herself. Moreover, British and American intelligence-sharing via the Five Eyes partnership[87] was infinitely more robust than that between EU countries and the EU Commission.

At the time, I chalked this discovery up to normal bureaucratic incompetence and the mysterious ways of the European Union. In retrospect, I understand that it was a symptom of the patterns of the Enduring Disorder that was already influencing the interactions among the Italians, British, and French in Libya. Libya was an important enough prize that interested parties chose not to share intelligence or security assets with each other or with the EU Commission, as that information might be used to forward their rivals' policies. The main players did not utilize UN and EU mechanisms to coordinate serious policy questions, as Libya was too important a matter for each country's national interests to be delegated solely to the UN and certainly not to the European External Action Service (as the EU's foreign service is known and from which the EU Commission's ambassadors are usually drawn).[88]

Right from the collapse of the Qadhafi regime, the major European players were tugging in different directions and suspecting each other's motives, clients, and actions in Libya, just as the memos sent by Blumenthal to Secretary Clinton suspected those of the British and French. The Western nations had acted out the ancient Bedouin proverb: 'Me against my brother, my brother and I against my cousin, my brother, my cousin and I against the outsider.'[89] This proverb evokes the structure of an archetypal peninsular Arabian or Eastern Libyan tribe composed of equivalent and mutually opposed segments. The founder of social anthropology and renowned historian of Libya, E.E. Evans-Pritchard, dubbed such tribes 'segmentary'.[90] Ironically, during the Enduring Disorder, this famous proverb came to apply to the ineffective Western efforts at foreign policy coordination. It also encapsulates the post-2016 tribalization of politics and culture in many Western societies and the inability of factions to put aside feuds to focus on shared interests until forced to by existential threats.

* * *

It required massive joint external threats to allow all the major Western allies to functionally coordinate. When faced with minor threats, the British and Americans could work together as could the Benelux, Germans, and the Scandinavians. But it was far harder for the Italians and French to work together, unless the threat to their shared interests was profound. In the absence of immediately obvious threats, it was each nation for itself trying to secure 'its interests' in the post-Qadhafian wilderness. It mattered not that Western countries were in agreement over 95 per cent of the decisions that needed to be taken concerning reconstruction and democracy-building in post-Qadhafi Libya. There was still enough disagreement, however minor, especially over the implementation details of how to fight terror, curb migration, and reform the economy. There were no effective coordination mechanisms or coherent institutional hierarchies to adjudicate between competing visions.

It should come as no surprise, then, that attempts to support the building of unified Libyan institutions horribly miscarried.

INTRODUCTION

The post-Qadhafi diplomatic scene in Tripoli was a game theorist's laboratory for modelling precisely how suboptimal outcomes emerge when self-interested actors fail to coordinate even on mutual interests.

When the Tubruq–Tripoli split emerged in the summer of 2014 and progressively deepened, suspicions among each of the Western powers developed into outright neo-colonial rivalries. This dysfunctional internecine behaviour among NATO countries could not have happened prior to 2003. The American juggernaut would have stepped in and deconflicted. Actions towards the Libya file post-2011 were symptomatic of the Enduring Disorder's paramount feature: suboptimally coordinated international policymaking, which developments in Libya then helped further reinforce. This hallmark of the Enduring Disorder—the inability of actors with a large overlap of shared interests to effectively coordinate—has only deepened as the civil wars in Libya, Syria, Ukraine, and Yemen have become protracted.

PART III
INVESTIGATING THE TRENDLINES OF THE
ENDURING DISORDER

Covid is yet another accelerator of the Enduring Disorder

We can use the Enduring Disorder framework to conceptualize the decision-making matrix of major international actors facing a whole slew of world events. Seen in this light, the Covid pandemic has significantly exacerbated the main dynamics that characterize this historical era. Most world economies are experiencing a recession, massive fatalities, heavy damage to global production, and the wholesale elimination of industries. Yet, many multinational corporations are recording eye-watering profits and global inequality is on the rise.

Due to their dependence on oil and tourism, North African economies' medium-term prospects are likely to be significantly worsened in the wake of the virus and possibly ripe for another round of popular protests.[91] Yet, major world powers could—if they chose to work together—seek to provide order for troubled hotspots like North Africa, cognizant that potential troubles there will feed disorder back home. Instead, they are focusing inward on their own domestic optics. Hence, in the context of the pandemic, all the dynamics of the Enduring Disorder that promote suboptimal coordination are accelerated and feeding off each other.

Depending on how the second-order economic implications of the coronavirus pandemic play out, it may be that deglobalization and decoupling of supply chains is a major trendline, which will further feed into the Enduring Disorder.[92] With less economic integration, willingness to coordinate would likely be even further diminished. Critically, the global response to Covid demonstrated the extent to which America is no longer the hegemonic convener, initiator, and shaper of multilateral responses to pressing global problems and that China has not stepped into the role—and will likely lack the credibility to do so for a long time. Hence, in the absence of the American president spearheading a global response to the virus, one has failed to emerge. When the Biden administration took office, they reversed nearly all of Trump's domestic executive orders, yet they were very slow to reverse the unilateral precedents he had staked out over Iran, China, and trade.[93] Biden also continued Trump's stated objective of withdrawing American troops from the Greater Middle East by making his first signature foreign policy move the complete withdrawal of the American military from Afghanistan. Seen in their totality, although Biden promised that a return to America's traditional alliances would be his showpiece foreign policy achievement, it appears he underestimated how the global forces emanating from the Enduring Disorder might impede his attempts in that direction.

Libya's chaos interacts with the fallout from the Covid pandemic and illustrates crucial facets about the current state of the world: the political implications of the globalization of a particular form of neo-liberal capitalism, the implications of America's retreat from the burdens of global hegemony, and the failure of the West to enshrine its Cold War victory into new global coordination bodies (the way the victory in the Second World War was institutionally cemented). Like a funhouse mirror, the closer we look at Libya, the more we see that the salient dynamics of the Wars of Post-Qadhafi Succession reflect selective distortions of the key features of our evolving international system and the post-pandemic world.

Mirror rather than emitter of the Enduring Disorder

This enlarged mirroring aspect holds true regardless of how strongly one believes that developments in Libya had an impact in fuelling neo-populism elsewhere, as discussed in Part I. Having made this argument at many public lectures over the years,[94] I know that some readers will reject outright those causation chains as impossible-to-demonstrate and pseudo-scientific—possibly invoking the argument, 'how convenient that a Libya expert is trying to tell us that Libya is actually super important globally and even led to Brexit and Trump getting elected'.

In response, I would suggest imagining a hypothetical world exactly like our own, except that the Arab Spring happens in 2017 instead of 2011. Would there be election wins for Brexit and Trump in 2016? I would argue not, as fears over migration and Benghazi and the Hillary Clinton email scandal were essential tropes in both insurgents' campaigns.

Fortunately, even if one rejects Libya's centrality in the causal chains that have led to neo-populism's ascendance and the specific timescale of its spread, this does not undermine the premise of this book. Whether or not Libya is a central causative factor in the Enduring Disorder or merely a peripheral victim of it, Libya still remains a convenient mirror in which we can watch the forces at play in the current global system reflected in real time. Libya post-Qadhafi is indisputably a society in flux—with new forms of social organization taking shape in the middle of a maelstrom of global pressures and international diplomatic, financial, military, and technological interventions. Hence, whatever we may feel about the extent of Libya's geostrategic importance or its ability to influence global developments, we can watch the logic of the Enduring Disorder unfold through our Libya-shaped spectacles.

Populism thrives amid disorder

Even if we choose to view recent events in Libya as merely reflecting the dynamics of the Enduring Disorder and not driving them, it is nevertheless a useful microcosm in which the interplay of the new global and domestic forces during the era of the Enduring Disorder can be clearly identified. This is epitomized in post-Qadhafi Libya by the rise to power of one aspiring strongman—the one man who remains the symbolic impediment to Libyans exiting the quagmire of their seemingly endless rounds of asymmetrical civil wars, General Khalifa Haftar.[95] The trajectory and timing of Libya's Wars of Post-Qadhafi Succession have primarily been shaped by his raw ambition, constant lies, mastery of the social media news cycle, creation of a narrative of victimization, perpetuation of Qadhafian methods of social control, and cult-like hero worship. Haftar is both a mirror for the forces acting upon Libya and their accelerator—much the way that Trump or Hungarian President Viktor Orbán reinforces the very same social grievances that gave rise to their political ascent. Just as Orbán was a canary in the coal mine for neo-populism's spread throughout the West,[96] there are many indications that Libya is a leading indicator for the spread of a new type of post-conflict outcome, which unfolds from the conditions of the Enduring Disorder.

Conflict zones in 2021 are tied by perverse linkages to the world's advanced economies. These ties are epitomized by flows of migrants, arms, aid money, corrupt funds, and disinformation campaigns across borders. In the Western world, these flows push democratic societies to become increasingly illiberal. In the world's trouble spots, they lead to conflicts that constantly simmer, while occasionally boiling over, but that major international actors refuse to work together to fix. It used to be that such enduring conflicts were confined to the fringes of the Russian sphere of influence—devoid of geostrategic importance, like South Ossetia or Transnistria, and lacking direct linkages back to major power centres. Yet, Libya is an enduring conflict quite near the heart of the international system.

Nowhere are these international linkages more apparent than in the outsized role that Ukrainian money, interpersonal connections, and narratives play in the politics of the US, UK, EU, and Russia. Rather than conceptualizing the Ukrainian tail wagging the American dog, in the contemporary globalized world, even the politics of the world's most powerful and geographically insulated superpower is 'fully penetrated' by dynamics that emanate from wealthy and geostrategically important hotspots mired in enduring conflicts like Ukraine and Libya.[97]

Bound to fail?

But independent of global dynamics and interconnectedness, wasn't Libya's transition after forty-two years of Qadhafi bound to fail? I think not. Libya's economy, oil wealth, geostrategic location, and absence of a legacy of civil war or major religious or ethnic fissures meant that a post-Qadhafi Libya could have been an enormous success story. Maybe not a Western democracy, but quite possibly a stable, wealth-generating, open society—akin to a richer, more capitalist, and more conservative version of Tunisia or a more socialist, more Islamic, and more decentralized version of Kuwait.[98] This book contends that a primary reason this optimistic scenario didn't transpire is because of global forces swirling around Libya emanating from the Enduring Disorder, penetrating Libya's political life, and corrupting its domestic players from the outset of its transition. The reason these forces penetrated Libya is due to the country's profound geostrategic importance and deep connections to global capitalism, oil markets, and jihadi and migrant flows.

It is well established that Libya's lack of social cohesion, dysfunctional institutions, absence of civil society, and other perverse legacies of forty-two years of Qadhafi's rule remain crucial and causative factors to how the Wars for Post-Qadhafi Succession have unfolded. Less widely understood is the role of Western decision-makers' misconceptions in exacerbating this legacy. My interviews with policymakers involved in the events reveal that top Western officials—from Foreign Ministers Alain Juppé and Hillary Clinton down to the relevant Libya desk officers—were ignorant or simply ignored the implications of how these factors would inherently bear upon attempts at post-conflict reconstruction and institution-building. The Western approach in the early post-Qadhafi years was to avoid confronting the potential challenges head on and to focus on the fact that Libya was wealthy, sparsely populated, and lacking major sectarian divisions or a legacy of civil war.[99]

Nonetheless, in a hegemonic international system prioritizing stability in geostrategic locations, these factors could well have been overcome. In the context of the Enduring Disorder, Libya's sources of conflict have been exacerbated—pushing the country, and in turn the world, towards ever-more frenzied disorder.

PART IV

ORDERING A STUDY OF DISORDER

Investigating the details of the Libyan case study

Post-Qadhafi Libya's seemingly endless civil war is truly the bastard child of the Enduring Disorder. The Enduring Disorder cannot be 'proven' to be a new historical period with certain fixed rules. Nonetheless, if we describe and analyse its key features through illustrative cases, we may arrive at a novel and useful perspective on the international system. To that end, this book will present deep background and interpretative analysis of five dynamics (one per chapter), each interlaced with the author's experiences of how the dynamics play out in the trenches of policymaking and at the rougher edges of contemporary geopolitics. The narrative exposition of each dynamic will be used to frame curated excerpts of the author's prior scholarship. Each excerpt will highlight the specific dynamic at play in Libya's civil war or the international community's actions, or lack thereof, on the Libya file.

The structure will attempt to illustrate what these five dynamics reveal about larger global trendlines. This multifaceted examination of the Libyan microcosm, along with shorter case studies from other hotspots, will help us trace the sinews of connection and causation that link the world's conflict zones to the larger international system. I will also seek to bring these abstractions to life by presenting assorted personal experiences showcasing how the novel features of the Enduring Disorder are lived.

The book has a decidedly economic focus, seeing structural economic dysfunction as the underlying root cause of many patterns in geopolitics. A recurring theme of these narrative morsels will be to illustrate the ways in which old myths and popular expectations about how geopolitics and capitalism are 'supposed to function' no longer appear to hold. To explain why this is the case, the book's last two chapters introduce the concept of 'incumbent psychology', namely how many powerful companies and political leaders have fallen prey to a type of reactionary psychological delusion whereby they no longer seek to foster free competition as they imagine that they can use their power to freeze the world in place and block new entrants to their privileged market niches. As a result of the increasing sway 'incumbent psychology' holds among political and business leaders in the West and their allies abroad, I propose the concept of neo-mercantilism as an overarching system structuring contemporary economic competition.

Starting off with an economic dynamic, Chapter 1, 'The Appeasement Trap', introduces certain unique characteristics of Libya's social fabric, especially those that differentiate it from other oil-rich Arab societies. In Libya, power has never been centralized. Social and political legitimacy exists at the periphery rather than in the centre. When combined with misguided international advisors and feckless domestic leadership, this social dynamic incentivizes appeasement. It is also directly connected to the lack of a global hegemon, multilateral coordination failures, and all the collective action problems that characterize the Enduring Disorder. To illustrate how this plays out in real life, I will relate my collision with a top UN advisor's theory that the NTC (Libya's first post-Qadhafi government) could 'temporize' itself out of 'the militia problem' by paying the militias off rather than having to confront them head on.

Appeasement is inherently attractive to decisionmakers who want to duck tough choices. The chapter's excerpt from 'Libya's Faustian Bargains: Breaking the Appeasement Cycle' showcases how a global leadership vacuum and collective action problems on the international side were mirrored in domestic Libyan politics. In retrospect, these interactions and newly emerging patterns were reflections that, by 2011, the world was passing from the structures of the early post-Cold War order to those of the full-blown Enduring Disorder. The chapter wraps up with my take on Ambassador Christopher Stevens' assassination and the cowardice of the American response. I demonstrate how that response epitomized the appeasement dynamic at play during the Enduring Disorder, and as such was occasioned by, and indicative of, the prevailing conditions of this current era of hegemony-less world order.

Chapter 2, 'Jihadis are Just a Symptom', seeks to explode the widespread myth that the prior existence of Islamic jihadism led to the post-conflict failures of the Syrian and Libyan states. The causation is reversed. The political vacuum and the Enduring Disorder are the root causes. The symptoms are the jihadi movements in those countries. The chapter's excerpt from 'The Origins and Evolution of ISIS in Libya' demonstrates how ISIS was actually a by-product, not a root cause of Libya's fragmentation. Expanding on this conclusion to the more general problem of ungoverned spaces, which policymakers face in Afghanistan, Iraq, Syria, Yemen, and many parts of Africa, I propose that the Enduring Disorder and ungoverned spaces symbiotically begot ISIS and prevent us from fully defeating it. Seen in this light, jihadism—like climate change—is a problem that can only ever be comprehensively tackled by coordinated, unified, and resolute multinational action. To explain why such collaborations have not emerged even to fight the universally acknowledged scourge of jihadism, I end the chapter with a couple of stories about Libyan officials and Western businessmen showcasing their shared desire to sweep the jihadi problem under the rug.

Chapter 3, 'Unregulated Cyberspace Leads to Neo-Populism', shows how during the Enduring Disorder, disinformation and narratives glorifying corrupt strongmen can spread like wildfire. Specific technological advancements over the last two decades have come to amplify the implications of the lack of coordinated intergovernmental action to police cyberspace. Moreover, with chaos reigning globally and the Libyan state hollowed out by appeasement, jihadis, and external actors pulling in mutually contradictory directions, the narrative of the strongman appeals to some as the perfect antidote. General Haftar's genius has been his creation of a narrative casting himself as the only solution to Libya's myriad problems. In this, Haftar has behaved in exactly the same way as other neo-populists. They all thrive on, and come to power as a result of, the same issues that they claim they will solve. Once in power, they exploit popular nostalgia, repressed longings for a strong leader, and a widespread desire for 'things to go back to how they were'. Even when Haftar is completely out of the picture—a reality that is now foreseeable due to his age and his star waning in the wake of the loss of the War for Tripoli—Libya's political narratives, coverage in the media, and relationship between strongman and follower will have been shaped according to the neo-populists' playbook. The chapter's excerpt from 'Kingdom of Militias: Libya's Second War of Post-Qadhafi Succession' delves deeply into the media narratives that underpin both the Government of National Accord (GNA)-coalition and the LNA-coalition. This investigation showcases how the Enduring Disorder begets the media environment in which regimes and individuals who promote disorder can thrive.

Chapters 4 and 5 constitute a unit on the Libyan economy, its global linkages, and its mirroring of the impact of broken post-statist economies on the functioning of Western democracies, international institutions, and multinational corporations. I start by adumbrating the various myths that exist in the foreign policy and business communities concerning Libya and the impact that multinational corporations and the globalisation of neo-liberal capitalism are 'supposed to have' on post-statist economies. The author's lived experience is marshalled to illustrate how reality is quite different from what these widespread myths or neo-liberal economics textbooks would suggest. A fascinating discovery emerges from this descriptive approach: Western corporations, trade associations, and specialized policymakers that interact with dysfunctional post-statist structures can end up progressively emulating them. This is a part of the self-reinforcing nature of the Enduring Disorder.

The excerpt in Chapter 4, 'Libya vs the Global Economy', is from 'It's the Economy Stupid: How Libya's Civil War Is Rooted in Its Economic Structures'. It explores how the unique features of the Libyan economy were constructed by Qadhafi primarily to be able to defeat internal accountability/scrutiny. As a by-product, they later developed the ability to take advantage of the global capitalist order and use foreign companies against the national interests of the countries they come from. Qadhafian structures were not actually inefficient when judged against their expressed goals. They simply were not created to maximize profit and avoid loss. Rather, they were constructed to maintain political control and avoid scrutiny—tasks they performed admirably—and they were bequeathed en masse to the post-Qadhafian world without meaningful reform.

Chapter 5, 'The US–Libya (Anti-)Business Association', describes how I sought to advance US business interests in Libya and discovered, counterintuitively, that the most deeply entrenched companies in Libya do not necessarily seek to increase their profit margins or find new business opportunities. In fact, they act quite similarly to the peculiar institutions created by Qadhafi with which they do business, obscuring transparency and protecting their ensconced fiefdoms. I detail an episode in which decision-makers at top global firms in 'old school industries,' like oil or security act according to 'incumbent psychology', fearing change and seeking to block new entrants. Seen from the outside, there is a macabre humour to these behaviours, as the actions in question benefit neither Libyans, nor Western governments, nor the firm's bottom lines. By eschewing positive-sum thinking, they create lose-lose, beggar-thy-neighbour type contests. This insight goes against received wisdom suggesting that the primary danger of public companies' quests to increase shareholder value inherently stems from the 'problem of the commons', namely that companies' 'rational' pursuit of profit puts them at odds with larger public goals, like protecting the environment. This chapter's perspective is more in line with breakthroughs in behavioural economics, which demonstrate that in certain cases neither firms nor individuals seek to maximize their profit or utility. This phenomenon is most pronounced when they are driven by narratives and institutional cultures that colour how they perceive utility and frequently lead to suboptimal decision-making. It also tells us quite a lot about why America and various corporate superpowers have drifted from incumbency to protectionism.

To illustrate all these points, I focus on the particularly striking episode of a proposed trade mission to Libya, which was requested by the then Libyan prime minister in 2017, supported by the US Departments of Commerce and State in 2018, and subsequently surreptitiously blocked by those very businesses who in the long run might have benefitted from it the most. This illustrates in microcosm a distinct feature about the era of the Enduring Disorder: with tariff barriers and trade wars emerging globally, many firms prefer privileged access over rational or reforming institutions. According to my analysis, due to the centrality of 'incumbent psychology', obtaining and maintaining privileged access has become the coin of the realm for multinationals during the Enduring Disorder. With this type of mentality becoming more and more widespread, it is strange that governments and institutions have not sufficiently adjusted their expectations of multinational corporations and continue to look at the private sector as 'part of the solution' rather than 'part of the problem'.

Drawing on these experiences, I then postulate that once we have exploded the myths about how the Libyan economy actually functions, we can understand that attempts at privatization or to 'introduce market forces' cannot 'cure Libya' because, as explored in Chapter 4, the country's economic system was set up to create perverse incentive structures for the firms and policymakers that interface with it. As a result, only an institutional approach rooted in a form of global collective action will be sufficient to oversee reforms to the Libyan economic system. This realization flows into an excerpt from 'An International Financial Commission Is Libya's Last Hope', presenting the only portion of this book's core chapters that proposes policy solutions—rather than recounting events, analysing chains of causation, or describing experiences and seeking to deduce patterns. The selection deals with how new forms of constructive global action can be formulated to create new institutions to deal with the Libya file. This type of institutional approach can only succeed if it accounts for, and seeks to counteract, the genuine forces at play during the Enduring Disorder and the psychology of decision-makers.

The final chapter, 'Conclusion: Quo Vadis?', engages in some blue sky thinking and a not-so-fanciful thought experiment. In Libya, as elsewhere, we have simultaneously more of a need for global governance than ever before and ironically less global governance than at any time in modern history. The current trend-line, as well as historical parallels, suggests a seemingly bleak upcoming decade or two, independent of how the Biden administration or its successors approach global leadership. Multipolarity or a rebalancing of powers will not automatically follow from the decline in America's relative power, just as the ensuing power vacuum in Libya in the wake of Qadhafi's ouster has not, by some cosmic law, elicited either the creation of a new durable organizing force to fill the void or incentivized a dominant outside power to provide order. There are various indicators that the world has become increasingly 'Libyan-ized' by becoming thoroughly penetrated by the key features of the Enduring Disorder. Developments in key nodes, like Libya or Ukraine, produce and emit the violence, hot money, ideology, and media polarization that feed the spiral of the Enduring Disorder.

Study of the philosophy of history and the discipline of forecasting does raise the possibility that the global populace might be in the process of gaining an increasing awareness of the interconnected nature of the seemingly disparate crises unfolding all around us. In the wake of such a realization, it is not impossible to imagine that electorates across the Global North will gradually reject the inward-looking, anti-expert ideologies currently in vogue and embrace a radically new form of expert-administered, consensus globalism. Nonetheless, despite this fringe possibility for the medium-to-long term, most indicators and trendlines predict that the Enduring Disorder is far more likely to deepen in the short-to-medium term.

The book is capped off with an afterword by Ambassador Jonathan Winer, who served as US special envoy to Libya from 2013 to 2019.[100] More than other types of diplomats (secretaries of state, ambassadors, Foreign Service officers) who conduct the day-to-day work of diplomacy, special envoys for issues (like combatting human trafficking) or to conflicts (like Libya or the War against ISIS)—particularly those hailing from the UN, UK, and US—are tasked with solving the collective action problems among interested states by mediating among divergent regional and international powers.

Drawing on his experience, Ambassador Winer recounts his perspective trying to mediate Libya's ongoing conflict and shares his unique insights into why optimal multinational solutions no longer emerge, specifically that the UN system was designed for the Cold War and early post-Cold War periods. It now has an Achilles' heel—when the Security Council is divided or ineffective, the UN simply cannot fulfil its designated functions.

For Ambassador Winer, the changing role of the US remains key to understanding the novel features of the current historical period. From the 1990s until the Obama years, the UN system and voluntary international norms largely worked—this is illustrated by the broad international unity in support of America's response to the 9/11 attacks. He engages with and problematizes the concept of the Enduring Disorder—agreeing with this volume's main premise that we are in a new historical era, although disagreeing that it is fundamentally different from the past or primarily caused by overarching structural features. He sees three US presidents as having botched international coordination that was otherwise functional: Bush over the invasion of Iraq, Obama by being overcautious in compensation to Bush's over aggressiveness, and Trump by giving in to Putin across the board and abandoning traditional allies on a range of foreign policy issues. Winer asserts that the consequence of these developments is a slew of competing regional power dyads: Iran/Saudi Arabia, Turkey/Egypt, UAE/Qatar, France/Italy, and so on. For Winer, this was exacerbated by Trump's cupidity and inexperience with geopolitics, which allowed Russia to rush into global hotspots, such as the Middle East, as the US withdraws. This dynamic has also made it harder to resolve divergent perspectives within the EU and larger Western bloc.

For Winer, the essential element of successful contemporary diplomacy is securing broad international consensus pertaining to any problematic regional context. He discusses how to go about achieving this, what happens when Western diplomats fail to do so, and what happens when major countries fail to protect their own national interests. For him, the Libyan case study illustrates how the absence of coordinated multilateral collective action is most certainly a critical feature of our current historical period.

In summation, this book presents multiple approaches (descriptive, economic, counterterror-focused, philosophical, forecasting-based, anecdotal, and diplomatic) to conceptualize the current world order. It draws upon twenty-first-century economics and psychology scholarship to critique realist and constructivist IR theory-based approaches by conceiving our global system as currently characterized by self-perpetuating, sustainable disorder—not multipolarity, nor a reassertion of the balance of power, nor the rise of a new hegemonic order. It seeks to tease out what this new era's defining features are, and why investigating Libya provides an ideal microcosm within which to discern the salient dynamics of our new global reality.

1

THE APPEASEMENT TRAP

The lack of leadership and coordination that characterized international actions towards Libya during and after the anti-Qadhafi Uprisings was mirrored in domestic Libyan politics. Each social group, town, tribe, ideological tendency, and institution suspected the intentions of the others and refused to pool resources or compromise. Qadhafi had been a tyrant, but everyone knew where the dinar stopped. In post-2011 Libya, a series of feckless leaders engaged in erratic acts of populist-style appeasement borne out of their own perception that they lacked sufficient legitimacy to lead courageously.[1] This is the primary theme of this chapter's excerpt.

Governance requires coalition-building in order to solve collective action problems. This can involve giving preferential benefits to certain groups in exchange for their participation or support. Appeasement results from giving away benefits to certain domestic groups or foreign interlocutors without receiving anything commensurate in exchange.[2] Appeasement can result from poor policy choices, miscalculations, or a lack of resolve. It is also a knee-jerk response of a weak government confronted by a restive population that is militarized and has significant popular legitimacy for its demands.

Although the decision to undertake specific acts of appeasement is meant to delay conflict or avert it altogether, it leaves the appeaser in a worse bargaining position after the action than before. Hence, it usually succeeds in postponing conflict but makes it more virulent when it does break out. Sometimes it is done to buy time or to curry favour. When it fails to do so, it can have disastrous consequences.

For a range of historical reasons, Libya has always been the only Middle Eastern oil country in which the 'periphery' (disparate social forces and communities) dominates the 'centre' (government and centralized institutions).[3] After the 2011 Uprisings, the institutions of the nascent centre felt a need to pay homage to the periphery. The periphery (i.e. armed youth from disadvantaged communities) had overthrown the Qadhafi regime. The men in suits representing the newly internationally recognized government had not. They attempted to claim the youth's victory as their own, but this claim was not widely accepted.[4]

Populist appeasement tends to arise in situations where governmental legitimacy is weak, while the demands or grievances of the people or specific interest groups are seen as inherently legitimate. The traditional social legitimacy of the periphery in Libya combined with its role during the revolution guaranteed that this would be the case after Qadhafi's ouster.

The very nature of the multipolar anti-Qadhafi uprisings led to the emergence of a multiplicity of armed actors, each with their own chains of command and *raison d'être*.[5] This multiplicity was inherent in Libya's social structure, its vast geography, and thinly spread population. Its history of governance from the Ottoman period to the present had reinforced primordial divisions—between the coast and the interior; east (Cyrenaica) and west (Tripolitania); non-tribal urban dwellers and nomadic pastoralists; the Sa'ada (or noble) tribes and the Murabatin (subordinate or bound) tribes, especially within Cyrenaica; and Arabs and darker-skinned, non-Arabic-speaking groups, especially in the south.[6] In addition to tribal, ethnic, linguistic, and regional divisions, Libya's coast has traditionally housed rival city-states. Given this history, it should come as no surprise that after Qadhafi's ouster each armed group claimed to be acting on behalf of its social segment and presented itself as possessing greater legitimacy than the new governmental authorities—many of whom had returned from the Diaspora.

Libyan history empowered the periphery

Italy's brutal occupation of Libya (1911–42) differed from most examples of British and French colonial rule in the Arab world as it involved the deliberate destruction of indigenous institutions and leaders rather than coherent efforts to co-opt them.[7] Afterwards, the British Military Administration (1942–51) governed Libya's historic regions separately. In the favoured eastern region of Cyrenaica, it was keen to 're-invent' supposedly native institutions, like tribal councils and Sanussi 'ministries', rather than to build a modern bureaucracy.[8] For the first twelve years of the Sanussi monarchy (1951–63), Libya was governed as three federal provinces. Identity and multiple corrupt layers of bureaucracy were rooted in the provinces. The Sanussiyya, as well as their British and American patrons, preferred this arrangement, as it allowed for the administrative separation of the more populated and Arab nationalist part of the country, Tripolitania, from the sources of the king's power, based in Benghazi, the Green Mountain, and the southern desert.

Oil was discovered in 1959 and exported in 1961. The extractive industries traditionally modify the structures of the regimes with which they come into contact—forging centralized (even if corrupt) institutions, which then engage in top-down decision-making about both rent extraction and wealth distribution. The need to manage a national oil industry and the wealth it produced led the Sanussi monarchy to abandon federalism in 1963 and embark on six years of genuine national institution-building. Nonetheless, favouritism and corruption were still rife while anti-colonial and anti-monarchical resentment festered.[9]

When Qadhafi came to power in a *coup d'état* in 1969, he changed the symbolic focus of the regime. His rhetoric stressed international issues, but its legitimacy came from local, regional, tribal, and communal identities. Qadhafi's views on direct democracy and deep suspicion of centralized meritocratic institutions inhibited the movement towards technocratic centralization and further reinforced the already deeply rooted trend of peripheral dominance over the sources of social legitimacy. Although Qadhafi preached radical decentralization and the diffusion of real power to the populace in his speeches and *Green Book*, it was only the Uprisings against him that made this a reality.[10]

In the wake of his ouster, pre-existing institutions were destroyed and power was therefore extremely diffuse. It was the ideal moment for a great unifier to arise, put forth a shared national vision, and harness the populace's collective energy. Tragically, what instead ensued was a crisis of leadership in which Libya's leaders appeased the militias, dodged the real governance problem, and adopted populist attempts to spend their way out of the crisis of legitimacy.

Islamist factions who advocated for sharia to be the basis of all law lobbied for Islamic banking and a traditional Islamic personal status law (*Ahwal Shakhsiyya*). They drew support from the Qataris[11] and Turks.[12] Those who advocated a civil republic, in the Tunisian vein, drew support from the French and Emiratis.[13] New Madkhali Salafist groups opposed both Sufis and political Islamists and followed the doctrine of *waliya al-amr* (a jurisprudential principle concerning the religious imperative to defer to the authority of temporal rulers as an obligation to God). They drew support from the Saudis.[14]

Contrary to how things might have played out in a bygone hegemonic era, the West did not swoop in to help Libya's post-Qadhafi leaders consolidate power by offering coherent on-the-ground security assistance, bureaucratic capacity-building and military training programmes. Most NTC politicians actively rejected any Western offers of on-the-ground security support, fearing it would undermine their authority relative to the militias.[15] Nonetheless, in the early days when the NTC was still popular, such an approach could have brought the disparate armed factions under central control by leveraging the popular goodwill that the new authorities had acquired by overseeing the ousting of Qadhafi.[16] Instead, certain international advisors advocated for the holders of Libya's purse strings to reject controversial Western security assistance programs and seek instead to 'temporize' by paying off militia members—to obtain their loyalty and incorporate the top militia commanders into the government apparatus. This went against every orthodox theory of how to create a security environment compatible with a transition to government control over the use of force through a demobilization, disarmament, and reintegration (DDR) process followed by security sector reform (SSR).

Temporizers versus de-centralizers

I was an early opponent of such populist appeasement, and experienced first-hand the fierce real world and scholarly debate over the issue.[17] In a peer-reviewed journal article submitted in late 2012 and written immediately after the July 2012 election for the GNC, my co-author and I traced the myriad errors of appeasement made by top NTC policymakers that impacted the subsequent meaning of the electoral results.[18] They had knowingly 'caved-in' to militia pressure—specifically over the role of the GNC in appointing the constitutional committee. After one journal rejected the article as 'not political science, but more like contemporary history', we revised it and resubmitted it elsewhere to include the then current instance of appeasement—a uniquely Libyan form of lustration (i.e. purging public life of former regime officials), known as the April 2013 Political Isolation Law. The reviewer asked us to focus less on the literature about appeasement and to present more political science literature about democratization theory and instances that could elucidate the theoretical case that the NTC could successfully 'temporize' itself out of the militia problem (i.e. with populist payoffs) rather than having to confront them head on.

In order to have our article published, we begrudgingly did so. True, the reviewer had put forth a persuasive case that the central government would become stronger over time while the militias could be bought off in the interim. Yet its eloquence did not make it truer. He was a man of conviction and consistent principles. He was a cheerleader for the 'success' of the 17 February Revolution and wrote articles in prominent journals and newspapers about how Libya was on a democratic trajectory.

The ensuing rounds of revisions delayed publication further. They were only brought to a close when a former American ambassador mentor of mine happened to be brought in as a third peer reviewer—presumably to adjudicate between the doyen's negative review and the positive review of another scholar. The ambassador wrote in support of the article's intellectual bona fides. By the time the paper was finally ready to come out—nearly twenty-six months after our initial submission and more than eighteen months from our first submission to the eventual journal of publication—the central government's security structures had been completely infiltrated by the militias, the First Libyan Civil War had just broken out, and chaos reigned throughout most of the country.[19] At the copyediting stage, the journal suggested that we retract the very same paragraphs that months earlier, the reviewer had advocated we put in. We had won the scholarly argument, but Libya had lost the war.

Ironically, while top advisors to the UN and respected chairs of academic political science departments had advocated for the 'temporizing' policy, grad students, newly minted PhDs, and diaspora Libyan twenty-year olds were cogently briefing about the dangers of this course of action. For example, the idea that 'temporizing' might ever work was the exact opposite of what my esteemed German colleague Florence Gaub had been advocating for. She and I were roughly the same age and on the identical briefing circuit—rubbing elbows at the NATO Intelligence Fusion Centre at RAF Molesworth and at various chancelleries across Europe. I recall one meeting in the British Old War Office—a glorious marble building a stone's throw away from Whitehall. She told the assembled audience that the militias were like the little furry Mogwai in the *Gremlins* movie. They start off nice and cuddly, and serve a useful purpose during the daytime. (And in Libya, this was true of the militias as they had ousted Qadhafi and then were essentially protecting their communities from looting and lawlessness in the ensuing power vacuum.) But like the Mogwai, if you fed them fried chicken after dark, their inner demons came out.[20] This was Florence's clever way of expressing what I had previously termed the appeasement trap. It was the post-Qadhafi authorities' decisions to subsidize the militias with free cash and preferential access to subsidized goods (such as petrol and letters of credit) that brought out their inner demons. By failing to follow the plot, Libyan policy-makers and their international advisors had fallen into the appeasement trap despite multiple warnings and clever metaphors from astute observers.

* * *

Appeasement begets a classical positive feedback loop—like so many of the destructive dynamics that characterize the era of the

Enduring Disorder. The more money the political class shovelled at the militias, the greater their appetites became, the more power they acquired relative to the political class, and the more enshrined they became in the institutions of state.

As soon as the political class met one round of militia demands, new requests surfaced, and the militias learned that they could boss the political leaders around while couching their demands as 'coming from the people'. They had also gained credibility within their communities and had spare cash to cultivate allies and hire more young men to join their ranks. Membership in a militia could provide an otherwise unemployed young man with a boost to his social status and income, both of which are a prerequisite to be able to marry.[21] The point of no return was reached when the UN unfroze the Central Bank of Libya's international deposits,[22] which had been under UN sanctions since the start of the anti-Qadhafi Uprisings. These assets were then used by Prime Minister Zeidan to pay off the militiamen that he believed posed a threat to his political agenda. After this point, it was impossible to return to a policy that was not based on appeasement. From then on, the militias ran the major institutions rather than the institutions being able to exert leverage over the militias.[23]

Roughly 10,000 men had participated in Qadhafi's overthrow. Yet, within three years of his death, over 250,000 had joined militias of one sort or another. Libya had fallen into the appeasement trap, with the nascent governmental authorities' military and institutional capacities being dwarfed by those of their militia opponents. The collapse of neutral and functional state institutions was an inevitable consequence.

Libya's implosion was the Global Enduring Disorder's first petri dish. Syria would be its second, Yemen its third, and Ukraine its fourth. As each descended into further disorder, those ungoverned spaces incubated and then propagated the core dynamics of the Enduring Disorder. America's, Britain's, and Brazil's subsequent turns to neo-populism, protectionism, and isolationism were fostered by the forces emanating from those trouble spots.

* * *

Selections from: Jason Pack, Karim Mezran, and Mohamed Eljarh, 'Libya's Faustian Bargains: Breaking the Appeasement Cycle', *Atlantic Council*, 5 May 2014.[24]

PART 1

THE CENTRE AND THE PERIPHERY: THE STRUGGLE FOR POST-QADHAFI LIBYA

The political process from NTC to present

Libya's leaderless 'Arab Spring' movement to overthrow Muammar Qadhafi began on 15 February 2011 as a series of disparate local uprisings. Individual towns and neighbourhoods erupted first in non-violent protest, though the movement later morphed into an armed insurrection against the Qadhafi regime. As the regime and its oppressive security forces attempted to suppress the rebellion via indiscriminate killings, militias and local governing councils formed spontaneously from local populations in the various pockets of the country where Qadhafi's control was contested or had evaporated.[25] These peripheral local councils and militias proclaimed themselves to be wholly new and revolutionary. Yet, they largely drew their solidarity networks from the pre-existing groupings in Libyan society such as locality, ideology, regionalism, and tribe. Certain municipalities came together and formed the National Transitional Council (NTC) on 27 February 2011 to secure domestic and international recognition and support for the uprisings, and to become the nascent legitimate national sovereign body of Libya, seeking to become a new centre of power. Considering former Qadhafi regime officials and reformers comprised its founders, many newly liberated towns and their militias were sceptical that the NTC had their best interests at heart.

In the wake of the euphoria of liberation from Qadhafi, many joined the NTC banner but viewed the alliance as temporary and provisional. As a result of the artificiality of the linkage between the NTC and the uprisings they claimed to represent, the nascent centralized authority in post-Qadhafi Libya was always weaker than the peripheral municipalities and their militias supposedly under its control.[26]

The NTC (backed by the Arab League) called for international intervention in the form of a no-fly zone, after the rebel forces suffered severe setbacks when Qadhafi forces launched a counterattack that brought the regime's forces within striking distance of Benghazi. The UN approved the request on 17 March by passing UNSCR 1973. The subsequent no-fly zone (NFZ) imposed by NATO-led forces stopped the Qadhafi offensive while simultaneously protecting pockets of anti-Qadhafi forces inside territory held by Qadhafi's regime.

Initially, although the NFZ and NATO airstrikes were sufficient to help the poorly-disciplined rebel forces hold territory, the rebels still failed to advance into Qadhafi-held territory. Foreign air support also enabled anti-Qadhafi rebels not formally affiliated with the NTC to survive within Qadhafi-held territory, so long as they controlled whole towns and could therefore be resupplied. Various towns used different resupply routes: for example, by sea (such as Misrata), or by the Tunisian border or helicopters (such as Zintan in the Nafusa Mountains). Without the NFZ these pockets of resistance inside Qadhafi territory would have either been crushed by tanks and planes or would have had to merge into the rebels' nascent political and command and control structures to stay alive. In short, the NFZ functioned like the internet as a democratizing force allowing any particular social segment or locality to create its own resistance brigades, control its own neighbourhood and create its own discourse.

As a result, from April–July 2011, disparate and peripheral local councils and militias spontaneously arose throughout Libya to contest the regime on a city-by-city basis; they also used the internet and satellite TV to put forth their own narratives of the uprisings. Unsurprisingly, although they proclaimed themselves to be wholly new and revolutionary, they largely drew their solidarity networks from the pre-existing groupings in Libyan society such as locality, ideology, regionalism, and tribe. Many did not swear allegiance to the NTC. Among those that did, they did not dissolve into the national army or voluntarily demobilize once Qadhafi was defeated, but remained as separate entities. The process of overthrowing the tyrant was transformative for the Libyan social landscape; previously buried social cleavages were transformed into numerous sites of revolutionary mobilization.[27]

Liberation from Qadhafi was declared on 23 October 2011, three days after he had been killed by Misratan militiamen in his hometown of Sirte. With its only shared goal of defeating Qadhafi accomplished, the NTC shifted its mission to knitting the country's disparate factions together. The NTC adopted an ambitious political transition timetable modelled on Tunisia and a rhetoric calculated to portray itself as a truly national and sovereign governing body controlling national institutions, including a unified military. In reality, Libya lacked national institutions. Each of Libya's parts had its own fighting force that could be directed to act for personal, local, tribal, or regional ends.

When the first post-Qadhafi NTC government of Abdurrahman el-Keib chose a new cabinet, some cities, most notably those represented by militias in Tripoli— Misrata and Zintan—were only willing to participate in this new government in exchange for large concessions. Due to the weak state of national army and police forces and the wholesale refusal among Libyans to invite in foreign peacekeeping forces, a paradox emerged: short-term stability could only be preserved via coopting militia groups and such stability was required to create an elected government, constitution, and the initially envisioned 'transition to constitutional governance' by June 2013. In an act of thinly veiled appeasement, those two cities were awarded the Defence and Interior Ministries, respectively, on account of their large militias. These and other initial concessions enshrined a form of social contract: that the militias would not rebel against the new government in exchange for subsidies, transfer payments, and political leverage at the centre.[28]

Multiple elements of the mobilized periphery clamoured to dominate the centre throughout the planning for a political process that would supposedly culminate in a transition to democracy and a new constitution. Long before Qadhafi was defeated and even before the NTC had control of Tripoli, the NTC established the precedent and framework for an elected government to replace itself by issuing the Temporary Constitutional Declaration (TCD) on 3 August 2011. Since that date, this document has been serving as a temporary transitional constitution and, in theory, the timeline laid down in it for the drafting and issuance of the permanent constitution still determines the legality and jurisdictions of Libya's current bodies.[29]

The TCD called for the NTC to organize elections for a 200-member General National Congress (GNC) within 240 days of Liberation from Qadhafi. The GNC as originally envisioned would have both replaced the NTC as a governing body appointed and overseen the constituent assembly in charge of drafting the constitution. It was also the GNC's role to elect a president and a prime minister, who would form a cabinet. However, due to a vocal minority in eastern Libya calling for Libya to adopt a federal model of government based on the three historical provinces from Libya's independence in 1951, the TCD was amended multiple times so that the constituent assembly would be elected by the people rather than appointed by the GNC and the sixty-member committee (also known as the Committee of Sixty) would be modelled on the original 1951 constitutional committee whereby twenty members would be from Cyrenaica, twenty from Tripolitania, and twenty from Fezzan.

Although lightly considered and easily granted, these concessions were fundamentally acts of appeasement by the Libyan centre to the Federalist periphery and they continue to exert a profound influence on the situation on the ground. Just as appeasing the militias with payments and cooptation into new umbrella units has enshrined them as the arbiters of power in Libya, so too has the decision for direct election of the Constituent Assembly and regional representation facilitated the rise of the militant wing of the Federalist movement and its bid to forge an independent Cyrenaica.

The successes and failures of the central authorities

Immediately after the revolution, especially in 2012, Libya witnessed a wave of economic and democratic successes, which raised expectations and created a window of opportunity for the central authorities to expand their support. Out of fear of being seen as despotic, the authorities failed to act boldly, and lack of trust and the cultural legacy of personalized rule hindered Tripoli from connecting with the country's fledgling local authorities. As a result, in 2013 the window of opportunity appeared to abruptly close after a series of inter-linked disappointments. The terrible state of affairs was the result of many factors: some rooted in the conduct of the revolution, some preceding it, and the most important ones deriving from the handling of the post-conflict period.

One critical factor was the political elite's failure to recognize that the 2011 Uprisings had exacerbated Libya's preexisting societal fissures, actually pitting various portions of the Libyan population against each other.[30] Only a national reconciliation where all sides publicly participate and make compromises could allow groups to transcend their legitimate grievances so as to forge a new Libya. The authorities' inability to genuinely begin the national reconciliation process has ensured the marginalization of at least one quarter of the population of the country, a demographic that has actively tried to undermine the stability of the state.[31]

A second critical factor has been the lack of recognition by the public and the government of the importance of foreign support in winning the war and overthrowing Qadhafi. The rhetoric employed by Mahmoud Jibril, Mustafa Abdul Jalil, and others baldly reinforced the view 'that the Libyans did it all by themselves' and that outside assistance was helpful but not essential to victory. This discourse has created the unrealistic expectation in the population that they could navigate the transition with only minimal outside help. It also signalled to the major foreign powers that the Libyans were more than happy for them to leave the country immediately after the Liberation. This, plus the legacy of Iraq, facilitated the Western countries' light-footprint approach towards capacity building, rather than a concerted, robust effort to harness the Libyans' good will in order to support the country's nascent institutions, strengthen them vis-a-vis their opponents, and create a security climate more conducive to the construction of a functioning state apparatus.

Despite the central government's remarkable achievement of pre-war levels of oil production by mid-2012, far sooner than initially imagined, production then stagnated until June due to lack of Libyan know-how and a security situation that impeded foreign investment.[32] Even worse, production was brought to a standstill by strikes and occupations of oil infrastructure from mid-2013 onward, such that production rates by the end of 2013 were less than one-quarter of 2010 levels. Similar to developments in the economy, the great successes in the political realm heralded by the GNC election in July 2012 (with minimal violence and high participation by over 60 percent of eligible Libyans) soon soured. The GNC has been unable to make significant headway on the multi-year task of DDR, establishing the rule of law, providing the security necessary to attract job-stimulating foreign investment, or most crucially, forwarding the constitutional process, supposedly the body's *raison d'être*.

No sooner did the newly elected GNC attempt to form a government in September 2012 than infighting torpedoed Prime Minister-elect Mustafa Abushagur's attempts to form a cabinet. During this moment of institutional chaos, US Ambassador Christopher Stevens and three other Americans were killed. When current Prime Minister Ali Zeidan was finally chosen in November 2012, there was a sense of great optimism that the chaos might end. That hope quickly faded in early 2013 as it became clear that the GNC could hardly secure its own premises, let alone take initiative on much-needed projects...

The successes and failures of the local authorities

In the absence of state control and widespread administrative incompetence, certain militias and their affiliated local councils [*became*] de facto substate governments in dispersing welfare, administering justice, providing jobs, and controlling the armed groups and politicians to which they disburse patronage. Moreover, the centre (the NTC and then GNC) [*was*] beaten by the periphery in the public relations battle to win over the hearts and minds of Libyans. The GNC failed to make an effective case to the Libyan people that their interests [*lay*] with a strong consensual constitutional government centralized enough to pursue coherent economic development strategies and to uphold the rule of law. Conversely, the periphery has excelled at channelling public interest and attention. It advocates populist causes that have a short-term impact. In this way, the militias act as armed representatives of various communities, successfully lobbying for narrow local interests and extracting concessions from the government...[33]

Misrata—the wealthiest, most powerful, and safest major city in Libya—is a prime example of the success of Libyan municipalities in achieving self-sufficiency in terms of security and administration of local affairs. Its security infrastructure depends entirely on its myriad revolutionary brigades, the by-products of the uprisings. Misrata suffered rape and pillage during its siege by Qadhafi's forces in the spring of 2011, which is likely why Misratans refuse to accept any security institution staffed by those who might have served the former regime...

[*As of the spring of 2014, there was*] no formal structure or agreement between the various successful cities of the periphery and the central government through which local power [*could*] be employed to strengthen the central government's position rather than undermine it. The so-called 'Gharghour incident' of November 2013 when notorious Misratan militias killed more than forty-four civilians is one illustration of the significance of local power. In the aftermath, public outcry mounted. Misratan militias refused to leave Tripoli until Misrata's Local Council intervened. The Local Council also decided to remove from Tripoli all government ministers and GNC members of Misratan origin, and ordered the Misratan units of the Libya Shield Force [*(LSF)—an armed organization formed out of disparate anti-Qadhafi groups in 2012*]—back to Misrata. In doing so, Misrata's Local Council bypassed the prime minister, the GNC president and the army chief of staff and successfully commanded individuals and units who should have been controlled by or loyal to the central government...

Tubruq offers another example of Libya's municipal diversity and the relative success of divergent local arrangements. The city is peaceful and does not currently have any militia units. The city's security forces are more or less the same ones that existed during the Qadhafi era with some *thuwwar* joining their ranks as lone individuals. This arrangement is the result of Tubruq's geographical isolation and its domination by traditional tribal structures. These same factors meant that during Qadhafi's reign, the regime had to rely on locals to police and govern their own city. The local authorities used this knowledge and structure to their advantage and have managed to keep the city relatively safe...

Given the central government's poor record of public communication and localization of authority, Federalists have also been able to capitalize on the public's emotions to frame the constitutional debate on their terms. In short, where local communities have successfully built institutions and security arrangements, they have used them in defiance of central authorities instead of in tandem with them, while in communities where there are feuding substate power structures—such as between Tubu and Zwai in Kufra or many other local, tribal, and ethnic feuds throughout the country—the central authorities have been unable to fill the power vacuum.[34] This means that success at the local level threatens the central government, and failure at the local level weakens and undermines it. Part and parcel of security sector reform and ending the trend of appeasement will be finding ways to connect the periphery to the centre through mutually beneficial linkages, as well as curtailing the most disruptive implications of transfer payments to the militias without provoking a widespread anti-government revolt...

PART 2
APPEASEMENT: ITS RATIONALES, COSTS,
AND ALTERNATIVES

The woeful state of affairs [*as of the spring of 2014*] could have been avoided if the NTC had demonstrated bold leadership and started to rein in the recalcitrant periphery during the honeymoon period after the declaration of liberation. Such leadership could have rallied the Libyan people to the side of the government, an invaluable asset which would have been more useful in building Libya's future than the $170 billion on-hand in sovereign wealth funds or top-notch outside technical assistance. Institutions cannot be built and security cannot be fostered without popular support... nor can these things be bought or manufactured by experts.

A counter-argument exists asserting that the abundance of arms dispersed throughout Libya in the wake of the revolution meant that bold leadership which eschewed appeasement would have been impossible or [*would have*] led immediately to civil war. Although it is impossible to conclusively prove or disprove either of these counterfactuals by conducting a truly 'controlled' experiment isolating the variable of appeasement, we must attempt to treat the issue of appeasement separately from the Qadhafian legacy and the proliferation of arms as if we were conducting such a 'controlled' experiment following the scientific method.

The proximal cause of Libya's current woes

Instead of bold leadership and enforcing the abstract principles enshrined in the 3 August 2011 Constitutional Declaration, the Libyan government was accommodating when confronted with armed demands from the periphery. This was certainly the path of least resistance, and the Qadhafian legacy of weak institutions and a culture of patronage networks, pushed the NTC, GNC, and various cabinets in that direction. Nonetheless, such behaviour has consistently been to the detriment of efforts to promote a democratic dialogue, discourage armed opposition, or build lasting political institutions vested with genuine authority. Although there are different schools of thought within the broader 'Libya field' concerning the government's performance, many prominent government experts, think tank analysts, and academics, view the NTC and GNC as 'appeasers'[35] who have abruptly changed their policies when threatened with force. The archetype of this behaviour was the NTC's action to 'placate' Federalist demands immediately before the July 2012 elections.[36] Seen from this point of view, Libyan authorities have over time appeased away a number of their powers and even 'appeased' themselves out of office in the case of GNC President Mohamed Magariaf, whose support of the Muslim Brotherhood and the Martyrs' Bloc in their demands for the Political Isolation Law led to him being forced to resign.

This [*think tank*] paper takes the train of thought a step further than merely identifying the problem of 'appeasement'. We argue that the proximal cause of most of Libya's current interlocked political and security problems is the central authorities' penchant for appeasement. This view seeks to cut the causal links between Qadhafi-era policies, Libya's primordial social and regional structures, and Libya's absence of institutions (like a national army or civil society) with the Libyan reality in 2014. In our view, the Libyan government and people have exerted agency in moulding their post-revolutionary reality and will continue to do so.

The GNC as appeasers

While Libya's historical social structures and institutions are certainly key components and to some extent the root causes of the current situation, the way in which these dynamics have manifested themselves in post-Qadhafi Libya has been inflected and exacerbated by the practice of appeasement. The implication of this is that prior to crafting policy solutions to address the morass in Libya, both the Libyan government and its international partners must address the sobering fact of appeasement head-on. Seen in this light, there is actually a silver lining to the current situation: it is far easier to correct the Libyan government's practice of appeasement than to change the country's tribal and regional structures while simultaneously constructing functional institutions out of nothing.

Study of the diplomacy leading up to the Second World War demonstrates that appeasement creates a vicious circle.[37] By rewarding destructive behaviour, it encourages it. In post-Qadhafi Libya, groups which have pursued their agendas through threats, force, blockades, and boycotts have been rewarded by having their objectives met, while those who have used the democratic process have been largely ignored. Unsurprisingly, given this incentive structure, the militias, Federalists, Islamists, and jihadists have all tried to extract maximum benefit from the current situation of a weak central government practising appeasement. In fact, most political, militia, ethnic, or ideological groups in Libya have been effectively transformed into 'rent-seekers' which seek to trade their potential to cause political or economic disruption to the country in exchange for material benefits or political positions for their top members.[38] Simultaneously, the silent majority of the Libyan populace has come to constitute an excluded demos, whose voices are not heard because they either respect the rules of the political game and are not sufficiently plugged in to elite and militia politics to pressure or lobby for their goals...

What if it had been different?

Although it is difficult to assert a counterfactual, there is much evidence to support the claim that most peripheral groups other than the jihadists would likely have played by democratic 'rules' [*had the government adopted an alternative policy incentivizing cooperation with democratic institutions*].[39] Given the prevailing incentive structure, moderate Islamist political parties which initially embraced the democratic arena and the trappings of government, most notably the Muslim Brotherhood's Justice and Construction Party (JCP), have later supported anti-government militias, such as those that demanded the political isolation law.[40] NTC Chairman Mustafa Abdul-Jalil and later President Magariaf knowingly encouraged Islamist militiamen to disrupt the political process and actively lobbied for their demands to be met, presumably hoping to garner their support and prevent them from disrupting the government.[41] By adopting Islamist and populist demands (e.g. polygamy, Islamic banking, subsidies, sharia law, etc.), they knowingly acquired short-term stability at the cost of later instability. Such short-sighted actions have weakened central government authority far into the future, as the appeasement of one group encourages others to follow suit, turning armed demands into an oft-repeated tactic. Moreover, with the case of Libya's moderate Islamists there is little doubt that these groups simply wanted their share of power and if they were forced to compromise and play by the rules to achieve it they would have done so. Study of JCP Leader Mohammed Sawan's speeches and actions reveals this.[42] This framework of analysis suggests that although it is impossible to roll back the gains made by the periphery through appeasement, future instances of appeasement can be avoided by creating a robust discourse about the Libyan state's interests that counteracts the appeals of populism in the public perception and by forbidding elected politicians from courting the support of extra-legal armed movements with legal handouts. Many apologists for former Prime Minister Ali Zeidan have asserted that he simply lacked the power to confront the militias and hence was fenced into the type of appeasement that Abdul-Jalil and Magaryaf engaged in willingly. This logic is hollow because in the twenty-first century the Libyan people are connected to the Internet and are forging nascent civil society organizations to which the country's leaders can appeal for support to counterbalance the militias. Therefore, Zeidan's successors would be wise to combine economic incentives with popular and regional outreach to make the central authorities emotionally appeal to Libya's divergent inhabitants.

Alternative views of the GNC: could they be classified as temporizers or over-centralizers?

While this [*2014 study*] sees the NTC and GNC as practicing appeasement, leading academics and practitioners have coherently argued for other paradigms. An alternative point of view sees the Libyan authorities as 'temporizers' whose failure to challenge their opponents does not give rise to a long-term weakening of central authority but instead is an astute move to buy time until they can build their forces. This framework sees Libya as gradually on a positive path where institutions are slowly forming and militias are being definitively rather than superficially coopted into the armed forces.[43] A third school sees the central authorities as holding too much power, rather than not enough. Instead of weakness, the central authorities are 'over-centralizers' engaged in a futile attempt to control the periphery from Tripoli and, in the process, setting the stage for corruption and inefficiency. According to this argument, those holding the strings of power are holdovers from the Qadhafi-era bureaucracy.[44] There is definitely some truth to both the 'temporizing' and 'over-centralizing' schools of thought, and it is for that reason that the government must 'localize' itself while also picking its battles carefully and not seeking to confront the armed groups which could openly defeat it. Despite those counterarguments, they do not negate the essential fact that appeasement has whittled away governmental authority.

The origins and implications of appeasement

The first major act of appeasement was the 5 July 2012 amendment to the temporary constitution. This amendment, Amendment 3, removed the GNC's authority to appoint the constitutional committee just two days before the GNC elections. Later in October 2012, armed militiamen from Zawiyya stormed the GNC assembly hall in the middle of the debate on Mustafa Abushagur's new post-election cabinet. Rather than calling in the army or even pro-GNC militias to disperse the Zawiyyan protesters, the GNC listened to the Zawiyyans' concerns over Abushagur's cabinet list. As a result, many members voted against the prime minister-elect and his list [*this is a critical episode that reveals a great deal about how patronage and political narratives work in Libya. I will revisit it in Chapter 3*].[45] In March 2013 armed protesters again took to the GNC hall to influence passage of the political isolation law; under duress the April 2013 TCD amendment specifically mentioned that any political isolation law would not be unconstitutional. The same amendment took the opportunity to maintain social peace by upholding the first major act of appeasement— the controversial July 2012 decision for an elected constitutional committee of sixty to be split among Libya's three regions.[46] On 5 May, as the Ministries of Foreign Affairs and Justice were surrounded, the GNC passed the political isolation law. GNC President Muhammad Magariaf himself acquiesced by abstaining from overseeing the vote and later resigning in accordance with the law.[47] Another example is recent reports [i.e. from the spring of 2014] that the head of the GNC Energy Committee may have tried to use government funds to bribe Ibrahim Jadhran's brother into ending the eastern oil strikes, actually creating lucrative incentives to engage in armed disruptions.

The Zeidan government repeatedly threatened to use force to break the oil blockades in Libya's east. Yet when the ultimatums expired, Zeidan did not follow through, thereby diminishing his ability to bluff, cajole, and instil fear in his opponents. Iterative game theory shows that being caught bluffing or not driving a hard-enough bargain leads in future negotiations to one's opponents calling one's bluff and subsequently driving a harder bargain. Therefore, Prime Minister Zeidan's ability to restore the government's credibility through bold actions and confrontations with the opponents of the central government was deeply compromised and culminated in his overthrow...

The origins of the problem

The Qadhafi regime long practised a policy of using oil revenues to provide subsidies and wage increases to suppress popular discontent. In a way, this was similar to the welfare model of most oil-producing rentier states which seek to minimize dissent without allowing political participation. The Qadhafi government subsidized health, education, and housing, while imposing price controls on many basic food items. Post-Qadhafi governments have continued with this same strategy of trying to buy peace as part of their social contract. However, lacking a coherent threat of violence or even the inner core of committed supporters which Qadhafi possessed, the NTC and GNC have had to resort to ever-increasing subsidies with constantly diminishing results (in terms of dissent averted).

In fact, the budget for 2012 increased subsidies for fuel, food, and electricity to 11 percent of GDP (i.e. far beyond the levels prevalent during Qadhafi's rule). The 2013 budget further increased these subsidies to nearly 14 percent of GDP. Furthermore, even though the economy was in dire straits in 2011, wages in the public sector were increased by 30 percent during the year. There was another wage increase of 27 percent in 2012 and a 20 percent wage increase was budgeted for 2013... Capital expenditure comprised only 20 percent despite the urgent reconstruction needs of the country, which have been estimated to amount to some $75 billion. Simply put, the Libyan state not only spurred inflation and a consumer goods bonanza, but it empowered its opponents, while almost entirely discounting the potential that intelligent use of government spending could have to create sustainable economic growth as well as to change the political incentives of its opponents. Simultaneously, since the oil blockades have come into effect, the government has not found ways to significantly reduce its spending. As such, on 25 March 2014, in the absence of an agreed upon budget, the government required a $2 billion loan from the central bank to cover its various operating costs.[48]...

In the short to medium term, the state will remain the dominant employer in the Libyan economy even if 99 percent of public sector jobs add little value to the Libyan economy.[49] Because the Libyan market offers the prospect of both lucrative contracts and wealthy consumers many foreign companies are willing to endure the hardships of working in Libya because they calculate that there will be a long term payoff. Nonetheless, foreign businesses are still largely dependent on the bloated and dysfunctional state sector or the unsustainable consumer glut, which is the result of government subsidies that cannot be sustainably continued in the long run...

Once it is understood that the appeasement is rooted in the authorities' inability to protect their offices, homes, and meetings places, it becomes clear that the government must make bold efforts to protect its premises and that of the country's parliament. The creation of economic incentives for militiamen to disband as well as the creation of an elite security force loyal to the abstract Libyan state, rather than a particular political faction, is essential to formulating a governance strategy not rooted in appeasement. Once this force is in existence it can be used to secure the premises of the Libyan authorities thereby allowing them to govern without constant threats to their lives and property.

PART 3

THE PLAYERS IN THE STRUGGLE FOR
THE POST-QADHAFI FUTURE

[*This section introduces some of the main militia groups discussed elsewhere in this volume.*]

Linking together the two concepts of the underlying centre–periphery conflict and the GNC's penchant for appeasement, it becomes clear that the Libyan government is trapped in a struggle with its myriad opponents to set the rules of the political game within which the struggle for post-Qadhafi Libya will be waged. The militias—and the social, local, regional, religious, ideological, and tribal cleavages which sustain them—have gained in strength over time as government policy incrementally transfers to them more funds and levers to both rally their supporters and pervert the political process...

Seen in this light, Libya's greatest security challenge remains the hundreds of militias that resist disbanding, impede the functioning of the country's official military and police forces, and threaten to interfere in the decisions of the post-Qadhafi elected transitional government. The continued lack of leadership and overall inactivity[50] demonstrated by former Prime Minister Ali Zeidan has allowed the militia leaders to view themselves as more legitimate than the national police and military as a result of the grassroots nature of brigade formation and the continued presence of Qadhafi-era officers in the military and police. With weapons readily available and trust in the country's politicians at an all-time low, armed brigades feel justified in influencing the highest levels of government by blockading or occupying government facilities, including the ministries, the floor of the GNC, and important oil and gas sites. The government does not have sufficient trained forces to counter these armed groups and to protect its own premises, and it will take many months, if ever, for planned training programs to have any positive impact.

Thus, the militias have only gained in strength with each attempt to disband or disperse them. This is because the NTC (Libya's first post-Qadhafi administration) chose to give the militias state subsidies. Since then, the militias have become formalized within the nascent institutions of the Libyan state as the government has tried to enter into an uneasy partnership with them to provide security. This means that at the forefront of security threats there are militias on both sides of the key issues: smuggling and human trafficking, mafia style crime, terrorist activity, assassinations in the east, and violent local disputes. Government forces are still too weak to fight these battles and hence for every rogue militia, a temporarily pro-government one has to be employed.

Unfortunately, brigades that have pledged to work with the Defence or Interior Ministries have frequently been the cause of armed clashes rather than a deterrent or solution. The Revolutionary Operations Room, the militia tasked with keeping Tripoli safe and reporting personally to the president, was implicated in the October 2013 kidnapping of the prime minister. The two main umbrella groupings of government-sanctioned militias, the Libya Shield Force (LSF) and Supreme Security Committees (SSC), frequently have clashes amongst their branches or with the civilian population. Egregiously, the major petroleum facilities of Libya have been occupied by the very Petroleum Facilities Guard sworn to protect them...

The creation of a coherent and accountable command and control structure is essential to breaking the impasse resulting from the penetration of the security sector by the supporters of the militias and extremists. Aiming to achieve this, the GNC had decreed that all unauthorized militias must leave Tripoli and Benghazi by the end of 2013 and in order to gain some positive momentum from this popular outrage, passed new laws regulating gun ownership effective March 2014.[51] However, as in earlier cases of government ultimatums for disarmament, the announcement that government payments will stop on 31 December 2013 to armed groups not registered to join the state security apparatus and that carriers of unlicensed guns will face penalties after March 2014 are not being followed through. Militiamen are still receiving their salaries [*as of Spring 2014*], and they have not been cajoled to abandon their arms or positions...

Zintan militias

During the 2011 Uprisings, Zintan (an Arab town in the predominantly Berber/Amazigh Nafusa Mountains) was never conquered by Qadhafi's forces. Benefitting from its proximity to the Tunisian border, it became a centre for rebel military organization from neighbouring areas, quickly building up the strongest Arab non-Islamist aligned militias in all of Libya. ... Zintan's militias are 'perceived as a counterweight to the range of Islamist groups'.[52]

The Zintanis, who have a small demographic base, have leveraged their control of the international airport and capture of Saif al-Islam Qadhafi for political power and prestige. It was via this control that Osama Juwaili was appointed defence minister in November 2011. This was a decisive appointment as the Zintanis have maintained control of the upper echelons of the Defence Ministry and have become something of a praetorian guard for the country's Liberal politicians. Despite that close alliance, the Zintanis have also disobeyed the government on occasion so as to maintain their power—most noticeably via not handing over Saif al-Islam for trial in Tripoli and by not vacating key positions in the capital...

Tripoli militias

Tripoli Military Council and Tripoli Local Council

The Tripoli Military Council (TMC) is comprised of former members of the Libyan Islamic Fighting Group (LIFG). They benefitted from Qatari monies and political assistance which made them unpopular with the citizens of the capital. Their former head, Abd al-Hakim

Belhajj, hails from the Tripoli neighbourhood of Souq al-Juma and was a prominent member of the LIFG.[53] Due to his association with Qatar, Belhajj abandoned his association with the TMC in order to run for office. After his unsuccessful bid with his Hizb al-Watan political party in the 2012 General National Congress elections he turned his attention to sending Libyan jihadists to Syria.[54] ...

Nawasi Brigade (Crime Combating Unit)

The 150-strong Nawasi Brigade affiliated with the Supreme Security Committee controlled the Mitiga airbase until November 2013.[55] Its leadership consists of [*Madkhali*] Salafists who pride themselves on fighting drug and alcohol related crimes, as well as activities that are deemed un-Islamic such as weekend parties, or Christmas or New Year's celebrations. At the start of their formation they wanted to be a copycat of Saudi Arabia's religious police...

Misrata militias

Misrata's more than 200 militias with over 40,000 militiamen in arms are the largest block of fighters in post-Qadhafi Libya. Their primary rivalry is with the Zintan militias. Their *esprit de corps* is high as Misrata faced a brutal three-month siege by Qadhafi and its citizens arranged themselves into brigades able to successfully defend the city. After ejecting Qadhafi forces, these brigades played a decisive role in the battle for Tripoli, the liberation of Sirte and the killing of Muammar Qadhafi. Over time, they have become increasingly aligned with the Libyan Muslim Brotherhood as they have felt isolated from the government of Ali Zeidan... This 'special relationship' was made clear as Misratan forces were the only forces deployed to Sirte in an attempt to retake oil terminals in the east...

Islamist militias

After Libyans who had fought in Afghanistan against the Soviets returned to Libya, they became a source of anti-Qadhafi activity in the 1990s, as many of them came together to form the Libyan Islamic Fighting Group (LIFG) dedicated to the overthrow of the Qadhafi regime. Libya's anti-Qadhafi activists and Salafi jihadists were concentrated in eastern Libya, and Derna in particular became a centre of Libyan jihadist activity. A captured al-Qaeda document known as the Sinjar Records listing the origins of foreign fighters in Iraq after 2003 shows more fighters from Derna than any other Middle Eastern city.[56]

On the one hand this concentration of jihadist influence in Derna is surprising, as eastern Libya was traditionally the home of the Sanussi Sufi order, which was antithetical to Wahhabi/Salafi/Jihadi doctrines. Yet on the other hand, this phenomenon reflects the perceived marginalization of eastern Libya by the Qadhafi regime and the rejection of Qadhafi's heterodox Islamic doctrines as heresy. Fascinatingly, this latter dynamic is playing out in [*circa 2014*] Libya. As the uprisings began in the east and the NTC's early leadership came from the east, many anti-NTC jihadist groups had difficulty recruiting. However, since the NTC's move to Tripoli, and the increasing sentiment among the inhabitants of Cyrenaica that their interests have been neglected and that the GNC's pursuit of constitutional governance and training of troops abroad is non-Islamic, it has become far easier for jihadi groups to garner support from this segment of the Libyan population...

Abu Salim Martyrs Brigade

This militia is based in Derna and comprised of former LIFG members. Its leader is Abdul-Hakim al-Hasadi who formerly engaged in militant activity in Afghanistan under the Taliban and was imprisoned by the US government in Guantanamo Bay.[57] ...

Ansar al-Sharia

The Benghazi branch of Ansar al-Sharia is officially led by Muhammed Ali al-Zahawi, who fought with the Rafallah al-Sahati brigade in Misrata. Other branches are in Derna and Sirte. Ansar al-Sharia is thought to be involved in the training of foreign jihadists in Benghazi, ultimately bound for Syria.[58] The most famous member of Ansar al-Sharia is Ahmad Abu Khattala, who denies being a member of the group and [was] considered a suspect [in] the 11 September 2012 attack on the US Mission in Benghazi that killed US Ambassador to Libya, Christopher Stevens, [which he also denies]. The group has certain sympathies [with] al-Qaeda but is not officially affiliated [to it]. A 28 December 2013 New York Times investigative report refers to [the role of Ansar al-Sharia in the storming of the US Mission in Benghazi] but concludes that there is no evidence suggesting that al-Qaeda played any part in the attack. [Ansar al-Sharia] is also implicated in the July 2011 killing of General Abd al-Fatah Yunis, [the] then head of Libya's rebel armed forces. This report suggests that [the group bears more responsibility] than any other non-Qadhafi aligned [jihadist outfit] for the failure of the transitional government to assert its authority over the

Islamist brigades in Libya.[59] This optic highlights that even though jihadists are supported by a miniscule fraction of the Libyan population and the Libyan state expends minimal funds and resources combating them (likely another instance of appeasement), the struggle against the jihadists is actually the primary battleground where the success or failure of the Libyan state will play out. This appears to be because although most Libyan brigades will not kill other Libyans or assassinate foreigners, the jihadists will. Clearly the US government has come to a similar determination when they declared Ansar al-Sharia in Benghazi and Derna as terrorists on 10 January 2014, not only because of their purported role in the attack on Chris Stevens, but also because of the tactics they use in internal Libyan political quarrels.[60] ...

The leader of Ansar al-Sharia's Derna branch is Sufian bin Qumu, who was once a driver for Osama bin Laden and formerly detained in Guantanamo. He is thought to be responsible for several attacks against former Qadhafi-era officials.[61]

The presence of Ansar al-Sharia in Derna has disturbed the local communities and tribes. Moreover, Derna was the only town in coastal Libya where the Constituent Assembly elections were unable to be carried out on either their initial date of 20 February 2014 or the rescheduled date of 26 February because extremist militias threatened both poll workers and anyone who would vote and the Libyan government has no traction in the town. In March 2014, there has been an anti-extremist campaign targeting Ansar al-Sharia, with at least thirteen members killed far including leading figure Ali al Darwi. The campaign is thought to be the work of relatives and tribes of the victims of the jihadist assassinations that engulfed the cities of Derna and Benghazi.

The election disruptions are only the latest in a long string of conflict between Ansar al-Sharia and the Libyan government... A similar dynamic evolved in the wake of the killing of US Ambassador Christopher Stevens, after which the people of Benghazi marched on Ansar al-Sharia's headquarters, chasing them out of the city. Yet due to a lack of government follow-up, the militia was able to reenter the town when the furore died down. This parallel is very instructive for future developments in both Benghazi and Tripoli as there is yet little concrete evidence that the government will be able to capitalize on the current outpouring of anti-militia sentiment. This is due to the lack of political will and unity over the issue of national security; additionally, many of these militias enjoy the support of powerful GNC members...

Armed eastern federalists

Ibrahim Jadhran's meteoric rise began when he was appointed head of the Petroleum Facilities Guard (PFG) for Central Libya, where the major oil terminals [then] under his control are located. Jadhran says that his observation of the government's unfairness in distributing resource wealth, lack of transparency and widespread corruption—specifically in the oil sector—are the main factors behind his decision to abandon his commission in the PFG and launch his bid for Cyrenaican autonomy.

By focusing on themes with a populist resonance, Jadhran quickly attracted the attention of many in eastern and southern Libya who could relate to his rhetoric. Despite the government's designation of him as a criminal, for his supporters he is a hero and the potential 'saviour of Barqa (Cyrenaica)' as some like to call him. To date *[spring 2014]*, Jadhran has capitalized on the government's inaction when his movement was beginning to take hold in early fall 2013. The operating budget, if any, and source of funds of the Federalists is not clear. Jadhran claims that his operating expenses are donated by 'businessmen who believe in his cause'.

While the government has sat on its hands, over the last eight months *[Fall 2013 to Spring 2014]*, Jadhran managed to transform his group from merely a protest group into an organized opponent seeking to carve out its own sphere of autonomy from the central government in Tripoli... However, his office and government have been unable to sell oil on their own in order to secure the necessary funds a true Cyrenaican government would need. ... The calling of a North Korean-flagged vessel at Sidra terminal on 8 March *[2014]* and its eluding the forces of the Libyan government to reach international waters on 11 March only to be captured in Cypriot waters by American Navy SEALs on March 17 constitute[*d*] a limited victory for Jadhran... Although Jadhran may have temporarily sparked the ire of various Tripolitanian militias who are ready to challenge his control of the oil terminals, this east/west clash appears to be increasing his popularity with the Cyrenaican populace who now feel under attack by Tripolitanians...

Worryingly, the GNC and Zeidan government were so caught up in their own power struggles that they were unable to take resolute action when a North Korea flagged tanker docked at Sidra and loaded a cargo of crude oil before the government started to react. The fact that the cargo could leave Libyan waters fully loaded caused such uproar as to provoke the fall of the Zeidan government. Many feel that Zeidan's enemies may have blocked him from taking coherent action so as to punish him when the tanker escaped. This appears quite likely as [*then GNC President*] Nuri Abu Sahmain was the commander and chief of Libya's army, and he and many other Islamists were in positions of power over the army, navy, and air force as it disobeyed commands to attack the tanker. The incident has caused much malcontent among the general populace over what has been perceived as theft of Libyan resources... Curiously, the *Morning Glory* tanker was owned by an Emirati company and directed by Emirati employers to call at Sidra.[62]...

PART 5

INTERNATIONAL TRAINING OF SECURITY FORCES

Table 1: Training by country, location, amount, and purpose as initiated or projected by each country as of February 2014

Country	Location	Number of trainees	Purpose
Libya	Various	15,200 [projected]	Police training
		10,000	Army training
France	Various	2,500 [projected]	Police training in counterterrorism
		75	Bodyguards to protect Libyan VIPs
		30	Air Force pilot training
		20	Navy officers
		72	Navy divers
Italy	Vicenza	60	Training Libyan border guard officers

	Army Infantry School in Cassino	362	Training Libyan infantrymen
	Tripoli	280	Training Libyan military police
		150	Training in using anti-drug sniffer dogs and forensic crime scene investigation
Jordan	King Abdullah Training City	1,900	Police training
Sudan	Karari Military College, Wadi Sayyidna	At least 60	Military cadets
Tunisia	Unknown	1,500	Training interior ministry officials
Turkey	Egirdir Commando School	3,000	Military training
United Kingdom	Bases in and around East Anglia especially Bassingbourn	2,000 [projected]	Army training in basic infantry skills
United States	Bulgaria	5,000–8,000 [projected]	Soldiers
	Near Tripoli	100	Special forces

Sources: Oscar Nikala, '220 Libyan Soldiers Start Military Training in Turkey', *DefenceWeb*, 11 December 2013, http://www.defenceweb.co.za/index.php?option=com_content&view=article&id=33026:220-libyan-soldiers-start-military-training-in-turkey&catid=49:National%20Security&Itemid=115; 'Insight: Libya's Training Honeypot', *DefenceWeb*,

17 December 2013, http://www.defenceweb.co.za/index.php?option=com_content&view=article&id=33068&catid=74&Itemid=30; 'First Libya Army Cadets Pass Out in Sudan', *Libya Herald*, 29 October 2013, http://www.libyaherald.com/2013/10/29/first-libyan-army-cadets-pass-out-in-sudan/#axzz2oB9OZhfS; Houda Mzioudet, 'Interior Ministry Staff Being Trained in Tunisia', *Libya Herald*, 17 December 2013, http://www.libyaherald.com/2013/12/17/reports-of-personnel-being-trained-in-tunisia-denied/#axzz2oB9OZhfS

The formulation of a much-needed comprehensive long-term plan to train Libyans by outside powers is inhibited by several factors: traditional Arab fears of a foreign military presence on Arab soil; Western worries for the safety of their personnel; and the risk of training militant Islamist sympathizers who may later use their weapons and training against Western interests.[63] Furthermore, the weak Zeidan government hesitated to be seen as embracing foreign training as a central plank of its strategy to bring stability, in spite of its clear necessity. Although at times, Zeidan 'threatened' his militia opponents with foreign intervention or with the acceleration of training programmes, he appeared unable to use the potentiality of outside assistance to actually strengthen his position inside Libya. Moreover, neither he nor others in the Libyan administration appeared to grasp that it was the lack of a professionalized security force able to protect government buildings and the person of the prime ministers and other ministers is what made exiting the appeasement trap impossible.

Even if Libyan authorities had grasped the critical importance of the creation of an internationally-trained security force, there were always hurdles to its rapid achievement. The initial iterations of various training programmes faced rather severe hiccups [*and multilateral coordination complexities as illustrated in Table 1*]. Jordan was the site of a short-lived 2012 effort to train

... police, but the programme ended due to bad behaviour by recruits, which culminated in a riot. US efforts to train a hundred army special forces at a base near Tripoli were halted when weapons caches and special equipment like night vision goggles were stolen from the base, possibly an inside job by the trainees. The programme was also criticized for selecting its recruits primarily from western Libya (mainly from Zintan), given that Libya's first minister of defence in post-revolution Libya was a Zintani.[64] Moreover, most cash-strapped European countries have found it politically challenging to commit resources to build such a force. As the Libyans have lacked the administrative skill to issue timely payments for training courses, only Italy and Turkey began their courses prior to receiving payment. The Italians may hope to recoup the cost of their training programme via defence sales, while Turkey hopes for a greater political say in Libya and possibly more business and defence contracts as a result. [*Seen in retrospect from 2021, the Italians failed to actualize this hope, while the Turks have notched up remarkable successes far beyond their initial ambitions. The global dynamics of the Enduring Disorder allowed this to unfold.*][65]

The UK has adopted a different approach. It has refused to begin its 'training programme' prior to receiving the relevant payment and as a result the arrival of the first tranche of trainees in the UK has been delayed multiple times. The British proposed [*as of Spring 2014*] to train 200 recruits in intensive courses over a span of 24 weeks at the until-recently mothballed Bassingbourn base in East Anglia, which is being refitted as a training centre...

The United States is structuring the financial and bureaucratic aspects of its training programme as a type of 'Foreign Military Sale', consisting of defence equipment, training, and logistical support. As such, the sale is supposed to not only further US national security but to employ Defense Department personnel and contractors, while providing an outlet for US military goods.[66] The sale must be discussed and approved by Congress.[67] ... In the wake of Zeidan's ouster many in the United States question if the United States has a governmental partner with which it can deal to coordinate the bureaucratic and administrative aspects of training.

With each country taking its own approach to funding and interfacing with the Libyans, no one country has asserted itself as either the leader or coordinator of the various multilateral efforts.

Despite the diplomatic inertia and organizational complexity, the United States, EU, UK, Turkey, Gulf Arab countries, and others intend [*as of Spring 2014*] to train 15,000 Libyan troops in a multilateral process, with varying degrees of coordination among Libya's international partners. The EU, largely through Italy and France, has committed to a two-year mission to improve Libyan border security forces. The UK has pledged to train 2,000 members of the General Purpose Force (GPF). The United States and Italy are also supposed to initiate a joint programme to train 6,000 to 8,000 members of the GPF in Bulgaria as the backbone of the future Libyan army, although this will take months to complete and will unlikely materially affect the balance of forces until after the constitution process is complete. Unsurprisingly, bureaucratic obstacles in Libya and in the United States appear to be delaying the start of this programme.

Moreover, questions abound about where these trainees will deploy upon their return to Libya, considering the lack of an infrastructure to absorb them into a national security apparatus. For example, will they answer to the existing army chain of command, or to newly created structures meant only for the GPF? Will the trainees be willing to serve the interests of the Libyan state against the militias of the regions from which they hail? Will the civilian leaders of Libya use the GPF as a praetorian guard to defend their own personal interests or those of the Libyan body politic itself?[68] The near total collapse of the legitimacy and efficacy of the Libyan government and GNC in February 2014 has exacerbated these doubts about what structures would absorb troops when they returned from training.

Despite these imponderables, if the training programme is even moderately successful and is paired with positive political developments, it remains the greatest hope for tackling Libya's militia problem, as all indications suggest that the militias will not voluntarily disband. To succeed it should be organized along a multilateral axis rather than overlapping bilateral commitments. The creation of a coherent multilateral structure could be... facilitated by a strong US, UK, French, and Italian political commitment, as signalled by a visit to a training facility or speech on the subject by a high-ranking figure.

The training debacle as appeasement and collective action failure

Looking back at the discourse concerning the Libya file in 2013–14 as showcased in the excerpt above, it should come as no surprise that neither US President Obama nor British Prime Minister Cameron exerted sufficient leadership to form a coherent multilateral structure to coordinate international attempts to train a Libyan army. Furthermore, no Libyan troops were ever trained specifically for the GPF. Among the few Libyan cadets who went to Bassingbourn for rudimentary training, some were involved in a rape scandal, causing the programme to be terminated,[69] while those that were sent to Italy rioted in their mess, throwing pasta at their trainers.

Was the wrong approach taken because the relevant strategic discussions never happened at the highest levels? No. Coordinating training efforts for the Libyan GPF were a high-profile discussion item at the G8 summit in Northern Ireland on 17–18 June 2013. They were mentioned as a magic bullet solution to the problem of the nascent post-Qadhafi state lacking a Weberian monopoly of force.[70] Yet despite this lofty rhetoric, each country engaged in its own sporadic and half-hearted attempts—barely informing its allies concerning their country's progress. Those countries whose programmes depended on Libyan pre-payment never got started; those that did not adequately vet the cadets tended to entrench the partisan connection between specific international actors and given factions on the ground. In short, the GPF never came into being due to run-of-the-mill failures of collective action.

The few returned trainees went back to their pre-existing militias—as no centralized command and control structure was forged to absorb them. Individuals trained by major Western nations later participated on rival sides of the First Libyan Civil War (2014–15). In retrospect, training could be conceived as an international attempt to appease the militias (by offering them coveted trips abroad and experience with advanced weapons systems) and not an investment of genuine political capital in sorting out the collective action complexities afflicting Western policy towards the Libya file or creating a genuine Weberian monopoly of force for the Libyan government.

The true costs of appeasement

In any post-conflict situation, a governance vacuum can only last for so long before outsiders attempt to take matters into their own hands to secure their own interests. Nonetheless, the absence of leadership on the Libya file in the international arena did not appear so crucial to a range of Libyan civil society commentators in 2012. In fact, due to forty-two years of Qadhafi blaming all of Libya's problems on foreigners meddling in Libyan affairs, many revolutionary fighters as well as prominent statesmen had drunk the anti-imperialist Kool-Aid and came to perceive foreigners as the primary threat that might derail the success of the revolution. In some way, their instincts were prescient given the extent to which later Turkish, Russian, and Emirati interventions would hijack Libya's political transition. But their inability to grasp which actors posed the real threat, led many to forbid well-intentioned Western technocratic experts from embedding within key ministries. This was a major contributing factor in the failure to build adequate Libyan governance capacity.

The new elites of post-Qadhafi Libya felt that they could use appeasement to cope with the power vacuum on the ground, as there seemed enough wealth and opportunity to go around so there was no need to make tough choices. By overthrowing a tyrant, Libyans had achieved freedoms of speech, civic organization and the ballot box. The populace was in the honeymoon period after Qadhafi's ouster, intercommunal violence was rare and hostile foreign powers were mostly keeping their distance. At that time, many commentators thought that the Libyan people would unite around a sensible path forward. Yet, as the microcosm of training illustrates, appeasement and collective action problems led to the squandering of the brief window, roughly 2012–13, that could have been used for effective state-building in Libya. It also illustrates that international actions towards Libya were just as muddled as Libya's myriad domestic factions.

Since 2014, the country has experienced the vicissitudes of war, the degradation of its infrastructure, and a haemorrhaging of truly unimaginable wealth: according to conservative estimates, at least 200 billion USD has been expended, wasted, or 'evaporated' since 2011 on corruption, subsidies, cash transfers, and smuggling—all forms of appeasement. It also seems that Qadhafian assets valued at roughly 100 billion have simply vanished; add to this the more than 170 billion directly lost from federalist (2014–16)[71] and LNA oil blockades (summer 2018, January–September 2020)[72] and the around 300 billion[73] indirectly lost because the security situation did not allow multinationals to upgrade Libya's out of date oil infrastructure. The point here is that the direct costs of appeasement—i.e. subsidy programmes and transfer payments—from Qadhafi's ouster to the present appear to be 'not that costly': only in the tens of billions or around a third of Libya's oil earnings in a regular year. But the indirect costs are certainly in the high hundreds of billions and quite likely over a trillion dollars[74] cumulatively over the first post-Qadhafi decade. In short, even using conservative estimates, by 2021 the overall costs of appeasement have exceeded the total wealth currently inside the country or sovereignly owned abroad.

Libya used to be a very wealthy, extremely sparsely populated place; tragically, the vast majority of its sovereign wealth either remains frozen by UN sanctions against the Libyan Investment Authority (LIA), has now vanished due to appeasement, corruption, and misuse, or is trapped underground with only inefficient ways to get it out (due to blockades, security issues, the global recession, and the expected future price of oil). The years that Libyan oil was largely taken off the market by blockades (2013–16) were ones with high crude prices, yet when Libyan oil production came back online after the most recent extended blockade in September 2020, it did so into an oil glut combined with decreased demand due to the Covid pandemic. Even if crude prices rally and Libyan production stabilizes, both of which seems likely in late 2021, the damage has already been done. Those untold riches and what they could have done for Libya's institutions, infrastructure, and human capital are genuinely lost forever.

Libya will now never be a Kuwait on the Mediterranean, but it is wrong to say that it never could have been. To my mind, appeasement is responsible for this lost future. Politicians believed that because Libya was wealthy, they didn't need to solve complex collective action problems about who gets what. They could simply pay off their opponents and supporters alike and that all would be well. Such magical thinking pervades appeasement traps elsewhere.[75] In fact, the legacy of appeasement has been a shared feature in other oil producers who have experienced institutional and state collapse during the Enduring Disorder. Venezuela is the most prominent example of an appeasement trap leading to the irrevocable squandering of far more than a trillion dollars of sovereign wealth, the complete implosion of state institutions, and the facilitation of a civil war. Venezuela has the largest oil reserves on the planet, and its geostrategic positioning and lengthy alliance with the United States granted it the opportunity to become a Latin Norway-on-the-Equator.

Appeasement's patient zero: Venezuela

Venezuela was the world's first country to become an oil rentier state. After the discovery of oil in 1914, the country's existing infrastructure and governmental structures were primitive enough to constitute a *tabula rasa*. Hence, its economy and society were completely moulded in line with its leaders' decisions vis-à-vis Venezuela's relationship to the global economy. In the early twentieth century, an aspiring strongman Juan Vicente Gómez seized upon the oil majors' preference to deal with a clear and consistent power structure to cement his one-man rule. During the Second

World War and the Cold War, the Venezuelan government and elites cultivated an alliance with a string of American presidents and diplomats, exploiting their fear of Communism to confront the American oil majors' interests and achieve for Venezuela a greater share of the proceeds from its oil wealth. Over the last century, it has been easier—both politically and intellectually—for the Venezuelan ruling class to buy off potential opposition than to figure out how to sustainably develop their country. Although such patronage politics arose in the aftermath of the discovery of oil, only since the collapse of the Soviet Union has appeasement metastasized into radical populism and indirect rentierism, roughly akin to the situation in Libya.

By looking at the Venezuelan reality, we see that appeasement-based populism has caused artificial scarcity of subsidized products while also promoting a culture of sectional grievances—where those who shout the loudest (or throw a mango at the President) get a free apartment.[76] In fact, Venezuelan appeasement-based programmes that were theoretically intended to benefit the poor, like subsidizing the price of petrol or giving preferential access to hard currency for the importation of basic foodstuffs, have given rise to criminal gangs and pressure groups that seek to take advantage of the loopholes these programmes create.[77] More recently, as the regime has come under threat, the military has been given preferential access to subsidized goods and racketeering opportunities to secure their loyalty.[78]

Once appeasement is adopted as a government strategy, it is devilishly difficult to undo. Decisions to appease inherently entrap future policymakers while spawning an addiction to free money among the recipients. As such, it should have been the priority of a well-coordinated international community to undertake the collective action necessary to prevent economically and geostrategically critical nations like Venezuela and Libya from falling into the appeasement abyss.

During the 1970s, Venezuelan civil society began to grapple with the ways in which sustained high oil prices were not necessarily good for the country. They artificially decimated domestic industries (Dutch Disease), promoted excessive government spending on red herring projects, and facilitated handouts to ease the wealth inequalities created by the oil industry. As this knowledge diffused through the populace, an opening for courageous political leadership emerged. Venezuela's economic structures had facilitated waste by promoting inflation, smuggling, and corruption just like Libya's, but during the 1980s, certain educated and far-sighted Venezuelans wanted to safeguard their nation's future and learn from the mistakes of previous economic policies. Then, in 1989, a democratically elected government sought to reduce the subsidies on gasoline, devalue the bolivar, and eliminate the most corrupt government agency—the Recadi, which was in charge of granting preferential access to subsidized dollars. The government adopted neo-liberal-style reforms that unleashed a wave of looting, riots, and protests in Caracas that elicited a repressive backlash from the regime, together known as El Caracazo.[79]

Failing to mobilize their supporters effectively, the government preferred to bash the skulls of protestors rather than making the case for the reduction in subsidies. The protests and the government's bungled response stopped the government from implementing its full package of economic reforms, which could have prevented future smuggling, corruption, and state collapse.[80]

Venezuelan politicians drew a perverse and incorrect lesson from this episode: that appeasement was popular and fiscal discipline was not. In the words of the foremost observer of contemporary Venezuela's economic system, *Wall Street Journal* reporter Raul Gallegos: 'Venezuela's democracy tempts presidents to use oil riches to perpetuate their hold on power. This means that future Venezuelan leaders must balance electability [against] a long-term view of the country's development.'[81] It was the shadow of democratic accountability, or the threat of removal from power, which led to, and perpetuated, the appeasement cycle in Venezuela, just as the threat of militias ousting the political class in Libya prevents them from cracking down on the militias' avenues for enrichment. Once those groups that benefit from appeasement have more power than the central government's technocratic economists, the game is lost.

El Caracazo and the inability of capitalist and globalist leaders to implement sane economic reforms contributed to the election in 1999 of the former coup-plotting paratrooper Hugo Chávez, who promised cheap products and a range of government handouts to his supporters, especially the military. He created and nurtured the self-reinforcing cycle of handouts, price controls, and opportunities for regime insiders and the military to enrich themselves that Qadhafi's policies did. Similarly to Qadhafi, while Chávez remained in power, the abuses of the system were kept within certain limits due to fear of his power and popularity. Then, analogously to after Qadhafi's fall, following Chavez's death in 2013, the perversities of the economic structures he had created became fully apparent. Nicolás Maduro, Chávez's successor as president, was no longer able to make sure that there were enough products in shops or petrol at the pump, as illegal gangs had arisen to smuggle these subsidized items out of the country. The gangs' supporters had also infiltrated the ministries, just as Libya's militias' allies did. Appeasement had so weakened the Maduro government (just as it had the central authorities in post-Qadhafian Libya) that it attempted to ban the main opposition parties from taking part in the presidential elections, touching off a pernicious civil war from 2018 to the present.

Venezuelan appeasement was facilitated by a range of domestic and global pressures and led to the implosion of the Venezuelan state. Appeasement also sucked in foreign involvement by powers such as Cuba, Russia, and Iran. It destabilized Venezuela's neighbours, especially Colombia, where rebel groups received funding and safe haven from Chávez and Maduro. Its perverse economic logic also engendered a bonanza of corrupt enrichment by a new class of cronies connected to the regime, which led to hot money flowing into the American and British banking systems while also creating a network of Western corporate entities vested in the continuation of the Maduro regime. All told, Venezuelan appeasement has been a major contributing factor to the Enduring Disorder. Venezuela's leaders want to work with enemies of the United States, especially Cuba, Russia, and Iran, all of whom, following the logic of the Enduring Disorder, are happy for Venezuela to remain an economic basket case so long as an anti-Western regime stays in power. Additionally, Chávez and Maduro wanted to export their unique brand of appeasement-based anti-capitalism to places like Ecuador or Bolivia. They too care little if those countries become highly destabilized so long as they do not support regime change operations or structural economic reforms in Venezuela.[82]

* * *

Seen in this comparative context, it is clear that appeasement is a type of self-reinforcing collective action failure, the corrosive effects of which can quickly cascade outwards. Nearly all Libyans and Venezuelans would reject the immediate gains of appeasement if they could choose roads, bridges, schools, hospitals, and scholarships to study abroad instead.[83] Most Libyans and Venezuelans also realize that their vast oil reserves, relatively well-developed human capital, and lack of sectarian cleavages could have granted them these things. Yet, due to tragically timed interventions of cowardly politicians, craven militiamen, corrupt thugs, and misguided protestors, they live in a state of perpetual civil war and state implosion. The international system has facilitated these suboptimal trajectories by preferring short-term unilateral solutions over longer-term coordinated multilateral policy. Western corporations and the movement away from genuinely free markets to a form of monopolistic neo-mercantilism have played their part as well—issues I address in Chapters 4 and 5.

In the spring of 2014, when the think tank report 'Libya's Faustian Bargains: Breaking the Appeasement Cycle'[84] was being written, the First Libyan Civil War had not yet started. Militias were manoeuvring, posturing, smuggling, collecting state salaries for fictitious persons, and attempting to infiltrate nascent state structures. This was not yet a full-blown civil war with sustained multi-day clashes with heavy casualties. In this environment, appeasement and populism seemed to me the primary cause of the post-Qadhafi authorities' inability to engage in genuine state-building or to exert Weberian sovereignty.

In hindsight, however, appeasement was merely a component feature of the structural vestiges of the Qadhafian economic model. These structures' reliance on subsidies and the market distortions caused by rival quasi-governmental economic institutions were the root causes of appeasement.[85] The Qadhafian economic model was a unique kind of indirect rentier state—predicated on buying off different segments of the population by giving them privileged access to opportunities for corruption—rather than directly via cash transfers as in the oil-rich and centralized Gulf states.[86] Haphazard appeasement of various social segments and the gradual expenditure of Libya's wealth without reaping commensurate benefits in improved infrastructure, human capital, or sovereign assets was the natural outcome of the Qadhafian economic model. This cynically dysfunctional use of funds expanded post-Qadhafi due to the old regime's fundamental economic structures not being overthrown, but actually being reinforced, especially by status quo domestic elites and international corporations who benefitted from the existing structures.

This is the main conclusion of my research into Libya's interactions with the global economy, which will be explored in greater depth in Chapters 4 and 5. It also demonstrates how appeasement pathologies can prevail even in states on the verge of financial collapse and how dysfunctional appeasement-based patronage networks can survive regime change events seemingly intact.

All these typologies are also demonstrated in the enduring civil war in Yemen. According to Yemen researcher Laura Cretney:

> [O]ne of the reasons the conflict in Yemen has become so intractable and difficult to resolve is that the country's highly complex war economy transcends the alliance structures and frontlines of the conflict. In many ways, the war economy is an extension of the neo-patrimonial system that existed under former President Ali Abdullah Saleh, whereby the President and his inner circle engaged in appeasement in the form of financial largesse, government contracts and public sector employment to various tribal and regional figures and their constituencies in exchange for their support, or to quell unrest or instability. Ironically, such appeasement made these various social systems, especially the tribes even stronger and more intractable than they would otherwise be.

> Post-Arab Spring, a similar system of patronage exists, though the networks themselves have evolved to encompass a plethora of new actors and now extend outside of Yemen's borders. Today, the appeasers are the foreign actors rather than the Yemeni regime, and the appeased are the armed groups on all sides of the conflict.[87]

The existence of appeasement networks weakening state institutions and promoting the continuation of the civil wars in Libya, Venezuela, Ukraine, Syria, and Yemen has major implications for understanding the dynamics of the Enduring Disorder. It suggests that due to appeasement and international collective action challenges, the collapse of the Soviet bloc and then the Arab Spring countries' political institutions did not inherently facilitate the creation of new economic institutions or even comprehensive efforts at economic reforms. Instead, the new regimes tended to witness the resilience of the most dysfunctional aspects of their former economic systems, albeit under new guises.[88] As these dysfunctional systems were progressively connected to the global economy, they went on to emit a contagion, 'infecting' the global economy writ large with those practices and perverse incentive structures. Seen in this light, many of the economic dysfunctionalities of the contemporary globalized order have a distinctly peripheral origin.

In the Libyan case, because Qadhafi's ouster was akin to popular multifaceted Uprisings[89] rather than a genuine revolution, appeasement of the victorious militias and populace was bound to ensue without farsighted leadership. Such bold attempts at root and branch economic reform did not materialize, as there were incentives for each group and their leaders to try to game the current system for their advantage. Each aspiring leader thought he could strengthen his faction by gaining preferential access to existing patronage networks rather than working together with rivals to attempt to forge a coalition with the legitimacy to reform state institutions to spend Libya's wealth more wisely.

Appeasement, and the ensuing proliferation of the militias, was therefore the result of a profound collective action problem on behalf of Libya's nascent political class. Game theory and historical precedent correctly predicted that militia demands would grow in proportion to the amount they were appeased. The phenomena of dispersion of power, a multiplicity of armed actors, populist handouts leading to increasingly outrageous popular demands, and the democratization of violence were all witnessed in post-Qadhafi Libya and are hallmarks of the era of the Enduring Disorder globally. From jihadists to white supremacists to criminal gangs, the ability to conduct violence or incite it has now been democratized globally by new technologies. Moreover, when violence hits at key nodes of global order (like US diplomatic personnel or major oil installations), the prevailing conditions during the Enduring Disorder facilitate feckless responses.

Vengeance denied

Jihadists and jihadi sympathizers wantonly murdered US Ambassador to Libya J. Christopher Stevens in Benghazi on 11–12 September 2012, and yet US diplomats and the military establishment initially did little in response. The immediate policy issue in the wake of the murder was not ascertaining whether his death was the result of a planned terrorist attack or a spontaneous protest. That was, however, the focus of media coverage—and the ensuing domestic American partisan blame game. The real policy issue was what the American response should be. This was neither discussed much at the time nor has there been much retrospective analysis or scholarship. If a similar episode involving the murder of a senior diplomat from the world's pre-eminent power had transpired in North Africa during the Cold War or during the British imperial heyday, it would have likely occasioned a swift and overwhelming American response. President Ronald Reagan had bombed Qadhafi's headquarters at Bab al-Aziziyya in response to the 1986 Berlin disco bombing. Despite the technical difficulties and the opposition of the French, the British dispatched gunboats to Alexandria when a mob threatened their citizens in Egypt in 1881; they subsequently took over the country when the populist anti-imperial Egyptian rebel leader Ibn 'Urabi threatened to default on loans.

By pointing out that America circa 2012 did not respond commensurately to the murder of a senior diplomatic official and his colleagues, and hence an affront to US international power, the way previous hegemons had done in similar situations, I do not mean to criticize President Obama or Secretary Clinton's handling of the lead-up to the episode or dredge up the ugly Congressional partisan blame game over the incident.[90] Having known Ambassador Stevens personally, as well as a few of the other key diplomatic players involved, I have unique data points[91] from which to conclude that the president and secretary did nothing wrong in the lead-up to the murder and that Chris was well aware of the danger he was facing by choosing to voluntarily go to Benghazi to open a hospital. My criticism has to do with how American policy evolved in the aftermath of the episode—and a lot of those decisions were shaped by the pressures and media optics created by the Republican attacks on UN Ambassador Susan Rice and Secretary Clinton. But it also emerged directly from the cowardly instincts of the Obama administration officials.

According to both common sense and the official findings of the House Benghazi Select Committee Report, the episode itself cannot be laid at the feet of high-ranking State Department officials.[92] Ambassador Stevens was not instructed to travel to Benghazi by a diplomatic cable from Washington. He knew the resonance and risks implicit in the date of 11 September; he knew that his friend and colleague Her Majesty's Ambassador Sir Dominic Asquith's convoy had been attacked in downtown Benghazi two months earlier. And yet, Chris chose to go to Benghazi anyway to open a hospital and an American cultural centre, without requesting additional security personnel.[93] This was Chris's decision, and he was most certainly the American government's foremost authority on the situation in Libya at the time.

Chris did not want America to act as a vengeful hegemonic power, he wished for it to serve the best interests of the Libyan and American peoples. I believe he was something of a willing martyr for his cause. Tragically, he could never have anticipated the extent to which his death undid everything he worked for in his life.[94]

Does this mean I am promoting a 21st century version of neo-imperial gun-boat diplomacy? By no means. Whether lashing out as a vengeful hegemonic power, lustily craving to restore order, is good or bad, moral or immoral, is simply not the point here. This book is an attempt to document the state of affairs in the global system circa 2021 and to point out how quickly things have changed since the Cold War. In 2012, the American hegemon lacked either the will to violate Libyan sovereignty or the ability to swiftly project preponderant force into it. America also lacked an acknowledged sphere of influence over Libya, which would have been recognized by its allies. These factors led to an American inability to achieve a consensus with their Western or Libyan allies about how best to respond to the tragedy. This played out during the hours of the mortar attack on the Benghazi Special Mission, when American rescue personnel could have been deployed from southern Italy but were not. It also played out long afterwards, as US and Western militaries and law enforcement agencies did not provide the GNC or anti-Islamist militias in Benghazi with the resources to pursue the attackers and reassert civilian authority over Benghazi. Quite the opposite; after Chris was killed most Westerners cut and ran from Benghazi.[95]

The Libyan people mourned Stevens, demonstrated against his killers,[96] and called for more American assistance, yet an abrupt and total American withdrawal was the response to his death, which is the exact opposite of what a similar incident would likely have occasioned a decade or more earlier, and of what Chris himself would have wanted and had told me personally he sought for Libya.[97]

Seen in retrospect, Ambassador Stevens's murder was the first demonstration of the post-Qadhafi authorities' and their international allies' wholesale loss of symbolic sovereignty over Benghazi, the birthplace of the revolution. But it was so much more than that. Just as chaos theory claims that a butterfly flapping its wings in Brazil can occasionally cause a hurricane in Kansas, Ambassador Stevens' murder led to the implosion of the post-

Qadhafian Libyan state's ability to secure territory, its bifurcation into two parts, and the flow of streams of sub-Saharan migrants through Libyan territory on their way to Europe. In turn, these phenomena deepened the Enduring Disorder, helping to facilitate Brexit and the election of Presidents Trump and Bolsonaro via the chains of indirect causation discussed in the Introduction.

This episode also demonstrates another defining feature of the era of the Enduring Disorder, which is in stark contrast to the Cold War or early post-Cold War periods: the reluctance of major Western powers to operate in dangerous areas either by committing civilian peacekeepers or reinforcing diplomatic missions to secure their interests.[98] This phenomenon is indicative not only of the weakening of political resolve in the West—about which there is a significant scholarly literature[99]—but also of the inability to coordinate such actions with allies because a coherent institutional mechanism is lacking to solve the inherent collective action complexities.

Even though Libya circa 2013 was a much safer locale than Iraq or Afghanistan had been a couple of years after their regimes fell, capacity-building assistance was harder to offer in Libya because in those other theatres the Americans 'ran the show' and decided whom to train, what to build, and when to delegate various tasks to the British or other allies. But in early post-Qadhafi Libya, it was unclear who should build the prime minister's praetorian guard, who should train the coastguard, and who should make sure that Libyan civil servants were paid on time. The Italians didn't feel the Brits should do it, the French wouldn't countenance the Italians leading the coalition, and the Americans who would have been acceptable to most parties had no desire to lead. Given this collective action problem, the will for joint action was sapped. Experienced US and European diplomats knew not to push for policies that they could not implement by themselves nor effectively coordinate with their allies.[100]

In the post-Qadhafian Libyan case, international actors lacked the ability and appetite to engage in capacity-building and were happy to offload the problem on to Libya's nascent political leaders and then hope for the best—only stepping in when their core national interests were threatened. This would avoid them being blamed for any failures, while also steering clear of any latter invocations of the Pottery Barn Rule.

In short, when the going got tough, the international community simply got going. Part of the reason for the Western states' inaction over Libya was the possibility that, by defending their own interests, they would be accused of neo-imperialism or hypocrisy. Conversely, as they did not have to worry about the optics of their actions, the militias and their regional autocratic allies could stand up to the international community, the United States, and Prime Minister Zeidan by simply calling their bluff. It was not the Libyan people but rather rogue Islamist militias who murdered Ambassador Stevens, pushed for the Political Isolation Law, briefly kidnaped Prime Minister Zeidan, and then harassed him into exile.[101] Miraculously, they got away with all of it. By late 2014, a few hundred ragtag militiamen had chased all the major Western powers and the bulk of the Global Fortune 500 companies out of the country.

Before their first terms, George W. Bush and Barack Obama both stated that they would stop using the US military as a global police force. In defiance of seven decades of precedent, Obama actually honoured his pledge. Was America inadvertently guilty of appeasement of Russia when it failed to honour its subsequent redlines in places like Syria and Crimea?

2

JIHADIS ARE JUST A SYMPTOM

Disorder is the cause, jihadis the symptom

Examining the causative dynamics of the Enduring Disorder is a complicated matter. Did anti-globalist, neo-populist ideology lead to the failure of global coordination, or did the failures and frustrations of broken systems of global coordination give rise to an era of neo-populist ascendency? Similarly, has the failure of Western policy in the Middle East given rise to the jihadis, or has the pre-existence of anti-Western jihadi movements caused the West's policies to fail?

Certain Western policymakers and military commanders excused their policy failings in the wake of the Arab Spring by claiming that the prior existence of active jihadi movements facilitated the post-conflict implosions of the Yemeni, Syrian, and Libyan states. This view reverses cause and effect. In reality, the causation is fairly linear: the conditions at play during the Enduring Disorder (epitomized by the international community's collective action failures vis-à-vis Syria and Libya) facilitated the post-uprisings political vacuum in those countries, which led to state implosion and ungoverned spaces, which, in turn, facilitated

113

the further spread of the already present jihadi currents. Although the jihadi networks long predated the Arab Spring, they would not have been able to expand and govern territory without the state implosions that they themselves could not occasion.

The Enduring Disorder and ungoverned spaces are the causes here.[1] They are 'the sickness' which in Muslim polities gives rise to 'the symptom' of jihadi recruitment and insurgencies. In certain instances of abject state failure, those movements then acquire territoriality and governance functions.

The last two decades in Yemen, Somalia, Afghanistan, Southern Lebanon, Syria, Iraq, and Libya showcase that jihadis can only ever acquire governance functions—like the ability to tax or provide justice and healthcare services—when both the domestic state and the international community have failed to prevent a governance vacuum from emerging.[2] Jihadis cannot create the governance vacuum if the regime and the population are united against them. Conversely, if the state has already imploded and the society is majority Sunni Muslim with a multi-sectarian, multi-ethnic, or highly tribal populace, it is nearly impossible to stop jihadi actors from filling such a vacuum.

ISIS differs markedly from its Sunni[3] precursors in being able to exhibit the ideological and institutional flexibility to foster, and then fill, governance vacuums across the Islamic world. One might wonder how ISIS burst on to the global scene with this novel capability. I argue that ISIS is a highly specific version of a Sunni jihadi organization perfectly mutated to propagate within, and then further promote, the prevailing conditions of the Enduring Disorder. Seen in this light, ISIS—and the white nationalist terrorist organizations that deeply resemble it—are simply the natural by-products of the selection pressures placed upon non-state organizations by the Enduring Disorder.[4]

In Chapter 1, we saw that Islamist and jihadi actors are uniquely placed to take advantage of the feedback loops unleashed by governmental appeasement and the international collective action failures that inhibit unified responses against them. In this chapter, we will now look at how these groups exacerbate the very conditions and dynamics in which they thrive, and why governmental actors tend to adopt short-term and whack-a-mole approaches to the systemic challenges posed by the jihadis while utterly avoiding treating their underlying cause—ungoverned spaces.

The Ancien Régime *Dictatorships beat the jihadis six ways to Sunday*

A connected misconception is the idea that Libya, Syria, and Iraq already contained active jihadi movements within them at the moment that their state implosions began. The reality is quite the opposite. In the late twentieth and early twenty-first centuries, all three countries had already comprehensively defeated jihadi insurgencies and were characterized by powerful intelligence services and repressive state structures able to prevent a relapse. In fact, the *ancien régimes* in Syria, Libya, and Iraq had been savvy, brutal and highly effective in devising mechanisms for quashing Islamist insurgencies in their territories while simultaneously exporting jihadis to other people's countries.[5] A case in point is the famous quip by Qadhafi's spymaster Musa Kusa bragging to Western intelligence services that 'he knew the name of every Libyan with a beard'.[6]

Although an exaggeration, it was not that far off the mark. Muammar Qadhafi and Saddam Hussein would have been exponentially more likely to have died of old age than to have succumbed to jihadi insurgencies. Hafez al-Assad showed at Hama in 1982 that he was quite capable of reasserting order when threatened by Islamists.[7] Even in the age of the Enduring Disorder, neither the al-Qaeda-linked Jabhat al-Nusra nor the core cadres of global ISIS were able to make a real dent against Bashar al-Assad's regime, despite receiving overwhelming support in the form of arms and volunteers from around the world.[8] Simply put, jihadis thrive in ungoverned spaces but lack the ability to create them *ex nihilo* or to stand up to brutal dictatorships willing to pull out all the stops to keep them in check.

Monarchies with a modicum of traditional Islamic legitimacy have proven themselves even more robust than the Arab nationalist republics in standing up to jihadism. For the past decades, the Kingdom of Saudi Arabia has been both the greatest source of jihadi fighters as well as their target. Yet the Saudi regime is still standing; these days its greatest threats stem from disinherited royals and angry Western liberals, not from radicalized Islamist youth.

Fertile soil

The *ancien régimes* in the Middle East were effective against jihadi insurrections but as rickety as a house of cards when faced with genuine popular insurrections. This is why an academic subgenre refers to the Arab nationalist military dictatorships as 'weak authoritarianisms'.[9] Lacking a broad base of popular support or robust institutions, the regimes could easily be derailed by popular non-violent opposition.

In the same vein, the core Middle Eastern societies are sometimes compared to powder kegs—so rife with social inequalities, resentments, ancestral feuds, and structural contradictions that only the slightest spark was needed to galvanize popular anger and elicit a conflagration able to wipe away the previous order. The implicit reasoning behind this fairly offensive analogy is that all the Arab states are inherently unnatural and permanently imbued with the misshapen handiwork of colonialism—lacking an ideological, territorial, ethnic, sectarian, or genuinely national logic holding them together.

A more rigorous application of these criteria yields a fairly good heuristic for where relative order and disorder reign post-2011 and where jihadi movements can most easily take hold. Those parts of the Middle East cobbled together from disparate Ottoman provinces and inhabited by non-homogeneous populations from a sectarian, tribal, ethnic, or linguistic perspective—Yemen, Lebanon, Algeria, Libya, Syria, and Iraq—are the least stable, while those with longer traditions of nationhood, monarchy, continuities among the ruling class, territorial integrity, or linguistic/sectarian homogeneity of population have tended to exhibit considerably more stability. Morocco, Tunisia, Egypt, and Oman were essentially fully formed nations long prior to their interactions with Western colonialism. As such, they have been able to maintain elite continuity and to avoid state implosion, even when regime change has occurred.[10]

Conversely, Syria and Iraq have known scores of coups, coup attempts, massacres, and terrorist attacks since their independence less than seventy years ago. In the nineteenth century, inter-communal massacres were a frequent occurrence, and the Ottoman authorities were never able to extend their authority to the hinterland.[11] Both countries witnessed major violent insurrections during the post-First World War mandates. Both during the mandates and after independence, their governing regimes have always rested on a minoritarian sectarian base.[12] One way of conceptualizing the primary dynamic of politics in the Levant over the last seventy years is: majority ethno-sectarian groupings (Sunnis in Syria, Shiites in Lebanon and Iraq, and Sunni Palestinians in Jordan and Israel) seeking to overthrow the unfair advantages that those groups blame French and British imperial rule for having bestowed on the minorities.[13] As such, Syria and Iraq have the maximum amount of potential to become particularly fertile ground for jihadi and Salafi movements due to their legacies of sectarian civil war, the illogicality of their colonial-era borders, and distrust between state and society.

117

These factors allowed those countries' long history of Salafi religious scholarship to become 'activated' into cycles of indoctrination and violence in the way that Egypt, which has the longest tradition of Salafi scholarship, has not.[14] The upshot is that Syria and Iraq are about the most fragile states on earth. They are truly the misbegotten bastard children of the San Remo conference.[15] This fragility has manifested itself in the myriad coups, uprisings, massacres, and sectarian conflicts from the creation of those states in 1920 to the present.[16]

* * *

Although on a similar spectrum to Syria and Iraq regarding state weakness, Libya is slightly less fertile ground for jihadis. Despite its horrific experience with Italian colonialism and the linguistic, tribal, and identarian cleavages among its three component Ottoman provinces, Libya is notable for its relative absence of sectarian differences,[17] lack of a history of civil war or intracommunal massacres, and the previous prevalence of Sufi-leaning forms of Islam. All of which has meant that Salafi jihadism did not propagate widely there in the twentieth century.[18] Rather Salafi jihadism predominantly spread as a form of resistance to Qadhafi rather than within an established Islamic scholarly tradition as it did in the Levant and Egypt.[19]

It was in this context that Qadhafi deliberately allowed Derna to become a hotspot for global jihadi recruitment (as discussed briefly in Chapter 1 and in greater detail in this chapter's excerpt), as he hoped to export the problem outside his borders—just as the Saudis had done.[20] This approach backfired for Qadhafi just as it had for the Saudis. Despite Salafi Islam and Muslim Brotherhood ideology having shallow roots in Libya, they were weaponized by their proponents to legitimate any opposition to Qadhafi as religiously permitted.

The jihadis who returned from Afghanistan formed the LIFG (*Al-Muqatilah*). They turned on the regime that had facilitated their acquiring training to fight against the Soviets—just as Bin Laden had done in Saudi Arabia. As a movement, they were largely defeated by the repression of the Cyrenaican insurgency in the late 1990s. As individuals, many were jailed and then 'rehabilitated' in the late 2000s.[21] In short, the jihadis and Islamists were starting from a shockingly low base in Libya from an ideological standpoint, as compared with Egypt, for example, with its robust tradition of both Salafism and the Muslim Brotherhood. Yet, in Egypt—where the state and national traditions have remained strong everywhere outside of the Sinai and the Western Desert—jihadis have been kept in check.

This broad historical exploration illustrates that in the complex context of the Middle East, it is easy to confuse root causes with symptoms, and hence to misread the meaning of trends. In Libya, as in Iraq after the US invasion of 2003 or Syria after 2011, state implosion allowed jihadism to spread, not the reverse.[22]

None of the Arab Spring states were toppled by jihadis. Yes, of course, repression by Qadhafi, the Assads, Ben Ali, and Mubarak facilitated the Islamification of the resistance to those regimes. But a dispersed network of jihadi cells trying in vain to overthrow the government is a completely different phenomenon from what we have witnessed in post-2011 Libya or Syria, where, due to state implosion, the jihadis conduct their business quite openly and have even temporarily acquired state-like structures to fill the political vacuum.

The increased churn rate

Like a multigenerational legacy of divorce in a particular family, a legacy of disorder in a given state or social group tends to breed further disorder via a positive feedback loop. But today's Enduring Disorder seems to be more intense and chaotic, just as today's jihadis are.

Twentieth-century jihadism was characterized by organized clandestine cell structures driven by certain core tenets of Salafi-jihadi ideology such as *takfir* and *imama*.[23] During the Enduring Disorder, coherent religious ideology has largely vanished from contemporary jihadi movements. ISIS behaves more like a digital mob nourished by fake news and inspired by social media influencers, rather than the disciplined orderly jihadis of yesteryear who assiduously studied *fiqh*, memorized hadiths, and did push-ups in caves.

A fascinating implication of the differences between old school and new school jihadism is that al-Qaeda is likely to out-last ISIS globally[24] because ISIS has behaved far too chaotically and brutally even for its self-interest—antagonizing the very host communities that it needed to shelter within. This is the first finding presented in this chapter's excerpt. It hints at a curious phenomenon at play in the Enduring Disorder—namely that the contemporary geopolitical and technological landscape is so unstable, and rapidly evolving, that it is not even a secure environment for jihadi groups! In fact, the Enduring Disorder promotes such unstable behaviours among its key actors that it seems to give rise to even more unstable actors replacing them through a positive feedback loop. Possibly there is no better microcosm of this phenomenon than the constant churn witnessed in former President Trump's cabinet.[25]

The masters of churn

Jihadi leaders are quintessential agents of disorder. Yet if you have ever met one, you would know that they are also generally capable of remarkable dynamism and innovation. All that testosterone, righteousness, charisma, ambition, and courage are fused together into a volatile stew—ready to be ignited by Quranic inspiration, hard drugs, or merely heavy doses of caffeine.

Psychological profiling shows that jihadi leaders share certain traits common among CEOs and politicians.[26] They have that rare cast of mind able to embrace goal-driven work, risk-taking, secrecy, and coalition-building. A significant mental impediment to Western publics' understanding of the Middle East is the prevalence of the condescending and racist stereotype of Salafi-jihadis as backward-looking, cave dwelling, subhuman, and incompetent.[27] In reality, it seems quite likely that most jihadi leaders know more languages, have read more broadly, and are far more tech- and media-savvy than the mid-level, desk-bound American policymakers administering programmes meant to kill them.

In fact, if certain jihadi leaders had had the good fortune of being born in liberal democracies, it seems quite likely they could have become successful congressmen, lobbyists, or oilmen. Like elected officials, jihadi leaders need to have a twinkle in their eye that make people want to believe them, work for them, and be willing to die at their command. Just as policemen and criminals sometimes share a psychological profile, the jihadi leaders I have met exhibited remarkable similarities to the Navy Seals and Special Ops fighters who pursue them. But more than any physical trait or pain tolerance, a jihadi leader needs to be like a hedge fund manager or professional gambler—willing to embrace random chaos and figure out how to profit from it.

My conceptual horizons have been expanded by close personal experience with one 'jihadi mastermind'. Noman Benotman is a Tripoli-born former commander of the LIFG turned London-based deradicalization professional. Noman used to be known as the 'Starbucks jihadi' due to his elite cosmopolitan background and addiction to espresso.[28] A handsome man of able body, sharp wit, and inspiring oratorical skills in both Arabic and English, Noman left a comfortable Tripolitanian existence to acquire the skills necessary to topple the tyrannical Qadhafi regime that had expropriated much of his family's property. He fought against the Soviets alongside Bin Laden in the caves of Afghanistan before returning to Libya to organize urban guerrilla warfare in Benghazi in the late 1990s. The failure of that venture and the 9/11 attacks led to his repudiation of jihadism, claiming that he could no longer tolerate the loss of innocent life and the defaming of the values of true Islam.

Over the following years, he adjusted to life in London as an exiled intellectual and became the president of the world's first counter-extremism think tank, Quilliam. He sought to promote deradicalization, not only among British Muslims but more controversially among white supremacists, who he felt were going through similar psychological struggles with globalization. Quilliam became famous for its controversial engagement with notorious Islamophobe Tommy Robinson, the founder of the far-right English Defence League.[29]

Eventually, Noman's successful deradicalization programmes and integration into the London policy scene helped him make his peace with the Qadhafi regime. When Saif al-Islam sought to employ deradicalization techniques to rehabilitate jihadis languishing in Libya's notorious Abu Slim prison, Noman was flown in to lend a hand.[30] These efforts gave Noman connections at the top of the very same power structure that he had dedicated his young adulthood to fighting.

When the Arab Spring came to Libya, Noman echoed the regime's line that there were 'no spontaneous uprisings'. Having finally secured access to the bastions of power, he was not going to abandon his new patrons that easily. In late February 2011, he went to Tripoli to try in vain to persuade former LIFG combatants not to join the anti-Qadhafi protests as they were 'foreign-led'. Then, as developments on the ground progressed and compelled him to admit that the uprisings were, in fact, spontaneous and Libyan-led, he then quickly pivoted again, proclaiming that Qadhafi would crush the protestors and reassert control.[31]

Despite this profound miscalculation, after Tripoli fell and Qadhafi was murdered in Sirte, Benotman saw clearly the real structural dangers that lay ahead for the new Libya. He counselled Western governments to engage in more capacity-building assistance, to build up a professionalized Libyan army, and to be cognizant of the dangers of Islamists infiltrating and then dominating the nascent security structures of the post-Qadhafi Libyan state.

His warnings were prescient and compelling. After hearing him address a British House of Commons Committee in 2012, I reached out to him. As part of getting to know each other, he and I co-authored a chapter for my previous edited volume—its most innovative scholarship derived from Noman's recollections of the Islamist milieu of Libya. Together, we coined the term 'Pakistanization' for the phenomenon of battle-hardened Islamists using their skills and networks to monopolize the upper echelons of the intelligence and security services, which are then tasked with combatting jihadism.[32]

Noman and I briefed the UK MoD together; he gave a stirring speech at the book launch of my edited volume in Cambridge in 2013.[33] It appeared to me that other than urging deradicalization of incarcerated jihadis in Britain and Libya, Noman's greatest passion was to advocate for greater Western, especially American, coordination and capacity-building assistance to Libya's legitimate authorities. Noman seemed to wish to solve the collective action problems that kept me up at night.

Then, in the wake of the Tubruq–Tripoli split in the summer of 2014, Noman underwent another change of heart—this time in the diametrically opposite direction from his earlier days in the Afghan caves. He deepened his ties with the anti-Islamist powers: the UAE and Saudi Arabia. More than just supporting Haftar, he proposed the sternest of counter-measures against the Islamists within the ranks of the Libya Dawn movement in Tripoli and Misrata. Within months, Noman had become an informal go-between connecting the American and European neo-populists with Haftar and the Emiratis.[34] In 2016, he rejoiced in Trump's presidential election victory on Twitter; Sebastian Gorka and Erik Prince returned the favour by invoking his name and parroting his analysis of the Libya conflict to the White House.[35]

Noman's public statements promoted the belief that Haftar could become a pro-Western strongman, forge order out of chaos, and purge Libya of jihadism. He also promoted the pro-Haftar talking point that the GNA was a ragtag collection of hoodlum militiamen deliberately harbouring unrepentant jihadis. By repeatedly stating these views, Noman ascended the heights of Twitter stardom and gained access to prominent Trump allies as an apologist of Haftar with a compelling life story.

Then, slightly before Haftar's ill-fated assault on Tripoli in April 2019, Noman presciently switched sides once again. He proclaimed that Haftar had become a tyrant and was on the verge of propelling Cyrenaica's sons to senseless death. Insiders I spoke with claim this change of heart was occasioned by Noman being rebuffed by Haftar when he went to Al-Marj in January 2019 during Haftar's southern offensive to discuss the position of national security advisor should Haftar conquer all of Libya.[36] *Al-Minassa al-Libiyya*, a news and commentary website, ran an exposé of Noman in February 2019:

> What is more controversial is the fluctuations in Benotman's positions: between backing the military establishment [meaning the LNA], to then opposing it and strongly disagreeing with the decisions of Haftar.[37]

Having conveniently switched sides just before Haftar's assault on his birthplace, Noman helped coordinate the GNA-aligned militias' defence of his old neighbourhood. He shared insights about the structures and tactics of the LNA with his erstwhile adversaries. As the war for Tripoli protracted, he cemented himself as one of Libya's leading Twitter personalities—with his live video chat sessions explaining to the populace what the war was 'really about' and why it was necessary to rally together to defend Tripoli from the invader. His detractors frequently spoke of his hypocrisy.

Conversely, his disciples in Tripoli embraced his pronouncements as gospel truth—conveniently ignoring the glaring contradictions with Noman's previous statements. Prominent Libyan TV pundit al-Sanussi Biskiri described 'the Benotman phenomenon' in the following way:

> With his fluctuation between being a Qadhafi regime supporter [after his post-9/11 rehabilitation from jihadism], to supporting Operation Dignity [i.e. the LNA, during the period 2014–18] to then becoming a supporter of the revolutionary Tripoli militias [in 2019], Benotman showed that some, or perhaps all, of his audience who responded to his sermons [by tweet, YouTube, and on TV] mentally or emotionally do not actually care about who Benotman is, what he represents, what he personally desires, what the sources of his information are, or even the degree of the credibility of what he says. What they care about is that he is [at that moment] on their side, be it Qadhafian, pro-LNA, or pro-revolutionary militias, and [due to his unique knowledge and connections can help them] exact their revenge on their opponents.[38]

Then as the Tripoli war ground on, Noman lost patience with those GNA military figures who were collaborating with the Turks to bring professionalism to the defence of Tripoli. He claimed that they were 'selling out the real revolution'. He spoke about instances of GNA corruption and claimed to be standing up for the individual Libyan solider, the real hero of the revolution, who was being abandoned by the political class. As this message became more mainstream and was taken up by incumbent powerholders like Interior Minister Fathi Bashaagha, Noman's popularity waned and he mostly reverted to private life.

Who benefits from churn?

In Trump's inner circle Michael Flynn, Paul Manafort, and Roger Stone exhibited many similar personality traits: bravado, eloquence, audacity, hypocrisy, hyperactivity, self-righteousness, extreme ideological fluidity, and bizarrely elitist claims to be standing up for the downtrodden. These traits would have excluded them from consideration as trusted lieutenants by old school political parties. Yet the conditions of this new historical period have incentivized such behaviour. In this world of chaos, characterized by abrupt reversals, those willing to violate conventions and change their stripes to fit the moment get ahead, especially if they have an uncanny sense of timing enabling them to ride shifts in popular opinion. In our example, in each instance, Benotman embraced a narrative or position that was ahead of the curve and then abandoned it just after its time had come and gone.

But other than crafty, faux-populist opportunists, who benefits from all this anti-establishment churn? Could it be that both the jihadis and their most vociferous opponents simultaneously benefit? It is worth remembering in this context that Ariel Sharon and Benyamin Netanyahu tacitly worked with Hamas against the Palestinian Authority, and that to this day Hamas tries to conceal the fact that Israel was instrumental it its formation.[39]

Nowhere is this synergy between the jihadis and those that fight them more evident than in Yemen, where a resource-poor regime with minimal control over its territory has used its ability to 'fight terror' to collect geopolitical rents while also simultaneously aiding and abetting the jihadis. One of the ways former President Ali Abdullah Saleh maintained his grip on power in Yemen for such a long time was by creating or exacerbating security threats in order to then offer a solution, extract financial support, or destabilise his rivals. According to Cretney:

Saleh practiced a policy of divide and rule which he referred to as 'dancing on the heads of snakes'—that is empowering different tribal and political figures at different times in order to keep his rivals weak and maintain his authority. He also tacitly allowed Islamist extremists to operate in Yemen—cracking down on groups like Al-Qaeda in the Arabian Peninsula (AQAP) only when they posed a direct security threat to his regime—in order to extract financial aid and political support from the West.[40]

Thus it is not that surprising that jihadism and its opponents—the Yemeni, Emirati, Egyptian, and Saudi regimes—share many traits. Both want physically to eradicate their opponents and remake Muslim societies in their own image. Although the UAE, Egypt, Israel, and Saudi Arabia claim to be leading partners of the West in the global fight against jihadism (and the Muslim Brotherhood, which they falsely equate with the jihadis), there is reason to believe that the churn and disorder that the jihadis foster actually supports these regional players' interests. So long as there is a global jihadi threat, these regimes can count on Western support against their domestic opponents. So long as there is a domestic jihadi threat, they can continue to engage in anti-democratic practices against segments of their own populations.[41] In early post-Qadhafi Libya, both the Islamists and their opportunistic international opponents were more than happy to support a polarizing agenda even if it allowed for all of Libya to drift towards chaos. Their aims were advanced through fragmentation and the evisceration of sovereignty.

Russia features heavily in this global alliance of strange bedfellows. The Russians seek to promote anti-Islamist regimes abroad while also benefitting from the type of chaos that jihadism causes. It is an economic tautology that Russia, the UAE, and Saudi Arabia benefit from sowing instability in other oil-producing countries, whereas the consuming countries in Europe have a stake in their stability. Furthermore, an increased flow of

migrants from Syria and through Libya drives European populaces towards the neo-populist, anti-EU, and hence, pro-Russian
right wing. Seen holistically, it is clear that the implosion of the
Libyan and Syrian states has directly benefitted the Putin regime.

Syria starkly illustrates this dynamic. Putin benefitted from
the existence of the very same jihadis that he used as a justification for supporting the Assad regime. As both Libya and Syria
show, if the jihadis are quintessential agents of disorder and
churn, so too are some of those who most vociferously claim to
be fighting them. The Enduring Disorder is self-perpetuating,
primarily because so many of its incumbent players benefit from
the disorder's continuation.

* * *

Selections from: Jason Pack, Rhiannon Smith, and Karim
Mezran, 'The Origins and Evolution of ISIS in Libya', *Atlantic
Council*, 20 June 2017.[42]

Findings

1. Brutality Backfires

Our data show that, over the last three years [*2014–
2017*], the Islamic State of Iraq and al-Sham (ISIS) has
become the enemy of the vast majority of the Libyan
people. By killing too many people and brutally crushing resistance, ISIS first lost Derna and in December
2016, lost Sirte. This fits into a larger regional dynamic,
where ISIS brutality occasions backlashes: ISIS lost in
Yemen because they were too brutal and acted against
tribal norms, undermining their ability to compete with
more established groups like al-Qaeda. Furthermore, in
Libya, ISIS has been doubly challenged by its inability
to rely on sectarian cleavages to marshal support from
the Sunni population as it has done in Iraq and Syria.

2. Statelessness Created ISIS

There is no such thing as a purely military strategy to defeat ISIS. ISIS is a symptom of broader Libyan problems, especially weak governance. The tyranny exercised by Libyan militias has been at the heart of Libya's instability for the past five years. It constituted a major contributing factor to the environment that attracted ISIS in the first place. Therefore, international and Libyan policy needs to treat root causes ... Merely evicting ISIS from Sirte has not and will not solve any of these underlying problems as ISIS cells maintain a presence in Libya and their ideology persists... The unique effectiveness of Libya's governance vacuum as an incubator for jihadist operations was showcased to devastating effect with the 22 May 2017 Manchester Arena bombing. ... Now that ISIS has lost its territorial control of Sirte, Western governments should provide further support for efforts to formalize, institutionalize, and restructure Libya's security institutions.

3. Necessity to Decentralize Authority

ISIS was allowed to thrive in vulnerable localities in Libya because previous central governments have been reluctant to devolve power to local authorities. Western policy must seek to get the militias and local councils to take ownership of governance and justice issues, rather than merely directing them to fight ISIS or other jihadists. The governance of Sirte in the aftermath of liberation from ISIS control is a case in point.

4. Marginalization in Libyan Society Enabled ISIS

ISIS has been able to exploit, and seek refuge within, communities that suffered in the wake of the 2011 uprisings. Communities vulnerable to ISIS's exploitation have included both pro-Qadhafi elements and more radical elements of those militias that supported the uprisings. True national reconciliation and inclusiveness in Libya, especially between formerly pro-Qadhafi actors and rebels and between anti-Islamist and pro-Islamist actors, is required to end the pattern of radicalization in Libya. This can be achieved by building a genuine reconciliation process into any new unity government plan and into the new Libyan constitution...

IV. Jihadist groups take advantage of the political vacuum

Since 2013: jihadist fighters return to North Africa

By the end of 2013, there was a new pattern of Libyan foreign fighters returning home from Syria, armed with the militant legitimacy that came with having fought in the widely popular Syrian civil war. If fighting for an extremist militia during the Libyan revolution was the equivalent of a 'college degree in jihad,' then fighting in Syria gave fighters an additional stature, similar to that conferred by a specialized post-graduate degree. The experience of returning from Syria to Libya allowed the 'graduate' to branch out on his own, and attempt to recruit others to work with him in Libya's political vacuum. Libyan fighters were joined by many Tunisians who chose to remain in Libya rather than transit through it, as Tunisia began cracking down on extremist groups like Ansar al-Sharia in mid-2013 through their relatively more robust security institutions.[43]

Buoyed by this trend, over the next three years, Libya would change its position on the global jihadist circuit from a transport hub to a bona fide destination. A wave of recruitment videos began to emerge, some aimed directly at Tunisian foreign fighters, calling on them to participate in jihad in Libya as a precursor to jihad at home.[44] In February 2015, for example, ISIS released a video calling on foreign fighters from Egypt, Saudi Arabia, and Tunisia to emigrate to Libya following Abu Bakr al-Baghdadi's formal recognition of an emirate in Derna in November 2014.[45]

Libya's terrain was particularly attractive to foreign fighters because it provided easy access to weapons, little pressure from weak security institutions, a somewhat permissive population, weak border security, no rule of law, and relative safety compared to Iraq and Syria. After it was established on 10 September 2014, the global coalition to 'degrade and ultimately defeat' ISIS put immense pressure on the group in Iraq and Syria, both through airstrikes and by targeting the group's finances. In contrast, only in mid-2016 did the air campaign against ISIS extend to Libya.[46] In the meantime, due to the persistent chaos and lack of a single undisputed government in the country, ISIS in Libya became one of the most effective governing structures in the whole country and was able to co-opt many local jihadists to its cause.

Derna: ISIS's first statelet inside Libya

Derna's historic connections to global jihadist movements, as well as the city's more recent links to jihadists in Iraq and Syria, meant that Derna appeared to be the logical choice to serve as ISIS's first headquarters in Libya. The city's isolation from the rest of the country meant that it was also the most feasible option logistically. Derna had never been integrated into post-Qadhafi governance structures in the same way other cities had. Elections for the Constitution Drafting Assembly in

February 2014 and parliamentary elections in June 2014 were unable to take place due to insecurity at polling stations, further isolating Dernawi residents from Libya's emerging democratic processes. Despite a fleeting revival of civil society organizations in the immediate aftermath of the 2011 uprisings, the city was quickly overrun by extremist groups who occupied the role that local councils played elsewhere in Libya during this period.

In this state of physical and political isolation, extremist groups, including an Ansar al-Sharia branch led by former Guantanamo Bay prisoner Sufian bin Qumu, took control of various neighbourhoods and battled among themselves for control of the city. In June 2014, the Islamic Youth Shura Council (IYSC), an extremist organization that announced its presence in Derna in April 2014, formally declared its support for ISIS. The group was then able to consolidate control over a number of strategic areas and impose ISIS's strict interpretation of Sharia law in these areas.[47] Throughout September 2014, clashes raged in Derna between the al-Qaeda-aligned Abu Salim Martyrs Brigade, Ansar al-Sharia's branch in Derna and the IYSC, each fighting for control of the city.[48] In October 2014, the IYSC and some members of Ansar al-Sharia met iteratively in Derna, ultimately deciding to pledge their allegiance to al-Baghdadi and ISIS, forming the Cyrenaica Emirate or *wilaya*.[49]

Al-Baghdadi recognized the Derna emirate in November 2014, and close communications have been detected between core ISIS figures in Iraq and Syria and affiliates in Libya since.[50] According to Aaron Zelin, within weeks of the declaration of allegiance, the social media profile of the former IYSC conformed to ISIS models, suggesting ISIS may have provided social media guidance to ensure the new *wilaya*'s online presence was harmonized with those of the core in the Levant, even if direct military or administrative orders were not enforceable from Raqqa.[51]

V. Filling the vacuum: ISIS's Libyan wilayat

High profile ISIS attacks in Libya

Shortly after al-Baghdadi formally recognized an ISIS affiliate in Derna, the group sought to demonstrate its growing capacity to terrorize Libya's residents and undermine its institutions, setting the groundwork to remain and expand in the country.[52] Through spectacular attacks that would make international headlines, the group would not only be able to increase global awareness of its presence in Libya, but also ramp up its recruitment drive. The group seized their opportunity following the death of Nazih Abdul-Hamid Nabih al-Ruqai, also known as Abu Anas al-Libi, in US custody in early January 2015. Al-Libi, a senior al-Qaeda leader, was awaiting trial on charges for his role in the 1998 US embassy bombings. He died of complications from a long-standing Hepatitis C infection.[53] Three weeks after his death, on 27 January 2015, ISIS took responsibility for an attack on the Corinthia Hotel in Tripoli, a prominent fixture in the capital that had regularly hosted government officials, Western diplomats, business leaders, and other prominent individuals in Libya. Ten people were killed in the attack, including five foreign nationals, among them an American citizen.[54]...

In December 2014 through January 2015, ISIS fighters kidnapped a number of Egyptian Coptic Christians, who were among the tens of thousands of Egyptian workers who still came to work in Libya after the 2011 uprisings despite the ongoing instability.[55] Targeted for

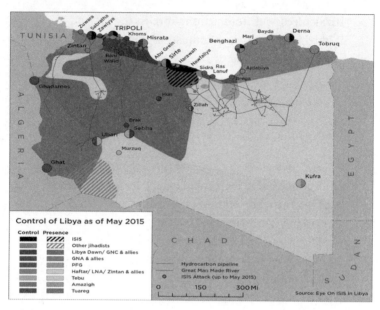

Map 5: showing control of Libya and location of ISIS attacks as of May 2015

their religion, these men were used by ISIS in Libya's second, and most spectacular, attack. On 15 February 2015, ISIS released a video depicting the beheading of twenty-one of these individuals on the shores of Sirte.[56] The international reaction to this horrific event was immediate. Egypt launched airstrikes in Derna and against ISIS strongholds in Sirte, where the group had been rapidly expanding. But the airstrikes were short-lived. In early March 2015, ISIS attacked eastern oil fields including al-Bahi, al-Mabrouk, al-Ghani, and al-Dahra. These attacks were apparently intended more to ensure continued state weakness in response to the ISIS threat than as a high-profile announcement of increased ISIS presence and strength.[57] Although there were few further high-profile attacks, ISIS *wilayat* grew and became more active throughout 2015.

ISIS's precarious headquarters in Derna

Despite the prevalence of jihadist fighters and institutions in Derna, ISIS's presence there was precarious because of the ongoing competition for dominance among extremist groups. In December 2014, shortly after al-Baghdadi recognized the Cyrenaican *wilaya*, jihadist militias opposed to IYSC and ISIS joined together to form the Derna Mujahadeen Shura Council (DMSC) coalition.[58] Both in the Levant and in Libya, ISIS had aimed to subsume all other jihadist groups, but it failed because its rhetoric and modus operandi put off certain core constituents of the jihadist population—especially those with deeper ties to their host communities and those opposed to ISIS's brutality and *takfiri* practices. Many of these groups also refused to pledge allegiance to ISIS because of their adherence to al-Qaeda allegiances and theology, as well as because it was a group imposed on Libya from the outside. Furthermore, although Derna has been a hub of extremist activity for decades, the population was not receptive to ISIS's particularly brutal approach to policing. Notably, foreign interference in Libyan affairs is a particular sensitivity for the population, and the fact that there were foreign fighters entering Derna and imposing foreign governance models on the city outraged many.[59]

ISIS attacks on prominent families and tribal leaders, designed to compel the population to be submissive, provoked residents to flee their homes instead. These tensions came to a head in June 2015, when ISIS killed two top DMSC commanders, Salim Derbi and Nasir Attiyah al-Akar. With local support, the DMSC was then able to drive ISIS largely out of the centre of the city before the end of the month.[60] Historical ties between jihadists in Derna and those in Iraq and Syria were not enough to keep ISIS in power there.

VI. Sirte: ISIS seizes territory in Libya

Ripe for the picking

Once evicted from central Derna in mid-2015, ISIS supporters occupied the peripheral sections of Derna until
mid-2016. Rather than losing key commanders in these
battles, ISIS was able to evacuate its critical personnel and
reconstitute its command structure in a new, arguably
stronger, headquarters in Sirte. Unlike Derna, Sirte, as
the hometown of the dictator, held a place of privilege
among Libyan cities during the Qadhafi regime. But after
the 2011 Uprisings, it joined Derna as one of a number of
cities and towns that failed to be adequately incorporated
into new governance structures. Sirte was one of the final
pro-Qadhafi holdouts in 2011, and was severely damaged
during the final bouts of fighting.[61] The town was also
subject to a fairly unique circumstance in post-Qadhafi
Libya—its inhabitants were disarmed and its key choke
points were occupied by fighters from the victorious
(mainly Misratan) militias. Tribes from Sirte such as the
Qadhadhfa, Warfalla, and Furjan—all linked to Qadhafi's
rule—were discriminated against by the post-Qadhafi
authorities who took no care to invest in or administer
Sirte, leaving it to fester as a battleground for rival militias.[62] Foreigners also frequently found it difficult to reach
Sirte by road or air. As the security situation worsened,
foreign embassy officials rarely ventured beyond Tripoli,
with the partial exception of the revolutionary cities of
Benghazi and Misrata; their absence from the vanquished
cities of Bani Walid and Sirte, fuelled the perception of
isolation in these communities.

From 2013, Sirte experienced its own jihadist/anti-
jihadist local conflict between the al-Zawiyya Martyrs
Brigade led by Salah Buhliqa from Benghazi and Ansar
al-Sharia's Sirte branch (formerly known as al-Faruq

brigade) led by Ali al-Teer from Misrata.[63] Buhliqa's forces eventually managed to kill al-Teer, yet, at the end of that year, Buhliqa died in a car accident leaving his group disorganized and weak.[64] Regional rivalries over control of valuable oil installations in the Oil Crescent and Sirte Basin have compounded the instability around Sirte, most notably during Operation Shuruq (Sunrise) in December 2014, when Misratan and jihadist elements confronted a coalition of easterners including Federalists, Haftar's Libyan National Army (LNA), and Special Forces (Saiqa) in an attempt to take control of the oil facilities and ports.[65]

Misratan militias used Operation Shuruq to consolidate their control of Sirte, kicking out the remnants of the Buhliqa forces which had become allied to their enemies, the nascent LNA in Benghazi. As a reward for jihadist support against the LNA in the Oil Crescent and in Benghazi, the Misratans essentially handed the security of Sirte over to Ansar al-Sharia.[66] It was at this key moment that jihadist elements faced no opposing forces to challenge their expansion in the city.[67] During this period of occupation, fighters from other hotbeds of jihadism throughout Libya and Africa flocked to the city. Domestically, jihadists came from places like Derna, Benghazi, and Ajdabiya, while large contingents of foreign fighters came mostly from Tunisia in 2014 and early 2015, but from late 2015 onward, Boko Haram and other sub-Saharan jihadist groups also sent large contingents to join them.[68] As this process unfolded, the jihadists came to oppose their erstwhile Misratan partners, establishing their own occupation of Sirte.

Resistance is futile

Sirte was empty of any national or local authority that could oppose these jihadist incursions. The fact that

ISIS was able to conduct more high-profile attacks in the Sirte area, including the killings of the Coptic Christians and early 2015 attacks on oil fields in the Sirte Basin, are clear indications of the relative freedom of movement the group had there as opposed to further east. In this context, ISIS in Sirte gradually took over more and more important civic locations. These included the Ouagadougou Centre (the site of many ISIS propaganda videos), the Ibn Sina hospital, and the port. Sirte's wealthiest families fled during this period. Their property was looted and productive industry and farmland was damaged.[69] The group was also emboldened by their defeat of the powerful 166th Brigade from Misrata in mid-2015. The Misratan 166th Brigade had fought against ISIS in the Sirte area between March and May 2015, but eventually retreated, preferring to focus their efforts on fighting Haftar's forces in the east. The 166th Brigade also complained that the contemporary GNC government in Tripoli did not provide it with enough resources to combat ISIS.

One of the most devastating examples of the futility of local resistance to ISIS during the height of its influence was in Sirte, where around 90,000 residents, or roughly 85 percent of the population, fled during ISIS's occupation.[70] ISIS would regularly target residents whom it accused of being spies for the Misratan 166th Brigade and subject them to gruesome public executions. Resistance to this brutality was repressed, including during moments when the group confronted challenges from the complex tribal landscape. In mid-August 2015, local residents, mostly from the Furjan tribe, tried to band together and derail ISIS's attempts at solidifying control over Sirte.[71] The impetus for the rebellion was the murder of local anti-ISIS Salafi cleric Sheikh Khalid bin Rajeb al-Furjani, who was killed during an attempted

ISIS abduction.[72] In reaction to the rebellion, ISIS fighters, including members of the Furjan tribe itself, killed over forty Furjan leaders and supporters, including members of the Warfalla tribe. They also targeted the local rebels by shelling their homes, mostly in the third district of Sirte. They beheaded twelve others and publicly crucified another four to send a graphic message to the rest of the community.[73] As a result, the rebellion was crushed within three days, quashing any further public opposition to their rule from the local population.[74]

The brutal repression of the Furjan rebels in Sirte also sent a message to the surrounding areas: it was futile to resist ISIS. By late September 2015, ISIS had established more checkpoints throughout Sirte and had begun requiring shops to close during prayer times and women to appear in public only with a chaperone. In Nawfaliya, a small town east of Sirte that the group had captured in February 2015 before entering Sirte itself, ISIS appointed local leadership to manage affairs there. The lack of resistance in satellite villages near Sirte, such as Nawfaliya and Hawara, particularly after August 2015, provided ISIS with a buffer to temporarily protect its growing headquarters.

Militia and civil society disunity

Unfortunately, ISIS's presence in Libya did not initially catalyse a unified military or political response from Libya's myriad factions and militias. Instead, the priority over the period of the rise of ISIS in Sirte in May 2015 to the launch of the Misratan-led al-Bunyan al-Marsus (BM)[75] offensive on Sirte in May 2016, remained the battle between Haftar's anti-Islamist Operation Dignity group and the pro-Islamist Libya Dawn camp.[76] Not only did this internecine fighting prevent progress toward resolving the political legitimacy crisis that had plagued

Libya since at least late 2013, but it also allowed ISIS to survive and thrive—sending out sleeper cells to various communities with a high proportion of returnee jihadists from the Levant such as Sabratha and Benghazi.

Just as many local militias had difficulties burying the hatchet to face ISIS, media and civil society organizations were similarly fractured. Local media in Libya engaged in practices that inflamed tensions between rival interest groups and prevented a unified response to the domestic, regional, and global threat of ISIS. According to Freedom House, gaining control over the narratives espoused by media outlets in Libya is a tactic used by rival interest groups to gain an upper hand in the ongoing conflict. Television channels and radio stations have been bullied off the air, journalists replaced with those more sympathetic to Islamist or anti-Islamist positions, and others have been intimidated and even assassinated for their positions, leading to pervasive censorship and inflammatory rhetoric.[77]... [*This phenomenon*

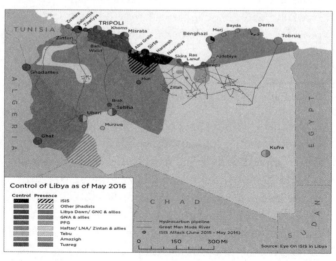

Map 6: showing control of Libya and location of ISIS attacks as of May 2016

and its implications for the global Enduring Disorder will be dealt with in Chapter 3.]

ISIS state-building activities

Libya has hosted various extremist groups for decades and for these groups, Libya served as a safe haven from which they could plot attacks against Western states and their regional allies.[78] By contrast, ISIS in Libya saw value in expanding territorial control within Libya itself and establishing state-like financial institutions, rather than just using the country's vast ungoverned spaces as a base from which to attack Western interests and assets. In the ISIS-controlled territories in Libya, the group destroyed Sufi shrines, implemented harsh punishments such as beheadings, crucifixion, and amputations and forced residents to participate in indoctrination forums and extreme religious observances.[79] Ansar al-Sharia's branches in Libya had sought to provide services and implement their strict brand of law and order in areas under their control in the past, providing a foundation upon which ISIS could build.[80] Once Sirte became ISIS's headquarters in Libya in mid-2015, the group evolved to conduct truly state-like functions: collecting taxes and providing public services, cleaning streets, ensuring grocery stores were stocked, and recruiting doctors, engineers, and lawyers to help run the new 'state'.[81] UN Special Envoy Martin Kobler remarked prior to the coalition assault on Sirte that ISIS had the most well-developed governance model of any group in Libya.[82] Because there was no strong central government in Libya to confront this type of organized territorial form of extremism, ISIS was permitted to survive and thrive.

ISIS also understood that the rise of any functional rival governance entity would embattle its progress. As such, it sought to expand outward and build its state, finances, and governance capacity. It also targeted the nascent UN-backed GNA by seeking to undermine its resources and support. For example, in early January 2016, ISIS conducted a major attack against a military training centre in Zliten, west of Tripoli, and also attacked checkpoints near Libya's most important pieces of oil infrastructure in Ras Lanuf and Sidra—hoping to deny both army recruits and possible oil export revenue to the nascent GNA.[83]

ISIS financing[84]

In both the Levant and its satellites in Libya, ISIS's territorial model of control depended upon loot, taxes, smuggling, corruption, and coerced donations. ISIS's governance template did not foster positive-sum economic growth. ISIS never controlled Libya's oil. Rather, its extractive approach to financing depended on acquiring progressively more territory to tax and plunder—a fact that would hinder the group's ability to resist the anti-ISIS offensive in Sirte in mid-2016, discussed below...

In Sirte in particular, many of ISIS's initial members drew state salaries due to their membership in various state-funded Islamist revolutionary militias.[85] Even after joining ISIS, this nucleus of fighters managed to remain on the state payroll due to poor public financial management practices and possible intimidation of finance officials. Another source of funding came from seizing the property of fleeing residents and distributing it among ISIS's fighters. ISIS imposed a tax on commercial properties, confiscating buildings for which tax had not been paid. Although this extractive system was far less developed than in Iraq and Syria, it is believed that by late August 2015, all shops in Sirte were paying a tax to ISIS.[86] It also relied on social media to promote its *zakat* (Islamic charity/taxation) programme.[87] Additionally, ISIS began charging road tolls on traffic along the east–west coastal highway (al-Tariq al-Sahili) that runs through Sirte and the road heading south towards Sabha.[88]

VII. Slow Western response

Early prioritization of the national over the local

Since the 2011 Uprisings against Qadhafi, Western governments and the UN have focused on developing relationships primarily with national-level interlocutors, reflecting Western governments' relative comfort working with state—as opposed to non-state—actors. Foreign capitals urged Libya's successive transitional governments to focus on elections, reconstruction, economic development, and the strengthening of national security institutions, including a national army and police force. While seemingly sensible areas of focus,[89] Libyan governments and foreign missions assumed that these matters should be handled at a national level. Yet, meaningful authority in Libya had largely devolved to the local level. While the series of national governments failed to achieve even minor accomplishments, some local authorities, notably in places like Misrata and Tubruq, made dramatic progress on reconstruction and building a coherent security infrastructure.[90]...

While the Libyan national government struggled to function, local militias across the country wielded actual power, and thrived on the Hobbesian struggle with their counterparts. They decided when oil could flow, planes could take off, border crossings could be opened, and when the national government was allowed to meet and pass laws. Western governments did not absorb quickly enough the reality that national-level interlocutors were too weak or corrupt to guarantee the success of such ambitious projects, and constantly urged their embassies to encourage one or another Libyan ministry to take various actions, which they were incapable of implementing. Acknowledging that there was no real government to work with may have required international capitals to commit to filling the void in post-conflict Libya in a more comprehensive manner than they—or their citizenry—were willing to accept, particularly given a decade of failed nation-building in Iraq [*and the collective action complexities it would entail as discussed in Chapter 1*].

Recognition of unity government legitimizes Western counter-terror support

After the split between the GNC and the HoR in 2014, Western governments focused their efforts on re-establishing a single central government in Tripoli. Even after the Libyan Political Agreement (LPA or Skhirat Agreement) was signed in December 2015, amending the August 2011 Temporary Constitutional Declaration and creating the Presidential Council (PC), an empowered unity government has been elusive... The GNA failed to unify what had become an east/west split, especially as it seemed to limit the role Haftar could play in any future government, which was unacceptable for many easterners.[91] The PC presented its cabinet list for the GNA to the HoR for ratification twice in 2016. However, after months of delaying the vote, the HoR rejected the proposed lists... [*The second HoR rejection of the GNA cabinet list happened in August 2016. The Skhirat Agreement lacked the relevant provisions to accommodate this initially unfore-*

seen outcome. When it materialized, it was unclear if it: (a) nullified the Skhirat Agreement; (b) remained in force but without the GNA being Libya's legal sovereign or (c) the Skhirat treaty remained in force and the GNA was Libya's legal sovereign, but the treaty lacked the necessary provisions, and the GNA the necessary powers, to promote a resolution to the conflict. Proponents of all three schools of thought embarked on an international effort to amend the LPA to respond to these legal difficulties. This new diplomatic tactic began in earnest with Ghassan Salame assuming the position of UN special envoy in the summer of 2017—months after this excerpt was published].

ISIS's presence grew during the course of the lengthy months of negotiations in 2015, but the international community still largely agreed that an effective, reunified central government was the sine qua non for initiating an anti-ISIS fight, despite evidence suggesting that local councils were viewed as the most legitimate governing bodies in Libya and could have been empowered to tackle ISIS themselves.[92] The moment Libyan leaders signed the LPA, the international community was eager to provide long-promised counter-terrorism assistance to their new, unified (if not locally recognized) interlocutors. Yet, no overt anti-ISIS, Western-backed military operations were initiated until the unity government was nominally in place [*that is installed in Tripoli, though never ratified by the HoR, so that*] actions in Libya could be billed as 'invited' support missions that were answering Libyan requests for help. The first example of this was in the western coastal city of Sabratha, where targeted US airstrikes in February 2016 scattered a growing ISIS cell.[93] The airstrikes in Sabratha in part successfully targeted Noureddine Chouchane, a Tunisian foreign fighter accused of having organized the Bardo Museum attack and the Sousse beach resort attack in Tunisia in 2015. With Chouchane dead after the attack, and Sabratha free of ISIS control at least temporarily, ISIS suffered a blow to its ability to attract foreign fighters from Tunisia and launch attacks throughout the region.

Tensions existed between foreign ministries that insisted on protecting the political settlement process above all else, and the security structures that watched ISIS's spread with deep concern. In the United States, this tug of war between the Pentagon and the State Department was pronounced; similar dynamics existed between the French Hexagone Balard and the Quai d'Orsay. [As of mid-2017,] the GNA remained the focus of Western diplomatic efforts, but quiet, direct support for groups fighting ISIS existed concurrently.[94] This covert military assistance was likely initiated as early as late 2014, with public evidence of it only available when special forces operators are killed in action or when rumours of activities are mentioned in the Arabic media.[95] Western powers [had by mid-2017] also provided support to rival factions in Libya despite public insistence on support to the GNA. France is the most notable for being overtly caught simultaneously aiding both Haftar and his Misratan opponents.[96] [This trend of certain EU members, including France, Greece, and Cyprus, outwardly supporting the GNA while tacitly supporting Haftar would increase after this excerpt was published in spring of 2017. From 2018 to 2020, the French would tilt further towards Haftar while also claiming enough 'neutrality' to mediate between the sides. President Macron and his Foreign Minister Jean-Yves Le Drian only attempted to rebalance their position after Haftar's stock waned in the wake of his defeat in the War for Tripoli.[97]]...

VIII. The battle for Sirte

Formation of an anti-ISIS coalition to attack Sirte

On 5 and 6 May 2016, ISIS fighters carried out two suicide bombings against Misratan Military Council forces at Abu Grein, a village situated roughly halfway between Misrata and Sirte, killing several Misratans. This was the first time ISIS had threatened to extend its influence westward into Misratan-held territory.[98] It appears this attack, and the direct threat posed by ISIS's proximity to Misrata, finally provoked Misratan militias to launch a concerted counter-offensive against ISIS. As a result, Misratan militias joined the Misrata–Sirte Operations Room (which became al-Bunyan al-Marsus, BM) which was established by the PC following the Abu Grein attack to coordinate military operations against ISIS in Sirte; in reality, the PC had little power over these militias even though they were nominally subsumed in the Operations Room umbrella group. Although the interests of both Misrata and the GNA were aligned in their desire to drive ISIS out of Sirte, the Misratans did not fight because they had been ordered to do so, nor necessarily to counter ISIS's brutal ideology and methods of governance. Rather, they fought because defeating ISIS and reclaiming Sirte would increase their own territory and power within Libya and prevent further ISIS incursions into Misratan-held territory. Haftar's response to the implied threat of losing control of the anti-ISIS fight to his rivals, was to set up his own, separate anti-ISIS military operations room to coordinate LNA forces southeast of Sirte. The competitive rather than cooperative undercurrents to the battle for Sirte would persist as no genuine coalition of anti-jihadist militias would ever be formed.[99]

When BM forces finally began attacking ISIS after a few weeks of propaganda, they made swift gains, with air support from Misrata allowing ground troops to advance to within 30 kilometres of Sirte from the west and southwest by the end of May.[100] By mid-June, BM forces had seized the strategic Sirte port, while Petroleum Facilities Guard (PFG) units under the umbrella of the GNA's Ajdabiya–Sirte Operations Room had seized the town of Harawah and advanced to within 50 kilometres east of Sirte.[101] However, by the end of June, advances against ISIS had significantly slowed. Although BM forces estimated that only 500–700 ISIS fighters remained in the city at that point, those ISIS fighters were able to use urban guerrilla warfare tactics to launch regular suicide and improvised explosive device (IED) attacks against the Misratan forces, killing and injuring hundreds.[102] BM forces surrounded the city, while Libyan naval boats half-heartedly blockaded the port in an attempt to cut off all ISIS's supply routes. It is unclear if the naval siege was ever conceived as comprehensive, given that ISIS fighters continued to have access to food, water, and weapons even though they were pinned into an area only a few square kilometres in area. It is likely that small boats were still able to reach ISIS's enclave as BM's naval capacity is limited and many of the Libyan navy ships do not have functioning radars, meaning smuggling vessels could easily slip in at night. Furthermore, the posturing between local factions prior to the assault on Sirte allowed ISIS to dig in and plant booby traps, while allowing its leaders to flee the city, scattering themselves into pre-existing jihadist cells throughout the country.

Turning point: US airstrikes

Increasingly frustrated at their lack of further progress after the initial blitz at the end of May [*2016*], on

25 July BM forces officially asked the PC to call for US airstrikes.[103] Since the GNA's formation many months earlier, discussion of airstrikes between Prime Minister Fayez al-Serraj, Western leaders, and Misratan commanders had been ongoing. Pentagon officials had been pushing the White House for months to authorize AFRICOM airstrikes over Sirte and, to force President Obama's reluctant hand, they had discussed the need for them in the press.[104] On 1 August 2016, after Serraj's public call for help, AFRICOM launched Operation Odyssey Lightning, aimed at helping the GNA and its militia allies deny ISIS a safe haven in Libya.[105] The result was much faster gains against entrenched opposition in Sirte than had been witnessed in Benghazi, where the international community had officially distanced itself from Haftar's campaign, especially since the formation of the GNA. The rapid progress achieved in Sirte by BM demonstrated the higher value of Western military assistance as opposed to Egyptian and UAE assistance. It also provoked backlash from Haftar's supporters rather than coaxing them to reunification. Haftar had been positioning himself as the best partner for fighting ISIS in Libya in order to press for the UN arms embargo to be lifted in a way that would benefit him. In reaction to US support for Misrata, he intensified his ties to the Kremlin, Egypt, and the UAE.[106]

Although the airstrikes, coupled with support from Western special forces and reconnaissance, initially reinvigorated the BM offensive, the dense urban landscape of Sirte meant they did not end ISIS dominance immediately. After seizing the Ouagadougou Centre on 11 August—which had been ISIS's headquarters in Sirte—BM forces fought a battle of attrition, slowly whittling away ISIS's territorial control and numbers, but suffering heavy losses from retaliatory suicide attacks, IEDs, and sniper fire in the process.[107] In mid-October 2016, the pro-GNA BM forces claimed publicly that ISIS[108] had been defeated militarily in Sirte; however, for the next two months, they continued to fight pockets of ISIS fighters who were entrenched in well-defended, booby-trapped enclaves in the Third Residential area of the city, as well as in recently liberated villages outside Sirte.

The intensity of US and Libyan airstrikes against ISIS positions increased significantly from mid-November, and on 5 December 2016, BM forces officially declared victory against ISIS in Sirte, with the victory formally recognized by PM Serraj.... In the days following the declared victory, BM forces began mopping up operations to clear the city of any remaining fighters, IEDs, booby traps, and bodies with continued support from US airstrikes.[109] In mid-December, the Sirte Municipal Council met in Tripoli to elect a mayor for Sirte; however, the Misratan BM forces felt the mayoral candidate was too pro-Haftar and the next day appointed their own military governor.[110]

Throughout the BM operation in Sirte, the siege on ISIS-controlled areas was occasionally lifted, ostensibly to allow the wives and children of ISIS fighters, as well as other civilians, to leave the embattled areas. Whatever its logic, these moments provided opportunities for key ISIS commanders to resupply and to escape.[111] Indeed, this trend was confirmed in late September, when clashes took place between fleeing ISIS fighters and BM forces south of Sirte in the wake of one of the humanitarian siege easements.[112] In late December, there were reports of ISIS fighters attacking a Man-Made River control station in southern Libya and setting up checkpoints in the area.[113] Then, on 19 January 2017—the Obama administration's last day in office—AFRICOM, in conjunction with the GNA, launched airstrikes against two ISIS camps 45 kilometres south of Sirte, reportedly killing as many as ninety ISIS fighters.[114] The head of AFRICOM, Marine Corps General Thomas Waldhauser, estimated in March 2017 that there were 100–200 ISIS fighters left in Libya that were most likely regrouping in southern Libya, and stressed that even with the success of Sirte, ISIS in Libya remains a regional threat.[115] Waldhauser also said that the United States would maintain a force to work with the GNA if more action was needed.[116]

The dangers of supporting a military coalition without political unity

Despite its clear military logic and record of qualified success, continued US support [from mid-2017 onward] to the nominally GNA-aligned militias was fraught with strategic, political, and security risk. As no genuine political anti-ISIS coalition was formed before the fight for Sirte began, the continued support of these forces [from mid-2017 onward risked shifting] the balance between factions on the ground and sparking greater conflict.[117] ...

The fall of Sirte [in December 2016 did] not represent the defeat of ISIS, nor end the threat of other jihadist groups hijacking Libya's post-Qadhafi transition, nor [did] the removal of ISIS from Sirte solve the city's concerns over governance, security, and marginalization. Jihadist groups have been woven into Libya's post-Qadhafi pattern of appeasement, deputization of militias, and statelessness. Only attempts to combat those issues, rather than simply to push ISIS out of specific territories, would be treating the root cause of the problem.

Parallels with Mosul

Striking parallels can be drawn between the Sirte offensive and the one against ISIS in Mosul, which began in October 2016, six months after the offensive against Sirte. In the Mosul theatre, various Shia militias are fighting against ISIS under the umbrella group Hashd al-Sha'abi. Although they are on the same side as the Iraqi government, this does not imply that they are actually taking orders from it. As with al-Bunyan al-Marsus in Libya, Hashd al-Sha'abi in Iraq are not truly under the command of the government nor are they one united Shia force; rather, just like BM, they are a loose coalition of different militias whose interests currently coalesce but could easily diverge when circumstances change. They are fighting with the aim of seizing greater power for themselves, Iran, and Iraqi Shia communities in the aftermath of the battle.[118] Just as the residents of Sirte risk feeling marginalized under a Misrata-dominated military government in their city post-ISIS, the Sunni residents of Mosul risk[ed] being marginalized in the absence of a clear political plan post-ISIS.[119] [*This is essentially what came to pass as Haftar was able to retake Sirte from the Misratans after the majority of the population defected to the LNA in 2019.*]

Consequently, both in Libya and Iraq, Western nations [*should have employed*] extreme caution when continuing to support anti-ISIS coalitions of militias, which have no underlying political agreement governing their temporary military alliance. When the battle is over, these fragile alliances will almost certainly fall apart [*as they in fact did*], prolonging the vacuums that allowed ISIS to exist in these areas in the first place.[120] Should Western nations decide to support certain groups as part of the global priority to rid the world of ISIS, they should also identify incentive structures for each of these coalitions and their members to determine how best to push all sides toward compromise, inclusiveness, and proper government after the military battle is won.

More focused diplomatic capital should be expended to incentivize genuine political coalitions and, when the opportunity presented itself, shared opposition to the systematic spoiling activities of jihadists should be used as a lever to cement real political alliances and grand bargains between factions. In this way, the war against ISIS could have been used as the turning point to finally forge a post-Qadhafi coalition capable of stopping the entropy that had characterized the post-2014 political cleavages. Similarly in Iraq, the opportunities for genuine nation-building in the post-Nuri al-Malaki age appear on the verge of being squandered. Defeating ISIS militarily is foregrounded by Western strategists, while the opening for correcting the implosion of Iraqi [*and Libyan*] state structures presented by the anti-ISIS fight is ignored.

Libya has regenerative properties for jihadis

Throughout 2014–15, ISIS prepared to make Sirte its last redoubt, should the battle turn against it in the Levant. Western and Libyan policymakers were slow to publicly acknowledge the extent of this threat—in fact, there was ample reason to believe they deliberately downplayed it and only acted when forced to do so—as the above excerpt has showcased and as the closing anecdote of this chapter will further illustrate. With Sirte declared liberated in late 2016, they tacitly agreed on abandoning the necessary mopping-up operations or engaging in the capacity-building and political coalition-building that was required to treat the root cause of jihadism—ungoverned space.

Tackling the problems of ungoverned space was just too complex a collective action challenge given the prevailing conditions of appeasement (examined in Chapter 1) and other dynamics emanating from the Enduring Disorder such as the polarizing media environment and dysfunctional economic incentives (to be addressed in the remaining chapters).

Furthermore, fighting and defeating jihadis can be used to score political points, while instituting procedures that bolster governance is tough and unglamorous work. Politicians face incentives to exaggerate the geostrategic importance of arenas in which they can score quick wins and minimize the import of more intractable problems. It should come as no surprise that other than for Italians and Maltese, for whom Libya's importance to their national wellbeing is an indisputable fact of life, Western leaders tend to downplay Libya's geostrategic importance to their national interests due to the collective action complexities implicit in tackling Libya's challenges head on.[121]

Yet, Libya's geostrategic import cannot be wished away by politicians. Libya's role as a key node of the geopolitics of the Enduring Disorder can be amply illustrated via the jihadi microcosm. It will remain impossible to defeat jihadi extremism in the Levant or globally if Libya's oil wealth, subsidies, permissive environment for smuggling and human trafficking, and massive artillery arsenals are easily accessible to global jihadis. This differentiates Libya from other jihadi hotspots outside of the Levant. ISIS cannot regenerate its power globally from Boko Haram in Nigeria, its affiliates in South East Asia, or even al-Shabab in Somalia. Libya has the money, connection to global networks, trained fighters, and armaments to resupply and regenerate any global jihadi movement that can exploit its state implosion and subsidy-driven economy.[122]

Fascinatingly, this regenerative function has always been the way jihadis have spoken about Libya in their recruitment videos.[123] Yet, from Foggy Bottom to the Pentagon, Libya remained a blind spot. Despite the writing being on the wall, and the Derna interlude providing another six-month head start, the Western response was reactive, poorly timed, and suffered from myriad collective action failures.[124] American involvement started late and ended early. Kinetic actions were ineffectively coordinated among allied nations. This meant that the opportunity to use the siege of Sirte to deal ISIS a knockout blow was missed. Simply pushing ISIS out of its stronghold allowed the top fighters to form sleeper cells, escape into the desert, and rebrand themselves by working with non-ISIS jihadi militias—exactly as I and other analysts had predicted would happen.[125]

Better a bloody fight to the death than a symbolic victory

If American, NATO, and Libyan fighters had been coordinating effectively, the assault on Sirte should have begun with a complete encirclement of ISIS territory combined with a naval blockade. Instead, due to the chaotic coordination that characterizes the Enduring Disorder, over the spring of 2016, the GNA held many press conferences about how it would defeat ISIS while refusing to attack Sirte or call for allied support in enforcing a naval blockade against it.[126] This allowed parts of ISIS time to dig in while allowing its most valuable assets to flee to fight another day.

The timing behind Serraj's request for US air support was also out of sync due to collective action problems.[127] The GNA had fantasized about taking on ISIS on their own in order to appear strong and legitimate to their populace.[128] They only called for American support when Banyan Marsus forces got bogged down in July.[129] At that point, airpower was less effective as ISIS fighters had abandoned their initially static positions and their leadership was already dispersed. As was happening in so many other political and military theatres, each actor was thinking about how their actions would be perceived in its own domestic media market rather than coherently coordinating with allies to achieve the best outcome.

No crisis too big to waste

Even larger than these military mis-timings was the political mis-ordering. A genuine anti-ISIS coalition—not only of Libyan factions but of international supporters—was needed before the fight for Sirte began.[130] Of course, it did not materialize. Due to this lack of effective coordination, as the GNA gained ground against ISIS throughout the autumn of 2016, it was at the lowest ebb of its legitimacy.[131] Its international support had frayed, the Central Bank of Libya (CBL) was refusing to fund its budget, key militias inside Tripoli had attempted to establish a rival administration, and it suffered a major coup attempt in October.[132]

These mistakes notwithstanding, because the jihadis were facing the full force of US airpower combined with a highly armed and motivated Misratan contingent they were eventually dislodged from Sirte in December 2016. As explained in the excerpt, the process was no doubt sped along by their loss of local support due to their brutalization of their Sirtawi hosts.[133] It was the first major success of the Obama administration's war against ISIS and the one in which collaboration with local Arab forces had worked most effectively. (Nearly all of the Department of Defense's militarily successful partners in Iraq and Syria were Kurds.) And yet, the fight against ISIS in Sirte was a wasted golden opportunity to unite Libya. Policymakers had chosen to solve the immediate problem in a way that was convenient for the short term rather than to harness it as an opportunity to address systemic, longer-term concerns. Truly 99% of the population and almost all of the major militia factions were anti-ISIS and viewed the group as a foreign incursion on Libyan territory. Most were open to embracing a shared effort against the group—if only the collective action compromises required from different groups could have been communicated and implemented properly.

It is worth reminding readers that most ISIS fighters in Libya have always been non-Libyan, and that ISIS was stigmatized even within Islamist-supporting communities as 'a foreign incursion' and 'dissimilar' to homegrown al-Qaeda-linked movements like Ansar al-Sharia.[134] From 2014 to 2017, most ISIS fighters in Libya came from Tunisia. This was starkly illustrated by the incident described in the excerpt of the February 2016 US airstrikes in Sabratha that killed thirty-six Tunisians but no Libyans. Then, after Sirte fell, ISIS became Africanized and a plurality of new ISIS fighters in southern Libya were sub-Saharan Africans.[135]

All major Libyan political movements claimed to want to evict foreign military forces from Libyan soil. Haftar and the LNA presented themselves as both the 'nationalist' and 'the anti-Islamist power' in Libya, yet they did nothing to participate in the fight against ISIS's occupation of Sirte. They talked the talk of being anti-jihadi without walking the walk.[136]

Although the GNA-aligned Banyan Marsus was a collection of various militias that worked together effectively to oust ISIS, no political unification proceeded from this military unification. In retrospect, this short-termism appeared to many commentators as simply inevitable, but it is actually quite unprecedented. Historically, it has been fighting against insurgencies, colonial occupations, incursions on national territory, or other shared enemies that had welded Arab political movements together.

A concrete opportunity to produce a twenty-first-century Omar Mukhtar was lost.[137] Hence, with ISIS evicted, the conflict among Libya's various factions proceeded more virulently than before—only with the Libyan state perilously weakened by the toll the jihadis had exacted on the oil storage tankers at Ras Lanuf, the pipelines south of Sidra, on Libya's global standing as a business destination, and on the populaces of Sirte, Derna, and Benghazi.[138]

The 'day after' problem

With ISIS in Libya deemed 'no longer a threat', Libya almost completely dropped off the global policy agenda for roughly a year. Italian, British, and American collaborations with militia factions, like BM, either stopped or were rolled back. This was exactly the time to double down and promote nascent Libyan institutional and governance capacity-building, especially at the local level in the areas newly liberated from ISIS. On the ground in western Libya, similarly to after Qadhafi's ouster, those foreigners who had helped defend Libya in its time of need were respected and their support coveted. Yet, America quietly abandoned those who had fought and died to kill its shared enemies, just as it had done in other Middle Eastern battlefields. The incoming Trump administration repeated the exact mistake that Obama had said publicly was his biggest foreign policy regret—not focusing enough on reconstruction and nation-building in the wake of a successful military support mission in Libya.[139]

This is the same pattern that later characterized Trump declaring victory against ISIS in Syria and Iraq—and then abandoning America's Kurdish allies in 2019 rather than helping them promote governance over the territory they had seized.[140] Instead of embracing the imperial or hegemonic burden of filling those political vacuums that prior American missteps had helped create, the few Special Ops and contractors who were deployed to Libya, Syria, and Iraq left without engaging in critical mopping-up operations to prevent a resurgence. 'Mission Accomplished' was declared too early. The Special Forces operatives simply returned home without sufficiently training their local counter-parties, abandoning the political capital they had gained from fighting.[141] Meaningful state-building efforts to fill the ensuing power vacuums—left by the jihadis' eviction—were not even discussed by major Western powers as serious policy options. I speculate that this was partly due to the collective action challenges they would entail.

Yes, some USAID funding was granted for Sirte and Mosul, at which point millions of dollars were spent on remote civil society trainings. Schools were rebuilt, municipal council trainings conducted, and health supplies sent via courier at huge cost.[142] Yet these efforts were a far cry from American and British state-building efforts during their hegemonic heydays in places like Japan and India, respectively. They also shared nothing in common with the heavy-handed nation-building that was attempted in Iraq in the wake of Saddam's ouster. In other words, the defeat of ISIS in Derna and Sirte led to the requisite alliances being disbanded prior to finishing the job or addressing the underlying structural problems that had given rise to the jihadis in the first place. As a result, the senior leadership cadre of ISIS melted into the vast expanses of Libya's southern desert regions and embedded themselves in the smuggling economy and inter-tribal/inter-ethnic feuds that post-Qadhafi Libya has become famous for. The jihadis then went on to exacerbate these inter-communal tensions to deliberately propagate the core dynamics of the Enduring Disorder in this new theatre.[143]

The West displaced the jihadis from the territory they occupied without addressing the inconvenient ungoverned space issue, which had caused the jihadi problem in the first place. No high-level effort was given to coordinating a global approach to impos-ing capacity-building assistance or fostering local governance. Certain donor nations outsourced poorly coordinated efforts to

international NGOs who further outsourced them to local implementing partners. Like my comment on page 110 in Chapter 1,
by pointing out these historical comparisons, I am not advocating for neo-imperial state-building policies.[144] Far from it.

Instead, my comparisons are meant to highlight how far the
global scene has changed over the last two decades and to postulate
the causality behind these shifts. Study of the coordination complexities of the Enduring Disorder provides compelling evidence
that they have engendered the Western dine-and-dash, bomb-
and-train approach rather than any genuine strategic calculation,
moral progression, or change in diplomatic philosophy.[145]

Victory even in defeat

The conditions of the Enduring Disorder also allowed ISIS to be
victorious even in defeat—just as its spokesmen had said it would
be.[146] The jihadis' strategy in Libya had never been to take over
the state but just to sow chaos—this dovetailed with the global
aims and media messaging of the neo-populist powers who benefit from, and propel forward, the Enduring Disorder. Jihadis
sought to pre-empt and block state-building efforts by denying
the possible resources needed by the nascent post-Qadhafi state.
ISIS was a symptom—not a cause—of Libya's fragmentation.[147]

Ungoverned space is a quintessential collective action problem

It takes a village—to govern a village. And in the contemporary
globalized world it takes many social and governmental layers
from the communal to the national to allied international actors
to bring genuine governance and capacity-building to a post-
conflict situation, especially when a vast array of actors is pushing
in the opposite direction. Study of the military successes (or lack
thereof) of al-Qaeda and ISIS definitively establishes the inability
of such jihadi movements to wage a successful insurrection

against an established regime. It also solves the chicken-and-egg conundrum showing that ungoverned space is the root cause—and jihadi expansion, the consequence.

According to Syria expert Joshua Landis:

> Neither Al-Qaeda, ISIS, or any jihadi insurgency has ever conquered a capital city. They have only succeeded in geographies that lack a tradition of state institutions or where the state has already been destroyed by a professional army. This is why we tend to see the co-location of unruly tribal areas with long histories of non-state forms of governance and the areas where Al-Qaeda or ISIS can establish themselves like in eastern Syria, Iraq's Anbar province, the central Libyan desert, non-urban Afghanistan, mountainous Yemen, and northern Nigeria. These are the places that Sunni jihadism can thrive because they are the pre-existing global epicentres of ungovernable space due to their unique human and physical geographies.[148]

The problem of ungoverned spaces facing Libya, Afghanistan, Iraq, Syria, Yemen, and many parts of Africa is one that can only be tackled via system-wide partnerships among international players and local actors. The fight against ISIS allowed the necessary players to temporarily solve their collective action difficulties for the immediate goal of preventing jihadis from governing territory. In the Libyan case, the period of proper international coordination lasted from September to December 2016. It took as its remit merely treating the symptoms and completely ignoring the root cause.

This blind spot is not only a Western one. Unfortunately, many Libyan policymakers failed to capitalize on those moments when Libya was front and centre of global attention by asking their allies abroad for a little help with state capacity-building, deradicalization, decentralization, or job creation to get militiamen off the streets. It would have been a fairly easy sell as the economics of the situation made it in everyone's best interest to help Libya establish better governance.

After forty-two years of Qadhafi's grandiose personal style and unreformed traditional Arab patriarchal structures, Libyan institutions exhibit extremely hierarchical structures—with executives unwilling to delegate authority and extremely reticent to outsource or request help.[149] Due to these traditions and issues of 'pride', most Libyan statesmen I have known are extremely unwilling to accurately diagnose the governance or jihadi problems in front of a non-Libyan audience. At some level, I understand this. In an honour and shame culture, it is particularly uncomfortable to admit publicly that one's society is in such a state of free fall, with such widespread underemployment and hopelessness that its sons are willing to join a suicidal cult or more frequently to harbour homicidal heretical outsiders.

Macabre humour

Mahmoud Jibril was Libya's first post-Qadhafi prime minister; on 5 April 2020, he became Libya's first public figure to die of Covid. I knew him from the Qadhafi period, where we interacted on various economic reform projects. He was, by all accounts, a technocratic genius. He was also a man with a rather high opinion of himself who was eager to flatter Western politicians with grandiose and eloquent promises but very quick to condescend to 'ordinary' Libyans, as well as Western Libya experts like me and my colleagues. I vividly recall a luncheon at the British House of Lords in late 2014 where Jibril was the guest of honour. The topic of discussion was how to continue to do business in Libya in the wake of the recent fighting over Tripoli International Airport, which had caused the Western diplomatic community to flee the capital and had splintered the country into two rival political administrations.

As we ate, Jibril gave his keynote speech on the advantages of Sirte and Hun (a remote desert community south of Sirte). He invited all the businessmen and British peers in attendance to join him in Sirte next year. He promised that mega construction contracts would be 'for the taking' by those swashbucklers willing to make the trek to Libya's central desert region and aid in its rebuilding. When asked by a Scottish businessperson about the threat from jihadis to travellers to that region, he brushed it off by saying that the jihadis were only in Derna, Tripoli, and Benghazi, and furthermore that Sirte was a central location, neutral in the feud between east and west, loyal to the former (i.e. anti-Islamist) regime, and in need of urgent rebuilding. Within a few months of Jibril's nonchalant promise, Sirte would witness the beheadings of twenty-one Christian guest workers in orange jumpsuits; within a year, it would become ISIS's main territorial acquisition outside of the Levant.[150]

I would love to say that Jibril's hubris was just a tragic character flaw. Yet to this day, Libyan leaders on both sides of the conflict periodically declare that 'Libya is open for business' and frequently downplay the jihadi problem as an 'inconsequential nothing' exaggerated by the media. When such Libyan grandees are visiting Washington, they usually prefer to meet with Department of Commerce officials or lobbyists from Fortune 500 companies rather than with genuine Libya experts—terrorism professionals they avoid like the plague. I have seen this dynamic at play in more government or trade association briefings with Libyan officials than I can count. Both the lobbyists and the Libyan officials enjoy playing a grown-up version of 'make believe'—discussing future business opportunities as if there was no militia or jihadi or security problem. The very word militias or ISIS is banned from such gatherings as if it were culturally offensive.

Media training, Libyan-style

I remember in 2018 being phoned by an American fixer for one of Libya's deputy prime ministers. He asked me if I was in

Washington. I said I was in New York City, but if it were truly urgent I could be in Washington the next day. He told me it was urgent: everything economic was on the table. Unfortunately, I was being conned: it turned out the deputy prime minister wanted to get my advice on how to facilitate American companies engaging in foreign direct investment for transshipment of goods to sub-Saharan Africa via the Misrata and Tamanhint Free Zones. Those in the Libya game will recognize this as an old favourite trope of politicians of an Islamist or Misratan background—who tend to be connected by personal and family links to those who skim money off the top of any deal made involving the Free Zones.

When the hoax had been revealed, I told the deputy prime minister, in Arabic, that it would be easier to sell ice to Eskimos than to secure investments in the necessary infrastructure for the transshipment of goods to sub-Saharan Africa via Libya. In response, he drew a map of Libya on a white board and explained to me that Libya has excellent highways, 2,000 kilometres of Mediterranean coastline, and that there was no militia or jihadi problem in the south, only great business opportunities. I responded that these transshipment ideas were never sound investments for Western companies, but they had a certain logic to them during the Qadhafi period due to the Brother Leader's deep economic and ideological investments in sub-Saharan Africa. In the post-Qadhafi political and security climate, they are completely irrelevant. I told him that I had heard roughly the same speech at a Libya business summit at the Corinthia Hotel in downtown Tripoli in 2008, at the FDI Libya Summit in Istanbul in 2017, and countless other times.

* * *

Compelling sound bites have a way of sticking around, especially when those who propagate them have a vested interest in doing so. Part of every Libyan official's kooky get-rich quick scheme seems to involve the standard 'brush-the-jihadis-and-militias-under-the-rug and pretend that we have the same business opportunities as we did in the Qadhafi era only better'. Many Libyan politicians seem to have imbibed this approach with their mother's milk. Yet, conversely, when the topic or the audience changes to a think tank or press conference setting, the same officials say that they are extremely committed to fighting terror and that, in fact, their side is the West's sole ally in the fight against jihadism. Tragically, on neither side of the Libyan political spectrum have we seen political leaders willing to acknowledge publicly the unpalatable truths about the root causes of jihadism and seek the necessary international help to bolster governance.

Building governance capacity is a long process, and most Libyan intellectuals acknowledge that it will not be completed without external assistance. To paraphrase my favourite Libyanist witticism, 'Libya lacks sufficient governance capacity to accept Western capacity-building assistance.' Nate Mason came up with this when he served as US commercial attaché at the embassy in Tripoli in 2012–13. It was true then and it is even more true now.

Libyan government officials need a phased plan to expand governance capacity through decentralisation, boosting capacity in municipalities, ensuring a transparent mechanism for equitable funding of all Libyan communities, and the gradual acceptance of sufficient technical assistance to engage in the tough day-to-day fight against jihadis and militias while simultaneously conducting the educational outreach and institution-building necessary to win the long war.[151] This is the only feasible way forward, but it has been assiduously avoided by Libyan leaders, even as it is championed by many civil society figures. Presumably, it remains unpalatable to Libyan politicians at the centre of power because they believe empowering local governance capacity would weaken them and that certain segments of the populace would rebel if they were pushed to give up the established inefficient ways of doing things. This is the exact same conundrum causing inaction vis-à-vis cutting subsidies and reforming the semi-sovereign[152] economic institutions—issues I will discuss in Chapters 4 and 5.

In order to undertake such a bold effort on either the economic or jihadi fronts, responsible politicians would need to construct a new narrative, one that simultaneously presents unpalatable truths to the Libyan people while also presenting a coherent plan to tackle them and addressing the legitimate needs and perspectives of the populace. In Libya, as elsewhere during the Enduring Disorder, compelling narratives have become the monopoly of the neo-populists. Why this is the case is the subject of the next chapter.

Tragically, during the Wars of Post-Qadhafi Succession, no major political figure has embraced a 'let's face the facts' approach. This is very much in line with the zeitgeist of the era of the Enduring Disorder. From 2014 to 2020, another narrative was winning the day in the Libyan microcosm—that ordinary Libyans had been victimized by outsiders and that only a paternalistic, anti-Islamist, anti-foreign strongman could make Libya great again.

3

UNREGULATED CYBERSPACE LEADS TO NEO-POPULISM

In Libya, as elsewhere, technology has shaped not only how messages are formulated and conveyed but also how rapidly and far they can spread. Media content is no longer exclusively local or national, as it can be produced anywhere and shared everywhere. Much commentary and reporting on Libya's civil war on Facebook and Twitter masquerades as being produced by Libyans but is in fact written by outsiders[1] or funded by them.[2] Unsurprisingly, when polled, Libyans exhibit a marked distrust of outsiders' political messaging about their domestic affairs.

This much is on par with global trends.[3] Unfortunately, Libyans are worse prepared than most—due to failings in the education system and a lack of experience with free media under Qadhafi—to handle the civic responsibilities of parsing all this information. In short, lacking both a coherent unifying nationalism and experiences with a multiplicity of media and political viewpoints, Libyans as individuals and as a society are ill-equipped to combat sophisticated disinformation campaigns.[4]

Protecting freedom of speech means allowing your enemies to beam propaganda into your country

Powerful institutions in liberal Western democracies—especially the United States with its rigorous, classically liberal definition of free speech—have seen blocking both misinformation and disinformation[5] as a form of 'policing freedom of expression', and hence, traditionally beyond the appropriate remit of government. Indeed, the advent of disinformation in the social media era has left them scrambling to keep up as the extent of this emerging threat has become more and more visible. At the international level, some global institutions and collaborations have been reactively created to address these problems, such as the 'Trusted News Initiative' (TNI), the 'European Centre of Excellence for Countering Hybrid Threats' (in Helsinki), and various EU frameworks against disinformation.[6] Yet as these online threats and belated responses have arisen during a period in which global coordination has been in decline due to the Enduring Disorder, the new institutions and diplomatic frameworks have been largely impotent at addressing the transnational governance aspect of the problem.

Selectively rooting out hateful, false, mislabelled, or counterproductive content, narratives, and myths while allowing healthy factual debate of political issues would be a massively challenging collective action problem, even for strong states dedicating massive resources and enjoying robust interagency cooperation. Conversely, individual states that wish to utilize wholesale bans on entire categories of political speech can do so quite effectively using information technology. Therefore, although other major Arab oil producers or Asia's autocratic regimes may have suffered from educational and civic engagement deficits similar to Libya's, they enjoy the advantages of strong states, effective firewalls, and populaces primed for nationalism.[7]

This exposes a fascinating paradox: only liberal democracies and weakened post-conflict states 'protect' unadulterated free speech—the former because they choose to and the latter because they lack the capacity to do otherwise. Therefore, in the Enduring Disorder, liberal Western democracies and post-conflict zones are the two areas where a free-for-all to set the cyber-narrative is unfolding. Neo-populists, racists, and jihadis possess tailormade messages to take advantage of this free-for-all.

Libya is a petri dish of free speech amid disorder

Disinformation and narratives eviscerating social trust are hallmarks of the Enduring Disorder. This type of messaging can spread like wildfire in these two types of regimes—not only due to contemporary technology but also because of the lack of coordinated intergovernmental action to police and regulate cyberspace. With the Libyan state hollowed out by appeasement, jihadis, and external actors pulling in mutually contradictory directions, disinformation has been used to promote the narrative of the anti-Islamist Arab nationalist strongman as the saviour of the nation.[8] This worked for President Abdul Fattah al-Sisi in Egypt and has found wide appeal with segments of the Libyan population.

In Libya, the country's problems are frequently portrayed as resulting from victimization by outsiders, lack of governance, unfair distribution of resources, and a civil war. The postulated solution of an older male strongman of the dominant religion and ethnicity returning the nation to past glories is actually in keeping with global trends. In the post-industrial West, the problems are framed partially differently: the decline of traditional culture, exploitation by migrants, the rise of wealth inequalities, and nefarious global actors trying to undermine the nation. Yet in both Libya and the post-industrial West, the neo-populists express their proposed solutions in eerily similar ways—stressing victimization by outsiders, the need for strong leadership, and the reassertion of the traditional culture of the majority.[9] In both democracies and weakened post-conflict states, the prevailing media environment of the Enduring Disorder has led to the rise of both jihadis and illiberal wanna-be autocrats who—lacking all relevant credentials—proclaim that they alone can fix whatever problem their nation faces.

General Haftar's initial rise to prominence fits this pattern to a tee. He and his media advisors understood the information landscape better than other contenders for power. They actively constructed a cult of personality. Like Trump, Haftar was a natural in the art of getting free media coverage. Although he was later the beneficiary of foreign financial, military, and PR support, Haftar initially catapulted himself on to the Libyan scene without any meaningful domestic or international backing, merely by making bold (and frequently misleading) pronouncements and claiming that he alone could solve Libya's problems.[10] He also constantly changed his message to suit the fears and sentiments of his audience at that exact moment. Insiders claim his goal has always been to be domestically and internationally acclaimed as Libya's strongman.[11]

Haftar's self-presentation as a political outsider with the right skills to save Libya from the pseudo-threat of 'a conspiratorial international Islamist movement' reveals a great deal about how neo-populism works and the kinds of ideologies and personalities that it brings to power.

In this realm, as in so many others, Libya acts as a funhouse mirror showcasing in enlarged fashion many of the key trends of the Enduring Disorder. Haftar's seemingly erratic behaviours, bold and contradictory pronouncements, disregard for advice from experts and allies, refusal to consult with his Russian, Emirati, and Egyptian backers even prior to major actions, and reliance on family members rather than seasoned military staff, all have striking parallels globally. They also give us unique insights into how political narratives and strategic communications operate given contemporary technologies and sensibilities.

Aspiring authoritarians understand clever slogans

Positive political narratives involving hope, faith, honesty, love, fairness, righting wrongs, and the fight for equality can successfully connect national policy issues to individuals' personal concerns. In the West, we associate such positive messages with public protest campaigns like 'Black Lives Matter' or electoral campaign slogans like 'Stronger Together'. Yet in dictatorships and failed states, narratives that resonate may be even more important in securing the buy-in of the populace.

The Egyptian army is adept at using slogans showcasing its positive solidarity with the Egyptian populace. The online Egyptian newspaper *Midan Masr*, known for its support of the 2011 anti-regime protests, commented on this phenomenon:

> The Egyptian army, represented by the Military Council, ascended to power [after 2011] and tightened its steel grip on the neck of the country in general after enhancing and beautifying this fist and wrapping it with Egyptian flags and with a lie: 'The army and the people are one hand.'[12]

In Egypt and Libya, aspiring strongmen have become masters of narrative—knowing how to use their slogans to justify the need for a strong anti-Islamist army. This approach has resonated especially well with a stratum of educated women who have long been concerned that Islamists would take away their freedoms. In Libya, Islamists had promised women concrete outcomes during the 2012 GNC elections and were then seen as not fulfilling them. For example, Libyan activist and lawyer Nayfin al-Bah (possibly not her real name) accused 'the Islamists' of robbing Libyan women of their rights and the freedoms that they enjoyed under Qadhafi. According to al-Bah:

> The current situation of Libyan women has become worse than under Qadhafi. Women were a winning card in the hands of the Islamists before the 2012 General National Congress elections [as the Islamists] raised compelling slogans praising the active participation of Libyan women and promising them more freedom, constitutional guarantees and greater representation in the parliament. But these were only promises.[13]

Anti-Islamist media in Egypt and Libya have built compelling propaganda narratives that Islamism inherently entails concrete and irrevocable losses of freedoms and economic opportunities for middle-class women.

Traditional Libyan politicians failed to articulate a compelling narrative

Most studies of Libya's post-Qadhafi period have analysed the country's politics by focusing on the military and the diplomatic actions of the legally sovereign authorities and their rivals.[14] Not enough scholarly and diplomatic attention has been devoted to looking at how those legitimate authorities—the NTC, then the GNC and the GNA—and their various rivals, attempted to craft a compelling national narrative. Such a narrative would seek to enlist the populace's overwhelming support for fundamental reforms addressing the core problems facing Libyans as individuals and communities: how to equitably distribute oil wealth, how to maintain security, and how to regulate the role of religion in social and political life.[15]

Libyans participated in the 2011 Uprisings 'against' a specific regime and 'against' specific instances of corruption and injustice. They did not fight 'for' a specific ideology or outcome.[16] Around 80 percent of the populace supported Qadhafi's ouster and shared a 'negative unity', meaning they were united against something.[17] As in other Arab Spring countries, the defining slogan of the 2011 Libyan Uprisings was: 'The people want the collapse of the regime.'[18] Positive unity was supposed to come later. Grasping the challenges inherent in this situation, the transitional authorities tried to mimic international best practices concerning interim governance. They used the 3 August 2011 TCD to structure electoral and constitutional processes that would allow a national conversation to unfold, hopefully culminating in positive unity around a certain type of governance and political programme.[19]

In the event, neither the constitutional drafting committee's selection process nor the various rounds of electioneering facilitated the body politic coalescing around either a uniquely Libyan national narrative or the desire to adopt international best practices for transitions. Conversely, Tunisians managed to use their constitutional drafting process as well as multiple rounds of elections to create a consensus narrative that allowed their leaders to embrace international best practices on certain issues like women's rights, religion, and the internet while rooting political identity firmly within the Tunisian constitutional (Destouri) tradition.

Libyans have had difficulty formulating positive national myths, but they have excelled at negative unity—being united in opposition to something rather than for something. This weakness may in fact have been the primary driver of the country's tragedy after Qadhafi's ouster.[20] Historically, Libyans were fairly united in their opposition to the brutality of the Italian colonization.[21] Later, they were motivated for independence via antiimperial rhetoric.

At different times, various social segments came together in support of uniquely tailored forms of Islamism[22] and Arab nationalism.[23] However, those ideologies were universalist or regional rather than national in orientation. Libyans have never been united for widespread political action by a purely nationally focused ideology. Qadhafi also stressed a range of universalist tropes alternating among Arab nationalism, Islamic solidarity, his unique Jamahiriyyan ideology, and pan-Africanism.[24] Therefore, both in times of peace and of national struggle, Libyans have lacked the type of pervasive national-centric myths and civic institutions that have characterized countries with authentic pre-colonial experiences of nationhood, such as Tunisia or Egypt.[25]

This has meant that Libyan politics for the last century and a half has been largely devoid of both a prevailing national ideology and concrete political programmes. As a result, the primary logic of Libya's post-Qadhafi political game has been what academics term clientelism or patronage politics,[26] and what Americans refer to more colourfully as pork barrel politics.

In the absence of a narrative, clientelism has prevailed

The shell game of Libyan politics is played not about ideology or rival political programmes but about controlling the distribution of resources and using them to obtain sufficient consensus to rule from certain regionally, tribally, and socially defined interest groups. As a result of this overarching political system, the composition of Libya's post-Qadhafi transitional governments tended to be determined via attempts to balance localities and interest groups. To win at this game, the aspirant to individual power (e.g. a prime minister-designate or elect trying to form his cabinet list) needed to favour those with the most collective power at that moment (specific militias, interest groups, localities, and tribes) while not offending other potentially relevant spoiler groups (other militias and tribes). Patronage politics tends to prevail when elites are disunited and unable to undertake an elite grand bargain regarding which national structures and unifying ideology should be adopted.[27] When combined with unearned wealth, patronage politics has a strong tendency to promote an appeasement trap. It also makes the selection of names for cabinet-level positions the most critical decision executives make.

In post-Qadhafi Libya, successful elite bargains concerning the distribution of positions of power to various tribes and regions tended to resemble an attempt to simultaneously appease nearly all interest groups, especially those with enough militia power to threaten the government.[28] As an example, the first two post-Qadhafi cabinets (those appointed by the NTC and GNC) featured Misratans and Zintanis in important military positions, as those cities occupied key power positions during the conquest of Tripoli, while members of each of the major sub-regions were also given lesser positions.

Doling out favours may seem an easy game to play, but it has proved the bane of many an aspirant to power. The first prime minister-elect of the GNC period, Mustafa Abushagur, had his cabinet selections rejected twice—preventing him from ever forming a government—as he was perceived as 'stacking the deck' with too many Tripoli-, Misrata-, diaspora-, and Muslim Brotherhood-aligned individuals.[29] Seeking to explain this bizarre episode—in which the same parliamentary body, the GNC, registered a majority vote for a prime minister and then resoundingly rejected two different cabinet lists that he proposed—Dr Naji Barakat, then minister of health in the outgoing NTC government, can provide us with useful insight. Writing contemporaneously to the unfolding events, he explained that the prime minister-elect actually had enough allies to pass the vote of confidence in his cabinet list by a reasonable margin. This made him overconfident. According to Barakat, Abushagur.

> ignored counsel from his advisors warning him to include some individuals [that he might have disliked personally in his cabinet list], especially a mixture of competent technocrats and moderates from the rival National Forces Alliance bloc. Abushagur brushed aside

such conciliatory advice [and tried to press his perceived advantage] choosing a list primarily from among his personal allies and the Islamist current.[30]

This pushed those who were on the fence about Abushagur but had selected him as a compromise candidate in the vote for prime minister to dig in their heels and oppose his government in both votes of confidence. GNC member Saleh Jadoua reported that 'massive discontent arose in the streets' against Abushagur as soon as the cabinet lists were published. The Libyan populace was shocked that neither of his cabinet lists deliberately pandered to those 'swing constituencies' that had just days earlier allowed Abushagur to be chosen as prime minister.[31] The meta message from this tragic episode is that, in Libya, the perception that a 'legitimate' power centre is being excluded from its justified share of the spoils is frequently enough to spur that power centre to spoil political progress, sometimes even violently.

As discussed in the Preface, the First Libyan Civil War broke out in 2014 as a result of fears by Western and Islamist-leaning militia blocs that the results of the 25 June 2014 election for the HoR had favoured the eastern and the anti-Islamist blocs— meaning that henceforth they would be at risk of not receiving their 'fair' share of power.[32] After the war concluded with the signing of the Skhirat Agreement on 17 December 2015, Serraj failed to gain approval from the HoR in 2016 for his cabinet list. One of the many reasons for this was that his cabinet list was widely perceived as having failed to grant sufficient favours to communities and personalities supportive of the HoR. As a result, Haftar had instructed his supporters within the HoR to not oppose the list. Furthermore, and separately from Serraj's cabinet list's rejection by eastern Libyan players, during his five-year tenure Serraj never cemented his domestic legitimacy, largely because his cabinet picks were not seen as adequately representative of all of Libya's power centres.

On the flip side, being a master of patronage can allow an executive of otherwise dubious legitimacy to cement his authority. In January 2021, Abdul Hameed Dabaiba was selected as prime minister-designate by the Libyan Political Dialogue Forum (LPDF), a UN-mediated pan-Libyan political body established in 2020 to appoint a new executive and Presidential Council as well as to facilitate elections.[33] In March 2021, he proposed a thirty plus person cabinet list—for a government that was only slated to sit for nine months to supervise elections. Within a week of proposing various options for his cabinet list, he offered to change his initial picks in an overt quid pro quo to secure the HoR's approval for a revised list by granting HoR allies minor cabinet portfolios.[34] This approach succeeded as Dabaiba brilliantly included enough cabinet members from those eastern and southern communities that would not traditionally support the candidacy of a Misratan billionaire with ties to the Qadhafi regime. As a result, his final cabinet list received unanimous approval in the HoR confidence vote. Power was rapidly transferred to his Government of National Unity (GNU), from both the GNA and the eastern parallel ministries, with none of the hold-ups that had marred the GNA's five-year quest for domestic legitimacy.

Having hit the ground running with surprisingly more legitimacy than other post-Qadhafi prime ministers, Dabaiba appeared to quickly notch a string of successes: unifying the eastern and western financial institutions, cutting subsidies, and promising infrastructure spending—all in his first month in office. A couple of months later, Dabaiba's approach floundered due to missteps and overreach culminating in the HoR delaying and criticizing his proposed 2021 budget bringing the rejuvenation of Libya's economy and the incremental integration of eastern and western institutions to a screeching halt.[35] Dabaiba's failure to get the 2021 budget over the line was also a failure to effectively play the patronage game for the long term. He had given away so many handouts to the HoR to get into power in February 2021 that he had no more leverage to compel them to compromise over the budget in the spring. Nonetheless, his initial use of patronage politics demonstrated that he was a power player in his own right, rather than a compromise candidate deliberately selected due to perceived weakness and malleability, as Prime Ministers Abdurrahim el-Keib, Abdullah al-Thinni, and Serraj had been.

The traditional Libyan clientelist approach to politics has usually meant that technocratic skills, governance experience, connection to key civic institutions, or the ability to articulate unifying rhetoric were not the reasons political candidates were selected or ministers appointed. Clientelism overtly perpetuates and reinforces existing social structures. By its very nature, it is conservative and anti-meritocratic. In post-Qadhafi Libya, this means that women and youth are largely excluded from senior political positions. As such, social media or making a career abroad are the only ways that young people, and women in particular, can make their voices heard.[36] Conversely, in Tunisia, where clientelism has not been nearly as prominent, women and youth have been able to occupy the mainstream political space to debate the issues of the day and have a direct impact on national life. The Tunisian transitional authorities also focused far less on balancing regional representation and far more on technocratic skills, historic legitimacy, and articulating a new vision of the rights and responsibilities of the Tunisian citizen.[37]

Despite the missteps caused by appeasement, ignoring the dangers of jihadism, and patronage politics during Libya's transition process, there have been many compelling opportunities for course corrections, especially in the immediate aftermath of seminal events: Qadhafi's ouster in October 2011, the first post-Qadhafi elections for the GNC in July 2012, and then the GNA-led eviction of ISIS from Sirte in December 2016. Each of these moments of Libyan national triumph were missed opportunities for the construction of a positive national narrative highlighting a collective goal. All three milestones witnessed diverse communities jointly rejoicing in the national milestone as their own. After each of these seminal events, Libyan leaders could have unfurled a compelling economic or social programme and convincingly presented to their compatriots the need to stand united behind this new shared mission. They could have invoked the recent shared victory—the defeat of Qadhafi (in 2011), the holding of free and fair elections (in 2012), or the ousting of ISIS from Sirte (in 2016)—and connected its symbolism to the need for a shared destiny and an ongoing collective national mission.

People are inspired by shared obligations and shared rewards. A widely appreciated example of this phenomenon is the manner in which British Prime Minister Clement Attlee framed the optics around the creation of the NHS and the Beveridge Report: he explained that all Britons deserved quality healthcare because of the sacrifices they made to win World War II. He proclaimed that all Britons would work together to make it a success. Attlee mobilized his fellow citizens so that they accepted higher taxes, austerity and rationing to achieve this national mission. A full seventy-five years later, Britons of all social classes remain uniquely proud of 'their NHS' because they were told that they personally sacrificed to build it.

Conversely, in Libya, elected or incumbent officials have had an uncanny knack for avoiding making concrete statements on specific economic or social programmes, even though the Libyan populace has been noticeably eager for a sense of direction and shared purpose. Similarly, many of the post-Qadhafi leaders have been woefully inadequate public speakers, in both Arabic and English. As a result, compelling national narratives have not been articulated by 'the forces of order', whereas many major militias have their own TV stations and Facebook pages to echo their catchy slogans. Tragically, we could say Libyan politicians perfected Abba Eban's quip about the Palestinian leadership that, 'they never missed an opportunity to miss an opportunity.'[38]

Prime minister as placeholder-in-chief

Although he was post-Qadhafi Libya's longest serving prime minister—remaining in office from March 2016 to March 2021—Libya experts and Libyans alike would have difficulty defining Fayez al-Serraj's legacy, economic programme, vision for demobilizing the militias or sharing Libya's wealth among the citizenry. Although he was advised by international media relations firms and had media relations professionals seconded to his office by European governments, he largely avoided speaking to the Libyan media. On those few occasions that he or his spokesman Hassan al-Huni engaged the Libyan public directly, they were unable to convey a coherent narrative of what Serraj stands for. In such appearances, Serraj decried those forces he claimed were deliberately blocking him (like the CBL Governor) and advertised his use of executive decrees to support those regions of the country (essentially Tripoli, Misrata, and their hinterlands) that backed him. As a result, his supporters felt that his job was simply to hold down the fort for their side—assuring them that his continuance as prime minister of the internationally recognized government granted legitimacy to their agenda.

Conversely, Serraj's rivals have been skilled weavers of bold narratives—artfully tapping into the zeitgeist of the Enduring Disorder to formulate an origin story that is crafted to appeal to Libyans' hopes, fears, and historical imaginary. Haftar's narrative appals many—and appeals to many. Importantly, it has the power to attract Libyans who do not necessarily come from the same region of those articulating it.

Haftar modelled his media strategy on that of the global master of narrative manipulation—Russia's President Vladimir Putin. And just as Haftar's army received training and support from Russia's Wagner Group, so too did its cyber warriors and media manipulators.[39] What they learned was to frame all their actions as part of a mythological narrative about purifying the nation from outside influences and restoring it to greatness.

Putin's media operatives have long championed the concept of a 'Russian World' (*Russkiy Mir*): a confluence of nationalism, revanchism, and support for both the Russian Orthodox Church and irredentist Russian ethnic communities.[40] Putin evoked the concept to justify the 2014 annexation of Crimea and give coherence to the cyber and influence operations accompanying Russian kinetic actions in the Ukrainian Civil War.[41] Andrew Wilson, an expert on both Eastern Europe and media narratives, has explained that Russian 'technologists' were arguably the first to expressly craft real world policies around which media narratives could be woven that lent themselves to going viral.

This new form of mythmaking for the digital age began in Russia and has diffused outwards. Wilson quotes Putin's former spin doctor Gleb Pavlovsky saying as early as 2007 that 'we live in a mythological era' and his colleague Sergey Markov noting in the same year that 'public opinion is made more and more by computers'. Both men were effectively predicting the wave of the future that they would help create.[42]

Politics is about mythmaking

National mythmaking has always been a crucial part of politics. In democracies and autocracies of every stripe, people are motivated to conceive of themselves as a community via the promulgation of a national myth evoking a shared past and shared future with their countrymen. In his seminal work *Imagined*

Communities: Reflections on the Origin and Spread of Nationalism, historian Benedict Anderson put forth the concept of 'Print Capitalism' to explain the structural logic behind the core narratives that sustained the formation of modern European nationalisms. For Anderson, the newspaper—with its unique format, market, and distribution channels—fostered the key features of the late nineteenth- and early twentieth-century national movements of Central and Eastern Europe. Anderson comprehensively showed that each national myth was fundamentally shaped by the medium through which it spread, as well as by the prevailing economic and social forces at play in that era.[43]

A necessary requirement of all successful political systems, religions, and international organizations is to create the narratives or myths that can allow disparate individuals with divergent interests to support those nations', religions', or institutions' approach to collective action problems. It used to be that stirring oratory, persuasive pamphlet writing, or even live military combat conveyed these myths to potential adherents. As the twenty-first century has progressed, technology has changed the tools leaders use to interact with their would-be followers. As the medium changed, the message evolved to fit it.

Libyans' media habits

Contemporary Libyans tend not to read print books or newspapers,[44] as both are extremely hard to obtain in Libya. Libya has only one famous publishing house that commissions works about Libyan history and politics, Dar al-Farjani.[45] Fewer than twenty thousand (non-pirated) book copies dealing with Libya-related content are sold in Libya each year.[46] Libya also has barely any general interest political bookshops (there are quite a few religious bookshops). This differs markedly from Egypt, Algeria, Tunisia, Lebanon, and Iraq, each of which are known for their long tradition of newsstands, bookshops, and even street ped-dlers focused on distributing non-religious books.

Although it is impossible to determine precisely, the penetra-tion of traditional print-media publishing in Libya is anecdotally among the lowest for any society of its wealth and literacy levels on earth.[47] This might seem surprising, as Libyans have a higher degree of literacy (especially female literacy) than any of their surrounding countries, as well as more hours of leisure time and more disposable income. The reason for these discrepancies in reading behaviour is therefore historical and cultural: before the discovery of oil, the Libyan media was largely unregulated. But at that point Libyans lacked money, leisure, and literacy. After oil wealth transformed their society and Qadhafi came to power, he undertook a campaign for mass literacy at exactly the same moment as he imposed rigorous press censorship.

Conversely, data shows that Libyans watch a great deal of political punditry on TV and spend more time engaging in political chat on social media and messaging apps than almost any other society on earth. This is particularly surprising given the low level of internet penetration in Libya.[48] *Yes Libya*, a digital newspaper, has cited global polling data showing that Libyans use Facebook significantly more than the global aver-age and that its penetration is more than tenfold that of Twitter. From this data—and similarly to other developing countries with resource wealth, but without a tradition of print journalism—we can infer that for many Libyans Facebook is their primary provider of political information, with TV sec-ond, and radio in third.[49]

The Media Mapping study conducted by my consulting firm Libya-Analysis LLC in April 2018 demonstrated that Libyans also listen to a lot of non-satellite radio in their cars, much of which is non-partisan in its coverage of national issues and car-ries a lot of local interest content.[50] Drawing on this empirical data, my colleagues and I formulated overarching observations about Libyan's non-social media consumption habits:

By Type: Radio stations constitute a far more popular and penetrative media tool than TV stations. They are also more neutral and tend towards more local and credible programming...

By Bias: Anti-Islamist, Pro-LNA media channels vastly outnumbered their contenders in 2018, the pro-Islamists/anti-LNA stations by almost 4:1, in terms of number, reach and popularity. While many Benghazi media channels are quite biased in favour of Operation Dignity [i.e. the LNA], media channels in Tripoli are more varied, presenting a more accurate picture of the population's sentiments.

By Spectrum: [Because] Libya's politics has many axes, we could have chosen to categorize most media on the pro- vs. anti-GNA vector as the main political axis, but our research showed that the primary fissure [referenced in broadcasts] was pro/anti-LNA (which mirrors and equates to anti/pro-Islamist). Views on the GNA were less salient for categorizing [and were discussed less frequently in] the Libyan media landscape than views on the LNA or Islamists...

By Ethnicity: The media outlets of Jabal Nafusa and Zuwara are deeply committed to building a sense of Amazigh/Berber identity and doing so separately from any of the main national level political divisions.[51]

Taken in total, this freeze frame picture of the Libyan media landscape in 2018 suggests that a new sort of 'primordialism' has set in. After Qadhafi's fall, Libyans had returned to pre-national forms of identity with town, sub-region, tribe, ethnicity, and extended family dominating the loci of both personal identification and media narrative consumption. Furthermore, our study showed that all major Libyan political movements—and even the major militias—are aligned with specific television and radio broadcasters. Usually there is a funding chain linking various media with either the GNA or LNA, or prominent and polarizing individuals like Grand Mufti Sadiq al-Ghariyani.[52]

Neo-populist media tactics 101

This rise of Haftar and the LNA is an indicative case study of how the Enduring Disorder allows neo-populists to create a bogeyman enemy and then make the media focus on them. My team's results showcased the overall success of the LNA's approach to media during the 2016–19 period: (1) in the popular consciousness, they had persuasively clothed themselves with the mantle of anti-Islamism—a narrative that resonated far better with the Libyan populace than Islamism—which was quite an achievement given the numerous Madkhali Salafist battalions in the LNA's midst and their overall failure to act against ISIS; and (2) they had made themselves the focal point of political discourse—and as such usurped in the popular consciousness both the internationally recognized GNA and the anti-establishment Islamists who had previously dominated the narratives surrounding political developments. In short, they followed 'international best practices' about manufacturing a personality cult, a bogeyman, and an overarching narrative.

Orbán and Bolsonaro are far more internationally known than previous leaders of Hungary or Brazil. International and American media of all stripes covered Donald Trump, debating his statements and actions far more than those of his rivals. This trend has continued into early 2021, even after Trump was no longer president and was unable to tweet. Neo-populists make the story about themselves and their enemies, not their political rivals or their programmes.

Haftar and the LNA mastered this. They left Serraj in the dust. When Serraj was the actual prime minister, most news stories about Libya still focused on Haftar. Even after Haftar was completely defeated in his attempt to take Tripoli by June 2020, it remained apparent that he had left a greater stamp on the Libyan polity and its cultural imaginary[53] than any of its post-Qadhafi prime ministers.

Libyans respect eloquence

Libyans' current pattern of media consumption and narrative formation represents a marked evolution from their traditional engagement with the media. It also encapsulates various continuities. Arab culture, and especially Bedouin culture, places a large emphasis on *balagha* (eloquence, especially in poetry or rhetoric). Additionally, during the anti-colonial struggles and early post-independence period, Arab societies, including Libya, consumed much more print and radio news than other countries at their education and wealth levels, notably relative to Latin America and Sub-Saharan Africa where the percentage of the population that had access to radio or second hand newspapers was far less.[54] Qadhafi cemented his power, as his idol Gamal Abdel-Nasser had before him in neighbouring Egypt, via his mastery of radio and live in-person oratory.[55] Both were seen globally as charismatic speakers and gifted at holding a range of audiences by weaving together local, national, and international themes.

Post-Qadhafi, Libya's cultural traditions still accord a special place to eloquence, especially as illustrated through in-person or live-streamed oratory. The security situation necessitated the use of TV and social media for the conveyance of political messages and the building of national movements. The Covid pandemic and the prior intensification of the war have merely exacerbated these pre-exiting trends. Although respect for eloquence, word play, and charisma has remained constant, what has markedly changed from the 1970s to now is the means of demonstrating those skills—short videos watched on smart phones have replaced lengthy speeches meant to be listened to on the radio. Libya's major political figures, militia commanders, and even heads of semi-sovereign economic institutions make YouTube videos and use Facebook Live to get their message out to the Libyan people.[56]

This is in fitting with trends globally. Libyans are representative of, or even ahead of the curve, with regard to global trends of media consumption. Their TV and radio stations have become stratified along local and hyper-partisan lines, with the phenomenon of social media 'filter bubbles' separating distinct online communities.

Myths motivate action

This is a media landscape that the LNA and its allies have mastered to disseminate their narrative. It has allowed them to gain collaborators from disparate groups who may not like Haftar personally but are willing to temporarily embrace his programme if it benefits their personal longing for security or their local community's struggles for representation or economic justice. Haftar's impact on transforming Libyans' national narratives will be felt long after he is gone, analogous to how the divisiveness of Farage or Trump will far outlast their times in the national spotlight. The disorder these figures have injected on to the international scene will certainly far outlive them. It may even facilitate the rise of similar figures in their wake.

Just as the previous chapters' excerpts have investigated the Libya conflict through the prisms of appeasement and jihadism, this excerpt will allow us to re-examine the main players and events in the Libyan drama from the perspective of their ability to hold media attention and to create compelling narratives. Successful narratives allow former enemies to join forces against a perceived or conjured joint threat, while their absence can prevent groups with a shared interest from successfully working together against a genuine shared enemy.

* * *

Selections from: Jason Pack, 'Kingdom of Militias: Libya's Second War of Post-Qadhafi Succession', *ISPI*, 31 May 2019.[57]

PART I

MACRO LESSONS ABOUT LIBYA'S ARMED ACTORS

Yet another war in Libya

The struggle for the post-Qadhafi future has been characterized by the dominance of non-state actors, feckless national leadership, endemic corruption stemming from the country's war economy and fluidity of allegiances. But more than any other trend, fragmentation has been the unifying theme (pun intended) for this long struggle.[58] Groups that fought together in the 2011 anti-Qadhafi uprisings later turned against each other in the first civil war which started in 2014, while groups that fought against each other in 2014[59] frequently fragmented into subgroups by 2018's late summer war over southern Tripoli. Some of those who fought each other in the western region in 2014, joined together to fight against the LNA offensive in Tripoli in 2019.

Alongside this fragmentation and shifting of alliances, groups rebrand themselves—then merge and subdivide—as new coalitions come into being. Since Libya's First Civil War broke out in 2014,[60] and the country bifurcated into two rival governments, only one entity has progressively grown in logistical coherence: the disparate collection of rank and file soldiers and civilian paramilitaries that call themselves the Libyan National Army (LNA). The LNA has spread outwards from al-Marj in eastern Libya and grown in complexity and sophistication. Its financial networks, supply chains, social media capabilities and international relationships all experienced incremental strengthening. Despite this geographic and capacity growth, the LNA has always been mired in contradiction. Like the famous quip about the Holy Roman Empire, the Libyan National Army is neither entirely Libyan (it occasionally relies on foreign mercenaries), nor is it national (initially the majority of its top brass hailed almost exclusively from certain Eastern and Central tribes), nor is it a regular army (it does not answer to a national sovereign authority nor are its rank and file drawn by national conscription or volunteerism). The conflict over Tripoli [*April 2019—June 2020 was*] the LNA's [*failed*] attempt to abolish these contradictions and become Libya's genuine Weberian sovereign by brute force alone. This second civil war, which [*was*] the second discrete phase of the struggle for the post-Qadhafi future, is characterized, then, by the LNA's quest to conquer the whole country politically, and to actualise some version of its leader's frequently articulated mantra of 'liberating Libya from Islamists'...

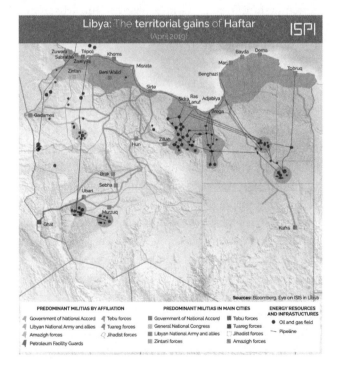

Libya: The territorial gains of Haftar (April 2019)

Sources: Bloomberg, Eye on ISIS in Libya

PREDOMINANT MILITIAS BY AFFILIATION
- Government of National Accord
- Libyan National Army and allies
- Amazigh forces
- Petroleum Facility Guards
- Tebu forces
- Tuareg forces
- Jihadist forces

PREDOMINANT MILITIAS IN MAIN CITIES
- Government of National Accord
- General National Congress
- Libyan National Army and allies
- Zintani forces
- Tebu forces
- Jihadist forces
- Amazigh forces

ENERGY RESOURCES AND INFRASTRUCTURES
- Oil and gas field
- Pipeline

Despite its claim to be the 'national army' of Libya, the self-styled Libyan National Army (LNA) is a collection of truly discrete military/militia units and tribal/regional-based armed groups.... Stemming from a series of smaller armed units that were component parts of the Libyan Army under the Qadhafi regime, the LNA emerged as a nascent force in mid-2014, when General Khalifa Haftar launched 'Operation Dignity' to eradicate Islamist militias in Benghazi.[61] Haftar had announced a coup earlier in February of that year, but as the Zintanis failed to follow his lead in the west of the country, his momentum quickly dissipated.[62] When Haftar tried again in late spring/early summer 2014, dynamics had shifted significantly as various Islamist and Misratan-aligned groups sought to cancel the 25 June [*HoR*] election results.[63]

The LNA's metanarrative

This was a propitious moment for Haftar: by seeking to defend 'the will of the people' and their 'elected body' while purging 'the enemies of the people' dubbed 'Islamists', Haftar had found a core metanarrative that would suit him well over the coming years. This narrative has helped his popularity grow as it has more than a ring of truth to it: the political entities targeted by Haftar—first in Benghazi, then in Derna, and now in Tripoli—have in certain instances embraced opportunistic support from extremist forces such as Ansar al-Sharia, the Libyan Islamic Fighting group, and on certain occasions even ISIS.

By March 2015, the eastern-based House of Representatives (HoR) designated Haftar as the Chief of Staff of the Libyan Army—i.e. the remnants of the former professional army that remained affiliated to the then internationally recognized HoR.[64] Over time, the LNA grew in cohesiveness and power, choosing to present itself as a 'security sector reform project' (i.e. an attempt to build a national army capable of bringing order to a lawless country). The LNA presented its main goals as purging Libya of Muslim Brotherhood affiliates and jihadists as well as exercising control over the country's other militias—either by eliminating them, demobilizing them, or incorporating them into its patronage networks and command structures. These goals have remained constant from mid-2014 to the present.[65] Through these public objectives, Haftar seeks to fulfil his primary personal ambition: securing autocratic power for himself or for the LNA as an institution.

As of April 2019, the LNA power structure relies on traditional business families from the eastern region, former Qadhafi-era top military brass, the nominally sovereign HoR legislature, and the Beida-based Abdullah al-Thinni government.[66] These groups embrace the metanarrative of a centralized command structure, which has gradually emerged as a reality via the LNA's gradual coalition-building, targeted payments, projection of power and public support for the emergence of a supreme authority—due to growing discontent from insecurity and lawlessness across the country.

The narrative's adherents

In eastern Libya, many young unemployed men are susceptible to the LNA's metanarrative, as they are imbued with a deeply rooted longing for order, personal dignity, and a centralized control of force as a legacy from the statelessness and arbitrary use of force during the Qadhafi period. Conversely, in western Libya, since the fragmented, Islamist-leaning or Islamist-accommodating factions have failed to deliver on their promises of restoring normalcy to the country, a portion of the public, especially those of an anti-Islamist and moderately educated bent, have turned their support to military-rule, even if this means authoritarian rule, which might offer a modicum of order to society. A paper by Clingendael based on polling in mid-2018 whose method likely implicitly overrepresents the educated and media-savvy, found that the Libyan public gradually evolved greater confidence in the 'protective capacity' of the LNA rather than the security institutions of the GNA.[67]

Over the years, the LNA has capitalized on these psychological and structural factors to gain support from specific communities in the western region, although acquiring the loyalties of certain groups does not necessarily mean the whole community or other militias from these towns or regions have become similarly aligned...

Stage 1: new territorial gains, new challenges; the siege of Derna

With the metanarrative fully in place to justify and rationalize any brutality against enemy combatants or civilian populations that might eventually surface on social media, in May 2018 Haftar launched a final assault on Derna with the stated objective of removing the city's al-Qaeda linked Shura Council of Mujahedeen (SCMD) [*this is the Italian acronym for the same militia which was called the Derna Mujahadeen Shura Council (DMSC) in Chapters 1 and 2*]. He had sporadically besieged the city since 2016, without committing significant forces to the campaign.[68] These attacks, like those in Benghazi before them, had led to significant human rights violations, occasionally captured on social media—particularly Facebook.[69]

Days after the concerted 2018 assault began, the SCMD rebranded itself as Derna Protection Forces (DPF), likely in an attempt to distance itself from SCMD-linked Islamist groups connected with terrorism.[70] The LNA deployed as many as twenty-one, if not more, different brigades during the assault and received overt support (logistics, armaments, and airstrikes) from Egypt and the UAE.[71] After a 'battle' that lasted nearly a year, the LNA announced the capture of Derna in February 2019.[72] This cemented its dominance over the whole of coastal eastern Libya and proved the group militarily capable of conquering and then incorporating originally hostile territories.

*Step two: cementing a national role—Operation
Southern Liberation*

On 15 January 2019, weeks after Libya's largest oil field had been closed by protesters, an LNA spokesman announced that its forces, including the Madkhali Salafist Khalid Bin Walid Brigade,[73] would undertake an operation to liberate southern Libya from extremist groups, and to 'ensure the public's continued ability to maintain and control Libya's oil and gas sector'.[74] This offensive marked the first time that the LNA was willing to extend its supply lines to undertake a major operation far away from its main base of operations in Libya's north-east. The LNA's mobilization into the southern region was on a much greater scale than the previous occasions from 2015 to 2018 when the LNA attempted quick southward forays to remove militant and extremist groups from the south.[75]...

The LNA's social media supporters up their game

The LNA went to great lengths to manage its perception and media coverage during the operations [*employing tactics similar to the hybrid warfare associated with Russia's actions in Georgia in 2008 and Ukraine in 2014*]. Indeed, the successful image carefully crafted by social media influencers concerning the LNA's southern operations did not reflect the reality on the ground.[76] Despite the very real gains that were made which facilitated the reopening of Sharara and al-Feel fields, rebel and opposition forces remained, though they were ejected from the main civilian centres. Regardless of this, the southern campaign was effectively utilised by LNA supporters on social media to present it as a supremely powerful and coordinated organization with the ability to guarantee genuine security free from oppressive tactics.[77] This image was meant to create a wave of positive support from local groups in the western region, which the LNA sought to capitalize on... [*The reopening in March 2019 of the Sharara oil field, which had been shut since November 2018, was an example of the LNA and its supporters 'solving' a problem they had created. It was an open secret that the Touareg militia that had shut the field did so in coordination with the LNA's international supporters.*]

But the momentum the narrative around it acquired enabled the LNA to channel its focus upon Libya's ultimate prize: Tripoli. In other words, the LNA leadership perceived that the moment had come to dominate the country's domestic and international narrative and that their media apparatus was strong enough to project themselves as the overlords of Libya. These lessons in projecting a narrative of effortless and continual victory honed in the Southern campaign were then deployed in the Tripoli campaign. Yet in the battle for Tripoli, a full-on social media war was launched with the aim of influencing international coverage of the fighting. In this effort the LNA's effectiveness was further enhanced by a coterie of Saudi-based[78] and Russian-trained pro-LNA social media influencers.

Step three—the battle for control of Libya's major militia prize: the Tripoli campaign

From the very start of Operation Dignity, Haftar stated that he intended to capture Tripoli—clearly demonstrating his understanding that no faction can truly be considered a 'national army' without it. He and LNA spokesmen have couched their desire for domination via the narrative of 'liberating' the capital from terrorist and extortive armed groups, thereby justifying a future assault on the city. In truth, Haftar has had long-standing ambitions to lead Libya without civilian oversight and to oversee a militarization of the state.[79] Haftar's decision to launch the offensive in early April [*2019*] appears to have been influenced by multiple factors: his increased international profile, his possible perception of being given a green light from foreign supporters and benefactors,[80] heightened confidence within the LNA leadership following its successful campaign to take southern Libya, improved reach and coverage on social media, a need for more cash to funnel through the LNA's patronage networks, and a view that the National Conference [*a UN-mediated pan-Libya meeting scheduled to take place in April 2019 and possibly to formulate a road map to elections*] would alter dynamics in the country in ways that were unfavourable to the LNA [*if it were to go ahead*]. The LNA's launch of operation 'Flood of Dignity' followed mobilization of its forces to Jufra, Sirte, and the northwest coastline over the preceding weeks. This coincided with outreach efforts to develop relationships with local municipalities, tribes, and militias along with the southern and western entrances to Tripoli.[81] Moreover, as shown in the preceding section, the southern campaign helped the LNA bolster its image domestically and internationally as a 'credible' national army-building project. By presenting itself in this manner, it has worked to entice groups to operate local LNA 'franchises' by providing them with both legitimacy and resources if they fly the LNA banner. For example, the LNA successful co-opted Tarhuna's Kaniyyat and Gharyan's Adel Da'ab.[82]

Despite these preparations and alliance shifts, the experience of Derna should have taught the LNA that an assault on Tripoli would not lead to a swift victory, but a rather long and protracted conflict. However, during the long Derna siege, many of the LNA's attacking forces were benefiting from 'relatively' local and supply lines secure, enabling ready access to capabilities and fresh troops. Conversely, during the [*War for Tripoli*] the anti-LNA forces benefitted from internal supply lines. Given these logistical issues, the LNA become a victim of overstretch...

PART IV

THE ANTI-LNA MILITIAS

The real axes of Libya's politics

For the majority of the GNA-aligned militias, it is not loyalty to the GNA that constitutes a group's primary allegiance, but rather its fierce opposition to Haftar and the LNA. In fact, a scientific way to conceive this grouping of actors is as 'anti-LNA' rather than 'pro-GNA'. A mapping of Libya's radio and TV stations conducted by

Libya-Analysis partner organizations determined that the primary fissure in Libyan politics was the pro-/anti-LNA and pro-/anti-Islamists axes (see figure below), whereas no pro-/anti-GNA axis existed in the discourse of Libya's media landscape.[83]

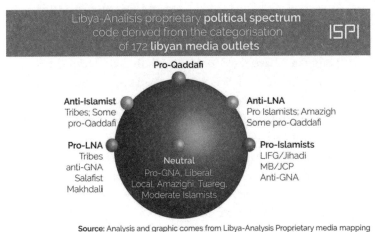

Source: Analysis and graphic comes from Libya-Analysis Proprietary media mapping

Fig. 1: Libya-Analysis Political Spectrum Mapping

The anti-LNA coalition's coherence and capabilities

Haftar's assault on Tripoli has forged all the above listed Western militias into a loose 'anti-LNA coalition', exactly as Libya-Analysis's militia mapping and the principle of balance of power would suggest. Yet, the coherence and sustainability of this coalition is highly fragile and susceptible to sudden fragmentation or even collapse... None of these groups had ever undertaken a joint operation, and have had little time to facilitate communications, but they seem to grasp the need to coordinate both their battlefield actions [*and their social media posts*] to jointly combat Haftar's media offensive...

PART V
THE OUTLOOK FOR LIBYA

Libya has never had a truly national army

All of Libyan history highlights this. The country has never had a national army. None of Libya's imperial rulers—the Ottomans, the Italians, or the British—ever unified Libya administratively or militarily. Its domestic potentates have fared only slightly better. During his monarchy, Idris al-Sanussi was a polarizing figure who drew support from very specific segments of the population and was terrified of creating a truly national army, correctly surmising that some disgruntled subaltern or colonel might eventually overthrow him. He preferred a Pretorian guard, the Cyrenaican Defence Force, which drew its manpower primarily from the [*sa'ada (or so-called noble)*] tribes of Cyrenaica.[84] During the Qadhafi period, the country was further unified economically and institutionally, but never militarily. Qadhafi eviscerated the army, creating his own Pretorian guard from the previously disadvantaged Magarha, Warfalla, and Qadhadhifa tribes.[85] He too was terrified that equipping and training a national army might lead to some part of it eventually overthrowing him—exactly as eventually came to pass.

Unlike other Arab States, even those with artificial colonial borders like Algeria, Iraq or Syria, Libya has, therefore, never had a coherent national army. In most Arab states cobbled together by the Imperial powers out of diverse Ottoman wilayat, mid-20th century state building was conducted by an army which acted as a sovereign. Not in Libya. Ability to distribute vast oil revenues to a small and dispersed population granted the financial centre of authority power, not the Army.

What does Haftar want for Libya?

> Haftar's intention was never to compromise on his desire to achieve complete leadership of the Libyan armed forces, unfettered by civilian oversight. His intention was to increase his power and leverage before the National Conference by taking control of Tripoli or creating a media perception of dominance, allowing him to dictate the terms of the political process or ignore it completely. Seen in this light, Haftar appears either stubborn or megalomaniacal. He was on the verge of being anointed Libya's most powerful actor by the UN political process, yet that was not enough for him. Psychologically, he appears incapable of accepting defeat.

He makes it all about him

Like many other leaders during the Enduring Disorder, Haftar simply chose not to acknowledge when he had lost militarily. The how-to manual for neo-populist leaders appears to instruct them to never admit to making missteps, losing a war or an election. Given this shared psychopathy, it should surprise no one that after Haftar had conclusively lost the War for Tripoli by June 2020, he came up with various ruses to demonstrate that he had, in fact, achieved his objectives, such as changing how revenues from oil are stored, distributed, and accounted for. His mythical narrative about 'always winning' served as a justification for his otherwise baseless assertion that he was destined to lead.

Yet, from his first attempted coup in February 2014 through to his assault on Tripoli in April 2019, Haftar has experienced many military victories and roughly an equal number of setbacks. Mopping-up operations that should have taken days were known to drag on for months, if not years. His true genius was clearly not on the battlefield.

Haftar's real skill was quite similar to many other icons of the Enduring Disorder: never having failures stick to him and employing erratic and bombastic messaging to stay at the centre of media attention. Just as Trump made himself synonymous with American politics and redefined political party allegiance into a litmus test of how a given individual felt about Trump, Haftar made his name synonymous with Libya's civil war. In so doing, he created a new sort of partisanship: realigning the Libyan political spectrum into a litmus test of how one felt about Haftar. This was demonstrated by the Libya-Analysis LLC Media Mapping, referenced earlier in this chapter. Through an extensive survey of Libyan radio, the study proved that by 2018 pro/anti-Haftar and pro/anti-Islamist divides had eclipsed citizens' attitudes towards the GNA, the UN peace process and the constitution as Libya's primary axis of political partisanship.

This is quite impressive for a figure who does not hail from a prominent family, has never run for office, never held an official internationally recognized governmental position, and returned from the diaspora with no personal power base. Haftar achieved this by pushing polarizing wedge issues to acquire free advertising or 'unearned media'. Trump used this tactic to brilliant effect during the 2016 US Presidential Campaign.

Despite their ability to obtain unearned media, drive polarizing political issues, and rally their bases, Haftar and Trump have not been successful in becoming autocrats. They are old men whose political and physical primes are behind them. Historically, they will be judged as overly ambitious and underqualified men whose political careers floundered as they tried to bite off more than they could chew. Nonetheless, due to the self-reinforcing nature of the Enduring Disorder, the narratives they inaugurated will have disorder inducing implications far outlasting their life spans.

Somewhere between 2014 and 2019, Haftar was able to switch the primary axes of domestic messaging about the Libya conflict from being about patronage politics to being about himself: his rightful political position, the role of 'his army' in national life, and the role of the narrative he constructed about Libya in achieving a path forward for the country. This is exactly analogous to how Trump hacked the news cycle of American mainstream media to make himself and his utterances the central aspect of US national debate.[86] Both are masters of distraction, able to refer to setbacks as 'victories,' and to make their pronouncements 'the story' rather than any inconvenient facts that might intrude.

Haftar's use of outright lies and bravado have possibly even outdone Trump. According to my team's media research, Haftar declared Benghazi 'completely liberated' on at least twenty separate occasions from 2014 to 2016, usually in the wake of adverse military developments that implicitly demonstrated that his opponents remained ensconced in neighbourhoods like al-Laithi, and were, in fact, killing LNA-aligned forces.[87] His declarations that 'Benghazi is liberated' would be covered by *Reuters* and *Bloomberg*, sometimes as actual news and sometimes to debunk them. Either way, other more factual stories were shunted aside. Haftar understood how to manipulate the news media's coverage of adverse events in a way that suited him. In fact, his pronouncements about military successes functioned quite similarly to Trump's claims in late 2020 that he had won the election.

On 27 April 2020, Haftar declared that he had unilaterally abrogated the 2015 Skhirat Agreement. He claimed that he alone had a 'popular mandate' for military control over eastern Libya and that he no longer relied on the appointment or acquiescence of the HoR to occupy the role of commander-in-chief. The move was perfectly timed to distract from the military failures that the LNA had just experienced with the losses of Surman and Sabratha.[88] In June 2020, he travelled to Cairo to declare a unilateral ceasefire with President Sisi and Speaker of the HoR Aqilah Saleh. This was exactly the moment that his forces were in full retreat, having lost all their major assets in Tripolitania over the last two months. These tactics were risible to most Libyans and Libya watchers, but they still convinced *Reuters*, *The New York Times*, and various Gulf media to cover the 'ceasefire' as the story and the LNA's military defeats as ancillary.[89] These moves would foreshadow Trump's tactics of declaring in advance of the 2020 election that postal voting was 'going to be fraudulent' and after the election that it 'was rigged', hence generating a landslide of coverage in right-wing media concerning election irregularities.

That Haftar failed to conquer all of Libya or that Trump did not win a second term (and that much of his policy agenda was promptly reversed) does not encapsulate the primary legacies of either man. They both reconfigured the media and political narrative landscapes in their countries, bringing it further in line with the trends and patterns of the Enduring Disorder. They had an intrinsic sense of how the current media landscape could be used to gain attention for their cause and promote the hyperpartisan climate in which their messaging would thrive.

Like Trump, Haftar's use of the 'social media bully pulpit' to distract from inconvenient facts has only been possible due to the prevailing technological and collective action conditions of the Enduring Disorder. Both effectively shaped their messages to suit the medium, while their opponents were stuck with 20th century style communications. Haftar's improbable ascendancy to power and the narrative he crafted for his political movement—as shown above in the excerpt—is a perfect test case to reflect upon the larger phenomenon of social media's role in crafting new forms of political leadership and narratives during the Enduring Disorder.

The power of these narratives will outlast their purveyors. With Haftar, we have seen that military actions were conducted for reasons of 'media optics'. Controlling physical territory was primarily useful in terms of how it would affect the media narrative.[90] This broader phenomenon of the multi-layered implications of military engagements are coming to characterize all wars globally. There is no longer such a thing as hybrid war or conventional war. Like the 2008 Georgian conflict and the Ukrainian civil war of 2014 that inaugurated this dynamic, Libya's civil wars exhibited a brutal competition among military actors vying to shape how events were reported and perceived. Rather than victors writing history as they have always done, contemporary aspiring tyrants dominate the news cycle and frame the depictions of the ongoing battles, independent of whether they are winning or losing. And their narratives survive even after they are defeated. This is a lesson with massive global implications.

Taking back control

In order to come to power under the prevailing conditions of the Enduring Disorder, the aspiring neo-populist leader must dominate the battlespace.[91] And the contemporary battlespace is social media. To do so, the aspirant must create a clear narrative by messaging about a 'problem' that he will solve and why specific 'enemies' must be defeated to solve this problem.[92] Where an actual problem exists, perfect. It can be reframed in such a way as to fit into the desired narrative template. Where a concrete problem is lacking, it can be evoked in their constituents' collective imaginary through referencing the disorienting implications of the technological and economic developments of the first two decades of the twenty-first century. For the creation of the 'enemy', neo-populism has carefully conjured a transnational shared imaginary of a cosmopolitan, capitalist, 'corrupt establishment'.

It is against this imaginary backdrop that Brexiteers wanted to 'take back control' and Trump's supporters wanted to 'Make

America Great Again'. To do so, both groups sought to prevent the 'cosmopolitan elite' from giving 'our jobs' to migrants and global organizations from 'telling us how to live'. Like the anti-Semitic tropes of the 1930s and 1940s, which they profoundly resemble, these slogans and solutions combine both right- and left-wing elements but are always nativist, nationalist, aggrieved, and reactionary. They can be directed against the outsider irrespective of her or his political persuasion.[93] It should come as no surprise that neo-populist movements the world over have made alliances with groups and individuals promoting an anti-Semitic ideology, which as a result is on the rise globally. Strangely, this is true even in Israel, where Binyamin Netanyahu has forged an alliance with anti-Semitic leaders like Orbán, and in the United States, where Orthodox Jewish communities have cultivated deep ties to President Trump's grassroots supporters, tacitly ignoring the fact that many believe in QAnon 'replacement theory'.[94]

All modern neo-populist ideology articulates anger over perceived victimization by outsiders and a desire to harken back to 'a time of old' when all was right with the world and the 'correct group' was in charge of one's country.[95] This reactive framing of 'taking back control' on behalf of its 'rightful' owners is an essential feature of many of the leading aspirants to political power during the Enduring Disorder. And the situation in Libya is no different.

Disinformation leads to cults of personality

Haftar's mythmaking has stitched together different support bases and given them a shared vision of Libya's current problems and future solutions. Haftar portrays Libyans as victims of an international conspiracy. He frames his movement as 'Arab' and masculine, while its enemies are purported to be homosexual, 'mixed-blood', and descendants of Turks, Berbers, and sub-

Saharan blacks. Enemies of Haftar are called such creative slurs on Facebook as 'Erdoğan's monkeys' or 'followers of the retarded prince of the gays'.[96] Haftar wishes to harken back to a time when Libyans adhered to 'family values', 'people were safe', and 'the state' exerted control. He does not overtly specify the Qadhafi period as the time that he wishes to adopt as his model, just as President Trump rarely explicitly invoked the pre-civil rights era and Boris Johnson dances around invocations the British Imperial heyday. Direct references would turn some people off and could be attacked as insensitive. So various dog whistles are used that work within the cultural imaginary of each country's national myths.

Haftar's genius has been his creation of a narrative casting Libyans as victims and proposing himself as the only solution to Libya's cultural, security, and economic dilemmas. In particular, his messaging has stressed four primary problems: outsiders meddling in Libya's affairs, Islamism/jihadism, corrupt/inefficient/Tripoli-centric economic institutions, and the lack of a strong army. All four are certainly legitimate crises. His communications team and international allies have honed their messages about them into an artform—precisely targeted tropes that hit the heart strings of their desired audience.[97]

However, as Haftar gained power throughout Libya, his actual policies gave rise to increased levels of each of the four problems that he claims to have launched his movement to solve. This is exactly the same way that other neo-populists work. They play on the emotional longings for a strong leader and the idea of a mythologized national/ethnic/racial identity. Yet, once in power, they exacerbate exactly the same issues that they drew upon rhetorically to come to power. But above all else, they use the contemporary news cycle and the ubiquity of information to craft a cult of personality and leader worship. In this media environment, being erratic is an advantage as it makes one constantly newsworthy with spontaneous pronouncements always front and centre in print media, Facebook feeds, and the national consciousness.

Making Libya great again

Haftar promises that he alone can solve Libya's problems and that he alone can 'make Libya great again'. Haftar's messaging and cult of personality encapsulate the causal relationship between the lack of international collective action to police hate speech and mis/disinformation online, and the ensuing rise of a novel form of neo-populist leadership via cults of personality.[98]

In a way, this is an ageless problem simply made more virulent by the media environment of the Enduring Disorder. In a letter written in August 1792, Alexander Hamilton diagnosed how human nature inherently gives rise to this phenomenon. He elaborately sketched for his readers a scenario in which the nascent American Republic could lose its democratic character and witness the rise of a strongman:

> Tired at length of anarchy, or want of government, they may take shelter in the arms of ... [a strongman] for repose and security ... When a man unprincipled in private life, desperate in his fortune, bold in his temper, possessed of considerable talents, having the advantage of military habits—despotic in his ordinary demeanour—known to have scoffed in private at the principles of liberty—when such a man is seen to mount the hobby horse of popularity—to join in the cry of danger to liberty—to take every opportunity of embarrassing the General Government & bringing it under suspicion—to flatter and fall in with all the non-sense of the zealots of the day—It may justly be suspected that his object is to throw things into confusion that he may 'ride the storm and direct the whirlwind'.[99]

Contemporary American political commentators have attached this quote to their critiques of President Trump, yet the precise text actually suits the problems of Libyans and the personal characteristics of Haftar even more accurately. If the Enduring Disorder leads to other state implosions like Libya's, it could be that both Trump's and Haftar's meteoric rises—and ultimate falls—will serve as preparatory studies for the mid-twenty-first-century's aspiring tyrants.

4

LIBYA VERSUS THE GLOBAL ECONOMY

Mysteries, riddles, and more myths

If Winston Churchill could be resurrected and appointed UN Special Envoy to Libya, his first quarterly report to the Security Council would probably contain an utterance like, 'The Libya problem is a riddle, wrapped in a mystery, inside an enigma, and its economic structures are perhaps the key'. In real life, the Libyan economy remains the most poorly understood aspect of the country and its ongoing civil war. It is also highly dissimilar from other Middle Eastern oil states. My guess is that it shares more structural features with Venezuela[1] than with either Algeria, Kuwait, or Saudi Arabia.

Despite its obvious importance, neither governments, nor think tanks, nor academics have systematically highlighted the post-Qadhafian Libyan economy's salient features. There are various reasons for this. Libyan economic entities are deliberately opaque. Journalists and academics of the Middle East have usually done their undergraduate and graduate training as Arabists—a rigorous professional formation that focuses on language, history, culture, religion, and politics but frequently lacks economics courses altogether. Businesses and consultancies that interact with the Libyan economy tend not to share information or publish their findings. Western think tanks specializing in the Middle East usually publish on diplomacy, counterterrorism, and women's issues, but not on economic structures. NGOs usually document human rights abuses and attempt to foster civil society.

There are some rare and noteworthy exceptions of dedicated NGOs and intrepid reporters uncovering episodes of corruption and vanished funds.[2] But their research rarely examines the deeper structures that have made them possible. By employing an organized crime lens, the implicit framing for the lay reader is that the Libyan state's institutions are not functioning properly or have been somehow hijacked by corrupt individuals. This is a conclusion I will contest below.

Nonetheless, the few ground-breaking exposés of this genre have indirectly revealed some of the Libyan economy's *sui generis* features and deeper connections to major financial centres like London and Paris or tax havens like Panama and the Cayman Islands. If we read between the lines of these exposés, the implicit message is how the lack of international governance over those nodes of global finance is a determinative factor in the evolution of the Libyan economy.

This long-standing absence of comprehensive investigations into the big picture economic structures at play in post-Qadhafi Libya only began to change from 2017 onwards, as my colleague at Chatham House Tim Eaton[3] and I separately published research papers implicitly attacking the received wisdom.[4] Our process of identifying, debunking, and then reformulating the myths about the Libyan economy reveals a lot about how capitalism and the economics of conflict zones are actually shaped by, and in turn shape, the Enduring Disorder. The Enduring

Disorder is so pernicious because most people—including policymakers and economists—still cling to specific myths about how the global economy 'is supposed' to function but in reality never actually did.

Over my twelve years doing business in Libya and advising others about its economic structures, I have encountered five key myths—each of which I outline below and then attempt to progressively demolish over the course of this and the next chapter. Only by exposing the shibboleths and self-serving fantasies of various interest groups can I attempt to finally present a systematic overview of Libya's actual political economy—and how global forces have been both detrimental to, and determinative of, its evolution.

1. The 'globalization myth' maintains that Qadhafi initially ruined Libya by imposing a totalitarian centralized command economy while simultaneously isolating the country from global capitalism—an eventuality that was then compounded by the post-Lockerbie UN sanctions. When finally faced in the late 1990s with his failure to create an Arab nationalist socialist paradise, Qadhafi was forced to reform or be overthrown. According to this myth, the Libyan version of the Arab Spring was, therefore, not caused by the failure of neoliberal reforms, as the Tunisian and Egyptian Arab Spring uprisings were. Quite the opposite: it was the success of the economic reforms of the 2005 to 2008 period that led to the collapse of the regime, as those reforms opened up Libyan public space. Then, like perestroika and glasnost, this facilitated the collapse of the old order.[5] Following on this argumentation, now in the post-Qadhafi present, if the refreshing air of capitalist competition could be further allowed to freely flow back into Libya, it would yield untold wealth for both the Libyan people and the international economy.[6] The multina-

tionals could turn Libya into Kuwait on the Mediterranean—if only the Libyan government and dysfunctional global regulators would get out of the way.

2. The 'greed is good myth' asserts that the multinational corporations and their trade associations were always fighting for the true interests of Libya. The corporates, especially the famous American oil companies that built Libya's infrastructure in the 1960s,[7] still maintain that they are Libya's only true friends. They alone claim to understand Libya's true importance to the global economy, which has been frequently overlooked by Western governments—that erroneously treat policy areas like counterterrorism or migration in isolation. If major governments would only listen to the wisdom and concerns of big business, the West could finally get Libya policy right.

3. The 'statelessness myth' maintains that Libya's problem under Qadhafi was that it lacked institutions and that everything was decided at the whim of Qadhafi personally.[8] Therefore, after Qadhafi's fall, Libyans would naturally reap all the advantages of truly starting from scratch and building from the ground up. Its unique 'statelessness' meant that Libya had a better chance of success than its Arab Spring neighbours who would have to destroy the corrupt institutions that they inherited from their former regimes prior to rebuilding them.[9]

4. The 'don't throw the baby out with the bathwater myth' contends that in the wake of Qadhafi's ouster, Western policymakers' primary goal vis-à-vis the Libyan economy should have been to protect Libya's oil, banking, and 'economic' institutions from the vagaries of post-Qadhafian political oversight and meddling, because those institutions alone were neutral, technocratic, and capable of safeguarding Libya's wealth. According to this myth, only the 'semi-sovereign institutions'[10] were capable of preserving Libya's wealth from

the turmoil around them, and hence reform of Libya's fundamental economic structures could only happen once a stable, legitimate, and sovereign authority had taken over with an unquestioned mandate to reform the economy. Proponents of this myth frequently make pronouncements in international meetings like 'you can't undertake economic reform, while there is a war going on'. As a natural contrarian aggrieved by such utterances, I have taken to punctuating my briefings with remarks like, 'you can't convene peace making conferences or try to hold elections, while there are dysfunctional economic incentives at work'.[11]

5. The 'war economy is a symptom' myth asserts that the Wars for Post-Qadhafi Succession were about politics, regionalism, Islamism, outside intervention, and bad leadership. Although control of the oil money was the prize for the winner, the structural features of the economy were not the primary driver of conflict. The war economy, corruption, and smuggling were symptoms of the conflict, not its root cause. Consider that Yemen also had a virulent civil war, but no treasure chest for the winners to conquer. According to this myth, Libya's civil war is just like all other Arab civil wars and is not fundamentally about the economy.[12]

In my experience of trying to brief policymakers, convince newspaper editors to run a story, or help businesses make money in Libya, these five myths tacitly undergird most private sector, academic, media, NGO, and governmental engagement towards Libya. Sadly, they are each misguided and only serve to perpetuate the status quo. Only in recent years, due to the upsetting experiences I describe in the next chapter, did I come to grasp how these myths are self-serving for certain incumbent players to propagate.

These myths can be grouped into two categories: the 'neoliberal' myths and the 'Libyan exceptionalism' myths. The neo-liberal 'globalization' and 'greed is good' myths deal with how global capitalism and multinational corporations relate to, and in turn shape, Libya. This chapter and the next will seek to debunk these myths by relating information gleaned from my personal experiences advising and interacting with the giant American companies operating in Libya. Then, in the extended opening gloss to the next chapter, I will include a series of anecdotes of my experience working in the trenches trying to promote US business interests in Libya and learning that—counterintuitively—certain global companies do not necessarily prefer to increase business opportunities, transparency, or free trade with the markets in which they are already embedded. Privileged access through established backdoor channels to key decision makers is the coin of the realm in the era of the Enduring Disorder.

Then there are the three 'Libyan exceptionalism' myths that claim to describe the internal workings of the Libyan state and its economic structures either by brushing aside Libya's true exceptionalism or by misunderstanding it. The excerpt below starts by attacking the 'statelessness myth'. The chapter's closing gloss debunks the 'don't throw the baby out with the bathwater' and the 'war economy is a symptom' myths by exploring how the unique structural features of the Libyan economy were constructed by Qadhafi to dole out patronage domestically. They also obfuscated accountability and took advantage of the lack of enforcement mechanisms to punish those who undermine global financial 'best practices'. A meaningful by-product of these institutions is how they have entrapped foreign companies to act as willing accomplices to the Qadhafian state's objectives and structures. Understood in this way, Qadhafian structures were not 'inefficient' when judged against their actual goals. They were not created to produce profit and avoid loss. They were constructed to maintain political control, avoid scrutiny, facilitate the flow of corrupt money into the international financial system, and convert their counterparties into advocates for the status quo—tasks in which they performed admirably. These perverse structures were bequeathed en masse to the post-Qadhafian state without meaningful reform.

The holding companies among Libya's semi-sovereign institutions are both fantastically wealthy and yet owe hundreds of billions to international firms from around the globe. They cleverly weaponized John Maynard Keynes' understanding of the double edged nature of debt, 'If you owe your bank a hundred pounds, you have a problem. But if you owe a million, it has'. In fact, the semi-sovereign holding companies are in so much debt to every major bank and construction company globally, that piecemeal reform is essentially impossible. Only global collective action to adjudicate competing claimants could ever succeed, yet the Enduring Disorder inhibits that form of coherent collective action from getting started. As a result, Libya remains trapped with its Qadhafian legacy institutions and the ensuing proxy conflict, because major corporations, governments, and international institutions lack the coordination mechanisms to work with pioneering Libyan reformers to devise and implement something better.

* * *

Selections from: Jason Pack, 'It's the Economy Stupid: How Libya's Civil War Is Rooted in Its Economic Structures', *IAI*, 19, 17 September 2019.[13]

1. Libya has institutions—they are just the wrong ones

The historical literature on Libya asserts that from the late Ottoman period onward it has been the paradigmatic 'stateless state'. Few historians of Libya are immune from this rhetoric: Lisa Anderson, Dirk Vandewalle,

John Wright, and my earlier writings all expound the unique reasons for Libya's twentieth-century stateless-ness.[14] And yet this scholarly axiom (Libya's stateless-ness) is only partially true and misses the real reason for Libya's uniqueness. Yes, the extent of Ottoman control of Libyan territory was quite limited, and the *tanzimat*, the Ottoman economic and constitutional reform pro-gramme that began in 1839, reached the country only in the late nineteenth century and was unevenly enforced.[15] Yes, Italian colonialism differed from its French and British cousins by tending to destroy Ottoman and tribal institutions, while avoiding building non-settler institu-tions.[16] However, despite these and more modern efforts to prevent state-building or undermine existing institu-tions, some institutions, notably those built from the 1950s–1980s and relating to the economy, have survived and even thrived in Libya. Before examining why that is, we must look at how Libya has frequently been a grave-yard for political, governance, and military institutions—leading to the myth that its proverbial statelessness and institutional void extends to the economy as well.

1.1 Deliberately partisan, but directly powerful political institutions

The statelessness argument for Libyan history ignores that the British Military Administration (1942–1951), the Sanussi monarchy (1951–1969) and the Qadhafi regime (1969–2011) all built a plethora of institutions in Libya.[17] The institutions which survive are those whose partisanship and power was the most indirect. Those were usually the economic institutions whose means of delivering patronage was circuitous, whereas Libyan political and military institutions have tended to be overtly partisan. The purpose of the most powerful of these institutions, like King Idriss al-Sanussi's Cyrenaican Defence Force (his Praetorian Guard of eastern tribesmen founded in 1945 and deriving from the elite units that fought with the British against the Italians during the Second World War) or Qadhafi's Popular and Social Leadership Committee (his council of loyal tribal elders founded in the wake of an attempted coup attempt by Warfalla tribesmen in 1991) was to strengthen a social segment that already favoured the existing ruler.[18] Those overtly partisan governance institutions have long since faded away, overturned by waves of retaliatory violence by those who they disadvantaged.

1.2 Semi-independent versus independent economic institutions

Yet, the economic institutions that were established with essentially the same aims in mind (strengthening/rewarding a social grouping loyal to the ruler or appeasing/buying off the populace) have not disappeared the way their political counterparts have. This is because like Qadhafi's Jamahiriyya, the sham direct democracy system brought into being from 1973–1979,[19] the innerworkings of Libya's economic institutions were deliberately masked by the dominance of informal structures of authority over formal structures—a paradox which epitomised Qadhafi-era Libya's uniqueness.[20] Because of this dominance of informal types of power (i.e. personal, tribal and geographic connections to Qadhafi's inner circle) rather than the formal power relationships of governance (as rooted in the official structures of the Great Socialist People's Libyan Arab Jamahiriyya), the partisan and corrupt functions of Libya's economic institutions were masked by layers of inscrutability.

To help create the complexity and opacity on which Qadhafi's Libya thrived, myriad committees, agencies, holding companies, public monopolies, and boards were established. These institutions took a few different forms: utilities like General Electricity Company of Libya (GECOL) and the Libyan Iron and Steel Company (LISCO); development/infrastructure funds like the Economic and Social Development Fund (ESDF), the Organization for Development of Administrative Centres (ODAC),[21] or the Housing and Infrastructure Board (HIB); free zones and special ports like the Misrata Free Zone; and many other categories. Each institution recruited from specific communities and favoured the needs of specific geographic areas or preferred businessmen.

In theory, Libya's alphabet soup of semi-independent economic bodies were accountable to the General People's Congress (GPC), the supposed font of all official authority in Qadhafi's Libya. In practice, the GPC held no power at all and was simply a rubber stamp for Qadhafi and his inner circle's whims. Qadhafi appointed cronies or key powerbrokers to run these semi-independent institutions, then funnelled them money, while rarely checking in on their outcomes.

Outside of the ambit of the GPC and Qadhafi's patronage networks, only two economic entities existed with a genuine degree of independence. They both traced their origins to the Sanussi monarchy period, when they were established in line with international best practices, as fully 'independent' institutions.[22] Before oil money flowed into Libya in the 1960s, power was quite diffuse, the surveillance capacities of the state quite limited, and genuinely independent institutions quite feasible.

The Central Bank of Libya (CBL) was formed in 1956. It derives from a UN institution, stood up during the decolonization process—the Libyan Currency

Committee, which was created as a technocratic commission with complete independence from political authority.[23] The National Oil Corporation (NOC) was founded in 1970, i.e. in the highly politicized early Qadhafi years. Yet it derives its institutional structure from the Libyan Petroleum Corporation established in the late Sanussi period, which sought to allow independent technocrats to remove the then-rampant corruption from the tendering and concessions processes and rationalize Libyan participation in international exploration and production consortia.[24]

1.3 Attempts to modernize Libya's economy only made things worse

Given their unique histories and institutional privileges, we can think of the CBL and NOC as the gold standard for independence of Libya's economic institutions. Slightly less independent is the Libyan Investment Authority (LIA), the country's sovereign wealth fund, which owns numerous other subsidiary investment vehicles. When it was established in 2006 at the behest of Western consultants affiliated with the Monitor Group, it was intended to mirror the CBL and NOC in its independence. However, as it was initially vested with over sixty billion dollars of Libya's oil winnings, its chairman Muhammad Layas was consistently pressured to work with allies of Qadhafi's son Saif al-Islam, such as Mustafa Zarti. Under their influence, the LIA lost prodigious amounts of money and engaged in spectacularly risky and corrupt investment schemes.[25] Despite their institutional protections, the 'big three'—CBL, NOC, and LIA—have frequently been subjected to political pressure and even to corruption scandals, but their fundamental laws and institutional design largely put them outside political control other than at the moment of the appointment of their heads.

These three 'independent' institutions have parallels in more normal economies, in which key functions like sovereign wealth management, oil production or setting interest rates are frequently detached from ministerial control to be run by formally non-partisan yet politically appointed technocrats. The distinction between the big three independents and the semi-independent economic entities is crucial to understanding the evolution of the Libyan economy.

The heads of the semi-independents could be changed at any moment and their institutional reporting relationships altered by new Libyan laws. When the semi-independent bodies like [ODAC], GECOL or the HIB were created, these behemoth economic institutions were given annual budgets of billions of dollars to be transferred to them by the CBL. They, in turn, doled out subsidized services (like free electricity) or highly inflated contracts for infrastructure projects. This system allowed key social segments to benefit from subsidized goods or preferential smuggling opportunities, while Libya's ruling class helped themselves to healthy doses of corruption carved out of inflated no-bid construction contracts. To facilitate this windfall of largess beyond the prying eyes of the Libyan citizenry, the semi-independents' relationships to Libya's ministries and between each other was deliberately obfuscated.

For example, ODAC and the HIB frequently built similar types of infrastructure such as housing, hospitals, schools and roads; they each contracted with foreign construction companies for mutually contradictory projects; blueprints were drawn, ground was broken, but no one technical authority oversaw a coherent masterplan of the Libyan economy.[26] Frequently, the actors themselves lacked an understanding of what their institutions possessed in terms of liabilities and competencies, nor did they keep track of the productiveness of the goods, services or infrastructure they produced.[27] They were simply given money, subsidized inputs and an expansive mandate to 'build stuff' or provide services. Yet, their actions were constrained by the ever-present threat of arrest or Qadhafi's sons demanding a piece of the action.

The logic of the semi-independent economic institutions was fundamentally that of a complex rentier system and not that of a market economy. Each town, tribe or ethnic group had preferential access to certain institutions, but not others.

Transparency was the enemy of the functioning of the Qadhafian economy. For example, according to Libyan law, GECOL has the right to seize crude produced by the NOC from the pipeline network, if that crude is deemed 'needed' to generate electricity, which is required by the Libyan people. Thus, one state economic institution can freely interfere in the operations of another with no thought to the impact this intervention may have on NOC operations, money flowing into the Libyan treasury, or ramifications on international consortia or lifting agreements.

When international experts were brought in from 2005–2010 with the task of helping to modernize the Libyan economy, privatize state holding companies and monopolies and attract foreign direct investment, they added onto the complex alphabet soup of agencies, another layer of 'reformist oversight institutions', most famously the Economic Development Board (EDB), the Privatization and Investment Board (PIB),[28] and the Public Projects Authority (PPA).[29] Unlike their predecessors from the 1980s and 1990s, these twenty-first-century reformist institutions were seen as sitting outside the formal Jamahiriyyan command structure (i.e. they were not answerable to the GPC). Rather they were made 'independent' like the big three and given the task of overseeing and directing expenditures of the pre-existing semi-independent economic institutions like the HIB or ODAC as well as trying to curtail the excesses of the monopoly utilities like GECOL and LISCO. As all businessmen, diplomats and experts who worked in Libya in the last years of the Qadhafi regime experienced, the constantly evolving and highly opaque power relationships between Libya's myriad agencies made implementing projects, collecting payment for services rendered, or even knowing who held authority over a given domain or project nearly impossible.

By 2010, the chain of command of Libya's economic institutions was so complex that Libyan policymakers hired outside academics and lawyers to examine, and then advise them, on the authorities, competencies and ideological justifications of various Libyan institutional bodies.[30] The rates of subsidies, public sector employ-ment and 'dead paper' (i.e. signed contractual obligations between Libyan semi-independent economic institu-tions and foreign companies entailing Libyan sovereign financial liabilities that would likely never be honoured) were shockingly high. By some accounts, on contracts signed before 2010 and pertaining to the next ten years, future Libyan financial obligations to foreign construc-tion, consulting, project management and oil field ser-vices companies would have been ten times greater than Libya's annual GNP.

Seen holistically, the late Qadhafian economy com-bined many of the worst features of both classic rentier petrostates (e.g. Qatar or Kuwait) and ideological author-itarian autarkic regimes (e.g. Turkmenistan or North Korea). On top of that, in Qadhafi's last years, Libya also incorporated the complex privatising and oversight mechanisms, which Western consultants set up in post-socialist economies (*à la* Ukraine and Russia). These were thought to 'simplify' complex institutional relationships bringing accountability and market forces to light. However, to the extent that they functioned at all in Libya, they actually allowed for the same outcomes that had transpired in Russia a decade before: crony privatization of state assets at fire sale prices, the rise of a new class of oligarchs, and further opacity and inefficiency introduced by the regulatory authorities. Hence, when the Great Socialist People's Libyan Arab Jamahiriyya collapsed under the weight of civil society protests, militia uprisings and NATO bombs in 2011, the economy that Qadhafi left to his successors resembled a Maurits Escher or Salvador Dalí painting: vast, hallucinogenic, bizarrely interconnected and recursive, and truly defying the capacities of the human mind to comprehend it.

2. Enter the Libyan revolutionaries

The self-appointed, leaderless revolutionaries who participated in the diverse anti-Qadhafi uprisings of 2011 were united behind only one goal: their desire to oust Qadhafi and his henchman, and discontinue their military and governance institutions. Conversely, most of them supported the existing economic institutions with the understanding that they were legitimate and served to support the social contract of providing goods and services free of charge to all Libyans. Qadhafi's obfuscations had worked. His opponents wanted an end to the rampant corruption of the semi-independent economic institutions, yet they failed to grasp his ruse—that the very structure of those institutions embedded inefficiency and corruption at the core of the Libyan economy.

2.1 Inheriting an economy without a blueprint

Most Libyans never interacted with abstract entities like ODAC and never took the economics courses that would have helped them understand the subversive implications of subsidies on petrol, electricity and bread. Among those very few militia leaders and rebel politicians who had the requisite training or had worked in the higher echelons of the Jamahiriyyan economy, there was no consensus on which economic institutions and subsidies needed to be eliminated. In fact, many of the political class of the 2011 Uprisings, most famously former interim Prime Minister Mahmoud Jibril, were associated with [*the 2005–10*] reformist attempts to preserve Jamahiriyyan economic institutions albeit in modified form [*presumably because these institutions benefitted entrenched elites and privileged technocrats with preferential access such as themselves*]. Others who ascended to positions of power in the wake of Qadhafi were connected to local and regional interests which were entrenched in the pre-existing forms of corrupt enrichment provided for by the subsidies and economic opacity of the semi-independent institutions.[31]

More naively, many felt that the economic reforms brought by outside consultants since 2005 had indirectly brought employment, opened up Libya to globalisation and created a sphere of advancement for the educated classes. Those economic reforms had coincided with increased foreign investment in Libya's oil sector. For many, the causation was unclear, and they felt that the reforms created a burgeoning middle class that had paradoxically led to the very revolution in which they were participating.[32] ...

2.2 After Qadhafi, the power of the semi-independents increased

This critical absence of a unifying ideology among Qadhafi's successors and disagreement about how resources should be divided have prevented the creation of a new social contract. Without such a joint vision connecting ruler and ruled, there has been nothing to anchor post-Qadhafi reform efforts—hence few reforms have been passed and even fewer implemented. As a result, the critical moments of 2013–2015 when global crude prices were high and oil was flowing were wasted. The inefficiencies of the Libyan economy could have been overhauled fairly painlessly then. Instead, money leaked out of the treasury due to increased subsidies, and much needed infrastructure was not built.[33]

During 2011, no consensus existed among either the fighters or the political leaders of the anti-Qadhafi uprisings as to the economic system that should be implemented when Qadhafi would be ousted. It should therefore come as no surprise that when Tripoli fell in August of that year and the TCD was issued earlier that same month, it did not directly address the issue of Libya's economic institutions. Similarly, the topic was not extensively discussed or legislated by post-Qadhafi Libya's first authority, the unelected National Transitional Council (NTC), or by its first elected body, the General National Congress (GNC). This behaviour was justified at the time by the fact that first the NTC, then the GNC and later the elected House of Representatives (HoR) and UN-appointed Government of National Accord (GNA) understood themselves as transitional governance authorities. None of these bodies truly possessed the attributes of unfettered sovereignty or domestic legitimacy rooted in a viable social contract.[34]

Amidst this vacuum of legitimacy, they wished to remain in the good graces of the populace who had shed blood allowing them to come into power. Therefore, the new authorities resorted to appeasement: putting militias on the government payroll, more than doubling state salaries, increasing subsidies on consumer goods and creating new semi-independent institutions, such as the Warriors Affairs Commission, to dispense billions of dollars in an attempt to purchase the loyalty of the most potentially disruptive segments of the population.[35]

As alluded to above, the problem of Libya's inefficient semi-independent institutions and their competencies, interconnectedness and myriad liabilities to foreign contractors was considered an issue that only a permanent government grounded with precise constitutional powers would have the necessary legitimacy to address. Hence, to many Libyans after the fall of Qadhafi, pre-existing economic institutions whose ostensible roles were to help the Libyan populace by producing electricity or building schools had a greater degree of legitimacy than the new political bodies, which were not overseen by a constitution and whose electoral legitimacy or governance mandate was frequently challenged.

The only main consensus that existed between ruler and ruled [*in the immediate wake of the 2011 Uprisings*] on the future post-Qadhafian economy was that the inherited vestiges of corrupt contracts should not be honoured. The [*new NTC*] authorities were well aware of the problems of corruption inside the semi-independents and the masses of dead paper they had issued. They did not wish to see the sovereign wealth they inherited from the Qadhafi period disappear into the pockets of former-Qadhafi allies abroad by having a full scale restarting of corrupt Qadhafi-era contracts. However, they didn't know which contracts were clean and which were dirty.

Hence, they issued a blanket freeze on implementation of construction contracts and seized upon one of the pre-existing oversight bodies, as the crucial vehicle to safeguard the country's wealth.[36] It was a Jamahiriyyan audit commission, whose formal name [*from the Qadhafi era*] was 'The People's Oversight [Committee]' (الرقابة الشعبية). Post-Qadhafi, it was renamed the Audit Bureau (ديوان المحاسبة). Thus rebranded, the Audit Bureau (AB) was progressively trotted out by post-Qadhafi politicians as the answer to corruption in Libya's semi-independent institutions.

The quintessential powers of the audit bureau since 2011 involve inspecting all public works contracts and approving those above a certain amount (traditionally 5 million Libyan dinars). These are essentially the same powers that the body had before 2011.[37] Tragically, these minor attempts to empower an independent oversight institution have not prevented an outflow of Libya's billions.[38] Furthermore, according to US and UK embassy staff present in Libya right after the revolution, no one central office has catalogued or recorded the grand sum total of Libya's contractual obligations or the destination of ongoing financial outflows. In fact, Libya's semi-independent economic, as well as economic oversight, institutions remain roughly identical in 2019 in terms of competencies and relationships—as when Qadhafi was still in power.

As a result of this structural stasis, the alphabet soup of Libya's economic institutions saw their degrees of sovereignty and independence, as well as their relative remove from oversight increase over the course of the post-Qadhafi period. In the Qadhafi era, the leaders of the semi-independent and independent institutions had to toe-the-line out of fear of imprisonment and murder. Now they are subject to very little oversight, as Libya's political class have neither the authority nor the competence to police their activities.

The primary reasons for this are twofold. First, in an environment where the heads of the economic institutions enjoy more legitimacy than elected and unelected politicians, the suitable government entities are unwilling to collaborate to remove them from office when their terms expire. Second, the militia leaders who dictate what elected and unelected politicians do benefit from the current economic system presided over by the semi-sovereigns. As such, the militia leaders [*continually*] pressure Libya's political class to not interfere in the opacities of Libya's economic institutions.

This [*chain of events was*] how these institutions acquired semi-sovereignty [*meaning, that throughout the post-Qadhafi period until the present day, these institutions have had no genuine domestic oversight and no effective way for government to monitor their actions or replace their leaderships*].

3. Sovereignty in post-Qadhafi Libya

The only tangible progress that the international community had made [*from 2014 to 2019*] in mediating Libya's ongoing post-2014 War for Post-Qadhafi Succession is the December 2015 Libyan Political Agreement signed in Skhirat, Morocco. It was constructed as a binding piece of international law, which, depending on one's viewpoint, has either been retroactively incorporated into Libyan law by constitutional amendment, a priori superseded Libyan law [*due to its being written into international law via UN Resolution 2259 endorsing it[39]*], or was never binding because it had not been properly ratified by the House of Representatives. [*As of April 2021, there is a related debate about whether or not the HoR's endorsing of the Government of National Unity (GNU) on 8 March 2021 caused the provisions of the Skhirat Agreement to be immediately superseded or if that only happened on 16 April when the UN Security Council adopted Resolution 2570 of 2021 welcoming the GNU as Libya's interim government and tasking it with overseeing elections. Another school of thought holds that it has yet to happen, that Skhirat is still in effect, and will only be abrogated if the Libyan constitution is amended to explicitly supersede it.*[40]] No matter one's perspective [*on these truly unanswerable legal complexities that Western diplomacy simply sidesteps and the relevant international legal authorities lack the coordination mechanisms to issue globally binding judgements*], all formal international community engagement in Libya [*from December 2016 until the final formation of the GNU in March 2021*] sought to build upon, amend, or transcend the Skhirat Agreement.

The major Western countries and the UN maintain[*ed during the period 2016–2020*] that the Libya Political Agreement builds upon the amended TCD of August 2011 determining where sovereignty and executive, legislative, and constitutional drafting authority lies in Libya. It is on the basis of the LPA that [*from 2016 to 2020*] all major international countries recognize[*d*] the GNA as the legitimate and 'nominally sovereign' government of Libya—even if they also work[*ed*] with the GNA's rivals. In short, even if it does not constrain their actions, legally the LPA [*was from 2016 to 2020*] the international community's 'last word' on Libya [*in that all other international conferences, UN resolutions, and peace-making efforts referenced it and sought to derive their legitimacy from it.*][41]

And surprisingly, a large number of the LPA's clauses, articles and annexes discuss the heads of the major economic institutions, seeking to enshrine their legitimacy and delineate what protocols should be used for replacing them. These texts comprehensively attribute sovereignty to Libya's economic institutions and their heads, yet fail to clarify the relationships among them and any future Libyan governments.

3.1 Semi-sovereign not sovereign

The Skhirat Agreement's Chapter 15 unequivocally grants 'sovereignty' to Libya's main economic institutions[42] [*but does not specify exactly which ones, presumably due to the extreme complexity of the Qadhafian economy— as this excerpt has detailed. The relevant, but highly cryptic passage reads, 'Libya's sovereign institutions play an essential role in upholding the long-term interests of the Libyan people. The Government of National Accord will safeguard the Central Bank of Libya, Libyan Investment Authority, National Oil Corporation, Libyan Post Telecommunications and Information Technology Company and other independent institutions, and will ensure that these institutions are permitted to fulfil their recognised role of safeguarding Libya's resources for the benefit of all Libyans.'*][43]
The intentions of the drafters of the Skhirat Agreement were presumably to safeguard the Libyan oil sector and the pot of treasure contained in the LIA and in the CBL against political machinations. However, they do not appear to have understood the unintended consequences of attributing them complete sovereignty as coequals with the government...
Looking back, it is clear that the semi-independent and independent economic institutions of the Qadhafi period have morphed [*during the chaotic 2014–20 period of Libya's bifurcation into two governments*] into far more powerful creatures as Libya's power vacuum increased.

The LPA was an attempt to codify that evolution... [*It remains to be seen if the GNU will consolidate its power in 2021 or if a successor government will ever emerge from elections with full constitutional legitimacy. In either case, it still remains unclear if the powers and semi-sovereignty acquired by these institutions can be fundamentally rolled back. My study of these institutions suggests that this will be harder than one might expect. History suggests it will only be possible to remove powers from these institutions if a consensus exists among all relevant political stakeholders. The institutions have heretofore successfully learned to expand the remit of their power whenever they are faced with political divisions among their political overseers.*]

4.1 What is known about the semi-sovereigns?

... All of Libya's major economic institutions are as deeply broken and counterproductive as they are entrenched. They employ many more people than needed, they block competition, they dole out resources according to a political—rather than an economic—logic. They sell utilities (such as electricity) at less than one-hundredth the price it costs to produce and yet only collect payment from half of commercial customers and less than one in a hundred residential consumers.[44] They subsidize petrol, making a litre at the pump in Libya the cheapest anywhere on earth [*some, like Raul Gallegos, have argued that it is cheaper in Venezuela, but this depends on whether you judge it at the official or black market rate of both currencies*]. As stated above, other than the NOC and CBL, whose lineal predecessors predate Qadhafi, those economic entities were designed either by Qadhafi as complex vehicles to buy off certain segments of the population and his loyalists or by international consultants who were trying to rationalize the excesses of the existing institutions. They were Soviet-style institutions never conceived to be efficient users of resources or be subject to genuine competition. Therefore, in Qadhafi's wake these institutions remain vessels of power, and pots of money, bereft of any coherent or systematic logic. That said, they do possess key competencies that are critical to safeguarding Libya's wealth, producing oil, investing funds, commissioning infrastructure, producing manufactures, facilitating business and putting Libya's wealth to use.

When the myths are debunked, an understanding of the Enduring Disorder remains

Since 1991, statist political systems have come tumbling down, yet their economic institutions were not necessarily uprooted.[45] And the historical record does not suggest that the abrupt introduction of multinational corporations after a regime change will necessarily push dysfunctional economic systems like Russia's or Libya's towards genuine reform or genuine free-market capitalism. Knowledge of the role of Deutsche Bank, McKinsey, and PwC in the Russian loans-for-shares scheme of the 1990s should have enabled policymakers to anticipate that a post-Qadhafi political power vacuum would lead to Libya's oligarchs taking over its semi-sovereign institutions, all the while being implicitly supported by foreign multinationals.[46]

The key connection between both episodes is that Western governments had unrealistic expectations for both the post-Soviet Russian and post-Qadhafian Libyan economies. They were also primarily focused on moulding the implications of political regime change rather than assuring that economic regime change transpired. Moreover, they neither coordinated their economic plans with the relevant Western private sector actors nor effectively regulated their actions. As a result, legacy financial interests in Libya and Russia 'learned' how to use private sector firms to undermine Western governments' reform programmes, while embedded Western corporates learned how to forge alliances with incumbent politicians that would protect established ways of doing business.[47]

Policymakers failed to unite the approaches and interests of divergent stakeholders, especially as the Libyan and Russian semi-sovereign economic institutions deliberately sought to create structural incentives to leverage corporations against their home states and their long-term potential profitability. Miraculously, they succeeded. Was this an aberration or is it more of a pattern throughout the world's emerging and post-statist markets?

My research indicates that this outcome is a key aspect of the Enduring Disorder—corrupt regimes creating opaque structures primarily for their own internal rentierism—but then these same structures are later inadvertently used 'to hack global capitalism'. They do this by enticing multinational corporates to work with foreign counterparts they know they shouldn't trust. The bait is usually sweetheart consulting, resource extraction, project management, or construction deals. Possibly, the CEOs abandoned their better judgment because the Libyans or Russians have leveraged those powerful decision-makers' preference for privileged access. Taken together, these phenomena may explain why progressively increasing globalization of capital, ideas, and knowledge paradoxically facilitated a world of decreasingly free markets. Or rather, that increasing globalization has caused Western countries with previously free markets to become 'penetrated' by the practices of post-statist institutions from other parts of the world.

To my sensibilities, there is also something quite amusing about this process. Dysfunctional post-Soviet and post-statist regimes that were not able to create domestic economic growth despite their enormous resource wealth, have nonetheless proven remarkably successful at performing sophisticated manipulations of the entire global capitalist system—outfoxing Western policy-makers, Western cyber defence systems, corporate CEOs, and international courts in the process.

The Organization for Development of Administrative Centres

Through my consultancy firm, as an expert witness, and as a trade association official, I have been involved in numerous due diligence projects, arbitrations, and investigations relating to The Organization for Development of Administrative Centres (ODAC). I was even engaged by a major international law firm to prepare to testify as an expert witness in Paris before an arbitral panel of the ICC in a case involving back payments owed by ODAC.

Despite the very seriousness of the billions of dollars ODAC has allegedly defrauded both the Libyan people and international construction companies, I can never say ODAC's full name without smirking. And the Arabic is even funnier (*Jihaz Tanmiyya wa-Tatweer al-Marakiz al-Idariyya*). Literally, ODAC is 'the entity' that grows, builds, develops, or incubates administrative complexes. I mean why on earth would Qadhafi have given it such a ridiculous name? Was it possibly to provide the punchline to the riddle: what would Stalin, Orwell, Qadhafi and Ayn Rand name the love child of their foursome?

Inside Libya, ODAC is widely referred to as *Jihaz al-Dubaiba* (the Entity of Dubaiba).[48] Ali Dubaiba came from humble beginnings to become one of the most powerful loyalists of Qadhafi. Along the way, he also transformed himself into a jet-setting billionaire with friends in powerful places. He was born in 1946 into an average middle-class family in Misrata. After completing high school, he became a geography teacher.[49] His ambitions, literacy, Nasserist Arab Nationalism,[50] combined with his social position outside the traditional elites of the monarchical period, perfectly positioned him to exploit the fluid revolutionary situation that prevailed immediately after Qadhafi seized power. Becoming mayor of Misrata in the early 1970s, Dubaiba was able to conduct asset seizures on behalf of the Qadhafi regime as different types of private property were abolished in the 1970s and 1980s. It remains unclear where all the seized assets went. What eyewitnesses' accounts clearly demonstrate is that it became increasingly difficult for anyone to stand up to him as he amassed a private empire in the pseudo-government sector by the mid-1980s.[51]

In 1989, as a reward for his services to the regime's ideological goals, Qadhafi created for Dubaiba his 'own' semi-independent economic institution.[52] ODAC's official remit was to unify the pre-existing public construction sector. In practice, ODAC's primary lasting accomplishments are the existence of a haphazard array of partially constructed airports, schools, office buildings, and meeting halls, many in the area around Sirte. Its actual *raison d'être* appears to have been to create discreet ways to finance Qadhafi's pet projects.[53]

With ODAC's creation, the old regime had perfected using enterprising individuals like Dubaiba as state enforcers in specific economic sectors. This is remarkably similar to what Putin would later do with his oligarchs. Loyalists were deployed to dominate specific sectors (or co-opted once they were there). And in both Russia and Libya, if these regime loyalists ever got out of hand or were caught lining their pockets a bit too much, a few weeks in jail plus some asset confiscation generally straightened them out.[54]

ODAC funds were used to purchase properties and invest in start-ups in Libya, as well as to create ODAC subsidiary companies in a number of countries including England, Scotland,[55] the

Channel Islands, Switzerland, UAE, Panama, the Caribbean, and Egypt.[56] Parallel to those official companies, accounts have been set up in the names of Dubaiba's relatives across the globe. Qadhafi attempted to tackle ODAC even before the revolution, but even he was unable to ascertain exactly what was going on and where the money had gone.

After 2006, Qadhafi sensed that ODAC's excesses were becoming an embarrassment. He also concluded that more foreign direct investment in the infrastructure sector was needed and could only be achieved by cleaning up the semi-independent public construction sector, such that Western firms seeking to work in it would not be in violation of the American Foreign Corrupt Practices Act and UK Bribery Act. Hence, as discussed in the excerpt, Qadhafi brought ODAC and the (less notorious) Housing and Infrastructure Board (HIB) under the authority of a new umbrella organization, the Public Projects Authority (PPA)—a new type of semi-independent entity, lacking true auditing powers, yet tasked with overseeing other semi-independents.[57]

Even despite his patron being deposed, Dubaiba never fell from his perch. As soon as the 2011 anti-Qadhafi Uprisings began, Dubaiba switched sides and began funding Islamist-aligned militias. In post-Qadhafi Libya, he initially had many arrest warrants issued against him.

But then he managed to get himself off the Interpol listing and set himself up as something akin to a neighbourhood oligarch in Misrata.[58] He was mentioned extensively in the Panama Papers,[59] but international states have never made getting this money back to the Libyan state a diplomatic priority—possibly because he had powerful friends in Britain, Canada, Malta, and the EU institutions.[60] Although the most likely explanation for his remaining at large is the coordination challenges faced by law enforcement bodies, it is also quite possible that certain powerful firms and individuals in the West would prefer if Dubaiba was never brought to trial. Seen from a global perspective, ODAC's creation, its so-called subordination to the PPA, and the role of Ali Dubaiba, all constitute an indicative microcosm showcasing how 'state capitalism' in Russia, China, Ukraine, or Libya is neither run by the state nor really capitalism.

The Dubaibas go to Tripoli

I actually wrote the initial draft of this chapter in the spring of 2020, when few non-Libyans regarded the Dubaiba clan as central to understanding Libya's relationship with the West or global financial markets. Since then, the dynamic of powerful people apparently seeking to protect the Dubaiba family has been reinforced after the selection in November 2020 of Ali's first cousin and brother-in-law[61] Abdul Hamid Dabaiba[62] as a dark-horse candidate, eligible for inclusion on a regional list, in the Libyan Political Dialogue Forum (LPDF) process.

The LPDF was a UN-organized body meant to reform the Presidency Council, which would then have a new prime minister, who would in turn form a new government to break Libya's institutional stalemate. Most commentators, myself included, thought that the LPDF process was a pipe dream—unlikely to produce a reformed Presidential Council and even less likely to culminate in a new government. Furthermore, it would be nearly impossible for any resultant government to gain the approval of the HoR and succeed in receiving a handoff of authority from both Serraj's Tripoli-based GNA and the eastern-based parallel interim government of al-Thinni.

Miraculously, Abdul Hamid became Libya's prime minister designate in January 2021 on the second ballot,[63] after his list had initially received fewer votes than the presumptive frontrunners' list containing Fathi Bashaagha and Aqilah Saleh. Within two months, Dabaiba proposed a cabinet list, got it approved by the HoR, and formed his government, which then took over the ministries of both the GNA and parallel eastern interim government. During this process, existing corruption and bribery allegations surrounding Abdul Hamid Dabaiba's candidacy, as well as the long-standing legal cases against Ali Dubaiba, have gone silent. A UN investigation into allegations of bribery dragged on for months with no conclusive statements.[64]

In 2020, the Libyan political commentator Muhammed al-Jarh alleged that a member of Ali Dubaiba's family and his assistant, both of whom were accompanying Dubaiba in his role as an LPDF delegate to the Four Seasons hotel in Tunis, offered other delegates inducements in exchange for their votes for Dabaiba to be a candidate on one of the executive lists.[65] The findings of the UN Panel of Experts report expressly looking into these allegations was finally published on 16 March 2021. The report referenced further concrete details beyond the initial hearsay reported by al-Jarh and others but had nonetheless chosen to hold back the findings in a confidential annex available only to certain UN officials. The public now knows that these details exist but not whether they conclusively implicate or definitively exonerate the Dubaiba family.[66]

Abdul Hamid's rapid ascendancy from relative obscurity to prime minister and Ali Dubaiba's initial path to business success give us certain insights into the longevity of the power concentrated in semi-sovereign institutional networks. This power has allowed the Dubaibas to remain in the shadows even as their opponents accuse them of operating multiple private militias. Moreover, few if any of Ali's financial actions were formally undertaken using his name—they were all under that of ODAC or his relatives—hence he has the power to discretely influence the Libyan (and especially Misratan) political and military environment to favour his allies, such as his cousin and brother-in-law.

Dubaiba's story is important because it is representative of the state of play economically during the Enduring Disorder. Fewer than fifty men—and yes, they were all men—had the privilege of heading powerful semi-sovereign entities during the Qadhafi regime, and they mostly used the institutions to amass money and power for their families, tribes, towns, and supporters. Now, post-Qadhafi, these networks of influence remain. As a result, the various oligarchs from the Qadhafi period have been active on all sides of the civil wars of post-Qadhafi succession.[67]

Regimes are temporary but the semi-sovereigns' power is forever

This dovetails with developments in other post-Soviet and statist economies. As corrupt statist oligarchic systems break down, history has shown that their economic structures will not be comprehensively replaced. This tends to leave the most powerful individuals as those with insider access to semi-sovereign economic institutions rather than those with the greatest entrepreneurial abilities.[68] In Libya, Russia, Egypt, and Ukraine during the Enduring Disorder, semi-sovereign institutions are where much real power has been vested—no matter how many changes of regime appear to take place. In Ukraine, in particular, post-Soviet semi-sovereign institutions[69] dictate the nature of political competition, as the lucrative opportunities for illicit enrichment they generate can be monopolized by the family members and loyalists of the current ruler—just as access to semi-sovereigns can in Libya. This trend was particularly pronounced during the tenure of Viktor Yanukovych.[70]

The types of illicit gains and the economic structures involved in Ukraine are eerily similar to those in Libya. Natural gas, for example, arrives in Ukraine from Russia and is sold internally and externally at non-market prices, just like refined petroleum products are in Libya. Ukraine traditionally overpays for its gas.[71]

And Russia uses those profits to support its favoured politicians in Ukraine in order to sustain the system.[72] Separately, subsidized gas is then illegally sold or smuggled at a price closer to the higher global market price (this step is done by the militias in Libya). Ukraine spends roughly 7.5 per cent of its budget on energy subsidies, and various preferred entities are able to use their preferential access to subsidized products to make staggering amounts of money.[73] If Libya was not a crude producer and had to purchase all its crude for domestic refining and import all the extra refined product needed for domestic usage while also then subsidizing it, such subsidies would account for 7 to 10 per cent of the typical Libyan budget. In both cases, a large part of these inefficient government subsidies simply goes into the hands of oligarchs, criminal gangs, and militias.

Another source of Ukrainian corruption comes from procurement fraud, whereby semi-sovereign entities issue non-transparent tenders for projects like airports, roads, and stadiums. They are then awarded to overpriced bids that have been placed by incumbent powerholders and oligarchs who use shell companies to pocket the difference between the services rendered and the fees charged. This is not wholly dissimilar to how ODAC procurement corruption operates.[74]

One result of the kinds of economic structures Libya and Ukraine possess is a fierce and sometimes violent competition among elites to maintain their control of the money-generating semi-sovereign institutions. The other is protracted low-level wars fuelled by cycles of hot money emanating from the semi-sovereigns. These conflicts also engender tacit alliances of status quo players from both sides who benefit from the conflicts' continuation as they impede fundamental economic reforms.[75] Another result is that institutional elites from former regimes are difficult to fully depose and usually retain the ability to make a comeback due to their embedded networks at the unelected semi-sovereigns.

Even Ukrainian President Volodymyr Zelensky, who ran for election in 2019 on an anti-corruption and anti-oligarch ticket, has been unable to quash accusations of being beholden to Ihor Kolomoisky, one of Ukraine's most powerful billionaires. Kolomoisky's wealth derives from his oil and media empire and his role in co-founding one of Ukraine's first private commercial banks, ingeniously named PrivatBank. He is currently under investigation in the United States for embezzlement and fraud of funds from Ukraine's para-statal institutions by PrivatBank. US courts are able to have jurisdiction due to Kolomoisky's surprising decision to acquire commercial real estate in Cleveland, Ohio of all places.[76]

The Ukrainian story is therefore not so dissimilar from events in Libya, where after ten years of chaos without a firmly established political sovereign, the first non-military personality to properly wield patronage networks to create genuine governance happens to be Abdul Hamid Dabaiba. He is also the first post-Qadhafi prime minister to have inherited the legacy networks of one of the Qadhafi regime's most powerful institutions, ODAC.[77]

This process is also similar to how the Egyptian Army and connected security apparatuses were briefly deposed from power but then returned with a vengeance. The Army has been the real power behind the throne since Gamal Abdul Nasser's death.[78] Its control over the Egyptian economy had become so vast that it came to function like a semi-sovereign institution.[79] Its decision to switch its support to the protesters in the early days of February 2011 brought about President Mubarak's downfall. A year later, the Army was briefly dislodged from power when its preferred candidate lost the June 2012 elections and Mohamed Morsi, the Muslim Brotherhood-aligned candidate, won the popular vote.[80] However, after less than thirteen months, Morsi was deposed in what amounted to a bloodless coup. He had proven unable to progress on his political agenda due to an inability to control the Army's power centres in the economy and ministries. Now, nearly eight years later, it is widely accepted that the 'new' Egyptian regime under Sisi is not so different from the old regime under Mubarak, as it derives its power base from the most powerful institutional networks of the old regime—the Army and the intelligence services. In the words of Egyptian political commentator and activist Sawsan Ghareeb: 'Al-Sisi's power base is the deep state. Both are simply an extension of Mubarak's regime. Sisi's regime derived its strength and survival from the deep state and the Mubarak network [otherwise Sisi would not have been able to retain power and Egypt would be ungovernable].'[81]

It is not impossible to imagine that moving forward, Abdul Hamid Dabaiba, his anointed successors, connected business tycoons, or rehabilitated old regime figures will be able to harness the power networks emanating from Libya's semi-sovereign institutions and use them to forge a genuinely functional Libyan regime. In so doing, they would conclusively prove that, in Libya, he who can make the semi-sovereign institutions do his bidding, possesses the levers to control its otherwise ungovernable complexity.

Tangential benefits

It would be incorrect to say that Qadhafi ingeniously created ODAC and its sister organizations to 'hack global capitalism' or to create an institutional powerhouse that would keep his allies in control of Libya after his demise. He created it and similar entities to help him govern Libya as well as to enrich his cronies and pilfer Libyan state coffers. Yet to achieve those aims, these organizations needed to employ special legal structures and have corporate veils constructed around them. It just so happened that once these structures were in place, they provided the tangential benefit of being ideal vehicles to pervert the tendering, invoicing, and legal conventions on which inter-state commerce rests.

Similarly, post-Soviet Russia's most powerful leader, Vladimir Putin, emerged from one of the Soviet Union's most powerful institutions: its intelligence services. Yet the Soviets did not cre-ate their intelligence services to hack Western elections or manipulate news coverage. Both the Soviets and Qadhafi created their signature semi-sovereign institutions to help them stay in power. Although they failed to achieve that function, their truly unique capabilities came to light later.

This is just like with drug development. Frequently, a new mol-ecule is initially identified as a promising therapy for a given condi-tion, but then fails in the clinical trial to show sufficient results. Yet having been created, catalogued, and stored, its truly 'killer app' is discovered at a later moment by another research team.

Why has global capitalism been so susceptible?

It is gradually becoming apparent that the West's centuries-old democratic institutions are less robust than had once been assumed. The same is true with our supposedly free markets. Markets rely on trust. No law and enforcement system can ever detect all the malevolent actors at play in the market, especially if certain legal structures like subsidies reward those who game the system.

To the extent that they ever functioned properly, free markets and open democratic electoral systems were always incredibly fragile as they rest upon various contradictions remaining sub-merged, most participants agreeing to play by the rules of the game, and most malcontents being unable to cause a raucous. Slightly more animosity, slightly less trust, and slightly more fake news always had the potential to tip the scales towards total system meltdown.[82] Given the inherent fragility of democratic socio-political harmony, it is not surprising that neo-populist contagion emerging naturally and introduced by social media from Russia was able to exacerbate previously submerged cultural conflicts in Western political institutions.

Equally important to the political story is the economic one. Authoritarian and post-socialist economies inadvertently devised genius vehicles for injecting similarly damaging contagion into global capitalism. In the case of Libya, this was done by the seemingly simple ploy of issuing lucrative contracts through vehicles that appear to be Libyan state entities but then cannot be proven in international courts to constitute parts of the Libyan state. This allows those entities to be able to break contracts with limited international legal liability.

In the case of China, this is still done by using continued market access as a bribe to silence political criticism and clamp down on free speech (e.g. by threatening to ban the NBA, specific movies, or whole companies unless they stop making comments about Hong Kong protestors or the Uighurs). Another ploy the Chinese use involves listing their parastatal companies on Western stock exchanges as 'genuine private enterprises' with very attractive (albeit often fraudulent) financial statements. This works to attract Western retail investment capital. Later, the firms claim artificial losses, hence pilfering the foreign investors' money while preventing any lawsuits. To keep this scheme alive and well, Chinese politicians use political leverage to protect their nation's accounting standards from being challenged by Western lawmakers and Chinese law punishes Chinese citizens with one year of manual labour for doing standard investigative due diligence on behalf of foreign entities.[83]

In the case of Russia, Venezuela, or mineral-rich sub-Saharan African countries, contagion is injected into global markets via entrapment into long-horizon deals in the extractive industries that require major foreign capital investment up front.[84] Investments or mining rights can later be confiscated at any time—the threat of which can be used to demand certain favours. Furthermore, the investment will only ever pay off if the companies help maintain the specific ruler or regime in power with whom they signed the contract.[85]

Traditionally, these stratagems have been explained as attempts to use global market capitalism to undermine the spread of Western forms of human rights and democratic accountability.[86] I'd like to analyse them instead as sophisticated ways of using the structures of multinational corporations and the psychology of their leaderships against the very institution of global free markets. Such efforts tend to be particularly effective when the Western multinationals dealing with these stratagems care more about maintaining individual or corporate incumbency than free markets or shareholder returns.

But why now?

This phenomenon of using capitalism against itself has only come to prominence relatively recently, partly because the communist and statist economies engaged in far less trade with the capitalist states than the post-communist and post-statist regimes currently do now. Until the 1990s, there were also far more hurdles to the global mobility of capital. From the eighteenth to the twentieth centuries, the vast majority of global wealth was held in the West and the majority of world trade was within Western-held possessions (including imperial territories). Since the end of the twentieth century, a majority of trade flows are now between the West and non-Western economies or within the non-Western bloc.[87]

Therefore since 1991, China, Russia, Ukraine, Algeria, Nigeria, and Libya have become increasingly important markets for multinational companies. My contention is that the specialized economic institutions in these (some former, some currently) statist economies have figured out a way of 'hacking globalization' and turning companies against the ideals of the free market and into vehicles that prefer privileged access.

The Miss Manners' Guide to Excruciatingly Correct Kleptocracy

To flesh out this argument in reference to the case study being examined in this book, let's look a little more closely at how this plays out in Libya—knowing that the Libyans are arguably more sophisticated in this realm of corruption, while most other African countries' approaches are generally cruder. Operationally, Libya created the aforementioned semi-independent economic agencies to consolidate regime power while avoiding accountability and scrutiny. This chapter's excerpt explains that the alphabet soup entities like ODAC and HIB were core elements of the Libyan state. These core institutions were primarily used to funnel money to regime cronies and secondarily to pervert counterparties' incentives. This was especially the case when Libya came out from blanket UN sanctions after Qadhafi paid compensation for the Lockerbie bombings and Libya was allowed back into the international marketplace. They also had a key tertiary function in obscuring the transparency of money flows.

Even in totalitarian autocracies, the populace will likely find out if the ruler's inner circle all of a sudden have billions of dollars of state money simply transferred to their personal bank accounts and start driving Ferraris ostentatiously around the capital city.[88] Aware of the risks of discovery by the Libyan people, the Qadhafi regime relied on tact, positing the correct 'etiquette' for totalitarian kleptocracies to use in ripping off their own people. A preferred method is to create a semi-independent entity such as ODAC and have it own multiple subsidiary joint-stock companies with interlocking boards of trustees, some of which overpay international contractors for project management services, which in turn overpay for construction contracts structured with demand guarantees. This type of transaction provides a double win for those in power. First, there is usually a difficult to trace kickback or pay-to-play bribe at some stage; secondly, if the projects never get built due to regime change or war, there is no reason to ensure the contractors ever get paid because of the layers of deniability linking the state to the contracting. Another time-honoured method is to have subsidiary holding companies in turn own subsidiary companies that 'lose money' on bad investment choices while also owning various off-shore companies in Panama or the Cayman Islands that then pay outrageous amounts on professional legal or investment services to fight legal actions against the Western investment firms that 'lost the Libyans' money'—all the while collecting favours and kickbacks from both the Western investment banks that managed the 'lost money' and the lawyers who billed a few extra thousand hours for suing them.

Well, you get the gist of it. But those are actually crudely oversimplified examples. Understanding exactly how the infamous Palladyne, Goldman Sachs, or SocGen affairs[89] defrauded Libyan citizens of billions of dollars is not the kind of thing that one can explain in a doctoral dissertation, let alone in a paragraph. The cases required millions of dollars of expert due diligence investigations and thousands of pages of legal filings because the scandals are almost as complex as the global economy itself. Just as Libya possesses the Platonic archetype of the semi-sovereign institution, it is also home to world-beating geniuses at corruption schemes. As an example, I participated in a fairly academic investigation relating to the confiscation of a Libyan-owned maritime asset that allegedly involved corrupt EU parliamentarians, bribed European judges, Maltese holding companies,

Liberian, Guamanian (and for good measure), Israeli-flagged vessels, former Qadhafi-era intelligence operatives, and wholly owned subsidiaries of Libyan semi-sovereign institutions claiming that they have been ripped off by Eastern European mobsters.[90] And years after the events took place, with much ink spilled and many depositions delivered, competing theories of the case remain. Was it an opportunistic asset seizure to exploit a loophole in maritime mortgage law? A conspiracy to commit insurance fraud? A creative way to collect a Qadhafian back payment? Or possibly an elaborate collusion among multiple parties seeking to defraud the Libyan state that later went astray?[91] We may never be able to say for sure. Teams of expert academics, forensic investigators, and even close associates of the players have not yet been able to determine what actually transpired. The Libyans are simply pros.

When the amounts escalate from the tens of millions into the billions, the Libyans generate a mind-numbing degree of complexity and interlocking corporate structures, all without a traceable paper trail. The upshot of this behaviour is that essentially no legal system on earth can untangle the web to see justice done. This type of corruption exists because it finds the weakest linkages of global institutions and then simply exploits the loopholes. And without coherent international collective action to crack down on it and change how tax havens and money transfers operate, this type of behaviour is metastasizing and becoming more prevalent.[92]

In short, from an elite Libyan perspective there have always been proper ways that these things are done. Libyan apparatchiks view Congolese officials as simply having no manners when it comes to corruption. They simply embezzle money directly from state coffers, force foreigners to include their entities as joint venture partners, or chop off the hands of villagers to seize blood diamonds to sell abroad.[93] In Libya, such forms of 'blatant' corruption and overt coercion would be seen as uncouth and are usually confined to new entrants to the field of illicit enrichment. And due to their decades of experience, elite Libyans have produced the unwritten equivalent of the Miss Manners' Guide to Excruciatingly Correct Kleptocracy. Most crucially, they have formulated definitive and enlightening answers to such thorny 21st century etiquette questions as: how many British Virgin Islands shell companies should you register for a dictator's son's third birthday party?[94]

Legal workarounds

In the late 1980s, when ODAC was formed, Libya did not have ministries in sectors such as housing because Qadhafi had abolished them as part of his goal of 'bringing housing to all Libyans' while also supposedly abolishing both renting and government bureaucracy.[95] As a result, there was simply too much red tape and too little capacity to do a project properly through the ministries. ODAC subsequently became the vehicle not only for funnelling state funds to Qadhafi's cronies but also for delivering billions of dollars of genuine state projects: schools, hospitals, and football stadiums. If you could name it, ODAC could build it—or at least they could commission it via a subsidiary shell company outsourcing overpaid work to Western project management companies who outsourced overpaid work to Turkish contractors, who would likely never get paid for the partially completed concrete monstrosities they produced somewhere in the Libyan desert.[96] ODAC contracts could prove useful for the Libyan regime to build key infrastructure, but they were also useful for so much more.

The distribution of contracts was also a major tool of Qadhafi's international diplomacy. The ODAC model was replicated for the creation of other 'implementing agencies', or *ajhiza al-tanfidhi-*

yya—the phrase Libya's law uses to refer to these bodies and that Libya's lawyers usually use to refer to their clients when they are being sued for non-payment of allegedly sovereign debt. These agencies were the 'implementers' of the Libyan state's development drive in the post-sanctions, détente period (2003–10). It was the sheer scale of that development drive and desire to entrap international construction and consulting companies that necessitated the creation and further elaboration of these entities as legal personalities. This is because the circa $175 billion in signed and registered commitments (the verbally promised or unrecorded commitments are likely in the low trillions) issued by semi-independent entities from 2005 to 2010 that formed the Libya National Development Programme could not, as per Libyan law, be accounted for alongside the state's GDP of around $40 billion per annum.[97]

Hence the semi-independents became a legal workaround—killing two birds with one stone, while breaking global capitalism and eviscerating the rule of international law merely as added bonuses. Behind this process was a conscious effort on behalf of the Libyan state to insulate normal-sounding state institutions and ministries (like the Ministries of Health or Housing) from debt and consequently increasing the exposure to financial risks that the implementing agencies' contractors (i.e. the major multinationals) would face. This strategy benefitted the Libyan state in some more nuanced ways as well. Qadhafi would gain the benefit of having companies of nearly every major global nationality hoping that the Libyan state did not collapse so that they could implement their projects and get their money. This approach turned the Libyan state into an arch-incumbent that many major global companies became deeply invested in preserving. Conversely, if and when problems arose, the hope of the Libyan state was that it could hide behind the fiction of the semi-independents as separate legal personalities acting as private implementing agencies not connected to the state.

Paradoxically, in the world of the Enduring Disorder, which lacks robust international legal systems underpinned by coherent interstate coordination, referring to state bodies created by Libyan law and clearly vested with state sovereignty and state monies as 'separate non-state implementing agencies' has largely been effective in protecting the Libyan state from being responsible for their liabilities in international arbitral courts. Libya is party to various investor–state dispute resolution mechanisms contained in treaties like the Organization of Islamic Cooperation formerly the Organization of the Islamic Conference, which can apply to companies with headquarters in most Islamic countries or the Austria–Libya Bilateral Investment Treaty or BIT (which can be used for companies within any EU jurisdiction).[98] Yet despite many back payment cases going to arbitration under the wide auspices of these two treaties, the Libyan state's strategy has continued to work.[99]

The implementing agencies had already contracted for hundreds of billions of dollars of construction projects using money that they did not have. This entrapped global companies into contracts that were backloaded so that, come what may, the companies would be incentivized to lobby their governments to preserve the Qadhafi regime and not sanction specific Libyan state entities in order to get paid. If anything went wrong, the Libyan state would assert plausible deniability, claiming that ODAC or HIB owed the money and not the Libyan state and that ODAC as an allegedly non-state entity could not be covered by any international investor–state dispute resolution mechanisms. Genius, right? Shame they couldn't have applied such skills towards building a genuine private sector and unleashing Libya's latent human capital.

But why do the multinationals continue to play ball?

So why in the post-Qadhafi period do major multinationals defend ODAC, HIB, and the very structure of the Libyan state even if it owes them billions upon billions?[100] This paradox has to do with what I term the psychology of incumbents. Simply put, once you have your foot in the door and a contract signed with one entity, you don't want that entity to disappear.[101]

On numerous occasions, I have witnessed colleagues advise international construction businesses to take the haircut and simply walk away from their investments in Libya or at least threaten to do so, attempt to negotiate a settlement, and then in the absence of a resolution sue to get their back payments. Usually, the companies do not adopt that approach. If they are owed a lot of money, they usually go back into Libya and deliver part of the previously signed project or even sign new projects hoping that by proving how essential they are to the Libyan economy, they will finally collect on their original debts.

To my mind, those firms that have chased new work when concurrently owed tens or hundreds of millions have exhibited the Global Fortune 500 company equivalent of 'battered wife syndrome'.[102] They keep going back to the Libyans because their pre-existing ties bind them so irrevocably that they cannot imagine breaking free. In short, the sheer size of the unpaid contractual obligations means that those construction companies and the states that they sign them with, enter into a permanent alliance. Games like this were played in the late twentieth century, but the monetary amounts were paltry in comparison to the size of the contracts that began coming into being in the early twenty-first century as formerly statist economies like China, Russia, or Libya began signing mega-contracts with Western multinationals.

The Chinese and Russians usually plan to pay for what they have commissioned, but to hack capitalism in other ways. The Libyans are simply the undisputed heavyweight world champions of this type of back payment fraud. And because these games all started in the late 2000s and the payments have come due in the late 2010s and are massively overdue and under litigation in the early 2020s, the requisite international collaboration and legal structures no longer exist to fix the problem. Doing business in Libya post-Qadhafi reflects what happens when the global Enduring Disorder impedes the international economy and transnational legal system from functioning properly.

Libya is suffocating under the crushing weight of dead paper

The phenomenon of 'dead paper' (introduced in the excerpt and used to refer to all back payments as well as unfulfilled pre-existing contractual obligations) means that nearly every major construction company on earth is owed or has been promised money in exchange for future work by some Libyan semi-sovereign entity. The size of these debts is truly unknowable but clearly far greater than a decade's worth of Libya's budgetary surpluses, even if oil prices were robust. So, Libya can obviously never pay them all back. Yet they are also unable to default on all of them, because unlike Argentina (which defaulted and then renegotiated around a hundred billion dollars of debts)[103] the Libyans do not claim to have any sovereign debts. Unfortunately, rather than the sane solution of adopting a technocratic commission to adjudicate all the claimants' cases, the Libyan authorities mostly treat legitimate and illegitimate debts the same and ensure that all domestic Libyan legal precedents are calculated so that the Libyan state can never be construed as taking responsibility for the actions of the semi-sovereigns, even though all the semi-sovereigns were established by Libyan law and vested with funds and natural monopolies by the state.[104]

This absurd situation means that many global construction and project management firms that are not already entrapped in Libya now know to never enter the market. Libya is simply suffocating underneath all the weight of the dead paper. Even if ten billion dollars could magically be injected into the Libyan economy and technocratic administrators appointed to spend it, it would not necessarily be possible to sufficiently upgrade Libya's infrastructure. This is because many of the most reputable international construction or project management firms will not accept the work even if it is relatively lucrative—and other firms with existing projects will not build newly required installations unless their old contracts are attended to as part of a package deal.

Given this conundrum, I hold the controversial position that the best thing for Libya would be to learn from the Argentinian debacle and pay off all its legitimate back payments at a negotiated discount rate and in more complex cases (usually involving *force majeure* arising from fighting in 2011 and 2014) adopt a less formalistic mediation plus direct negotiation process, as opposed to oppositional arbitration.

I have tried to help firms litigate against the Libyan state and usually due to the sheer complexity of the semi-sovereign institutions' legal positions within Libyan and international law, the claimant law firms cannot proceed with their cases and may not even know how to effectively use expert witness information to help their clients. The unsatisfactory results of these court rulings have the perverse effect of driving companies that are owed money back into Libya: seeking to complete their projects or land new ones, hoping to work to earn the Libyans' good favour and eventually get some of their back payments addressed.

Imagine a situation where every court globally tended to side with abusive husbands. And due to some legal technicality, wives who sued for abuse and then lost were forced to forfeit all future chance of getting an alimony. That is roughly the perverse incentive structures at play in Libya at present. The Qadhafian and post-Qadhafian state institutions—as well as those of many of the post-Soviet states—have introduced a Trojan Horse into global capitalism, by using the technicalities of capitalism's legal systems against the proper functioning of free markets. The lack of international cooperation at the heart of the Enduring Disorder allows them to do it.

Clearly, there is no purely domestic solution to the question of Libya's dead paper issue, and due to ever present global collective action failures, it has never been addressed in any of the major international treaties and conference communiques issued by the international community about Libya. Most policymakers have seen the issue as both controversial and tangential to the conflict. In reality, it is central to the conflict and I fail to grasp what could be controversial about asking a country to honour its existing debts as a requirement for re-entering international life and reclaiming its international assets currently frozen by UN sanctions.

Due to this absence of international collective action, each country tries to help its firms get their monies back without ever mentioning the larger issue that there can never be a lasting peace or an effective reconstruction plan in Libya if the dead paper issue remains unresolved. And because it is widely known that there is not enough money to go around, sometimes countries actively tie various diplomatic outcomes to their firms' back payments being prioritized. In fact, back payments in the construction sector was one of the primary reasons that Turkey escalated the extent of its intervention in the War for Tripoli—saving the GNA from likely defeat in late 2019 and early 2020.[105] So John Maynard Keynes was spot on. When you owe a truly prodigious sum, it is the debtor who has all the leverage and the creditor who must do everything possible, including in this case inventing new forms of drone warfare, to save him.[106] The Enduring Disorder has many such hundred billion-dollar elephants hiding in the room and surreptitiously guiding policymakers' decisions.

The multinationals' role in post-conflict zones

Just as the Libyan economy's relation to global capitalism is shrouded in myths, so too is the role of corporate power on societies in transition.[107] Neither set of myths accounts for how the world works in practice. In the contemporary interconnected world, it turns out to be much more difficult for technocrats and statesmen to reform a country's deeply entrenched and thoroughly globalized economic system than it is for protestors or armed revolutionaries to overthrow that same nation's political system.

It also might be that foreign governments and corporations are willing to embrace political reform to remove recalcitrant dictators but less than eager to embrace genuine reforms of entrenched economic structures when the current structures either owe them money or appear to offer privileged access and 'someone competent to talk to'. I am not a Ukraine or Russia expert, but cursory study of those countries reveals that analogous false myths about the underlying state of their institutions were at play when the Soviet Union collapsed, as when Qadhafi was overthrown. The 'greed is good' and 'globalization' myths were deeply held by Western policymakers relating to how exposure to Western capitalism would change their post-authoritarian economies.[108]

The forms of dysfunction and crony privatizations that transpired in Ukraine and Russia were partially the results of coordination failures between Western governments and the multinationals.[109] The economic system during the Enduring Disorder is highly penetrable by certain kinds of disorder emanating from the periphery, especially if it speaks the language of neo-liberalism and can interface seamlessly with its institutions.

One underappreciated similarity between Libya and the post-Soviet countries is that many of the same personnel from the major management consulting and accounting firms (e.g. PwC, Booz-Allen, Mackenzie, and Monitor Group) helped with the implementation of the crony privatization of the semi-sovereigns.[110] Frequently, these privatization gurus wrote the same sorts of neo-liberal recommendations in both instances, knowing that the people in power would disregard the critical details and cherry pick certain neo-liberal concepts as cover for their crony enrichment schemes. More directly, personnel continuity among elite management consultants helps explain how the 2008–10 Libyan Economic and Social Development Fund scandal—which involved handing out to each Libyan adult nominally tradeable shares in supposedly privatized Libyan semi-sovereign entities— was so remarkably similar to the schemes of the Yeltsin period (referred to collectively as the 'loans for shares' scandal) in which supposedly privatized parastatal companies issued shares to the Russian people. In both instances, the shares were supposed to inculcate a spirit of entrepreneurialism among the people. Somehow, they ended up being purchased and consolidated at artificially low prices by a new class of oligarchs, who happened to be those connected by familial and social ties to the heads of the semi-sovereign institutions.

The psychology of incumbents

Mid-twenty-first-century capitalism (both in supposedly 'normal' Western societies and supposedly 'dysfunctional' post-conflict ones) seems to have rather different features than economics textbooks, Wall Street gurus, CNBC pundits, and our politicians might lead us to believe. Americans, in particular, seem prone to the myth of the rational, and purely profit-maximizing, corporate actor. The Libyan state never rationally maximized the amounts in its bank accounts, so why should corporations with shareholders necessarily act any differently? Aren't both the heads of semi-sovereign institutions and the heads of major multinational companies connected by a deep-seated fear of losing their positions? The entire politics of the Saudi monarchy has been described as a ceaseless quest for security,[111] while Libya's militias, semi-sovereign institutional heads, and senior politicians are dubbed the status-quo party,[112] so why should corporate power players, especially those in declining industries, not succumb to analogous reactionary ideation?

My personal experiences in Libya demonstrate that multinational companies frequently choose suboptimal decisions for their long-term profitability and create highly complex structures whose very opacity blocks even the potential for change—just as powerful and dysfunctional governments like the Libyans have done. Essentially, the former statist economies (most crucially China and the sub-Saharan African resource kleptocracies) have subtly encouraged the multinationals to mirror their structures as a precondition to getting their foot in the door.[113]

In fact, the psychology of incumbents is part of the way in which power corrupts and absolute power corrupts absolutely.[114] My research of the British and American imperial systems suggests that reigning incumbents (both geopolitically and commercially) prefer the status quo and cannot easily envision alternatives, and hence prefer fighting rear guard actions to preserve the status quo—no matter how dysfunctional—rather than preparing for the economy or politics of the future. For example, between the two World Wars, British viceroys and officials at the Indian Office could have prepared for a form of Indian independence that would have been favourable to their nation's economic interests and world standing. However, despite certain high-ranking officials privately acknowledging that independence was inevitable, they remained institutionally opposed to publicly acknowledging the concept until events were far beyond their control, at which point they were forced to accept a version of Indian independence that was deeply harmful to their global standing.[115]

In a way, we are all familiar with the phenomenon of incumbent power-holders preferring the status quo over embracing a new way of doing things. Consider how global energy companies exert themselves to fight against regulations meant to curb climate change. The companies' rear-guard actions are fundamentally counterproductive for those firms' long-term interests. If they chose instead to get ahead of the curve, at best, they might make billions in the renewable energy field, and at worst, the political backlash and punitive regulations against them would surely be mitigated. But decision-makers at those firms behave like powerful incumbents—they fear change and hold powerful myths that guide their actions. Moreover, decision-makers who suffer from 'incumbent psychology' appear primed for alliances with similar individuals and entities.

Possibly a new sub-field?

The field of corporate and political decision-maker psychology is underdeveloped, and it would be fascinating to see what further study in this area could turn up. Major research would be needed to diagnose the personal and psychological mechanisms through which entrenched power players in places like Ukraine, Libya, Turkey, and the UAE make common cause with leading firms and politicians in Western countries. After being united by 'the psychology of incumbents', it is quite easy for elites from other societies to use hot money and carefully crafted narratives to forge alliances with Western corporate and policy elites who share their fear of change and genuine transparency.

Americans have seen such alliances in action in the bedfellows kept by the likes of Rex Tillerson, Rudy Giuliani, Paul Manafort, and Roger Stone. It used to be that such alliances were limited to a few industry cartels. In the late twentieth-century world of free trade and mostly self-contained national conversations, the potential for cross-cutting alliances of reactionary incumbents was limited. Today, in a world where borders are re-emerging for goods and people, but narratives and cash flow faster than ever, this nascent natural alliance among global incumbents destabilizes democratic accountability and rational policymaking in the West.

From the imperial period onwards, Western elites have generally found ways to forge alliances with elites in other societies. What has changed of late is that in a globalized world, the sheer volume of money flows between the West and the rest of the world is at an all-time high. Additionally, as discussed in Chapter 3, social media's ability to cross borders is largely unregulated. Hence international political and corporate actors are able to forge alliances and narratives across borders like never before. With all these media and monetary flows, ideological and structural cross-pollination is an inevitable outcome.

Quantitatively, this change is particularly noticeable in the period from the 1980s to the 2020s. In 1986, the USSR's trade with the United States was less than two billion dollars a year, while in 2020, the smaller geographical entity of Russia's trade with the United States is over $28 billion even during an economic downturn.[116] The story is even more stark as pertains to the Emirates. In 1986, US–UAE trade was under $600 million annually, and in 2020 it was over $10 billion.[117] In short, US trade with Russia and the UAE has increased roughly thirty-fold in thirty-five years, while trade with the UK has increased roughly twofold over the same period. When it comes to investments, which are even more politically salient than trade, the Emiratis have increased their investments in the United States by over a thousand-fold in the same period.[118] Correspondingly in the 1980s, media narratives of Russian and Emirati origin in American politics were vanishingly small and had no significant implications. Today, even a small country like the UAE is a genuine player able to use incumbent linkages and privileged access, not only when it comes to investment, but also in influencing media coverage to swing both elections and specific policymaking decisions.[119]

LIBYA VERSUS THE GLOBAL ECONOMY

This is the main conceptual linkage between the global neo-liberal capitalist system and the conditions that eviscerate forward-looking leadership and promote the spiralling effects of the Enduring Disorder globally. Further study is clearly needed of the Libyan, Russian, and Ukrainian economic systems to uncover all the ways in which dysfunctional semi-sovereign institutions 'over there' intimately affect how capitalism and political fundraising plays out 'over here', in the hubs of the global networks—places like London, New York, Switzerland, and Washington. As our knowledge of how these complex networks operate increases, we may come to understand when, how, and why the prevailing modalities of global capitalism stopped promoting free trade and open markets and became driven by the psychology and decision matrix of incumbents, allowing them to make cross-cutting alliances to prevent change.

Global capitalism to the rescue?

Seemingly conspiratorial left-wing theories about prevailing forms of global capitalism stifling competition have always sat uneasily with me. Doesn't the globalization of markets favour insurgent actors and creative disrupters against incumbents? And how can a system built upon creative destruction enshrine incumbents?

According to this line of myth, global capitalism was never meant to be pretty. It virtually says on the tin that it will be the race of all against all, filled with creative destruction, and ruthless competition. Some firms, individuals, and occasionally whole countries will go bust whereas others will innovate and prosper. Most Anglo-Saxons are raised to believe that in a genuine capitalist system the best ideas, products, and organizational cultures get their fair chance to come out on top. Yes, such a system will likely be highly unequal at distributing wealth. Nonetheless, historically the Anglo-American view has been that it is preferable to correct those injustices on the back-end, after buyers and sellers have made their choices, rather than on the front end, through regulations that might stifle competition or inhibit innovation.

What if this traditional view is just another myth? What if neo-liberal capitalism as actually experienced today in many global industries and global markets during the Enduring Disorder is not really about free markets at all, but rather, due to the psychological profile of incumbents, is primarily about monopolists forging effective ways of shutting down further competition? According to this analysis, the alliances of Western corporate incumbents with the perverse structures of non-free market economic systems have gradually morphed into an incumbent-driven 'neo-mercantilism': a competition to secure preferential market access, monopolistic market domination, access to government regulators, and in the Libyan, Russian, Ukrainian, and many Sub-Saharan African cases, preferential access to heads of completely opaque semi-sovereign institutions.

As a classical Liberal, a New Yorker, and a fourth-generation entrepreneur, it has required a personal journey for me to accept that such practices were widespread and were the rule rather than the exception. The idea that major Fortune 500 companies behave as neo-mercantilist incumbents rather than as job-creating innovators feels like the explosion of a key aspect of the American dream. Yet this is actually an old and well-established idea with a fine intellectual lineage. In the 1930s, the famous Austrian economist Joseph Schumpeter argued that most companies and entrepreneurs seek monopolies rather than competition, and that Anglo-Saxon ideas of market competition arising spontaneously were always a myth.[120]

According to this line of thought, what has made global capitalism function fairly effectively from the end of the Second World War until the dawn of the twenty-first century was government regulation and an international order that kept the inherent anti-competitive practices, which arise naturally from incumbent psychology and the pursuit of monopolistic advantage, in check. Seen in this light, we can appreciate that since Reagan and Thatcher, global economies have been de-regulating at an astonishing, almost exponential, pace. In fact, it might have happened at such breakneck speed that almost all of us missed the exact moment that truly free market competition had ceased to be the norm, but rather an exception that now only prevails in certain quaint and specialized marketplaces.[121]

5

THE US–LIBYA (ANTI-)BUSINESS ASSOCIATION

The neo-liberal fairy tale of the Libyan unicorn

Looked at from the vantage point of 2008, Libya held the prospect of being a unicorn: a completely non-partisan space where Presidents Clinton and George W. Bush, the British, the Chinese, and most of the Libyan people all wanted the same outcome. My joke in those days was that Libya was the only country where Amnesty International, Greenpeace, ExxonMobil, Pepsi, Boeing, the Republicans, and the Democrats had the exact same policy goals: to get the oil flowing. At that time, it seemed to all players that the only way to get the oil flowing was to open up Libyan society to 'capitalism', the internet, globalization, and respect for human rights. Given the above, when the opportunity arose to transition out of my prior academic studies in the Syria and Israel/Palestine fields and move to Tripoli for consulting work, I did so eagerly, thinking I would be leaving contentious zero-sum partisanship behind.

Shaped by this naïve logic—and its exponents who were decades more experienced in Libya than myself[1]—my view was that doing incremental business in twenty-first-century Saudi

Arabia or Qatar was largely zero-sum, but Libya could constitute the very definition of a positive-sum environment. That Libyans are known for their inveterately zero-sum thinking about their domestic politics and economics seemed to me neither here nor there. I thought that it was the structural factors that mattered. I was still blissfully ignorant of the 'psychology of incumbents' and their cross-cutting alliances; I was still a virgin when it came to the semi-sovereign institutions and their Western allies; I had not yet heard of the Office of Development of Administrative Centres (ODAC); I believed that we lived in a world tending towards more order and that Western corporates would be key forces in bringing us that order.

My simplistic thinking went as follows: if the Saudis want to build a mega-hospital and 'firm a' from America wins the contract due to their preferential access to US or Saudi government decision-makers, 'firm b' from Belgium inherently loses the deal. The Saudis already have lots of hospitals, and their markets and institutions are about as transparent as they are likely to become given the rigidity of their political system. Furthermore, each year the Saudis only need to do a limited number of new mega-projects—so they dole them out as benefits to senior princes and trusted international allies. In this scenario, helping 'firm a' win the contract over 'firm b' is not a particularly noble thing to do unless you are a shareholder of 'firm a' or a nationalist from its country.

Yet in Libya, the calculus should be different: if Libya remains broken from a security or corruption perspective, then no hospitals can be built at all. Conversely, if foreign businesses work with the Libyan government to help build state capacity, reform the economic structures, and create jobs, then Libya will need—and can pay for—multiple mega-hospitals, roads, university buildings, and entertainment complexes. All the companies of every interested nation can each build one. Everybody wins.

According to this logic, if Libya ever became coherently governed and safe enough from a physical security and a payment security perspective to systematically upgrade its oil infrastructure, then truly all of the 10,000 kilometres of pipelines, the myriad tanker farms, and terminals would all need to be repaired.[2] Schlumberger, Halliburton, Bechtel, J&P, Sinopec, Orascom, and Sonatrach could all get a piece of the action.

The new technocratic Libyan authorities could even commission some serious innovations. It is worth remembering that the last time Libya was governed coherently, the Libyan oil law of 1955 created world-leading incentives for exploration while assuring a business-friendly, free-market environment. As a result, the Libyan oil industry ramped up from nothing to three million barrels a day in less than a decade—still the fastest virgin growth in a country's oil production in history.[3]

In fact, if Libya ever truly became 'open for business' and the world economy was not in a recession, the entire oil field services space globally might not have enough spare capacity to service Libyan requests for upgraded infrastructure. And in this scenario, the GDP and purchasing power of the Libyan citizen would expand considerably—generating a surge of demand for goods and services that would create more than a million jobs globally.[4] And as the icing on the cake, due to Libya's geography, geology, climate, and the need for a complete overhaul of the existing infrastructure, a greener energy industry could be created, harnessing the environmental advantages of sweet crude, solar power, and proximity to Europe.

It was this positive-sum aspect of business in Libya that had captivated my imagination from my very first trip to Tripoli in the late Qadhafi period: the tantalizing prospect of participating in a truly virtuous cycle. In this way, Libya seemed to me like the Wild West in the late nineteenth century. If it remained lawless, it would be a shady and dangerous place to do business—

with people ending up shot and villains making off with the cattle. But if a new sheriff came to town and law and order prevailed, the boom could last decades and there would truly be enough to go around. According to this logic, the key thing was to help Libyans reach a tipping point towards a virtuous cycle. I initially imagined that the Anglo-American private sector, and especially DC lobbyists, could be instrumental in that. I thought that their greed could be good for everyone, not in the Gordon Gecko style, but more like Adam Smith's invisible hand.

Back in 2008, my contrasting experiences in Syria and the Gulf had led me to believe that further exposure to global markets would tend to push a country towards order, not its opposite. However, that naïve train of thought misunderstands the role that the international system and global markets play on fragile political vacuums. I assumed further exposure to global markets inherently increases the flow of expertise and investment creating wealth into a country. Sadly, this is not always the case, especially in our current times. In fact, it was my professional experiences from 2017 to 2018, which I present below, which disavowed me of the notion that Libya could be a positive-sum unicorn.

Unicorns don't exist and it was just a neo-liberal fairy tale that opening up a formerly statist autocracy to global forces would inherently push it towards order and stability. Just as researchers have scrutinized the post-2001 claims of American statesmen to be spreading democratic values through their diplomacy, so too should we scrutinize American corporate actors' statements concerning their desires to increase trade, strengthen bilateral commercial ties, and export genuine market-based capitalism.

Witnessing from 2017–18 how American corporations behaved towards their investments in Libya conclusively demonstrated to me that the Enduring Disorder was afoot. This is actually quite similar to how former UN Special Envoy Ghassan Salamé extrapolated outwards from his experiences in trying to mediate the Libya conflict to the related observation that certain global actors' policies and the manifest lack of coordination among major allies were actively pushing the international system towards disorder.[5] Corresponding with me in April 2021, Salamé wrote: 'I truly think that the combination of unregulated neo-liberal policies and the concentration on anti-terrorism actions by major powers have helped in the emergence of highly corrupt political classes in post-conflict countries such as Lebanon, Iraq or Libya.' Salamé also remarked that this dangerous brew of forces is self-reinforcing: increasing disorder further inhibits the formulation of effective global initiatives to rein in the ever-expanding disorder.[6]

Looking back upon the personal episodes I will relate in this chapter, I now observe in them specific dynamics of the Enduring Disorder that I have sketched in earlier chapters—namely appeasement, focusing on terrorism rather than ungoverned space, the prevalence of media narratives favouring protectionism, populist nationalism, global collective action failures in efforts to reform broken economic institutions and incentive structures, 'incumbent psychology', and neo-mercantilist thinking.

Into the belly of the beast

Over the years, the DC lobbyists and government relations professionals of Fortune 500 companies have created preferential access channels to US policymakers, visiting foreign dignitaries, and the media influencers in the foreign policy space. These channels span personal relationships to diplomats and Congressional staffers, trade association events, sponsored think tank publications, and specialized government relations media firms. They are particularly influential when it comes to the opaque world of Middle Eastern policy and its emphasis on face-to-face social access to decision-makers.

Planning to head into that K Street jungle, I accepted that the power of the lobbyist to utilize preferential access could be used for good or ill. In my own reckoning, it was less than ideal when oil and defence companies were swaying policy in favour of the Saudi or Emirati royals—known for their inhumane treatment of dissidents and controversial acquisitions of billions of dollars of American armaments destined to flatten Yemeni hospitals and wedding halls. Conversely, I assumed that the power of the Fortune 500 lobbyist would be a positive good (even from a climate change perspective) if they were trying to make Libyan oil flow.

Libyan crude happens to be about the sweetest on earth and among the least energy intensive to extract, and it is also located extremely close to consuming countries. In short, extracting Libyan crude is far better from an environmental perspective than fracking in the Permian or Bakken basins, extracting from the Canadian shale sands, or refining and transporting heavy Venezuelan crude.[7] Making Libyan oil flow consistently requires investment, collaboration, skills transfer, increased security, job creation, and the opening up of the Libyan economy.

Going into my DC job as executive director of the US–Libya Business Association (USLBA), I thought I knew the strengths and weaknesses of the role played by lobbyists, trade associations, and big corporates. USLBA billed itself as the only trade association focused exclusively on the US–Libya business relationship[8]—the one place that Libyan grandees visiting Washington make sure to 'drop by', and incoming US government officials desired to be briefed on American commercial interests in Libya.

USLBA seemed outwardly to stress that American businesses had a positive-sum role to play not only in advocating for training programmes and creating jobs to get militiamen off the streets but also in bringing Libya to prominence as an international destination for investment and a strategic location for the

American government to play the role of neutral order builder. Moreover, USLBA messaging stressed that Libya had the money and the resources to pay for the best quality American products and services on the open market, if only the bureaucratic and institutional hurdles could be overcome and the correct person-to-person ties between Libyan officials and American companies[9] could be forged.

I believed that running a trade association should be like a type of informed matchmaking—connecting those with a need and those with a solution. And without connections to American or Western goods, wouldn't the Libyans be doomed to subsist on inferior Chinese, Russian, and Turkish products and services which would come with less knowledge transfer, less of a commitment to free markets, and less of a commitment to democracy? The logic seemed flawless. By pushing USLBA's agenda, I would be promoting a more ordered international system, even if the companies were simply motivated by greed. It had an irrefutable Adam Smithian logic to it. The global capitalist private sector would inherently help bring stability to Libya.

It never occurred to me that big American corporates were not necessarily making decisions based on long-term profit but on far more cynical calculations. It never occurred to me that we might be living in a world of Enduring Disorder.[10]

The Sage from West Virginia

My former boss from my first stint at USLBA in the late-Qadhafian period was a jovial, hardworking, quick-witted, and quirky man from West Virginia. I have always admired him and told others that he was the best boss I ever had. His ability to remember names and assess people's true character was a unique gift.

I had never wanted to work in Washington. I had ended up there by accident, but he made me love it. His mentorship had made the intricacies of DC begin to make sense for me. When I heard he had resigned from his executive directorship of USLBA in 2016, I was in northern Greece. I phoned him to touch base. Knowing how my mind worked, he warned me not to apply to be his successor. This advice was not a surprise. The board member companies were accusing him of being past his sell-by date; he was accusing them of being bureaucratic, dogmatic, and unable to see their own best interests. I assumed there might be bad blood between him and the board, and that, therefore, his advice would not necessarily be appropriate for my situation. He would need more distance from his personal experience before his advice would be relevant for me.

On a subsequent call when I explained that in spite of his advice, my goal was to succeed him, he counselled that once I was on 'the inside', I would see that USLBA was not as I envisioned it (he was right). He forecasted that I would eventually resign for similar reasons to him (exactly what happened). He warned that I would find myself engaged in a kind of kabuki theatre with the lobbyists and government affairs professionals strutting their stuff in front of Libyan grandees and American officials but not actually taking the concrete steps to facilitate increased US–Libya business ties. He warned that if I ever tried to actually accomplish anything meaningful, I would notice that bureaucratic procedures would tie my hands behind my back (100% right and again deeply paradoxical). In other words, he warned that we were living through the Enduring Disorder.

Headstrong, I believed that my background as an Arabic-speaking, Oxford-educated, card-carrying Libya expert (rather than the Sage from West Virginia who was a former Congressional staffer and Department of Commerce official) would allow me to quickly become indispensable to USLBA companies. Moreover, if I could help them make tens of millions, I assumed I could leverage that success to restructure my working environment. In short, during my time in the job I mostly ignored the implications of the most essential parts of his advice: that the USLBA member companies were not ignorant of how the semi-sovereigns worked but were simply exhibiting incumbent psychology and hence did not want to improve their bottom lines or make new deals to grow the US–Libya commercial relationship.

There was, however, one piece of advice that I was essentially forced to take. On subsequent phone calls, the Sage from West Virginia inserted a final piece of wisdom: 'If, against my counsel you do take the job, don't sign anything. They will never actually let you fulfil the job of a real executive director, so don't shoulder any of the legal responsibilities by signing official documents that evince fiduciary responsibility.' As no official documents were ever presented to me, I was essentially forced to take this advice. Despite receiving my pay, health care, new office furniture, and business cards stating that I was the executive director in English and Arabic, I was never asked to sign anything legally binding pertaining to my stewardship of USLBA, as would be normal for an executive director of a 501(c)6 non-profit with DC articles of incorporation.

Initially, to begin the job, I was presented with what I suspected was a legally invalid contract.[11] When I protested and suggested we seek the neutral opinion of an employment lawyer, I was told 'not to worry and to save the money—it was just boilerplate anyway'. When that non-legally binding, first-year probationary contract expired and I was verbally invited to stay on, I asked for a contractual renewal at least to set out the terms of my continuation. I was told that that was not necessary, that the contract was 'inherently rolling' and was at-will employment. (By this time, I had consulted a lawyer who informed me that the whole contract had no legal bearing on the question of whether or not I was the executive director, and even if it did, it had no evergreen clause and was most certainly not 'inherently rolling' as it specified a fixed duration.)

Therefore, I ran the day-to-day affairs of USLBA on an expired, non-legally binding contract. Could there be a more perfect representation of how working with statist and post-Soviet semi-sovereign economic institutions indirectly incentivizes Western entities to mirror them? USLBA's contractual arrangements certainly gave their 'executive director' relevant experience from which to sympathize with his Libyan counterparts when he hosted them on their visits to Washington.

As I initially penned these lines in mid-2020, the heads of the NOC, CBL, HoR, and GNA (the then four most powerful internationally recognized institutions in Libya) had all stayed on beyond their legal mandates and should have lacked standing in either Libyan or international law to be leading their institutions. Yet despite those legal niceties, the leaders of these institutions were all treated by international organizations, world leaders, and multinational corporations as the rightful heads of those institutions—because the alternative would have been a chaotic vacuum. When it came to Libyan officeholders, possession was nine-tenths of the law.

In a similar vein, I was never asked to sign a non-disclosure agreement or take any of the fiduciary responsibility that is normal for executive directors of non-profits under DC law. Initially, I thought that having a legal binding contract or non-disclosure agreement would protect me. I repeatedly asked for them. When they never materialized, I was disappointed. But, in reality, not having one protected me. Legally, I had less executive power than the association's accountant or IT administrator. Was I experiencing the classic Libyan case of informal power bossing around formal authority? I was certainly experiencing a novel microcosm of how the global economy works during the Enduring Disorder.

It may indeed be the case that according to the laws of the District of Columbia, I was never actually the executive director. Non-profit lawyers have informed me that having the business cards, office, pay cheque, and my name on the website would not affect my standing before the law. There were other quirks as well: the association took its website down during most of the Arab Spring when outside interest in Libya was at its peak and the association could have made the greatest impact in forwarding US–Libyan commercial ties; it refused to change the membership fee structure despite the fact that it depressed operating capital and discouraged new members from joining; and it also refused to conduct effective marketing, publicity, or media to attract members and allies.

As I reflect on these arrangements, they had no discernible advantage for either the organization's effectiveness or the member companies' business interests. They most certainly did not help the association promote business between Libya and the United States or engage in the 'public educational' functions that were mandated by the bylaws. The only thing I can imagine that they achieved was potential future avoidance of legal or public accountability on behalf of the board member companies for the (in)actions of the association. Perhaps the initial founders felt that the more bizarre and non-legally binding administrative layers separating the board member companies from the association's governance, the more plausible deniability on behalf of the board member companies would exist to legally distance themselves from the association and help them if trouble ever arose. The upshot of all of this is that it would be essentially impossible to sue USLBA for anything, since doing so would be like suing a Libyan semi-sovereign entity—impossible to legally prove who is in charge, what the chain of command is, and where accountability lies. Little did I grasp it at the time, but USLBA's organizational structure and overall actions embodied the Enduring Disorder in a microcosm. Just like with ODAC, obfuscating transparency and accountability might have been its ultimate *raison d'être*.

My credo

Returning to our narrative, despite the weird institutional arrangements of USLBA, I didn't initially grasp that they would impinge upon my goal of promoting US–Libyan political, educational, cultural, and commercial ties as per the organization's stated objectives in the bylaws and mission statement. Recalling the charming eccentricities of Oxbridge life, I thought the fact that DC lobbyists have their own oddities might add to the charm of my new life. At the start, it didn't seem nefarious in anyway.

I sought to wake up every day knowing why I was going into the office: I have always maintained that Libyans would thrive from a more open and more competitive economy where the murkiness of corrupt Qadhafian statism would be progressively blown away by the clean air of open markets. This capitalist renewal would be promoted by Western firms seeking to sell the best soft drinks, the latest telecoms technology, and the most cost-effective pipeline repairs. I felt especially good to be promoting US and UK businesses because their companies are covered by the rigorous American Foreign Corrupt Practices Act (FCPA) and UK's Bribery Act respectively, which encapsulate international best practices to combat bribery and promote free and fair market competition. To wit, the FCPA and UK Bribery Act actually do work.[12] (They are one of the few myths that experience hasn't burst for me.)

In practice, it is very hard for a US- or UK-headquartered company to bribe a Libyan official to get preferential access— those that have tried, like Och-Ziff, have paid large fines.[13] One does not need much experience in Libya to see that Southern European, let alone Middle Eastern and Asian firms, do not operate under such stringent anti-corruption legislation and do not face such penalties. As a result, the impact of their businesses on non-democratic societies usually tends to reinforce corrupt practices, where they already exist, while those of US or UK firms tend to change the societal norms, the tendering processes, and the operating procedures towards cleaner practices.[14]

Rationally, it seemed to me that promoting US–Libya business ties would be a win-win for both countries,[15] something I could put my heart and soul into and wake up every morning feeling good about going into the office—even if, in reality, I was operating within a bizarre contractual arrangement and usually hosting lunches rather than my preferred vocation of influencing actual outcomes in Libya by writing articles or advising decision-makers.

What I didn't know and was shocked to gradually uncover was that big American businesses were using their government relations professionals, their lobbyists, their clout, and their preferential access to obstruct the development of further business ties between the United States and Libya, to hinder the reform of the Libyan economy, and to implicitly prevent political processes that might lead to greater diplomatic and commercial ties between the US and Libya. Yes, the Sage from West Virginia had hinted that this might be the case. But at first blush, it seemed too conspiratorial to possibly be true. None of the academic literature or even the word on the street in Tripoli suggested it could be the case.

Like most other Middle Eastern societies, Libya is filled with an active conspiratorial rumour mill, yet the idea that some incumbent American businesses were trying to prevent the growth of US–Libyan business ties was too weird to even exist as a fringe rumour. It took me about a year in the job to realize that this dynamic was fundamental. The very structure of USLBA had been progressively evolving, subtly guided by personnel changes due to retirements. First, new board members replaced founding board members, then there was the arrival of a new president of the larger trade association, NFTC, which held USLBA's management contract. The new personnel were not emotionally connected to the narrative of 'bringing Libya in from the cold' and helping to grow its economy. They were younger and had implicitly imbibed the changing global paradigms, where even mega-corporates were no longer advocates of unfettered free markets but had tacitly adapted to the playbook of the Enduring Disorder. Hence, they discretely oversaw the erection of barriers for new entrants to the US–Libya business relationship. So, from an organization that during the late Qadhafi period was instrumental in getting Libya removed from the terrorism list, US sanctions lifted, and new business ties forged, USLBA had evolved into treating Libya like their proprietary closed shop, but perhaps that had been its purpose all along.

* * *

It would require a separate book to tell the tale of my personal discovery of these subtle and not-so-subtle practices. Below, I will merely highlight some revealing anecdotes and analyse what they tell us about the era of the Enduring Disorder.

Writing twenty-two centuries ago, Polybius, the Greco-Roman statesman, general and captive from Megalopolis, recommended that those with first-hand experience of events should write the corresponding history. He advises aspiring historians to relate what they have personally experienced and try to draw larger conclusions about the global system.[16]

Furthermore, Polybius invites historians to assess the impact of institutions and culture on the flow of history and then to sit in judgement over decision-makers. He understood the psychological and institutional/constitutional component of historical causation and how it could only be accurately captured by those who had participated in the events and witnessed the various forces operating on decision-makers, in real time, as they bumbled through the decisions surrounding whether to go to war or not (or in my case, to go to Libya or not). Given his focus on causation, decision-maker psychology, passing judgement on those responsible, institutional/constitutional structures, and the participant observation method, a strong case can be made for considering Polybius the true father of history rather than Herodotus or Thucydides.[17] Possibly, if today's history and political science scholars were guided by him, we would soon acquire a better conception of the new world order we inhabit.

All too often, academic political science texts and journalists' books ignore the salient behind-the-scenes dynamics of insider testimonials—focusing instead on those few incidents that captured headlines or resonate with an academic theory currently in vogue. For this reason many of the drivers of Libya's unwritten history—especially those which pertain to its economy—remain obscured and wildly different to what the newspaper articles, academic literature, or even think tank reports might suggest.

I know that many Libyans from taxi cab drivers all the way up to the heads of semi-sovereign institutions genuinely trust American businesses, especially oil companies, as Libya's supposedly truest and oldest friends, while simultaneously distrusting American diplomats, experts, and academics, as undercover spies acting in their own interests. Ironically, many of the government relations professionals of major American oil companies are former Agency spooks, and most of the American intelligence operatives in Libya in the late Qadhafi and early post-Qadhafi periods posed as investors or businesspeople in order to gain high-level access. Conversely, I have never met a US ambassador, American academic expert, or Western journalist of Libya with any sort of intelligence background. How tragic, then, that throughout the MENA region graduate students, researchers, retired diplomats, and journalists are accused of being spies as a pretext to hold them in jails without trial[18] while corporate businessmen, lobbyists, and oil executives are generally fawned over by the regime higher-ups and local citizenry alike?

Morally, it is the refuting of this prevalent and dangerous myth, which I consider truly paramount. Intellectually, my over-arching contention is that the Enduring Disorder has made anti-competitive practices more common, and that taken in their totality, these practices do not constitute a true 'order'. In fact, neo-mercantilism and rear-guard actions by incumbents are the antithesis of order—they are a free-for-all. Therefore, by telling my USLBA story, I hope to draw out larger lessons about preferential access, market capture, and the interconnections between 'over there' and 'back home' that define the world in which we now live.

Now that we are inside, please help us close the door

Roughly six months into my tenure at USLBA, the board members set their mind to amending the bylaws—something which had not been done since the organization's founding. I was not opposed to the idea, hoping we could find a way to broaden the scope of potential companies eligible for membership. The board had other ideas. They voted unanimously to give existing board members a veto on new companies joining the association or the board.[19] They cited concerns of possible corruption and unethical business practices by potential new member companies. In practice, this policy essentially allowed companies to block their competitors from gaining access to the Libyan statesmen and the heads of the institutions that USLBA would host. For example, imagine that 'company x' is in sector z that sat on the board of the U.S.-Libya Business Association. If another company in sector z wished to join the association so that they could attend events with US policymakers and Libyan grandees, 'company x' could block their entrance to the association by citing their rival company's questionable ethics and lack of a specific industry certification. Although I was successful in enlisting new members in sectors where there were no current members, the addition of any members in sectors where there were already existing board members proved harder to achieve.

This was an example of market protection writ large: not illegal at a private non-profit trade association but deeply against the spirit of USLBA's stated purpose and original bylaws. The association was now being used to pigeonhole Libyan grandees and USG officials. The community of DC-based lobbyists and company reps interested in Libya is inherently small. Therefore, visiting Libyan dignitaries assumed that by meeting with USLBA they were meeting the totality of the US business community interested in Libya. After all, the organization's name conveyed as much. Hence, they would usually reserve their public-facing, commercial engagement meetings to be hosted by USLBA for member-only, off-the-record conversations. As a result, Libyan grandees would generally not end up meeting non-member companies' DC reps. This was the exact opposite of the practices of the Libyan British Business Council (LBBC), whose fee structure was more rational, events far more widely attended, and from which no potentially suitable members are blocked if they meet the neutral criteria for admission. Partly, these differences derived from the fact that LBBC's institutional structure gave power to the former ambassadors who traditionally occupied its unpaid appointed executive director position, while USLBA's structure gave complete power to the lobbyists, former Agency, and military personnel who occupied its Board.

As USLBA's true ethos gradually came into focus, I thought these trends were inadvertent rather than deliberate and likely recent in origin rather than foundational. Hoping to right the ship, I tried to nudge the organization towards promoting new entrants to the US–Libya business arena through a variety of initiatives. In one telling instance, I sold the top sponsorship to an open public event (rather than a formally closed association meeting) to a non-member firm, 'company y', so that that it could experience the benefits of membership and have a chance to appear before an important set of Libyan and State Department officials. This was not a violation of the newly amended bylaws, which only applied to board members blocking membership in the association, not sponsorships of association events. According to common NGO practice, sponsorships are exclusively the executive director's remit. This has to be the case for practical reasons, as board members compete against each other to be the Gold Sponsor of the most desirable events or to sit next to the top official at an event.

And yet, the board member from company x operating in the same sector was not pleased. They retaliated by demanding that their logo be placed in 'as prominent a position' as company y's and that their representative have the same preferential seating as company y—essentially demanding to be treated as if they had sponsored the event. Company y was attempting to position itself on the front lines of connecting Libyans with American capacity-building skills—their hoped-for success in Libya would have been positive-sum and led to business opportunities for other firms.

Such petty jealousies and attempts to block competitors from gaining access to charitable dinners seemed to me small potatoes, not worth the few thousand bucks that the board companies were willing to pay to achieve them. I had learned long ago that the Libyan grandees did not care who happened to sit next to them or sponsor an event in their honour. Conversely, the Libyans cared deeply about whether a given company (or academic expert or political actor) was connected to the 'right' Libyan factions and had the 'right' legacy from the Qadhafi period. This was something the company's DC representatives were generally astoundingly ignorant of—and no amount of sponsorships could change.

Almost all Fortune 500 companies that had been in Libya for decades maintained continuous relationships with their trusted local partners, who in the olden days needed to be connected to officials from the former regime to be able to function. As such, according to the ebbs and flows of Libyan politics, their contact networks fell in and out of favour. Yet, this primary dynamic of doing business in Libya was something that most of the billion-dollar companies I represented were either ignorant of, or in denial about.

After the sponsorship episode and other foibles, I faced my conscience and decided I could easily live with such petty 'sponsorship jealousy' and the silliness of DC-lobbyist visions of how to do business in Libya. These prejudices didn't seem to really harm anyone and derived simply from ignorance. Except for the sprinkling of Lebanese-Americans among them, the lobbyists, government affairs professionals, retired military and intelligence personnel, and businesspeople who were USLBA's members spoke no Arabic and possessed little relevant regional experiences or subject matter expertise.

On the other hand, attempting to freeze US–Libya business relations and not seize a major opportunity to build commercial and diplomatic momentum that could help bring peace to Libya was something I could not abide. Initially, it was difficult for me to spot such behaviour. When petty episodes of sponsorship jealousy were playing out, I did not yet grasp that larger forces having to do with incumbent psychology and the neo-mercantilism of the Enduring Disorder were actually behind them as well. Years before, when I had worked at USLBA in the late Qadhafi period under the tutelage of the Sage from West Virginia none of these forces were yet in play. The Sage would not have abided them either. The Enduring Disorder was not then in full force—free trade and open markets were still in the ascendance.

In 2010, the post-Cold War world order appeared to be in full swing: experts were not yet vilified nor influence peddlers praised. Yet eight years later, with President Trump occupying the White House, the green light had been given to all who wanted to play transactional, zero-sum, neo-mercantilism with sharp elbows.[20] The Enduring Disorder's anti-competitive forces had thus created a corporate culture in Washington where not everyone actually wanted to promote economic growth in Libya (or Ukraine, Turkey, Yemen, Venezuela, Syria, Nigeria, Equatorial Guinea, etc.). Seen in retrospect, when I thought the lobbyists and former Agency types were being petty, they were likely actualizing their boss's priorities and mentalities quite accurately. In retrospect, they have all earned my grudging respect for being good at achieving their benchmarks. Unfortunately, when they appointed me to represent them, they did not have the courtesy to explain to me what those really were.

Commercial diplomacy

Of all the tools at USLBA's disposal in the post-Qadhafi period, trade missions were the most effective way to expand business ties and to get the US government further vested in commercial and traditional diplomacy with Libya.[21] During the days of the massive European overseas empires, the adage was that 'trade follows the flag'. In the twenty-first century, the causation is frequently the reverse:[22] political engagement, especially in capacity and peacebuilding, happens where bilateral business ties already exist—motivating governments to step in to help protect their businesses' interests when they are threatened by political strife. Hence in Libya, US companies gaining new contracts or even just getting their back payment issues addressed would almost certainly have the effect of luring the US government to expend further energy trying to provide a security umbrella to protect those companies' ongoing operations.

THE US–LIBYA (ANTI-)BUSINESS ASSOCIATION

These days, it is quite clear that the flag follows trade. Variants of this important theory have a long and distinguished scholarly pedigree.[23] Applying them to today, we would imagine that the US government is inherently incentivized to provide its 'hegemonic ordering services' where US firms have—or are attempting to acquire—a major commercial stake. In short, a trade mission would inherently bring together the business and diplomatic aspects of America's overseas might. That synergy could provide the classic win-win that would benefit Libya, the US private sector, and global governance.

When is a trade mission not a trade mission?

On the margins of the UN General Assembly in 2017, I hosted Prime Minister Serraj for a state dinner-style event focused on promoting US–Libya business ties. The optics surrounding the dinner were quite successful. In its wake, the prime minister's office expressly invited me as USLBA's executive director to organize a trade mission to Libya. Such a trade mission should have been the bread-and-butter of USLBA—a yearly or at most biennial staple. USLBA's bylaws stated that the organization existed for three primary purposes and conducting trade missions was one of them. USLBA's sister organization, the Libyan British Business Council (LBBC) had undertaken such missions both during the late Qadhafi period and every year from 2012 to 2019. Conversely, USLBA had conducted missions during the late Qadhafi period, then once in 2012 just prior to Ambassador Stevens' murder, and then never again.

Was this because of the security situation, a lack of American business appetite, or an absence of Libyan governmental interest in American companies? When I had applied for the executive director job in late 2016, I said in my interview that my ambition was to conduct a trade mission. I was told that that was a great goal, but we would need to wait and see if the security situation improved. That seemed a more than reasonable response at the time. But by the autumn of 2017, the security situation *had* partially stabilized, and I'd secured the invitation of the Libyan Prime Minister.

Personally, I thought that the trade mission was a wonderful opportunity for hundreds of millions of dollars of memorandums of understanding to be signed, tens of millions of back payments to be wired, and productive contacts established that could help support infrastructure repair and job creation in Libya, as well as increase US governmental commitment to reforming the Libyan economy and pushing for a political resolution to the country's civil war.

For nearly eight months, sorting the details of the forthcoming trade mission became my eighty-hours-a-week obsession. As I worked on making it happen, I found myself thwarted at every step, but not by 'devious' Libyans or 'rigid' government bureaucrats.

Prime Minister Serraj and his people figuratively rolled out the red carpet, and the heads of the semi-sovereign institutions like the CBL, GECOL, NOC, and LPTIC were willing to keep their schedules open until we picked a date for the mission and to use their private jets to fly their personnel to Tunis for working sessions. The interagency complexities between the Commerce and the State Departments—and their constant turnover of personnel—presented concrete challenges, but they too could be solved. The Trump administration had made the promotion of US 'exports' a priority, and hence the institutions of the US government were willing to put in the necessary work to help me with the trade mission to secure new markets for US exports.[24]

The first round of difficulties began as the non-oil board member companies expressed a willingness to take up the prime minister's literal offer of 'meeting him in Tripoli'—flying in and out during the daylight hours to meet him and the heads of the semi-sovereigns for quick photo opportunities in their offices and calling it a trade mission. Conversely, the oil companies asserted that their legal teams and insurance policies would not allow them to go to Libya because the country lacked a functioning US embassy. The companies that could not go to Tripoli preferred to scupper any mission inside Libya rather than allow other companies to go to Tripoli without them.

Hosting the event in Tunis or Malta was the obvious answer. Both are safe and tourist-friendly destinations where much business relating to Libya is conducted. LBBC has had trade missions to both over the years.[25] Tunisia has the advantage that Libyans, Brits, and Americans can go visa-free. So Tunisia it was.

With a quick jaunt to Tripoli nixed by the big oil companies, the board members agreed that they would only go to Tunis if I was able to secure the official blessing of the US Departments of State and Commerce for USLBA to constitute 'an officially sanctioned US private sector trade mission'. Fortunately, those officials were keen to promote such a mission as their own creation. Their commercial staff in Tunis could piggyback off the mission to show to their bosses back in DC that they had fulfilled their remit of promoting US exports.

There were many forms to fill out, many phone calls to make, many divergent interests to massage, and collective actions problems to solve. Most of my waking hours had become about perfecting the tiny details concerning the trade mission, and yet due to what I would characterize as the myopia of one who is academically trained, the real obstacles were entirely out of my field of vision. It really didn't occur to me that there might never be a mission at all. The prime minister had personally invited USLBA, after all. I knew that if he died, was removed from power, or there was a major terrorist attack in Tunisia we wouldn't be going, but barring that, I couldn't see how something like a major trade mission that had already achieved the blessing of the American and Libyan governments might just 'fall through the cracks.'

Suffice it to say, I certainly didn't understand what I was experiencing as I was living through the chaotic tumble of events, while trying to actively mould them. Neither did Polybius, so it shouldn't be shameful to admit as much. Hence, with the historian's advantage of hindsight and extensive retrospective interviews of other participants and observers, I can now see many possible ways to relate the causative linkages and account for the motivation of the participants. A corporate diplomatic history approach is possible, yet in this instance, having revisited the extensive email paper trail, what emerges most vividly are three indicative episodes. I will relate them in a narrative fashion, present some interviews with relevant officials for their perspectives, and let the reader draw appropriate conclusions.

Three bewildering episodes

I flew to Tunis in March 2018 to scope out the venue for the trade mission and to build the relevant personal connections with the US *Chargée d'Affaires* (essentially the acting, but not Senate-confirmed, American ambassador), the commercial officer at the embassy, and some relevant Libyan interlocutors. I was under strict instructions from the USLBA board chairman to not mention the possible dates on which the trade mission might happen, even though we had internally fixed two windows of target dates. I explained to the board that not telling the *chargée* the prospective dates might make us look amateurish. Even if the dates might be pushed back, would it not be better to give her tentative dates so that the embassy could start planning receptions, or laying the ground work for meetings?

I still remember vividly my meeting with the then American *Chargée d'Affaires* Stephanie Williams. We made interesting chit chat about our prior experiences in Syria and Iraq. We discussed how Libya was a different kettle of fish, especially when it came to the role of economic structures in facilitating the conflict. When talk turned to the trade mission, I should have anticipated that her most pressing question would be: 'Can you please give me a date that you want the mission to happen, so we can begin our preparations?' When the issue came up a second time, I said the association was still deliberating internally. She asked for a date by which I would be able to get her the likely dates of the mission. I said I could not say. I instantly realized that no amount of academic credentials or knowledge of Libya's economic institutions could make me look like a serious person heading a serious institution after having delivered such answers. As such, despite her openness to greater contact with USLBA and her genuine desire to help make any trade mission of US companies a success, the association would have no more direct contact with Williams while she was the highest-ranking American representative at the Libya External Office.

It was quite the missed opportunity. When Williams was replaced by a permanent US ambassador a short number of months later, she became the deputy special representative for political affairs at the UN Support Mission in Libya (UNSMIL) from June 2018–January 2020 and then later served as acting UN Special Representative of the Secretary-General at UNSMIL from February 2020–February 2021, the most powerful post in shaping the international community's policy towards Libya. In the latter role, she was instrumental in resuscitating the UN peace process, laying the technical groundwork for Haftar to lift his blockade on Libya's oil production (which the Russians sought to take credit for through the September 2020 Sochi Agreement), brokering the 23 October 2020 ceasefire agreement that formally ended the War for Tripoli, and most crucially seeing the LPDF to its successful completion in early 2021.

* * *

The second episode was even more bizarre. My board members had made it clear to me that their bosses back in Houston wanted to have the trade mission in a hotel where the conference room had windows overlooking the Mediterranean. Tunis has only three or four top international hotels with the requisite facilities to host an international trade mission for which much of the Libyan cabinet, the heads of the semi-sovereign institutions, and possibly the prime minister himself would all be in attendance. All of those hotels had guest rooms with glorious sea views, but only one had a conference room with windows.

After a retired British ambassador had vouched for my credentials with the relevant hotel's top staff, I used my French and Arabic to get a deal on a block of hotel rooms and the rental of the conference room for the most likely of the tentative dates for the mission—which also happened to be during high tourist season. The manager of the hotel explained that he could even give me a significant discount if I might use his hotel for such events in future years. I assured him that if all went well this year, we would certainly be back, possibly annually. He had one condition: I had exactly two weeks to wire a deposit to confirm the rooms.

Back in the United States, I informed the board members of my coup—I had not only secured a hotel with a conference room with windows but had gotten a discount that would reduce the costs to their companies of participating and likely increase our ability to use the trade mission to get new members into the association. A classic win-win seemingly secured.

I explained that the only catch was that we needed to give the go-ahead to secure the dates by the next Sunday. The chairman said he would get back to me. When the Friday before the Sunday deadline approached, I wrote emails and left voice messages reminding him of the Sunday deadline. The deadline passed, and I neither got a thumbs up nor a thumbs down from any of the board members.

THE US–LIBYA (ANTI-)BUSINESS ASSOCIATION

As I now look back at this, I made a grave strategic error given my stated goal of trying to promote US–Libya business ties in the long term. It was fully within my rights as the executive director to simply wire the money or give the hotel my corporate credit card to fix the dates of the trade mission. This was not something about which the board needed to be consulted. The concept of the mission had been *pro forma* approved at the last board meeting, the money was in the relevant year's board-approved budget, and the bylaws stated that the organization existed to conduct such missions. My job was supposed to be to execute, and I shouldn't have had to 'ask permission' to do so. With hindsight, I should not have worried that the various board members or their companies would not attend if the wrong dates or a window-less conference room was selected. In retrospect, I partly believe that if I had just wired the money to reserve the hotel rooms, then it would have created momentum and the companies would have eventually snapped into line. Would the chairman of the organization have failed to attend the biggest event the organization had initiated in over five years because the conference room lacked a sea view?

* * *

The last episode is truly the weirdest. I had spent months trying to arrange a private audience with the Tunisian ambassador to the United States for myself and the USLBA chairman to discuss how the Tunisian government could help facilitate the US–Libya trade mission, which for logistical and security reasons we proposed to conduct in their country. This would be the first time that USLBA had ever had a private meeting with the Tunisian ambassador—who was something of a rock star around Washington, due to his skills, seniority, and the influence he had back in his home capital. In the wake of the board's non-decision over the hotel rooms, I knew that this was likely the make-or-break meeting for the trade mission. Then, completely out of the blue, the USLBA chairman asked me to cancel the meeting and explain that 'something had come up'. The meeting was only a day away. I explained that cancelling would be extremely rude. I could go alone if he couldn't make it. The ambassador had offered to arrange for the Tunisian economy minister to attend our reception and possibly invest Tunisian personnel and political capital into making everything work smoothly on the ground. That could be invaluable.

The chairman said I should write to the ambassador that another meeting had 'come up'. I explained that that would be even ruder than just cancelling, as it implies that another person was more important to meet than the Tunisian ambassador. I mean seriously, who in our area of interest could be more important—were we going to pretend that we had invitations to the White House?

I stressed that his message would be perceived in Arab culture as a grave slight. The chairman was not an Arabist. I told him that my years in the Middle East had taught me that, if he insisted we cancel, then the way to go was to say something like, 'due to Haftar's recent bombings we were unable to get away from pressing obligations'. Saving face, social graces, and polite apologies are of course crucial aspects of all cultures, but in the North African context they could make or break diplomatic and business interactions. Yet, the chairman insisted that I forward his template message using the exact language he provided (saying essentially that another lunch meeting 'had just come up') and cc him on the email. Again, I should have trusted my instinct that this was not something that a chairman of a board of a non-profit could tell its executive director to do. Instead, at the last moment I doubted myself and thought maybe this slightly older gentleman with much more DC experience than myself knew something I did not know. So, I sent the email as instructed. Predictably, it burned both an institutional and a personal bridge with the Tunisian embassy.

I then threatened to resign a week or so later anyway if the overarching issues were not addressed: namely if the board did not commit to dates for the trade mission and make the relevant hires within a relevant period. Not receiving any timely response to my ultimatum from a board whose internal coordination was likely itself burdened by collective action complexities, I finally built up the courage to pull the plug—publicly resigning and citing association governance issues. Over the next couple of years, I sold my house in Washington and moved back to where I had grown up to reassess my next step—all just as the Sage from West Virginia had done and had presciently predicted I would do.

* * *

What did it all mean? One analysis of the logic behind these three seemingly disparate and paradoxical episodes, is that the board member companies would only want a trade mission to take place if they could minutely choreograph its details, dates, and invite list to provide certain optics. Another hypothesis is that the board members didn't want the mission to happen because other companies would gain access to the heads of Libya's semi-sovereign institutions. They already had their business interests in Libya and key connections in place. They had come to enjoy using USLBA to pigeonhole the Libyan grandees when they came to Washington. A trade mission would simply allow too many new players into the space and introduce new forces beyond their control.

A final hypothesis was that there was no overarching plan at all. No given board member was determined to have a trade mission and none of them were resolutely opposed to one either. Some wanted to go to Tripoli, others to Tunis, and some would have preferred to stay home. The collective action challenges were such that an undertaking of the complexity of a trade mission simply could not be brought to fruition with the state of the association's governance structure—just as collective action to address global warming or fake news cannot be achieved through the UN. Seen in this light, even coordinating among a few similar companies, an executive director, and various US government officials whose interests should all have aligned was simply too complex in the institutional climate of the Enduring Disorder. This is an era that favours obstruction over compromise and in which many actors are willing to make an impassioned stand over the need for windows in the conference room or how an email cancelling a meeting should be worded rather than compromising to secure long-term mutual advantages.

Looking back, I cannot help but feel that the board's scuttle was at least partially deliberate—albeit certainly not minutely choreographed. Each of the given episodes seemed so ridiculous that they struck me as neither strategic nor deliberate but their opposite: spontaneous, haphazard, and full of disorder. As I was living in the realm of the details, I was missing the bigger picture: USLBA was a placeholder, it existed to prevent another more active trade association from arising in its patch.

USLBA was acting as a prototypical incumbent. It was not functioning in line with its bylaws and stated public purpose to increase bilateral cultural, diplomatic, educational, and business ties. It was therefore a fitting representative of a stratum of companies who during the Enduring Disorder do not actually try to maximize their future earnings.

Whatever the board's rationale, past performance told the whole story: the LBBC had held at least six trade missions in the previous five years, while USLBA had held none. Why did I think that rational argumentation or a letter from the Libyan prime minister on official stationery could change that? Had the association simply outlived its initial post-Cold War purpose?[26] Or perhaps its real institutional purpose was not encapsulated in its bylaws, which were likely just tweaked from the boilerplate of other non-profits? Or could it be that the organization as a whole and its officers in specific were dutifully fulfilling the organizational founders' intentions, as its clever institutional design and seemingly haphazard contractual arrangements were still in fact guiding their actions?

History is destiny

Whatever the reality, USLBA was always a tiny organization and barely a player in global commerce in its own right. It was merely a microcosm of the multi-billion dollar companies on whose behalf it was acting. Even at the organization's peak of membership in the early post-Qadhafi period, it never had more than three staff members and only received yearly dues of a few hundred thousand dollars.

USLBA's failure to organize a trade mission may strike some as inconsequential to the bigger picture of the Enduring Disorder. However, having given the issue much thought, I believe the abortive trade mission episode can be seen as a highly indicative microcosm of the broader Enduring Disorder—helping us examine key American political and corporate actors' drift over the last few decades from leadership to incumbency, and then towards neo-mercantilism. It also brings into sharp focus the type of suboptimal outcomes that emerge from failures to solve collective action problems.

To better contextualize this story, I will now attempt to unearth the history and foundational purpose of USLBA. As no published research exists on this topic and the organization's files do not capture anything about its founder's real intentions, I interviewed every personal contact whose Washington experiences positioned them to be close enough to USLBA's founders and chairmen to provide educated speculation on their intentions.

Below, I present a précis of my three most revealing interviews, which tell us a lot about how corporate America behaves during the Enduring Disorder.

A former American ambassador who has long been in the DC Libya game speculated:

> It seems likely that the major US oil companies had initially been advised in the early 2000s by their lawyers or government relations professionals to create a trade association as part of their strategy to push to return to their oil concessions and get the sanctions against Qadhafi lifted as he fulfilled his benchmarks in paying off the Lockerbie families. You have to keep in mind the amount of knee-jerk opposition to normalization with Qadhafi that existed in Congressional Washington, and especially amongst the East Coast Jewish community [who had suffered heavy casualties from Lockerbie and also felt that Qadhafi was an unrepentant supporter of Palestinian terrorist organizations]. A trade association could present the optic of a united business community which advocated for a policy of rapprochement with Qadhafi as a counterweight to public sentiment which opposed it.

> It would never been known to policymakers or Congresspeople that the association was essentially controlled by only those oil companies who had legacy positions in Libya. Hence the potentially divergent approaches to the country between those who wanted to protect legacy business interests and those who wanted to enter the market afresh would be pre-empted by the incumbents. Additionally, a given oil company with legacy interests could use the association for the purpose of hosting Qadhafian officials or lobbying Congress on behalf of getting Libya off the state sponsors of terrorism list or trying to defeat the Lautenberg Amendment to the Iran–Libya Sanctions Act without the risk of ever being singled out in the media as supporting Qadhafi.

THE US–LIBYA (ANTI-)BUSINESS ASSOCIATION

As I participated more in USLBA events over time, the organization had moments of opening up beyond the big oils, but then the pendulum would swing and the big oils would become afraid of losing their position of dominance within the association—and the DC Libya business universe more generally—and would steer the ship more towards being a closed shop.

According to his theory, USLBA was for incumbents only, and its legal and membership structure was meant to discourage new entrants and freeze a status quo system in place in which the big American oil companies treated Libya as their private sandbox. Moreover, it was also supposed to act like a BVI shell company or a semi-sovereign entity, creating another layer of deniability that could be used to separate the board member companies from the actions of the association, if the need ever arose for such a legal or publicity shield, as pertains to lobbying or hosting.

Another colleague who worked at the Department of Commerce and attended scores of USLBA events provides a different twist:

The association's governance and overall approach was created to keep the 'Libya issue' or the companies' direct involvement in meeting Libyan officials out of the limelight of the US media. Somewhere back in Houston the 'big bosses' felt that doing business with Qadhafi in the 2005–2010 period or later after the 2012 'Benghazi' scandal would be seen as toxic for their branding and should be hidden or obscured. That this perception concerning the extent of reputational risk in dealing with Libya existed—but not about China, Equatorial Guinea or Saudi Arabia where mass-scale regime-directed human rights violations were going on constantly—reveals how much of American corporate capitalism's risk tolerance is about the vagaries of optics and popular sentiment of the moment. Just look at how corporate America has responded to Black Lives Matter issues, but not to Chinese concentration camps for Uighurs.

All told USLBA hosted many great events and was always an aggre-
gator of incredibly useful commercial knowledge about Libya. It was
just a deliberate policy to only share that knowledge selectively.

Personally, I have always been proud to be doing business with
Libya or trying to bring a Libyan point of view to the United
States, so it never really occurred to me that I might have become
the executive director of an association predicated on helping its
members obscure their connections to, and advocacy for, Libya.
Never in my wildest dreams would I have thought that a trade
mission to a commercially important business destination could
present a negative optic for a big company. But as this inter-
viewee pointed out, since the Benghazi fiasco American politicians (and hence possibly businessmen as well) appear to shy
away from doing anything publicly connected to Libya and might
be reluctant about being seen to go there.

Lastly, conversations with a former Department of Treasury
official with extensive experience with USLBA suggested to me
the following insightful analysis:

> The association never existed to promote business between the US
> and Libya per se. It exists to pigeonhole visiting Libyan officials
> when they come to DC, so that whenever they want to host a net-
> working event, meet the private sector, or even be introduced to
> USG officials or Congresspeople, they end up always seeing the same
> companies—the USLBA board members. Due to the structure of
> the association, these same few individuals are therefore literally
> always present wherever the Libyans want to go. This is thought to
> have a powerful psychological and structural effect on the Libyan
> officials as they then believe that they need these specific companies,
> not only if they are going to upgrade their pipeline network or fix
> their electricity grid but also if they are to have access to the US
> governmental bureaucracy. Traditionally, Libyan ambassadors to DC
> lack the structural tools to navigate the complexities of the US gov-
> ernment in the way that more established Middle Eastern ambassa-

dors do. Hence, corporate lobbyists seem to offer Libyan diplomats a privileged access point into US government.

Given this, the association is a minnow that has learned to cast the shadow of an elephant. It creates an optic of corporate power in the DC Libya world on behalf of the incumbent players and as such gives those players much greater leverage in their negotiations with their Libyan counterparts over business dealings. And those board member companies happen to also be the legacy oil companies who are essentially rent seekers squatting on the oil fields they discovered and developed in the 1960s and have barely invested a dime in since.

This lobbying-for-incumbency tactic only works in America, as most developing country politicians believe that having America on their side is critical to their own personal incumbency and that the American government will do whatever American businesses need. Never mind that this perception is fundamentally wrong on both counts as USLBA and similar organizations have next to no pull with the US government, especially as they have miniscule budgets and no real lobbying capabilities. Nonetheless, because America is perceived as a hegemon whose might is brought to bear upon the developing world via corporate lobbyists, this in turn gives these lobbyists an aura of power that similar trade associations simply can't exert in London, Rome, or Brussels.

This last account struck me as the most revelatory. It never occurred to me while I was running USLBA's day-to-day affairs that American firms were more likely to be anti-competitive or status quo-oriented than European firms. In retrospect, and seen through the lens of the Enduring Disorder, there is something appealing about this conjecture, as it explains how today's global order encourages the most powerful incumbents to seek to block change while simultaneously creating optics that portray incumbents as 'the only game in town'. Very Trumpian, yet long predating Trump. This observation about the psychological and branding implications of trade associations and corporate business to government networking events seems highly applicable to the government affairs behaviour of other American mega-corporates in sectors like tech or investment banking.

Why blocking trade is no strategy and constitutes no order at all

Whether or not it was consistent with USLBA's founders' intentions or was to avoid troublesome optics for the big bosses back in Houston, blocking the trade mission would not secure the board members' companies' true interests in Libya. It would disadvantage less established American companies far more than theirs, that is true, but primarily it would give new entrants, from other nations, the leg up. USLBA's continued advocacy for its major corporates' interests in Libya was not exactly leading to many success stories. In 1970, Libya produced three million barrels of oil a day on average and more than half of it was produced, lifted, and marketed by American oil companies. American companies had achieved that dominance partly by piggybacking on American military hegemony but primarily because they were nimbler, more open to taking risks, and decades ahead of the competition when it came to prospecting, engineering, and financial instruments.

A few decades later, when the post-Lockerbie sanctions on American firms operating in Libya were finally lifted and new business ties were forged during the détente period of 2003–10, no fewer than eight American major and supermajor oil firms returned to their sizeable holdings in consortia and exploration and production sharing arrangements in Libya.[27] That is not to mention the oil field services space into which American capital and experts returned.

Over the course of 2020, Libya produced fewer than 600,000 barrels a day on average, due to off-and-on blockades and rusting infrastructure. Less than 8 per cent of that was allotted to the two remaining American majors due to existing crude sharing arrangements. Over the last few years, American oil interests in Libya have been dropping like flies—Chevron left in 2012, ExxonMobil in 2013,[28] Occidental sold to OMV in 2016, and Marathon sold to TOTAL in 2018.[29] Among the reasons that the American oil companies have left Libya is because they no longer enjoy significant engineering or financial advantages. They are also unwilling to leverage American geopolitical might to advocate for American global leadership.[30] Conversely, they face various bureaucratic, cultural, and structural hurdles to operating that make them less able to make a long-term profit in a challenging environment than their more nimble European competitors, who generally act more in step with their governments.

Blame the messenger

I can now see that allowing the trade mission to happen would have been going against everything the board members were doing in Washington and the whole direction of travel of the US–Libya commercial and diplomatic relationship. Foolishly, when I did resign, I still thought that a new person would have to be brought on swiftly and that the organization would be essentially forced to promptly conduct the trade mission as the Libyan prime minister's office and the US government would expect it to do. How could mere corporations stand up against the expressed wishes of the very governments that held their business interests in their hands? Again, my assumptions proved wrong.

From the firms' perspectives, the psychology of incumbents dictated that they go into a defensive shell the more they were threatened. Moreover, the big corporate incumbents have become experts at pushing governments around. There is a profound asymmetry of wills. Civil servants and government officials do not usually get promotions and bonuses for achieving their bosses' desired outcomes, while corporate lobbyists do. Furthermore, American corporates have a different approach to government than European multinationals—the Americans tend to think government exists to either serve them or get out of their way. Conversely, European corporates envision themselves in partnership with their governments and societies. Due to the American attitude and pervasive collective action problems, these vastly different types of institutions (oil companies and government departments) usually cannot coherently negotiate with one another to achieve the most mutually beneficial outcome.

* * *

I will never know what exactly happened behind the scenes about the trade mission or in the calculus to create and maintain USLBA's governance structure and relationship with NFTC. I had provided the elbow grease to push the trade mission forward, and my departure could be used by the board as a brilliant excuse to explain to the State Department and the Libyan government why the mission could not happen, without the companies having to directly face the blow-back from their own actions. However, this analysis might be too conspiratorial. The only thing I can assert beyond a historian's burden of proof is that the Fortune 100 multi-billion-dollar corporates I interacted with were not particularly concerned about increasing US–Libyan business ties in the abstract nor concretely via their own person-to-person business ties. They were clearly keen to fabricate excuses to not have to conduct the trade mission and nearly all of the major American companies were loath to invest actual OPEX or CAPEX into Libya, while their European counterparts were willing to do so.

The CEOs of major European firms flew to Tunis and Libya frequently to meet with their Libyan counterparts, while even government affairs heads and regional managers of US firms did not. The big US oil companies wanted to extract crude from assets they developed decades ago, while most of the other American multinationals were keen to collect back payments by deepening privileged connections to the heads of the semi-sovereign institutions. The few firms that did want to go into Libya in a big way were happy to ramp up their presence only through the non-free market approach of securing exclusive US government or UN contracts for security, training, or contracting work. Doing business in a rentier state like Libya seemed to have turned those who interacted with it into unabashed rent-seekers.

Neo-mercantilism had reared its head

More than three years have passed since my resignation and USLBA's true colours have become even more apparent. After many months with no full-time staff in place and the thought of a trade mission withering on the vine, my former intern was hired to replace me as her first job out of undergrad. No inklings of a USLBA trade mission to Tunisia or Malta to meet Libyan officials emerged. Action for a trade mission would likely have to wait for another American trade association to pick up the baton—one whose governance was led not by multi-billion-dollar corporate incumbents but by a single, highly dedicated entrepreneur.

But it would still be an uphill battle. The mere existence of USLBA profoundly inhibits the emergence of another DC-based trade association that could host a trade mission or advocate for economic reform in Libya. Due to fifteen years of successful branding, Libyan grandees visiting Washington 'know' that they need to meet USLBA to see the business community, while American officials 'know' that they need to consult USLBA to get the private sector's wisdom on Libya. Mission accomplished. Game, set, match for the incumbents? Not so fast. Protectionism and incumbency is not a permanent solution. The world refuses to stay static. As it relates to a trade mission of US companies to Libya, creative and entrepreneurial Libyan and American businesspeople will at some point find a way to sidestep the incumbents. And advocates of such endeavours, myself included, will always be found waiting in the wings, to lend support and experience to forward their efforts.

But don't all the companies just want to make money?

My bizarre experiences at USLBA appear to be both a leading indicator and funhouse mirror exaggerating various global trends. Big American businesses are now playing capitalism by mid-twenty-first-century rules, not twentieth-century ones. They simultaneously followed the lead of President Trump[31] and adapted to the statist rent-seeking environments in which they were operating. Even when Trump tried to assiduously apply his 'principles', he did so as an agent of disorder. In the Libyan space, smaller UK firms were mostly playing by the beneficial let-the-best-man-win, we-rely-on-our-comparative-advantages, and anyone-can-join-our-trade-association rules of the twentieth century. The institutional cultures and organizational dynamics of USLBA and LBBC were about as similar as Liberty University and Oxford University.

When did colossal American firms switch from fostering market competition to seeking rents and monopolistic market capture? And how did we all miss this? During the Enduring Disorder, the global economic system has made an abrupt U-turn and has now become about securing privileged access, not about destroying trade barriers and fostering free competition.

No longer the post-Cold War world

The twenty-first-century American origins of this anti-free trade, incumbency thinking may stem from hegemonic complacency at the tail end of a seemingly unipolar world. It did not characterize American political or business leadership during the Cold War or early post-Cold War periods.

American firms outside of the tech sector have declined in relative competitiveness vis-à-vis their global counterparts over the last decades. And this has led to a greater desire by their leaderships to insulate them from competition. As a result, over the last decade or so, major American-headquartered firms have either played an oversized role in setting these new anti-competitive norms or have seamlessly adapted to them. More recently, Trump channelled the zeitgeist of certain CEOs in declining industries like coal, oil, and steel. Yet, those industries will not come back merely because of Trump's or other politicians' reactionary policies attempting to freeze time.[32]

Today, free trade is a risky platform for American politicians of both parties. The American far left and far right both oppose free trade for a variety of reasons. The Biden administration has shown wariness about embracing a free trade agenda and have already reinforced certain Trump tariffs and has spoken of continuing to shield domestic industry.

Economically, this does not make sense. But psychologically it does. America's proportion of global exports and global GDP have been decreasing for decades now. Incumbency appears to have become bipartisan.

One of Biden's first executive orders was to strengthen Trump's Buy America programme.[33] Similarly, the first piece of major legislation of the Biden era was the Covid relief bill, which was immensely popular with the American public, partially because it contained many populist and anti-market provisions, most famously giving $1,400 stimulus cheques to about half the US population. In short, although Biden represents a profound reversal on many salient dynamics of the Trump legacy, he is not an unabashed advocate of global free markets and is not keen on shaking the corporate apple cart. This is especially true now that mainstream corporate America has increasingly abandoned the Republican party and has sought to back the Biden administration as the moderate,[34] pro-establishment party in the wake of the 6 January 2021 insurrection and the April 2021 Republican-backed Georgia legislation to restrict voter rights.[35]

* * *

Returning to my experiences with American firms doing business in Libya, prior to 2017 I had received warnings of American corporates seeking to freeze the status quo in place, but initially they seemed to be so counter-intuitive and conspiratorial that I dismissed them. On the face of it, why would they try to prevent reform to the notoriously inefficient, subsidy-laden Libyan economy that was holding back their assets from becoming even more valuable? Why would they oppose the replacement of the heads of various semi-sovereign Libyan bodies who were both refusing to pay their companies' back payments and maintaining the inefficient laws that prevent the value of their assets from skyrocketing? Why would a Fortune 100 company with billions of dollars of investment in Libya try to block a trade mission of US companies to Libya?

I cannot say for sure. But the answer appears to lie in the inherent preference of dominant market players for a form of status quo that blocks new entrants. This psychology of incumbents tends to prevail when the dominant firms or dominant nations have lost their prior competitive advantage and no longer believe—whether subconsciously or otherwise—that they would win in open competition. This psychology leads to a preference for resting on one's laurels and hoping to collect a kind of 'rent' for ownership of choice assets, technologies, stakes in consortia, and preferential access to the levers of power.

I was witnessing in microcosm what the news headlines were whispering: we no longer live in a world where America cultivates and polices a 'fair' global economic order.[36] Instead, the coin of the realm for both countries and multinational companies during the Enduring Disorder is privileged access. For the Tech Giants, as well as the Big Oil companies, it was 'One Man, One Vote, One Time.' They had won the first round of the competition and wished to use their dominance to cancel subsequent rounds. They might have thought they were substituting a free trade order, for one of incumbent dominance. But the Chinese, Turkish, Russian, and other players were not getting the message that they were supposed to keep out of America's patch. They have continued to rise and encroach.

Putting the pieces together

Seen holistically, Libya's economic dysfunctionality and deep interconnections to major global corporations provides a fascinating insight into how capitalism actually functions during the Enduring Disorder. In some instances, it plays out as multinationals pushing for authoritarian stability in places like Qadhafi's Libya, Putin's Russia, or Obiang's Equatorial Guinea. Tragically, when it comes to approaches towards post-Qadhafi Libya or post-Maidan Ukraine, many have chosen to embrace the corrupt and dysfunctional status quo, where things may be crazy, but at least your company has the WhatsApp number of the guy who controls the Central Bank and can, in theory, wire you the money you are owed. This is unfortunate as the multinationals would almost certainly have better long-term returns on their investments in a more functional and economically competitive regime. But maintaining the status quo—where the money keeps coming in with minimal risk and in the process blocks competition—probably makes it easier for these organizations to meet their short-term performance targets. It also suits their current psychology and corporate cultures.

As discussed in Chapter 4, incumbent psychology's attractions for CEOs, lobbyists, trade associations, and dominant firms has not been treated sufficiently in the literature, unlike the detailed scrutiny that has been given to the corrosive effects of bankers' bonuses being tied to short-term performance targets. Popular books about the dangers of the oil industry to global geopolitics and human wellbeing, such as Rachel Maddow's *Blowout* or academic ones like Thane Gustafson's *Wheel of Fortune: The Battle for Oil and Power in Russia* and *All the Kremlin's Men: Inside the Court of Vladimir Putin* by Mikhail Zygar[37] all assume that Western multinational energy companies are coherently pursuing shareholder value and long-term profits in a rational way in their dealings with unsavoury autocrats and broken semi-sovereign institutions. Those authors' perceptions are that devoid of democratic oversight, Western citizens face the externalities caused by the companies' rational pursuit of profits.

Having worked with the major corporates of the Libya space in close quarters via my USLBA experience, I analyse their actions from more of a Freudian or Polybian perspective than a Hayekian, Smithian, or Leninist one. What I witnessed is that CEOs and lobbyists of major multinationals are operating under their own delusional myths, reinforced by the short-termism of the quarterly earnings reports. Therefore, multinational companies frequently choose suboptimal decisions that harm their long-term interests. So do governments and individuals. The psychological component here is profound and cannot be explained away by charts and graphs of expected earnings.

As wealth inequality grows globally, this 'status quo paradox' is increasingly familiar to most of the world's population. Global elites seem quite good at preserving the current economic model, which generally keeps their stock prices going up and their taxes going down—independent of whether it is actually good for their long-term economic wellbeing or the planet's. This dynamic is widely acknowledged and studied. Nonetheless, it is an under-researched feature of this neo-mercantile, yet hyper-globalized world that there is frequently a tacit understanding linking leading multinationals and incumbent wealthy and corrupt regimes. Big corporate power tends to mediate the interplay between entrenched interests in places like Ukraine, Libya, Turkey, Russia, and the UAE to the hubs of the global economy in London, Houston, Singapore, and New York. Furthermore, corporate channels sanitize the flows of hot money from conflict zones into our democratic politics. This is the main conceptual linkage between the mid-twenty-first-century neo-mercantile economy and the political conditions in the West that eviscerate coherent, forward-looking leadership and promote the Enduring Disorder.

Our understanding of these issues would benefit from more graduate students and think tank scholars working on the real implications of the psychology of incumbency and how it is shaping the world we live in. Western societies should encourage up-and-coming economists to do what their eighteenth-century forebears did and popularize their theoretical research which proves that mercantilism doesn't work as an economic system.

Where to go from here?

Even before all the necessary research is conducted and the popularizing op-eds are penned, we still need an interim global game plan for the world's hot spots, where prevailing conditions have in certain instances made the multinationals become a part of the problem rather than the spear tip of the solution. The prevailing conditions of the Enduring Disorder have pushed major multinational companies, especially in certain industries, away from being good collective citizens and collaborative players. This process has been particularly noticeable in a place like Libya, where existing semi-sovereign institutions evolved the capacity to offer perverse incentive structures for the international companies that interface with them.

As such, the major collective action problems must be solved by connecting the Libyan populace, Libyan reformers, and Libyan intellectuals directly with their international allies—not mediated via the prevailing economic logic of the Enduring Disorder. The top dogs of the global private sector will remain advocates for the status quo ante in Libya because the existing institutions either owe them money, are making them money, or are providing some kind of psychological security blanket for incumbent players. But international institutions and governments should not be driven by such short-term calculations—they should be worrying about the systemic instability that emanates from ungoverned spaces like Libya in the forms of terrorism, rent-seeking, migration, cults of personality, and arms proliferation. In an ideal world, subject matter experts and veteran technocrats would be able to override their political bosses' incumbent psychology to tackle head-on the collective action complexities surrounding major global challenges. Our reality is very far from that dream.

If not global capitalism to the rescue, what then?

By 2019, the experiences I related above led me to conclude that the mythical rational, profit-driven multinational corporations simply did not exist. Hence Fortune 500 corporations would not be the answer for Libya's ails. Therefore, this chapter's excerpt presents a piece of think tank scholarship calling for governments and international organizations—in alliance with Libyan reformers and young people—to step forward to deal with the genuine drivers of conflict and economic dysfunction by forming an international financial commission to coordinate the collective action complexities that currently impede coherent action. Once reformed institutions are in place, creating different incentive structures, then big businesses will not fight for the old order— they will be forced to adapt. However, some firms will have to be dragged kicking and screaming, so that they don't prevent genuine reforms from coming into place. This could well be a lesson applicable to multiple theatres across the Enduring Disorder.

* * *

Selections from: Jason Pack, 'An International Financial Commission Is Libya's Last Hope', *Middle East Institute*, September 2020.

> For a range of reasons... the 21st century's international system is more fractured and therefore promotes proxy intervention while consistently hampering mediation efforts... Globalization, the internet, and the withdrawal of American hegemonic power all reduce the relative importance of controlling strategic pieces of territory. Of course, airports, roads, oil installations, military barracks, and ethnic heartlands still retain military importance—but over the last decades—institutions, economic structures, and media narratives have gained increasing strategic weight. As a result, many twenty-first-century conflicts are no longer fought primarily over territory or even rival national visions but for more obscure and hybrid logics, whereby control of territory is merely one dimension of a multidimensional, multiplayer chess game.
>
> In such multifaceted wars, it is impossible to bring peace to a war-torn nation without addressing the complex root causes of the violence. Merely returning the combatants to their antebellum territorial locations will not suffice in instances where territory was militarily

contested only to provide leverage over an economic institution or grant one side an optic of victory.

* * *

Nowhere are these complexities on starker display than in Libya, where since 2011 the country's seemingly endless Wars of Post-Qadhafi Succession have not fundamentally been fought over the control of territory but rather over the control of economic institutions, patronage networks, and the amorphous optics of legitimacy and international support...

Back in January 2020 [*when the below policy recommendations were written*], I called for the main heads of Libya's political bodies and semi-sovereign economic institutions to request international help in convening a technocratic commission to: Firstly, make transparent to the Libyan people where their money is being spent, where their subsidized products are being transported, and where the billions are actually kept; and then secondly, rewrite the rules of Libya's economy in a transparent way, taking into consideration genuine expert advice and the will of the Libyan people...

The military stalemate [*as of September 2020 when this preface to the recommendations was published*] is partially useful as it ends needless suffering and allows improvements in the security situation so civilians, technocrats, and businesspeople can return to Tripoli and communities across the country. Yet on its own, the military stalemate will not end Libya's Wars of Post-Qadhafi Succession. No lasting political deal can emerge if the underlying causes of violence remain unaddressed—the semi-sovereign prerogatives of Libya's new breed of oligarchs who have overstayed their legitimate mandates, the unfettered access to secret funds, and the corrupt distortions of the market mechanism that are embedded in Libya's current economic institutions [*and that many international corporations tacitly seek to uphold*].

No matter how many power plants and mobile electricity generation units are added to the Libyan power grid, load-shedding will still be necessary every summer if electricity remains subsidized and demand growth is unchecked by the functioning of a rational market. No matter how much oil revenue flows into Libya, fights to control key institutions in Tripoli will continue until transparency mechanisms are created to showcase how funds flow to and from Libya's communities and institutions. No matter how peaceful Libya becomes, there will always be an incentive to join a militia if doing so can provide preferential access to subsidized goods.

Intelligent and civically-minded Libyan patriots, especially those of the younger generation, are willing to put the past behind them and forget old grievances about whose cousin, and which tribe, started which war. They need the help of their genuine allies abroad to provide the protection, technocratic expertise, and political cover to actualize their visions of reform and renewal.

Prescribing a workable solution in ten policy recommendations

[*The reinvigorated UN-mediated peace process (which was rechristened the Berlin Process after major heads of state including Chancellor Merkel and Presidents Putin, Macron, and Erdoğan, came together in Berlin in January 2020 to discuss Libya) can claim remarkable successes when it comes to ceasefires and transitions of power. But it has failed to demonstrate much progress on economic reform through the so-called economic dialogue track. As such, the below recommendations, which were drafted before the January 2020 Berlin Conference was organized, could now serve in the Spring of 2021 forward as a way to supplant the moribund economic dialogue track and capitalize on the legitimacy of the GNU.*]

1. Establish an International Financial Commission (IFC) with its headquarters in Malta, Tunis, or London. It will have offices in Tripoli, Misrata, Sabha, Tubruq, Baida, and Benghazi, but it is essential that top Western officials can easily brief it and that its Libyan members are not subject to militia intimidation. To achieve Libyan buy-in, the main Libyan political, economic, and institutional players will initiate the creation of the IFC by requesting it and then formally participating in it—initially by allowing audits of their institutions and other transparency promoting mechanisms. If there is hesitation on behalf of specific relevant Libyan stakeholders to convene the commission, then those who are willing can promote transparency and audits of their institutions, which will build momentum for the full-blown IFC and make it more difficult for spoilers to resist.[38]

Because optics matter, the international community will not formally request or convene the commission, but rather the Libyan semi-sovereign institutions and top political brass... will initiate it—acknowledging that the Libyan economy is dysfunctional and needs the help of Libya's allies to be reformed. As noted above, the author of this paper has spoken with many of the heads of Libya's most important semi-sovereign institutions (including the NOC, Libya Post, Telecommunication, and Information Technology Company (LPTIC), CBL, and the Libyan Investment Authority (LIA); many have assured me that were the right mechanisms in place they would call for such a commission to help them do their jobs more effectively, and that they would want to sit on the IFC, acting as both stakeholders at the commission and reform agents for it. Moreover, the institutions which possess sovereign wealth (LPTIC, CBL, LIA, and its subsidiary the Libyan Local Investment & Development Fund (LLIDF) would be willing to fund the IFC's activities if it brought increased Western engagement, capacity-building, and protection of their institutions from militia intimidation...

An IFC is necessary to undo the corrupt incentive structures that operate at present. A genuine supranational commission with sovereign powers to reform the institutions of the Libyan economy is needed... International technical experts embedded in the Libyan ministries won't work—as, in Libya, the ministries have relatively little power, and their functions are duplicated at the semi-sovereign institutional level. The process of embedding technical experts without country-specific expertise was tried and failed after the ouster of Qadhafi. The IFC will differentiate itself from previous training experiments by having Libyans and Western experts of Libya as its core components. Libya is too complicated for outsiders—other than those that have dedicated a significant portion of their professional lives—to fix it.

The IFC will start by cataloguing and auditing the Libyan economy—financial and petrol flows as well as subsidies, institutional architectures, debts to foreign companies, and the competences of various authorities. Only once the research is done and the findings promulgated will the IFC engage in the action phase of announcing and implementing reforms. It should have an equal number of voting members from Libya and from the key international and regional powers. The chairmanship should rotate among a Libyan, a Briton, an EU official, and an American.

[*The first step to reforming Libya's economy must be fully understanding it. Over the course of 2020 and 2021, a forensic audit of the CBL was conducted by the international accounting firm Deloitte. The then-Acting UN SRSG to Libya Stephanie Williams was instrumental in surmounting the political hurdles that stood in the way of the audit's progress, just as she was in pushing the LPDF to its conclusion. She even tried to expand the remit of the audit to accomplish some of the functions that I had called for the IFC to do in this paper.*

Later, in an email conversation with Stephanie Williams in Spring 2021, she explained to me,

> I believe the story of how the audit was actually implemented is important and illustrative of the broad 'sovereignty' theme you outline (in your think tank papers and book). The invocation of 'sovereignty' (by Libyan political figures and heads of semi-sovereign institutions) when it suits the status quo as a blocking mechanism to processes which may shed light on corrupt practices, versus a reliance (by these same vested Libyan interests) on internationals to protect these same institutions (from domestic scrutiny) when needed. I do believe the fact that I achieved the audit somewhat broke that model.

Williams' perspective explains how the modicum of sovereignty vested in Libya's economic institutions, due to the Skhirat treaty and the processes I have described in Chapter 4, constitutes a blocking mechanism to acquiring accurate information about their functioning. It highlights how an essential aspect of any International Financial Commission is for it to have the requisite powers to compel transparency and systematize information about the Libyan economy.]

At present only internationals have the capacity to devise the technical mechanisms needed to fix the Libyan economy in a transparent way. Mid-career officials from the foreign ministries must also staff the commission, not only technical experts. This is essentially to signal the political will from, and the direct connection to, the key policy makers back in London, Brussels, Rome, and Washington to vest the commission with the requisite political clout and power.

2. The first act of the commission will be the creation of a website—with easy access via social media and the internet—that can communicate the actions of the IFC to Libyans and worldwide in Arabic and English.

Libya has one of the highest rates of social media and Facebook penetration in the world and its citizens are highly involved in the country's political discourse. To date this has been a point of polarization; it can equally be wielded as a point of inclusion. Libyans should be able to easily submit evidence to the commission via an online platform.

3. After the website is operational the second step of the commission should be to figure out how Libya's economy actually works at present. It will hire academic experts and retired Libyan and international businesspeople and diplomats to create a map of Libya's economy and its stakeholders. This work will demonstrate the formal and informal power relationships and existing laws that constitute the architecture of Libya's economy and institutions. Its findings will be published on the web in Arabic and English for all to see.

This will facilitate domestic Libyan buy-in for the proposed reforms.[39] Unlike in other societies, Libyans do not have a constitution, fundamental law, or monarchical charter which explains how power flows in their society. The Libyan people are educated, involved, and deeply curious. The IFC must not engage in spin or propaganda. It must simply present the facts as verified by experts. This step will create enormous goodwill for the IFC and allow for a conversation with the Libyan people in a way that previous attempts at National Dialogue have not.

4. Create a system to transparently monitor flows of refined petrol.

A GPS tagging system for petrol trucks and a special website which allows for tracking the movement of petrol across the country in real time should be established. All petrol for the Libyan domestic market can be tagged with a special compound so that it can be traced if it is smuggled abroad. The NOC has recommended this step previously.[40]

5. Create a system to transparently monitor financial transfers into and out of the CBL and into and out of ministries. At present, only the functionaries of the rival branches of the CBL and military leaders know how the Libyan economy truly functions. Top officials in the government are unaware of how various sums are spent.

Complete transparency of allocation of money to ministries and municipalities must be achieved immediately. It must also be clear what they spend it on. The results should be published online in Arabic and English. Corruption has thrived in the dark and will be progressively minimized by the light. The CBL is not solely to blame for the current state of affairs; it is a result of the Qadhafian legacy. However, without the CBL's buy-in this plan cannot be implemented.

6. Complete an audit of Libya's semi-sovereign economic institutions. Make the resulting document of 'who has what and where' public for all Libyans.

7. Achieve buy-in from the Libyan people about what a fair and just Libyan economy would look like by

conducing social media and telephone polls, culminating in a national conference on the topic.

8. Undertake subsidy reform, currency devaluation then flotation. The plans should first be promulgated and then implemented. [*A one-off devaluation of the dinar happened at the start of 2021 and was a big success in undercutting the structural incentives for smuggling subsidized goods, but future devaluations or flotation will likely still be necessary due to the weakness of Libya's macroeconomic picture in the face of fluctuating global crude prices and Libya's erratic oil production figures.*]

9. The laws governing Libya's semi-sovereign institutions should be re-written by the IFC and then implemented by those very institutions in concert with relevant government authorities.

10. New technocrats—especially young people and women—should be chosen via a meritocratic process and installed within the reformed institutions. They should receive ongoing training and communication from the IFC as they reshape the Libyan economy....

2011 was not a revolution: That is why the economic fabric of the ancien regime (the semi-sovereign institutions) survived

What happened in 2011 was merely a series of disconnected uprisings.[41] A genuine root and branch revolution (like France in 1789 or Russia in 1917 or the Warsaw Pact Countries in 1989) would have destroyed entities like the Economic and Social Development Fund (ESDF), the Organization for the Development of Administrative Centres (ODAC), CBL, and LIA—expropriating their monies, replacing them with more functional or more 'revolutionary' institutions answerable to the new regime's logic, and doling out funds at the behest of the new order. Tsarist Russian institutions were destroyed, their liabilities or hard currency either erased or ransacked by new structures...

Yet in Libya, due to the absence of genuine leadership or a unifying vision of what post-Qadhafi Libya should look like, the multibillion-dollar behemoths are all still intact. Salaries and subsidies have been raised on multiple occasions, yet the mechanisms and institutional logic of using oil revenues and extreme centralization to buy-off the Libyan people's complacency was never altered. Today, the General Electric Company of Libya (GECOL) and the LIA, as examples, appear as much facts of Libyan life as the Sahara Desert—immutable and eternal, filled with vast economic resources and huge opportunities for inefficiencies, smuggling, and self-dealing.[42] Due to their perceived permanence and prestige, there is an incentive for Libyans to fight to control these loci of power [*and for foreign firms to fight to preserve their privileged access to them.*]

Paradoxically since 2014, as the rival governments' abilities to govern or control territory have been steadily weakened, they still fight tooth and nail over the right to officially run Libya's semi-sovereign economic institutions. In fact, their legal 'rights' to appoint boards of directors of institutions or award access to contracting vehicles are the only real powers that either government possesses. In short, in a country where no government holds genuine sovereignty, it is these semi-sovereign economic institutions that (in certain instances) are the only functioning parts of the Libyan 'state'. They have more than merely cash—they are still vested with power and legitimacy, whereas the governments' ministries are not.

It follows, then, that as Libya's post-Qadhafi chaos has failed to offer up any legitimate social contract to the Libyan people, a perversion of the existing Qadhafian social contract has emerged. Each Libyan region, locality, tribe, ideological grouping, and individual feels that they are as entitled as anyone else to the money and power vested in Libya's semi-sovereign institutions. People do not care that the rationales for those institutions no longer exist, they simply want their piece of the pie. And they are willing to fight for it.

Is the international community sovereign or partly sovereign in Libya?

Why should the international community have any role or legitimacy in remaking Libya's economic structures and complete the trajectory of the anti-Qadhafi Uprisings?

Firstly, because since 2014, the Libyan conflict has become a penetrated system whereby the armed actors and institutional heads function primarily due to the support or legitimacy that international actors bestow upon them. Secondly, [*as shown in Chapter 4's excerpt*] Libyan institutions were semi-independent under Qadhafi, developed semi-sovereignty in the political vacuum in the wake of Qadhafi's ouster, and via the Skhirat Treaty process international stakeholders have granted them a claim to complete sovereignty.[43] In short, the 'sovereignty' of the CBL or the Housing and Infrastructure Board (HIB)—in as much as they exist— has been granted by the UN and international actors, not by Libyan law. The reason for this is twofold: firstly, these institutions are merely shells from the Qadhafi period, and it is international actors' willingness to accept them as legitimate that has enshrined them in the Libyan scene, and secondly, since 2014, Libya has legally lacked a sovereign authority.[44] Rather than using its position of authority to undo this institutional morass, much of international policy since 2014 has sought to insulate the CBL, LIA, Audit Bureau, and the NOC from the civil war and from partisan meddling, as if they were true sovereigns in line with their designation in the Skhirat Agreement.[45] In fact, as I have demonstrated elsewhere the UN mediation process overtly granted sovereignty to Libya's economic institutions to make sure that the diplomatic and business communities have interlocutors to deal with.[46]...

By issuing protections to status quo ante institutions, the international community has treated these institutions as if they truly operated in a vacuum of governance and sovereignty and hence had become completely sovereign entities. The wording chosen in the Skhirat Agreement text in 2015, actually accords with the UN Support Mission in Libya's and major international players' ensuing actions. This wording and complimentary political actions defy both reason and facts. The key, therefore, to untying the tangled knot of the Libyan crisis lies in acknowledging the semi-sovereign status of the country's economic agencies, and hence, their accountability to both the Libyan people and subordination to the international institutions and treaties from which Libyan sovereignty derives. This legal realization gives the legitimacy for key Libyan stakeholders and their international allies to call for the creation of the IFC...

One school of thought [*which I am sympathetic to on intellectual and legal grounds*] holds that after the fall of the Qadhafi regime and the failure of a non-interim sovereign government to emerge within the time limits set out by the 3 August 2011 temporary constitutional declaration, the international community, and the UN in particular, became effectively obligated to act as *in loco regis* for the vacant Libyan sovereign (as they did in the period 1947–51 after Italy chose/was compelled to abnegate its claims to sovereignty after losing the

Second World War, but before independent Libya was formed).[47] Seen from this legal perspective, the international community and the UN might have both the right and the duty to exert their sovereignty and either dismantle or reform the alphabet soup of semi-sovereign dysfunction. In the eyes of most Libyans, the more that they became aware of them over time, the institutions created in the Qadhafi period (e.g. ODAC, HIB, LIA, GECOL, LPTIC, ESDF, etc.) are as illegitimate as the pots of money squirrelled away by Qadhafi cronies offshore, frequently by using the semi-independent prerogatives of these institutions.[48] [*The increasing spread of knowledge about these institutions, transparency about their financial flows, and their connections to the global economy and major multinationals is creating the correct environment*] for key stakeholders to call for an international commission.[49]...

Leverage and how to deploy it

Prior international attempts to help in Libya's post-uprisings reconstruction (2012–13), to avert civil war and the fracturing of the country's institutions (2014), to reunify those institutions and create a pathway to elections (2015–18), and to halt the offensive against Tripoli (in 2019) [*before it became a protracted war*] have all failed because the international community has not deployed the leverage or goodwill that it possesses effectively. The UN and most Western nations have relied on press releases and diplomatic carrots, while the regional powers, which support spoilers, have deployed hard power in the form of arms, mercenaries, and cash... Western nations must finally threaten to use their stranglehold on international economic institutions and transactions to force Libyans to the table and to penalize outside actors that offer perverse incentives to militia leaders.

Simultaneously, genuine naming, shaming, and sanctioning of spoilers must be applied multi-laterally and comprehensively against all sides. There must be no picking of favourites. Recent UN Sanctions Committee reports and U.S. Congressional legislation provide the information and the teeth to do this. The United States and the UK are viewed on the ground as relatively neutral actors, even if the UN is not. With these sticks in place, even previously recalcitrant Libyan technocrats might prove quite eager to participate in the IFC. Once they express that willingness, they need to be protected. Spoilers who benefit from the status quo war economy will likely attempt to hijack the process. They will be unable to do so if foreign support to such spoilers is profoundly penalized and boxed out and key militia leaders involved in Libya's economy and willing to participate are given a real seat at the table, rather than being treated as elephants in the room, as in previous negotiation processes.

Conclusion: avoiding another 'Oil-for-Food' fiasco by having a genuine Libyan-led process

Financially and diplomatically, Libya's civil war is among the most complex and globalized of the twenty-first-century's major conflicts. As such, international policy must finally come to reflect the reality that the devil is in the details. No one actor can dominate the country. No single military or political event can cut the Gordian knot of corruption and bad incentives. It is for this reason that the conditions that allow this mess to persist must be studied in depth and untangled bit by bit—by diagnosing drivers of conflict and chokepoints to progress and then systematically eliminating them. The easiest such drivers to eliminate are subsidies, the dinar rate, and the blocking power of vested economic players who allow the current morass to persist.[50] Once those are out of the way, another layer of spoilers, militia chokepoints, and command and control blockages will need to be dealt with. The IFC process can achieve the requisite degree of specificity, research, implementation, and pooling of political will... It can be framed as a consensus international approach to dealing with Libya's ongoing civil war deriving from Libyan political leaders and semi-sovereign institutional heads, who will request it and facilitate buy-in and transparency.

For the IFC to work, lessons must be learned from the Iraq 'Oil for Food' debacle, which scarred a generation of UN and P5 diplomats. The main lesson which must be applied to Libya—as told to the author by retired diplomatic participants—is to focus on transparency (both of financial flows and of decision criteria) while having Libyan institutions and stakeholders call for the IFC rather than having UN fiat decree it upon them. Fortunately, top Libyan political and economic officials frequently request increased US and UK engagement in their country and have stated in London and Washington that they are willing to publicly request more engagement. Moreover, relative to Iraq in the 1990s, the current information technology and its broad penetration in Libya means that transparency is arguably easier now than it was at the time of the 'Oil for Food' programme. Today, it is possible to engage in diplomacy directly with the Libyan people by publishing in real time the workings of the commission on the internet and social media and making the reformation of the Libyan economy a collective nation-building project.

Libya is filled with economic opportunities. At present these economic assets and the economic needs of the Libyan people are being used to enable corruption. These assets and needs can be turned into even greater opportunities to release the productive capacity of the Libyan people... This can only be accomplished if a neutral caretaking technocratic commission creates new institutions and agrees on the rules of the economic game prior to the free-for-all power grab of elections or jockeying for position in a post-civil war appointed government.

Policy recommendations born out of a personal journey

After years of working on Libya from a variety of perspectives—as an academic, a consultant, a representative of large multinationals, an advisor to diplomats, a media pundit, and a think tank scholar—it had finally dawned on me. Big business was not the solution, it had become a part of the problem. Because of its influence and the circumstances of the Enduring Disorder, even the most ideally targeted 'silver bullet' policy recommendation stood no chance of being implemented, let alone of succeeding without coordinated international governmental buy-in. The logic of a Libyan coalition of righteous and well-intentioned actors getting others on board was simply not feasible in a country with a fragmented social and political legitimacy being manipulated by the discordant puppet masters of a non-hegemonic world in disarray.

Yet even if the international components were miraculously fixed, attempts to get the different Libyan factions to march in step would be denounced inside Libya as neo-colonialism if they came exclusively from outside. Hence the policy suggestions presented in the above excerpt advocate for unity to be achieved first by a bloc of relevant Libyan domestic stakeholders, institutions, youth representatives, and power players. They would then be able to create the legitimacy for the relevant partnerships with the international community needed to fix Libya's perverse economic incentive structures. Only then would they request outside help in bringing forth the necessary conditions to make their vision into a reality.

From the domestic Libyan angle, this might not be as far-fetched as it seems. After nearly a decade of the Wars of Post-Qadhafi Succession, many prominent Libyan intellectuals and technocrats of all stripes and factions—even those who had initially decried outside support—had finally admitted publicly that they could not fix Libya's problems by themselves.[51] Their country's economy and conflict had become completely internationalized and penetrated by the centrifugal forces of the Enduring Disorder. Every institution that Qadhafi had devised to entrap foreign firms had ended up tethering Libyan institutions further to the status quo. Having abandoned the initial hope that foreign powers would leave them alone to pursue their own internal affairs, major Libyan technocrats have spent the last few years begging the international community to solve their collective action problems.

This acceptance of the need for foreign mediation finally bore fruit on the political front. Libyans of many political stripes, regions, and ethnicities accepted the late 2020 LPDF process, even though it was invented entirely by the UN and culminated in an oligarch with ties to the Qadhafi regime being selected as Libya's new prime minister.

That Libyans successfully rallied around a consensus process suggests that they have already become sufficiently tired of dysfunction and factional infighting so as to be both willing to accept foreign mediation of their disputes and to turn a blind eye to the faults in the process so long as it yields results. It would seem that a similar model could now build on these political achievements and be applied to Libyan economic issues.

Tragically, on the economic front, the Libyans may have been trusting the wrong interlocutors. What many Libyan officials have consistently failed to grasp is that the US private sector is not organized as a coherent, rational, profit-seeking collective bound together by shared goals of profit maximization and positive-sum collaboration with Libya's best interests. This is not to say that there are no US businesses that want to help Libya and make a buck in the process. There are many. They merely face difficulties solving the requisite collective action challenges to work together and forge win-wins, unless a functional institution, dynamic individual, or appropriately constructed entity arises to lead them.

In response to Libyan requests for more American businesses in their country, the US government could have stepped in and conducted their own trade mission to Libya, the way that many continental European governments' trade promotion agencies do. Those private sector actors who wanted to come along for the ride would benefit enormously, and the relevant Libyans institutions would have embraced them with open arms. Only governments, corporations, and societies working together can solve massively complex collective action problems. As Benjamin Franklin said: 'We must all hang together, or, most assuredly, we shall all hang separately.'

The US–Libya (Anti-)Business Association is totemic of the Enduring Disorder

On my resignation from USLBA, the president of NFTC, the trade association with USLBA's management contract, made a kind and respectful gesture. He offered me the 'rights to all the intellectual property' from the research I had produced about the Libyan economy. However, to acknowledge what I had really learned, it would have been more fitting for him to have awarded me an MBA from the K St school of neo-mercantilism. In late 2016, I thought I had been hired to analyse the finer points of the Libyan commercial scene and seek market expansion opportunities for the firms I represented, but by mid-2018, I realized I had inadvertently signed up for a crash course about American multinationals drifting towards protectionism in the age of the Enduring Disorder.

The mega-corporates had long ago fallen prey to the psychology of incumbents. They were privileged powerholders who feared change and were either too lazy to plan for its inevitability or were expressly instructed by their leaderships not to do so. In retrospect, it seems, then, that I had unwittingly agreed to be the figurehead of the US–Libya (Anti-)Business Association—lending it, albeit very temporarily, the whitewashing that came with my scholarly credentials and long track record of helping Libyans. And yet, despite all their attempts to control the optics surrounding their business endeavours, the companies were still not achieving their goals. The board member companies' investments in Libya were not thriving. By the rigorous logic of markets, smaller and more nimble firms and trade associations were bound to come along and challenge the incumbents.

And this trajectory encapsulates a larger truth: attempts to close borders, block change, and prevent new entrants in a globalized commercial contest do not constitute a comprehensive strategy or a sustainable alternative order. As market conditions evolve, there will always be those who stand to lose from progress and hence have an incentive to block it. Yet, the zero-sum nature of blocking progress is generally seen as shameful and needs to be enacted in the shadows. Hence, such retrograde action manifests itself as the disorderly, ineffectual, and haphazard enterprise that it inherently is. Mercantilism and protectionism are not only bad economics; they are simply unsustainable. They do not even achieve the goals for which they claim to be designed.

Despite claiming to put America first, Trump's policies hurt the competitiveness of many American firms abroad. From his first few months in office, it seems unlikely that Biden will reverse this trajectory. Similarly, trying to protect their decades-long fiefdoms in Libya, USLBA's strategy had inadvertently presided over the replacement of American firms by their more nimble Turkish, German, Italian, French, and British competitors.

CONCLUSION

QUO VADIS?

Aren't neo-mercantilism and neo-populism just alternative forms of order?

This book's investigation of the dynamics underlying the current era of the Enduring Disorder has unearthed many paradoxes. The biggest one may be the assertion that simultaneous and coordinated attempts by many actors to embrace neo-mercantilism and illiberal populism actually constitute the antithesis of any systemic order.

This conundrum can be explained as follows: this volume has laid out the case for the recent birth of a new historical epoch defined by novel forms of global collective action failure. At the same time, it has demonstrated the presence of powerful individuals, corporations, and quasi-state institutions, which potentially in unison, carve out privileges in order to grant themselves certain sustained structural advantages—like privileged market access or geopolitical or commercial 'rents'.

This raises the question: if the illiberal neo-populist regimes and the anti-free trade multinational corporations are all pushing in a certain direction, couldn't that be analysed as the opposite of disorder? Does it not merely herald the emergence of a different kind of order—one that is more monopolistic and less Liberal than has prevailed across the Global North in the second half of the twentieth century? According to this line of criticism, this volume has been right to identify that the post-Cold War era has ended due to global structural changes but possibly wrong to argue that the new era is defined by disorder rather than simply being an illiberal order.

My treatment of the phenomenon of neo-mercantilism and incumbent psychology in the last two chapters foreshadowed my rebuttal of this criticism and the exposition of a paradox. I contend that the political approach of aspiring autocrats and institution-breakers in the West, wannabe-tyrants like Haftar in war-torn countries, or corporate entities trying to stem the flow of trade are all unsustainable. Like the ghost ship whose passengers fight to briefly steer the vessel into choppier waters, even if they succeed in directing the vessel on to their desired course, their actions will only cause more instability and necessitate further rapid course corrections. Plato understood this. He did not think that letting the passengers steer the ship was an alternative order to having the navigator at the helm. He understood that it was no order at all.

Unlike traditional monarchies, global empires, republics, or liberal democracies, the political currents of neo-populism, leadership by cults of personality, and neo-mercantilism do not enjoy a track record of fostering long-term stability—they either inadvertently or deliberately create more instability. Their policies and ideologies are as rapidly shuffled as Noman Benotman's Twitter pronouncements. In the case of the corporate actors blocking access, controlling optics, or trying to protect a dominant position, the fact that their rear guard actions inherently promote instability is probably not grasped by those actors, as they have fallen prey to incumbent psychology. Conversely, those political players who promise their followers monetary handouts, job creation, and better versions of international treaties knowing that they cannot sustainably deliver them probably do realize that they are agents of disorder. Either way, from this perspective, the ascendency of the neo-mercantilists or the neo-populists does not constitute an alternative order but rather the facilitation of the rapid churn and reversals that I have sketched as defining this new historical period.

The reader is, of course, free to disagree with this proposed resolution of the aforementioned conundrum.[1] But this logic explains why these illiberal forces feed upon, and in turn, chose to reinforce the Enduring Disorder—and will not voluntarily produce a new, more stable international system.

Neither Biden nor any Western leader acting alone can change this. Most of the problems besetting Western states, from deficits to inefficient public services to coordination failures in confronting geopolitical foes like Russia and China, have all been getting worse. Although popular misconceptions have blamed Trump for much of the current global dysfunction, it actually has longer institutional antecedents. According to the editor-in-chief of *Bloomberg*, John Micklethwait, and the political editor of the *Economist*, Adrian Wooldridge, leaders of all mainstream Western political parties over the last four decades have been systemically ignoring the root causes of our current disorder, while choosing to exclusively fight symptoms.[2] This is why the Enduring Disorder will far outlive Trump, Brexit, and Putin. Self-reinforcing structural factors have been unleashed that separate our current era from the post-Cold War one that preceded it.

But was there ever a global order?

It is impossible to say with any certainty if a global 'order' has ever or will ever exist. Did the Pax Britannica or Americana really 'order the globe', or was disorder still prevalent in those times?

There is a compelling argument to be made that disorder has prevailed over the span of human history, and that any sort of global order was only a three-and-a-half-century aberration due to unique economic and military realities that lasted roughly from the Peace of Westphalia in 1648 until the end of the Cold War in 1991.[3] Order and disorder are of course relative and not absolute.[4] They are also qualitative and immeasurable. Pockets of order exist within a disorderly system, just as pockets of disorder exist within an orderly one.

I have sought to present an abstract thought experiment born out of my own experiences, observations, and analysis, hoping to push the scholarship and the debate forward. It is impossible for this exercise to be completely scientific. It has not attempted to 'prove' anything but rather to intuit trendlines and the direction of travel. My contention is that study of the Libyan microcosm reveals that, over the last decade or more, new sources of systemic disorder have been unleashed and that, under the current conditions, these trends are self-reinforcing, especially in how they shape post-conflict societies in transition.

Even as these sources of disorder are multiplying and reinforcing each other, that does not mean that new ideologies of order cannot rapidly emerge to combat them. In fact, there are numerous philosophical frameworks to underpin such speculations. It behoves us to consider the implications of these optimistic expectations: the world system and the human race may gradually be rationalizing itself in a Whig or Enlightenment sense; undergoing a process of self-realization in a Hegelian manner;[5] going through overarching world historical cycles in a Viconian sense;[6] or progressing towards spiritual and eschatological unification according to Baha'i or other related theologies.

Just as new political movements have arisen over the early part of the twenty-first century stressing difference, division, and nationalism, the peoples of the world may in fact be on the cusp of becoming fed-up with divisive politics and ready to put aside national, religious, and parochial identities to forge new, cross-cutting alliances. There are minor indications of this in global protest movements like the Extinction Rebellion of 2018[7] and the mass protests in the wake of the killing of George Floyd in the spring of 2020,[8] but contraindicators remain dominant at the institutional level and overshadow these brief flashes of spontaneous, non-hierarchical, and non-institutional global collective action.

None of this speculation or examination of the evidence proves anything beyond a reasonable doubt. Hegelians, futurists, and Viconians do not believe that an accumulation of standard evidence will likely precede their anticipated trendline shifts. In fact, the emerging science of futurism or super-forecasting is not necessarily evidence- or research-based in the way that other disciplines claim to be.[9] It instead calls for intuition, experience, discipline, forecasting trends, and imagination. Hence the book's treatment of the phenomenon of the Enduring Disorder has not been evidence-based in a traditional sense but more intuitive, descriptive, trend-conscious, and experience-based.

A novel coalition of previously rival states could spontaneously emerge to combat an existential threat like global warming, deepfakes,[10] or a global pandemic—just as the alliance of the United States, the UK, and the USSR in the early 1940s to combat Fascism would have seemed a complete impossibility in the early 1930s. Or looked at more philosophically, from a Hegelian or Baha'i perspective, a culmination of mass striving for collective consciousness could well yield new ideologies and global institutions that solve the current coordination complexities, possibly by using artificial intelligence or as yet undiscovered technology.

Much historical, philosophical, and spiritual wisdom suggests it is always darkest before the dawn. Yet, even for the analyst steeped in intuitive forecasting methods and examination of trendlines, the evidence pointing to the Enduring Disorder deepening in the short-to-medium term seems to outweigh the contraindications. One of the primary impediments to the paradigm shifts and cross-cutting alliances that the philosophers have envisioned is the failure of our international institutions to reform themselves to shepherd those bottom-up movements to completion. There is no doubt that many global youth movements and more than a few aspiring political leaders would like to end global warming or racism while solving wealth inequality and poverty. Yet, doing so requires functioning global institutions to coordinate multilateral action to solve the problems.

Without reforming the UN and the other international economic and governance bodies that comprise the post-1945 institutional legacy, it will be impossible to coordinate the collective action complexities that tackling these global goals or dealing with the possible problems of the future—like deep fakes, regulating artificial intelligence, or genetic manipulation. The fact that every new UN secretary general tries and fails to reform the UN, because of vested interests on behalf of those member states that the current system favours, means that global leadership cannot emerge from the very organization that was crafted to provide it.

In its current form the UN lacks an independent political will and is only ever able to express or embody the will of those member states with veto power. As such, the UN is another ideal microcosm for investigating the paradigm of the Enduring Disorder—why it has emerged and why it is deepening. The UN was created to resolve the problems of the post-war world. But the further we get into the new millennium, the less fit it is for that purpose. Its successes and failures and the types of collective action it can and cannot coordinate are directly analogous to why the situation in Libya has evolved in the way it has.[11] At present, the UN only works effectively when all major member states want to solve a problem and are flexible at delegating the coordination to an external body. The UN is completely useless at envisioning the problems of the future and setting up the institutional entities to deal with them. It is a deliberately reactive body constructed to provide legal cover for sovereign states' actions to deal with geopolitical issues. And it can only fulfil that role in those instances when the five permanent security council members are in agreement. Ambassador Jonathan Winer covers this issue in depth by drawing on his personal experiences in his Afterword. We both agree that, as bad as the UN is at coordinating Libya policy, there is every reason to assume it will be worse at policing deepfakes or regulating the use of artificial intelligence, gene manipulation, or cyberwar.

What has the Libyan microcosm demonstrated about these intangible processes?

Examination of the connections between the Libyan microcosm and the larger global system has illustrated connections among seemingly diverse phenomena such as appeasement, ungoverned space, jihadism, divisive/xenophobic rhetoric, cults of personality, influence operations, corruption, incumbent psychology, and the collapse of genuinely free global markets. These disparate yet interconnected phenomena in many of the world's societies in transition indirectly stem from the relative decline of both American hegemonic leadership and voluntary interstate coordination over the last two decades. Taken together, these two sets of phenomena reinforce each other through a positive feedback loop, epitomizing the historical era of the Enduring Disorder. In this brave new world, with a plethora of forces pulling in contradictory directions and lacking an overarching unifying power or alliance, actors and messages best suited to exploit the new vacuum naturally emerge.

LIBYA AND THE GLOBAL ENDURING DISORDER

In the Libyan arena, the perverse economic incentives created under Qadhafi and exacerbated by various post-Qadhafi tendencies are now the primary drivers of the conflict. Fixing them remains impossible without global collective action. Hence there is no 'Libya-only' solution without systemic reforms to the global system or isolating Libya from the global system through some kind of boxing out of outside powers. Similarly, most of the intractable problems of the contemporary world—climate change, demographic challenges, pandemics, disinformation, ungoverned space, jihadism—appear to derive from collective action problems—precisely because the current international system has not devised any newly functional mechanisms to coordinate collective solutions to them.

We are, in fact, fighting twenty-first-century problems with twentieth-century global institutions.[12] The result is that the problems have metastasized, and the global system has morphed far quicker than our prevailing theories of it. The current international system as presented in this book has proven itself incapable of formulating a coherent solution to a complex, multi-layered problem like Libya. A truly new form of global coordination seems to be required. The experiences this book has presented of how global corporations interact with Libya suggest that the global private sector is unlikely to spontaneously foster open markets, win-win solutions, or lasting reforms. This is unfortunate, as there are economic benefits for all actors to reap should they figure out how to work together—not only in Libya but on challenges like climate change.

Western (especially American) multinationals have been converted into incumbent powerhouses with their leaders succumbing to zero-sum and flawed incumbent psychology, in many instances fighting against their very own long term profitability to keep the global order roughly the same as it is. Schumpeter appears to have been prophetic when he argued ninety years ago that 'mainstream' Anglo-Saxon economists were always pedalling a self-serving myth by postulating that free and fair market competition emerges naturally in a laissez-faire world.[13] Rather, it emerged only when hegemonic powers worked in concert with their allies to create the national and international regulatory frameworks in which it could thrive.[14] And whenever those frameworks break down, inequality skyrockets and social mobility plummets. We are in one such period, but the difference is that unlike at the end of the nineteenth century, during the Enduring Disorder governments lack the capacity to deliver coordinated action, even if national electorates suddenly execute an about-face—voting and/or protesting for globalism rather than nationalism.[15] This does not bode well for President Joe Biden, European Commission President Ursula Van der Leyen, UN Secretary General António Guterres, or any of their successors to reverse the trendline. Nonetheless, it is great to see this new crop of committed globalists unfurl multilateral initiatives focused on creating global standards for corporate taxation, carbon emissions, or human rights. However despite their best intentions, these leaders simply lack the institutional tools, even if political currents start to shift away from nationalism and towards globalism.

If Libya is a representative example, there is every reason to believe that new economic incentive structures are needed to address the underlying causes of the current disease and give rise to the correct kinds of institutions. And then, with proper incentive structures in place, corporations and interested nation-states could become part of the solution. At present, there are few indications to anticipate such structures will be built, but it is nonetheless conceivable.

Extrapolating outward from Libya

What is true regarding collective action complexities in Libya's conflict is logically analogous to other major international problems like money laundering, tax havens, climate change, controlling infectious viruses, and regulating destabilizing emerging technologies like artificial intelligence and genetic manipulation. At present, the inability to create coalitions for global action has little to do with whether the solutions are known or unknown and everything to do with the hollowing out of international institutions and coordination among allies from 2003 to present. It also has to do with the power, competence, and legitimacy of Western nations, institutions, and ideologies to order the globe having been starkly eviscerated over the past decades. Multinational companies, and now Western political systems, have increasingly come to resemble the post-Soviet and non-Western structures with which globalization has brought them into increasing contact.[16] This is similar to the observations of military theorists such as Clausewitz, Van Creveld, and Sun Tzu about the involuntary mimicry that transpires between opponents during war.[17] We can understand this as a type of modernization theory in reverse.[18]

To tackle these challenges and formulate coherent solutions, there are two main options—a rising global hegemon that cultivates its ordering capacity, or a new form of publicly motivated sovereign collective such as a bloc of nation-states acting as a single unit for certain clearly delimited purposes. As discussed in the Introduction, reform of existing international institutions is not a particularly feasible approach to cure the collective action problem, as the very premise of the existing institutions is the legal supremacy of national sovereignty, with 'pooling of sovereignty' into international institutions only happening voluntarily by member states signing treaties.[19]

Because reforming existing institutions is unlikely to be sufficient and because no new hegemon appears looming on the horizon, the world is more in need of global coordination institutions than ever before, and ironically, has less global coordination capacity and fewer enforcement mechanisms than at any time in modern history. China has the economic muscle, state capacity, and ability to engage in long-term planning but lacks the requisite ordering and international coordination capacities, has eschewed developing them, and may have promoted the Enduring Disorder.[20]

This same paradox was highlighted by the global response to the Covid pandemic. National-level responses in major countries could not be optimized without an effective global response. But with no global leader and no effective coordination mechanisms in place, countries initially adopted divergent approaches to quarantine, travel bans, mandatory mask wearing, and vaccine research.[21] Nonetheless, global coordination in this specific domain gradually improved out of sheer necessity over the course of the pandemic, but so far it has not led countries to engage in an equitable vaccine-sharing scheme, create a global vaccine passport system, or embed global health institutions that would prevent the rapid spread of the next pandemic. Could these successes and failures provide some insights into the current global system? Does this suggest that in this hegemony-free era, new coordination mechanisms will only be generated when collective threats grow so existential that our very way of life is on the verge of being irrevocably altered, and even during that process, nation will fight nation for access to precious resources like vaccine doses?

Surveying recent events, it does seem that during the Enduring Disorder reactive coordination in the face of a pressing shared danger has a better chance of success (such as mask mandates and coordination of vaccine research) than pro-active coordination (like vaccine passports or creating new institutions to stop the next pandemic).

Collective action problems and decision-makers' psychology

This book has sought to challenge the prevailing wisdom that climate change is a collective action/game theory problem while the conflicts in Yemen, Syria, Libya, Venezuela, and Ukraine are not. In the historical era of the Enduring Disorder, all major international issues are at their deepest level collective action problems. Rather than being a tautology, this contention contains more novelty than one might suppose. Since the start of their subfield after the Second World War, Realist IR theorists have argued that the USSR/Russia, the United States, and other global actors have fundamentally opposed interests and hence are each fighting 'rationally' to push for their preferred outcomes.[22] Drawing on extensive studies of the European balance of power from Westphalia until the Second World War, such theorists have also asserted that nature abhors a vacuum and that power vacuums invite in 'order-providers'. And for centuries now, historians, political scientists, and policymakers themselves[23] have waxed poetic about the self-correcting nature of the balance of power.[24]

I have bucked this trend and presented the opposite case, arguing that there is no Newtonian-style balance of power at work. Furthermore, major corporate, governmental, and political actors are not actually maximizing their own long-term gains. Not the Libyan factions, not the international actors, and certainly not the supposedly profit-driven corporations. I am suggesting that IR theory needs as fundamental a corrective intervention[25] as the one that the field of classical economics (partially) experienced with the introduction of behavioural economics from the 1980s onwards.[26] The behavioural economists successfully critiqued the prevailing rational actor assumptions and determined that they were flawed and that the predictive power of their research was deeply undermined by proceeding from incorrect assumptions.[27] In short, they attacked the myth of the rational *homo economicus* and introduced psychological insights into economics.[28] IR theory is ripe for exactly the same transformation. Without both this mentality shift among thinkers and structural changes in the international system, the world's new conflicts appear set to remain intractable collective action problems in which suboptimal outcomes will prevail for all involved.

Is the Enduring Disorder durable?

Civil wars in the early 2020s tend to be more multipolar than those of the Cold War and post-Cold War periods, also inviting in a wider range of foreign intervenors.[29] More so even than the destabilizing implications of communications technology, it is the prevailing international system that leads to contemporary conflicts being pulled in a range of contradictory directions by the gamut of international forces acting unchecked.[30] The sheer multiplicity of uncoordinated actors facilitates state collapse in post-conflict situations, even if no particular foreign power desires this.

Over time, these imploded states might essentially transition from hot civil wars into frozen conflicts that simply cannot be coherently addressed under the global conditions of the age of Enduring Disorder. In the past, enduring conflicts were able to persist in places like South Ossetia and Transnistria because they were in the borderlands between the two major superpowers and also of very little geostrategic or economic importance.[31] Syria, Libya, and Ukraine are quite the opposite. They are in areas of extreme geostrategic importance and do not sit on the geographic fault line of the twenty-first century's superpowers.[32]

These new enduring conflicts appear to be feeding into the very global disorder that caused them because of the way they emit migrants, hot money, terrorists, and international discord, as well as stimulating a longing for protectionism and isolationism inside Western electorates. This insight highlights the value of having examined the Libyan microcosm's interplay with the larger global system. Like a classic positive feedback loop, until the structural drivers and incentive structures are changed, and the prevailing psychologies upended, the Enduring Disorder will simply beget more Enduring Disorder—no natural law of geopolitics or human societies is 'inherently' going to provide a fix. The 'balance of power' was always operated by humans and their ideals, not by the laws of physics. Despite its centrality, geostrategically and economically, it is not far-fetched to imagine that Libya—as well as Syria, Yemen, Venezuela, Eastern Ukraine, and the next global hot spots—could all remain mired in perpetual conflicts for years to come if the underlying conflict drivers are not modified and if the global system remains fragmented.

The ghost ship of state

Judging by the last two centuries of history, when a coherent consensus solution is needed to resolve a multifaceted problem, Anglo-American leadership of a coordinated Western bloc has been the only successful approach.[33] New combinations led by the EU, India, China, and the G20 may emerge, but as of yet there is no precedent or blueprint.[34] Consensual global leadership has been strikingly lacking since the Iraq debacle and the concomitant loss of Anglo-American moral authority and coordinating power to lead global coalitions. It appears unlikely to re-emerge in the near term, and therefore the disorder around us appears to be enduring, independent of who occupies the White House or 10 Downing Street. Without genuine coordinated leadership, outcomes like those in Libya seem all the more likely across the globe—rending states asunder, spurring economic implosions, and setting off previously buried fault lines.

Over the last two decades as the ghost ship of state has drifted to and fro without a captain, the very knowledge that leadership in international politics is about managing vast collective action complexities appears to have been lost. The art of compromise and diplomacy has been replaced by ideology, rhetoric, and polarizing debates on Twitter. Neo-populist ideology on the right and anti-globalization identity politics on the left reject the very notion that the main goal of politics is to forge more perfect forms of global collective action. They occupy moral universes of right and wrong—victim and abuser. Centrifugal forces have multiplied as fringe beneficiaries on both right and left have come to the fore. Consensus ideas and centrist political movements able to stem the centrifugal momentum have not yet appeared on the horizon.

For those in America and abroad who think that Joseph Robinette Biden Jr. has been anointed by the accidents of history as the centrist Messiah and will now usher in a new form of coordinated, consensus politics, I have bad news. His first few months have seen the escalation of the feud with China rather than its amelioration.[35] They have also witnessed the Republican Party unanimously double down on a strategy of voter suppression. The healing of America's partisan divides is nowhere in sight. As I pen these lines, Biden has sent signals about leading a coordinated NATO response to the Russian and Chinese threats, but rather than 'doing anything' or creating new institutions to project multilateral Western power, he has chosen to make his first signature foreign policy move the withdrawal of US troops from Afghanistan—a move which diminishes America's global leadership credentials. America thus remains in an unlikely spot to be a global unifier when the American polity is so internally disunited and the major world powers are at loggerheads.

Seen from the spring of 2021, the disorder looks set to endure. Unless, of course, humans do what they have done periodically in the past: surprise everyone with radically new ideas and organizational principles.

Putting humans at the centre

From the ancients onward, certain prophets, theologians, philosophers, and political commentators have envisioned that the golden age was behind them and the trajectory of human civilization would be irrevocably downward. There is no scientific evidence to suggest that this—or that its opposite, the Panglossian view of progressive progress—is inherently accurate.

What trajectory are we on at present? Though technology and globalization have helped level the international playing field, diversify the actors, and degrade nearly four centuries of Western global hegemony—all of which have in turn factored into the Enduring Disorder—those same forces might also provide exactly the mechanisms and cultural innovations needed to forge new ways of doing global geopolitics. The study of Libya suggests that if major domestic and international players could work together, great results might be achieved and externalities avoided. Is this likely to happen in the short-to-medium term? Both the quantifiable and anecdotal evidence suggest not.

And yet, scholars, policymakers, and businesses making long and short bets on every type of commodity must consider alternative possibilities in order to do their jobs properly. This book has argued that the smart money is on the current disorder deepening in the short-to-medium term and that even new American or European initiatives such as green energy, infrastructure, and global corporate taxation, or massive improvements in the relationships between the West and China (or Russia) would also be insufficient to buck the trendline. Nonetheless, it is conceivable that the populaces and leaders of major countries could engage in a backlash against nationalism, neo-populism, and the myth that America, Britain, China, Italy, or one Libyan faction can 'win' while other countries or factions 'lose'.

As wild as it may sound, global governance might become a rallying cry of the people and mainstream politicians, rather than the curse word of right-wing conspiratorialists. To deal with global warming, a global demos might demand a curtailing of individual freedoms to enforce demographic and consumptive limits set by international institutions. Or slightly more probable, the leaderships of certain major Northern hemisphere states could simply enter into a new form of strategic alliance—this time not constructed against a rival political bloc like NATO was but against various problems of the commons such as climate change, deepfakes, ungoverned space, genetic engineering, demographic challenges, monopolistic corporate giants, and cyber criminals.

Again, pointing out the need to prepare for and consider these possibilities is not to say that they are likely in the short term. Like a pendulum, the momentum of the Enduring Disorder makes its polar opposite more likely in the medium term as well. What seems increasingly less likely is a short-to-medium-term return to the status quo ante that prevailed in the late Cold War and early post-Cold War period. The pendulum of historical change has far too much momentum for that at present. The old certitudes are simply gone.

Just as the Second World War gave rise to a period of prolonged peace, economic growth, and the construction of novel political and financial institutions (the UN, NATO, and the Bretton Woods institutions), there is no reason that a worsening Enduring Disorder cannot eventually do the same. Throughout history, pandemics from the Black Death to the Spanish Influenza have heralded novel conceptualizations of human societies and international geopolitics. In fact, it is in the wake of such order-upending events like pandemics that new ways of organizing human affairs have tended to emerge.[36]

The key thing to stress is that there is no reason to believe that any such reimagining or reshaping will happen by an automatic law of global geopolitics, akin to a Newtonian correction to the physical 'balance of power' by an inertial force inherently acting on history's pendulum. The international system can just as easily tolerate an Enduring Disorder as a Pax Britannica. The historical pendulum this book has sketched is not affected by gravity and inertia but by human ideas, organizations, institutions, technologies, and decisions.

The First World War ended with the new mechanisms that had been created to coordinate global politics proving unsuitable for the tasks they were designed to solve. Realist IR theorists have explained this by stating that after the First World War, the world was multipolar with a genuine competition for dominance underway; whereas after the Second World War, bipolarity was a mirage with American hegemony actually accepted by most major players, which allowed for the creation of a coherent world system.[37] That is certainly one analysis. But another, equally compelling one would stress the contingencies of America's fall into isolationism after President Woodrow Wilson's untimely incapacitation[38] and the vengeful and acquisitive imperialist logic that dominated British and French post-First World War thinking, as opposed to the gospel of Western unity in the face of Communism that prevailed after the Second World War. Although American hegemony and coordination of a Western bloc was likely what made the difference, there is every reason to believe that voluntary collective action and shared ideologies after 1945, as opposed to the zero-sum competitive ideologies after the First World War, were also at play—and not the inherent structural forces between rising and falling powers.[39] There is no way to test such a hypothesis but every reason to inject into the debate the possibility of psychological and ideological factors being as important as structural, economic, and military ones.

Blue sky thinking and the global collective

Part of the reason Brexit, the Covid pandemic, and Trumpism have had such destabilizing effects is that policymakers, thinkers, and businesspeople were caught wildly unprepared. This book is a warning call urging them to prepare in detail for all of the implications of the Enduring Disorder deepening in the short-to-medium term—independent of the current Biden administration's or its successors' attempts to return to the structures and order of the early post-Cold War world. Nonetheless, when it comes to the medium-to-long term, we should prepare for the opposite as well.

Therefore, despite it being an unlikely scenario, it is quite possible that with increasing popular clamour for collective action on climate change, cybercrime, social media manipulation, and global public health, it will be easier for policymakers and global populaces to see conflicts like the Libyan, Syrian and Ukrainian ones as the collective action crises they really are. In the wake of such a realization, it is not impossible to believe that electorates across the Global North will gradually reject the inward-looking, anti-expert ideologies currently in vogue and embrace a radically new form of expert-administered, consensus globalism.

There are of course many hurdles. In fact, there are many deep psychological hurdles that could prove even more difficult to overcome than the structural ones. Advocates of libertarianism, identity politics, woke political correctness, and different strains of national exceptionalisms of all sorts would have to sacrifice cherished narratives that stress the freedom of the individual or the unique destiny of their national, ethnic, or religious subcommunity. These ideologies all stress individuals', communities', races', ethnicities', markets', or nations' rights and perspectives above that of the global collective. As such, these cultural movements on the right and left are all inherently impediments to forging a truly global consensus for undertaking collective policymaking aiming at maximizing overall utility rather than protecting the interests of specific segments.

At the beginning of the twenty-first century, ideas surrounding the universal equality of individuals and the concept of individuals' freedom to choose their associations and lifestyles rapidly gained ground and achieved considerable policy successes. Yet by the mid-to-late twenty-first century, it is also possible that a reversal will come about with the concepts of the 'global collective', 'involuntary obligations', and 'collective responsibility' becoming realities rather than buzzwords. Although this does not appear to be the direction of travel in the early 2020s, there is no way to forecast what will come next and where the tipping points will be. The Arab Spring, the rise of neo-populist nationalism throughout the West, and the concomitant backlashes against experts, global coordination, and free trade were not predicted by mainstream political theorists, futurists, commodities traders, or government scenario planners of the early post-Cold War period. So, there is no compelling reason to believe that even with increasingly advanced computing, we should be able to predict the next great ideological, sociological, or geopolitical transformation.[40]

* * *

As we look out towards the horizon, I hope that thinking about the interconnectedness of global events via the paradigm of the Enduring Disorder has been a useful intellectual exercise. It has highlighted that any future geopolitical or ideological rebalancing is not 'inherent'. Multipolarity or a rebalancing of powers will not automatically follow from the decline in America's relative power. Similarly, in the wake of Qadhafi's ouster, the vacuum of power in Libya has not, by some cosmic law, elicited either the creation of a new, more durable domestic organizing force nor incentivized a dominant outside power to provide order. Such collective efforts and communal achievements must be the work of humans—especially those who are willing to put aside their previous flawed myths to forge new alliances and embrace novel ways of acting for the collective good.

Jason Pack, April 2021.

AFTERWORD

HOW GLOBAL COMPETITION LED TO CHAOS IN LIBYA

Jonathan M. Winer[1]

ABSTRACT

Former US Special Envoy to Libya Jonathan Winer presents his take on Libya's post-Qadhafi history, seeking to offer a slightly different perspective than Jason Pack's on what Libya's trajectory demonstrates about the current state of global affairs. For Winer, the Enduring Disorder took root in Libya due to the repeated intervention of foreign states from the beginning of the 2011 Libyan Uprisings to the present. These ten years of continuous interventions have led to massive disruption of Libyans' ability to build their own future. If international players started honouring diplomatic standards and norms, this could still help Libya move beyond the Enduring Disorder to greater stability, equilibrium, and an opportunity to build a better future.

The decade that followed the 2011 Libyan Uprisings was not a happy one. Instead of the liberation from the mercurial whims of Muammar Qadhafi providing renewal, opportunity, democracy, and freedom, the collapse of the old order brought terrorism, violence, criminality, civil conflict, foreign intervention, and

351

recurrent evidence of the failure of the Libyan state to provide essential state services.

Jason Pack describes this result as both an expression of our current historical moment, which he labels the 'Enduring Disorder,' and a cause of that continuing disorder. His work marshals a range of evidence showing Libya's travails as both cause and effect.

The task of establishing a new regional order, when an old one falls, is often fraught with stress. When empires collapse, achieving stability can take years—or even decades, as demonstrated time and again in the post-Ottoman Middle East and North Africa. There is not always special providence in the fall of a dictator: the aftermath can be as brutal as the dictatorship was, or worse, if an array of sadistic actors vie for control through ruthlessly applying violence until the opposition submits.

After Qadhafi's fall, Libya could never have had an easy time of creating a stable government. The country's institutions were too weak and deliberately dysfunctional, having been designed to be subject to Qadhafi's manipulation as discussed in Chapter 4. There were also real grievances, especially in the east and the south, that needed to be resolved, as well as the problem of disarming and reintegrating the militias into civilian life or reconstituting them as part of a national security force subject to civilian control. But the engagement of foreigners trying to pick Libyan 'winners' and 'losers' according to their particular national, personal, or corporate agendas, as discussed in this volume's Introduction, made finding solutions to these problems impossible. The result was that the competing agendas of various states and personalities to shape the post-Qadhafi era magnified Libyans' differences and rewarded Libyan politicians, political groupings, tribes, and warlords for refusing to compromise. Creating functioning post-Qadhafi governance, therefore, posed a classic collective action problem.

AFTERWORD

Mr Pack has asserted that the current historical era is uniquely poorly equipped to handle this sort of challenge. The collective action complexities arose early, were in full force within two years after the Uprisings, ebbing and flowing thereafter based on the situation on the ground and in significant part on whether they themselves risked negative consequences for magnifying Libya's conflict.

As outlined in detail by Mr Pack, Libya's disorder reflected, and was shaped by, the global conditions around it. Libya was not the only country to go through the 'Arab Spring' and cast off a prior regime. It was part of a mass movement that threatened even those governments in the region which were never directly challenged by mass protests. The complicated and interacting responses of those governments—especially Turkey, Qatar, Saudi Arabia, and the United Arab Emirates—played out on Libyan soil, as well as elsewhere, and the conflicts among them played a central part in exporting the dynamics of the Enduring Disorder.

I will try to use this Afterword to engage with this volume's primary thesis by drawing on my own experiences to shed light on how we arrived at the current moment and to what extent the dynamics of the larger international arena impacted Libya's post-Qadhafi trajectory. I will place relatively greater weight on the causative dimensions of US policy under the Trump Administration and the related issue of Russian actions, rather than Mr Pack's focus on systemic global forces. Seen from this vantage point, I will also attempt to make the case that the Biden Administration has the potential to reverse the recent direction of travel, not only in Libya, but of the Global Enduring Disorder more broadly.

* * *

LIBYA AND THE GLOBAL ENDURING DISORDER

Solving Libya's Problems Requires both Domestic and International Compromises

For a new domestic order to be achieved, Libyans will have to seize the chance to exploit Libyan-to-Libyan dialogue and reduce the negative impact caused by foreign intervenors. Libyans will need the aid of the United States and other countries who have no particular dog in the regional fight, as well as of the help of the United Nations, and the moral support of other relevant international groupings, including the African Union and Arab League. For this to happen, collective action at the global level is needed. Reshaping competition into cooperation is a primary policy challenge during the current historical period. As the Biden Administration undertakes its work, that remains the clear goal of US policy on Libya.

Regardless of the positions of the foreign actors, Libyans will need to look beyond the competing agendas of the foreign patrons who have turned Libya into their political and military playground, and insist on reaching agreements with one another to enable Libyans to determine their own future. Internationals will need to give up the goal of installing any of their preferred candidates to 'run' Libya, as well as the idea that they can maintain permanent zones of influence along geographic lines, which exclude other regional powers. Instead, the foreigners will need to accept solutions in which Libyans share power through formulas that are inclusive, rather than excluding disfavoured groups. For stability, the solutions will likely need to embrace geographic diversity; economic sharing, so that oil revenues are distributed both to municipalities and to Libyans on an equal per capita basis; and, as part of Libya's post-conflict rebuilding, the welcoming of foreign companies and workers from many countries, not just those who intervened in the Libyan conflict seeking commercial advantage. These ideas are not idealistic fantasies, unsuited to

Libyan realities: they are actual necessities for the country to move ahead economically and politically, and therefore to secure stability and provide for the physical security of its territory.

A decade after the Uprisings, these ideas have vitality within Libya. They are the kind of ideas that are attractive to a wide range of Libyan constituencies, rather than rival ideas, such as: restoration of Qadhafism or its equivalent under Saif al-Islam Qadhafi or a similar figure; military rule under a dictator, elected or otherwise, such as Khalifa Haftar; one-party rule, such as that of the Muslim Brotherhood, which to date draws the support of only a few percent of Libyan voters; partition, an option which remains preferred by a small number of politically active people in Libya's east, often under the euphemism of 'federalism'; or rule by an Islamist terrorist group, such as the Islamic State or its more home grown equivalents, which for periods of time gained control of Sirte and Derna.

To establish a stable democratic order, Libyans will have to reach compromises with one another to share power through an inclusive approach. Redistributing an existing pie, even a big one, requires either an outsider making and enforcing the allocations or the domestic initiation of binding deals among the distributees, when more for you may mean less for me. This is the very essence of a collective action dilemma. With Libyan national revenues remaining well below those generated during the Qadhafi years, deals among Libyan groups to share the wealth could become true win-wins, addressing both 'greed' and 'grievance' with benefits for anyone willing to be part of the solution. To get there, Libyans will have to think of their goals first, and accommodate the foreigners only to the minimum extent needed to prevent them from continuing to act as saboteurs to Libyan progress. They may also need to devise strategies to insulate themselves from a new international system of the kind described by Mr Pack, which seemingly thrives on scuppering such deals so the free-for-all of the self-reinforcing Enduring Disorder may continue.

The Libyan Agenda

Foreign meddling aside, the end of the Qadhafi era created an inflection point for every Libyan, and those who experienced grievances under Qadhafi quickly sought to redress them. Indeed, some of these groups had already been seeking change in the years directly prior to the Uprisings.

Some groups had done well under Qadhafi, others less so. Have-nots included the Tubu in the south, who had generated their own militias going back to 2007 after Qadhafi stripped them of citizenship due to their purported lack of loyalty in Qadhafi's wars with Chad. They also included much of the political and popular classes of Cyrenaica, which felt, rightly or wrongly, that for decades Qadhafi had given Tripolitania the lion's share of the oil wealth, which was generated from underneath their soil.

By 2009, Cyrenaican protests were added to ongoing Tubu unrest in the south, prompted by the economic stagnation and lack of jobs that accompanied the global financial crisis—a problem faced throughout North Africa. Qadhafi tried to mollify the protestors with money, but the cash was too little and too late. Libyans were sick of the corruption, sick of the human rights abuses, sick of having little-to-no control over their lives, and fed up with their eccentric leader. For four decades, Qadhafi had told Libyans that every one of them was equal and a king, even as he alone allocated the country's only meaningful source of revenue, the proceeds from its oil production, for whomever and whatever he deemed Libya might need. With his overthrow, to follow the metaphor used by Mr Pack in the opening pages of this book, Libya lost the captain of its ship of state. However crazy the captain had been, at least Libya had had one. With his removal, there was no obvious successor to steer the ship.

* * *

Unlike after most revolutionary upheavals, no unified ideological political camps emerged. Rather the spectre of permanent partisan groupings were conjured up whole cloth by their opponents and branded with misleading labels. In reality, cohesive blocs with genuine political programmes and coherent ideology did not exist, but opponents of each tendency labelled their myriad enemies as if they were a coherent bloc embracing a specific political programme and ideology. The ones I usually heard about while I was the US Special Envoy for Libya were the supposed opposition between the pro-former regime 'Qadhafians' and the anti-former regime 'Islamists.' The former label was applied by their enemies to people who were among the 'haves' under Qadhafi and who generally hailed from certain regime supporting tribes (like the Magarha, Qadhadhfa, and Warfalla). They had either been given government jobs or lucrative contracts and relationships with the government to import goods or benefit from contracts deriving from Libya's oil wealth, then generating some \$60 billion a year. The latter label was used by their opponents to describe people who participated in the military aspect of the Uprisings against Qadhafi, or for individuals which hailed from Misrata, Derna, or certain neighbourhoods of Benghazi (like al-Laithi) or Tripoli (like Suq al-Juma'a). In reality, these labels made little sense except as weapons used to delegitimize those who were in an opposing political camps. The various geographical and tribal entities grouped together haphazardly under these labels did not share the same political goals nor did they coordinate their actions.

Some reckoning to address legitimate grievances in Libya was essential.[2] The country's resources needed to be divided up anew so as to enable all Libyans to feel that they were getting some share of the national patrimony that Qadhafi had often said belonged to them. Such a redivision of the spoils was especially needed to integrate the interests of the eastern coastal parts of Cyrenaica with those of Tripolitania; to assuage and address the long-standing injuries inflicted on the Tubu and other nomadic southern peoples in Libya; and to provide opportunities for a generation of younger Libyans, frustrated by economic stagnation in their efforts to move forward.[3]

Mr Pack describes the process of the succession of interim governments succumbing to those Libyans making armed demands for additional shares of the national wealth as a form of 'appeasement.' The process might also be characterized as merely 'patronage politics,' handled poorly by a political class that had not gained much experience of how to make decisions on such issues.

The patronage bargains struck with the various Libyan groups did create an entitlement system that enabled militias to retain local power without having to give up their autonomy to state institutions. The political class tried to offer decentralised wealth sharing to secure fealty from local leaders and armed commanders but lacked the credibility and leverage to do so successfully. Therefore, it became far easier for both politicians and militia leaders to avoid compromises with each other, instead looking to foreign mentors to secure immediate advantages. That instinct proved to be fundamentally destructive to the possibility of Libya becoming a functioning state.

The conflicting agendas of the major foreign intervenors

The bubbling caldron of interests seeking advantage in post-Qadhafi Libya then became stirred by a range of foreign powers with their own diverging interests in the country. As Mr Pack has shown, what Libya needed from the foreigners was steadiness, engagement, business deals, capacity building assistance, and patience. What it got instead was their competing national agendas, and these brought the pot to boil.

Those agendas directly conflicted with one another and turned Libya into a conflict zone that was a playground for the national goals of the foreign intervenors, which principally included Egypt, Qatar, Turkey, the United Arab Emirates, and later, Russia. Other intervenors included, France, and secondary actors such as Jordan and Saudi Arabia in support of Egypt and the Emirates.

Amid so much change, major regional actors saw both threats and opportunities.

In the UAE, the ruling family of Abu Dhabi, especially Crown Prince Mohammed bin Zayed, saw the Muslim Brotherhood and Islamism as a threat that could gain a foothold in one or more of the less wealthy and more religious sheikdoms that make up the UAE.[4] Saudi Arabia similarly perceived a threat of Shi'a encirclement, from Bahrain and Iraq in the north to Yemen in the south, as a threat to its own legitimacy and authority, especially given Iran's heightened influence in Iraq post-2003.[5] For both the UAE and Saudi, a religiously-based challenge to the status quo in any country in the region created the risk of contagion at home.

Once President Abdul Fattah Al-Sisi was in place as of June 2013, Egypt had the more immediate goal of countering the risk of any return of the Muslim Brotherhood. It also faced ongoing threats from a range of Islamist terrorist groups which operated especially in the Sinai and in Egypt's western desert near the Libyan border. The public beheadings of Egyptian Copts in Libya by the Islamic State in February 2015 added to Egypt's justified concerns about instability along the entire range of its western border.[6] In response, Egypt intensified its support to Khalifa Haftar's effort to create a so-called Libyan National Army (LNA) that would become Libya's equivalent of the Egyptian army by pacifying Libyan cities, taking direct control of governance, and generating contracts that would give Haftar and the LNA an ongoing economic role and the opportunities for building an extensive patronage system.[7]

By contrast, Turkey and Qatar both saw opportunities for themselves with Islamist-based political movements. Under President Recep Tayyip Erdoğan, the secular nationalist state established in 1923 by Ataturk had been replaced in Turkey by a government that combined centralized leadership with transnational Islamism centred around the idea that Turkey could mould Islamic movements in other countries to establish aligned local governments in a 21st century update of Ottomanism. For Qatar, using its oil wealth to support pan-Islamist movements was a form of soft power, enabling it to leverage influence despite its small population, size, and limited capacity. It did so by funding the purchase, mostly through Turkey, of massive amounts of weapons which went to a variety of Islamist forces opposing Qadhafi in 2011, and continued funding them for a variety of purposes in the years that followed.[8]

The interests of these five governments in particular began to play out quickly following the Arab Spring. In June 2012, Mohammed Morsi, the head of the Muslim Brotherhood, was elected President of Egypt. Qatar invested tens of billions of dollars in his government, lent funds to Egypt's Central Bank, and even provided free tankers of liquified natural gas (LNG).[9]

In response, the United Arab Emirates initiated contacts with the Egyptian Army, and provided financial support both to anti-Morsi protestors and to the Egyptian military with the goal of securing the coup by which Abdul-Fattah Al-Sisi became Egypt's leader in June 2013.[10] This was followed by the UAE providing billions in foreign aid to Egypt after Sisi took power, with the success of its operation proven by Sisi remaining firmly in place in 2020 following elections in 2018 in which he received some 97% of the vote, just as he did in Egypt's 2014 presidential elections.

Meanwhile, in neighbouring Libya, both Turkey and Qatar had retained warm ties with Islamist political parties and militias, as well as with the loose grouping that prevailed in the General National Congress (GNC), backing them when they and their armed militia enforcers enacted the Political Isolation ('lustration') law in May 2013 to prevent members of the Qadhafi regime from holding public office for the remainder of the country's transition.

Taken together, the lessons for all of the intervening countries were obvious: control of Libya, and its tens of billions of dollars in annual oil resources, was up for grabs, and victory would go not to the peacemakers, but to those willing to use enough force or guile to ensure that their side won. Over the following year, the Emirates would spearhead a coalition of like-minded Arab countries that included Egypt, Jordan and Saudi Arabia to support resistance to the 'Islamist' government in Tripoli, and seize upon the problematic figure of Khalifa Haftar as a potential dictator-in-waiting who could be used in the meantime to organize an alternative to those in Tripoli they saw as representatives of the Muslim Brotherhood. In the meantime, Turkey and Qatar continued financial and military support to their 'friends' in Libya—with Sudan providing weapons-for-cash to both sides.[11]

By 2014, the influx of weapons and funds from outside Libya had produced the sorry result of two Libyan parliaments and two governments, one based in the west in Tripoli and the other in the east in Bayda (for the government) and Tobruk (for the parliament). Neither 'government' was meaningfully functional.[12] They provided little in the way of governmental services to the Libyan population, who continued to receive salaries from the Central Bank of Libya if they were registered as anti-Qadhafi fighters or government workers. (As discussed in Chapter 1, the former category of payments went to at least ten times the number of people who actually fought against Qadhafi, but these payments helped keep Libya's population able to buy food and other basics.) Neither government was especially legitimate, either politically or in its claims to derive from Libyan law. Neither was able to exercise a monopoly of force beyond the particular coastal cities they controlled. Each relied on local militias for much of the security that was in force.[13] And neither stopped the emergence of true terrorists, in the form of the Islamic State, from taking up residence in the central coastal city of Sirte, and using terror to build territorial control, which at its maximum in 2015 extended along some 120 miles of coastal Libya as described in Chapter 2.[14] Thus, after a mere three years of post-Qadhafi foreign intervention, the competing visions for Libya of the foreign countries had so weakened Libya's security environment, that it enabled the 'worst of the worst' terrorist group, the Islamic State, to emerge as a viable alternative governance model.

The role of the United States and her allies

The crucial question of 'where was the United States during all of this,' has had different answers in different periods.

The U.S. was first actively engaged in helping Libyans overthrow Qadhafi through the deployment of American airpower as part of a coalition of foreign forces that worked together under the umbrella of NATO to enforce a no-fly zone over the country from March 2011 until Qadhafi's death in October. The US provided initial advice to the National Transitional Council, worked to ensure its recognition by other countries, and appointed as ambassador a US diplomat who had previously served in Libya as the Deputy Chief of Mission and had helped the National Transitional Council from the outset of the conflict. Then, just four months after his return to Libya, the new US Ambassador, J. Christopher Stevens, was murdered in a terrorist attack in Benghazi, together with three other Americans.

AFTERWORD

As discussed in Chapter 1, Ambassador Stevens' murder was an inflection point that reduced US engagement at a critical moment for Libya, less than a year after the fall of the Qadhafi regime. The event was highly politicized in the United States, leading to many Congressional hearings, aimed largely at damaging the political prospects of the likely Democratic Presidential nominee, Hillary Clinton.[15] One result was that a new US Ambassador, the highly regarded Arabist Deborah Jones, was not appointed until April 2013, and was not posted to Libya until the fall of 2013. It was during that year—from September 2012 through September 2013—that the foreign interventions in Libya deepened and that the country began to come apart. This was not a coincidence.

While it was terrorist extremists who were responsible for killing Ambassador Stevens, one result of his death was to unleash the appetites of competing Libyan groups to secure control over Benghazi, Libya's second largest city, and former joint capitol during the Kingdom period. The terrorists responsible for Ambassador Stevens' death were associated with Ansar al-Sharia, a jihadi group that was using terrorism in an effort to secure control of the city. But they were competing with a range of other militias and law enforcement bodies—all with shifting allegiances, uncertain loyalties, and lethal capabilities.[16] With the US having effectively withdrawn from the territory, and the Libyan government having no national forces to deploy, Ansar al-Sharia, and those aligned with it, slowly but systematically over the course of 2013 took control of much of Benghazi. Others in Benghazi, desperate to avoid the puritanical Islamic rule promised by Ansar al-Sharia, reorganized especially around the focal point of those tribes traditionally hostile to the de-tribalized urban neighbourhoods, where the Islamist militias recruited heavily.

By 2014, forces associated with a number of local Libyan tribes made common cause with other Libyan forces in the east under the command of Khalifa Haftar,[17] with support from the Emiratis, Egyptians, and by 2015, the French. Chapter 3 demonstrated how Haftar's narrative was masterfully calculated to seize upon the new media landscape of the Enduring Disorder, while offering Benghazinos pie-in-the-sky style solutions to their pressing security problems.

This constellation of forces in turn consolidated an opposing one, in which Misratan and Tripoli-based militias teamed up with certain elements labelled as Muslim Brotherhood and 'Islamist', who dispatched contingents to counter General Haftar's effort to take the city. The civil war was 'on' and at this point, foreign powers had their sides, with Turkey and Qatar supporting elements of the 'Libya Dawn' coalition against General Haftar's 'Operation Dignity.'[18]

And so Benghazi, the very city that sent the United States into mourning and retreat, became the place where Libya's civil war first coalesced, and where the United States was for a critical period, functionally absent. As President Obama later acknowledged, the failure of the United States to do more was 'the biggest mistake of his Presidency.[19] Others have referred to it as 'a debacle.'[20]

The "mistake" identified by President Obama of not doing more in Libya between 2012 and 2014 was not something unique to the American approach to Libya. As discussed in the Introduction, it was part of an overall approach undertaken by President Obama of operating multilaterally and seeking international coordination for American actions, and avoiding both imperial overstretch and the arrogance of a superpower telling other countries what to do. For the United States, there were benefits to this strategy in other theatres, such as enabling the US to reach agreements and undertake initiatives on the basis of common interest. But this approach was also seen by some in the Gulf and Turkey, in particular, as a form of imperial retreat, where the US was no longer willing to take actions to police other countries, creating space that those nations could instead fill themselves.[21]

The gap left by the US retreat after the murder of Ambassador Stevens was not filled by another historically important imperial power with its own special history in Libya. The United Kingdom had governed Libya from 1943 until its independence in 1951 via the British Military Administrations of Tripolitania and Cyrenaica. It had retained an active involvement in Libya affairs until Qadhafi took power and nationalized British assets there.[22] In the final years of Qadhafi's rule, the UK had returned to Libya, invested again in its oil infrastructure, and played a critical role in the NATO-led military intervention that helped to oust Qadhafi.[23] But under Prime Minister Cameron, the United Kingdom undertook a policy of retrenchment and withdrawal from exercising influence beyond its shores. This indirectly culminated in Brexit,[24] and in practice, limited the UK's ambitions globally and its ability to focus on Libya—leaving its Tripoli-based ambassadors no longer receiving top-level support from 10 Downing Street.

This left France and Italy as the main Western powers directly engaged in the field in Libya; both had their own colonial legacies in the country. The former derived its Libyan policies from its interests in Libya's neighbouring Francophone countries. France was therefore interested in building Libyan military capacity to counter terrorism on a regional basis. By 2015, this drove France to provide covert support for the wars of Khalifa Haftar.[25] When I raised this issue with the French Ambassador to Libya during this period, he told me there was no French military support to Haftar, and that the reporting in *Le Monde* was mistaken. I did not believe him, but I did believe he was communicating the official position of the Government of France, especially as the UN Arms Embargo for Libya remained in place.

Italy, whose brutal 30-year occupation of Libya (1911–1941) still remained a sore point in Italian-Libyan relations seven decades later, sought primarily to protect the oil interests of ENI and therefore to promote cordial relations with whatever Libyan government was in place. It also became increasingly focused on combating illegal migration from Libya, focusing on whatever arrangements it could secure with whomever was in control locally in areas where the migrant trafficking was concentrated, such as Sabratha and Zuwarra.[26]

In this environment, competing domestic groups and rival international power blocs contesting the future of Libya and fuelling its conflict, drove Libyan security into two primary camps: that of General Haftar in the east, and that of a range of militias in the west. In response, the Obama Administration re-engaged on Libya in early 2014, and by the end of December 2015 had played a central role in bringing to fruition a Libyan Political Agreement to establish the Government of National Accord (GNA), having secured the support of each of the competing foreign powers.

* * *

I played an ongoing day-to-day role in mediating the Skhirat Accords (aka The Libyan Political Agreement), while other senior US officials sought to press Egypt, Qatar, Turkey, and the UAE to tell their respective clients in Libya that they needed to compromise and achieve an integrated government. Those doing so included President Obama, Vice President Biden, National Security Advisor Susan Rice, UN Ambassador Samantha Powers and Secretary of State Kerry, among many others. The team effort included a notable gathering of Gulf State leaders by President Obama at Camp David which resulted in a declaration on 14 May 2015 committing them 'to move in concert to convince all Libyan parties to accept an inclusive power-sharing agreement based on proposals put forward by the UN and to focus on countering the growing terrorist presence in the country.'[27]

Notably, the Skhirat Agreement, which created the legal and political framework for the GNA, followed just six months later.[28] The emergence of an order, however temporary, from the previous disorder, was only possible in response to the active efforts of the United States to convince the major foreign interventionists that their strategy of divide and conquer was in no one's long term interest. With each international actor attempting to maximize their interests in Libya, they had inadvertently created a space in which no one was winning, other than the terrorists.

In short, when they focused their attention on offering order-providing services, the US was able to help restore some semblance of political cohesion. The subsequent failure of the GNA, however, resulted in substantial part from the efforts of another major power, Russia—who sought to create disorder, reward Haftar and other spoilers, and gain advantage in the process. From the spring of 2016 onwards, Russia intervened to give support to spoilers in the east to enable them to avoid moving forward with supporting the formation of the GNA. That process began quietly, became increasingly brazen as the US elections approached, and turned into triumphalism following Donald Trump's ascension to the presidency and his approach to Libya becoming clarified, which amounted to a withdrawal of US engagement.

Russia's pernicious role in disordering Libya

There was always a risk that the Skhirat Agreement would not be fully implemented and that one or another spoiler would use its economic, political or security resources to stop the GNA from moving forward. During early 2016, the GNA was able, with Italian help in particular, to establish itself in Tripoli. But the GNA was denied the ability to secure a vote on forming a government by the House of Representatives (HoR) in Tobruk acting under the authority of its Speaker, Aqilah Saleh, who in essence refused to convene the HoR whenever there was any chance it would approve a GNA cabinet.[29]

According to briefings I received at the time, when faced with the reality that a majority of the HoR was ready to endorse the GNA's geographically-balanced cabinet, Aqilah and his similarly minded colleagues locked the doors of the HoR and turned off the electricity. One of the participants in this denial of democracy proudly told me he personally participated in the lockdown to ensure no vote would take place. Rather than approve any GNA cabinet list, Aqilah preferred to play the role of perpetual spoiler and maintain his independent power in the east, derived in substantial part from the economic exploitation of eastern-based institutions, including the region's banks, and from the patronage networks being built by Haftar. He was able to do this due to the prevailing international climate of the Enduring Disorder.

Central to those networks was the sudden, miraculous, influx of counterfeit Libyan currency printed by Goznak, the Russian state printer, and given to Haftar, Aqilah and their hand-picked 'Central Bank' head, Ali al-Hibri, which they were free to use for whatever purpose they wanted, regardless of any national budget. Over the next four years, the Russians provided some 14.5 billion counterfeit Libyan dinars (US $10 billion at the official exchange rate at the time), to Haftar and Aqilah through the branch of the Libyan Central Bank located in Tobruk that they controlled.[30] Together with the forced issuance of 'loans' to the eastern government and to Haftar by commercial banks in Libya's east (which decapitalized them in the process), the Russian funds provided the basis for a massive patronage operation, enabling Haftar and his coalition of militias under the banner of the LNA to build up control of a growing number of cities in Libya's east, and then to move south.[31]

Russia used its relationship with eastern Libyan spoilers to empower them to counter efforts by the US, supported by the UK, Italy, and to some extent, France, during the last nine months of the Obama Administration, to make the GNA able to function. Russian diplomatic efforts also played a direct role in ensuring that the Libyan military would not unify around an integrated command under civilian leadership, as needed to stabilize the country. Russia did so by encouraging Haftar in his dreams of securing power through conquest and by giving Aqilah and affiliated eastern elements the means to frustrate the GNA's efforts to form a government without facing unified international censure. Russia also began to introduce military trainers and materiel to Libya, in violation of the UN Arms Embargo; in the aftermath of Donald Trump's Russian-aided victory over Hillary Clinton, to participate in discussions with the Emiratis and Egyptians about how to secure total victory for 'their side' through steady support of Haftar.[32]

Russian and Emirati support in the east was the foundation for the east's ability to reject the GNA from the start. On a technical level, Russia and the UAE's support of Haftar enabled him to build up his military capabilities to the point where he was willing to attempt to conquer all of Libya by invading Tripoli on 4 April 2019.[33] The attack took place precisely at the moment that the UN Support Mission in Libya (UNSMIL), under the leadership of Ghassan Salamé, was in the process of convening a national conference to arrange moving forward with Libya's political transition to an elected government. Haftar was thus wilfully sabotaging the conference.[34]

Having ensured that Libya would fall into disorder, Russia directly engaged to maximize the enduring nature of that disorder, and in the process increase its military presence in the country, potentially for the long-term. This process illustrates in microcosm the thesis of this volume—that some international actors benefit from disorder. Rather than seeking to impose an alternative order, they prefer to stir the pot and keep conflict going. For them, this has more than one benefit. First, it creates problems for, and weakens, certain foreign competitors. It also provides a demonstration of what can happen when a tough, authoritarian government like theirs is not maintained.

In short, the same Russian statesmen who endorsed the Libyan Political Agreement of December 2015 then sought to destabilize that very agreement and to ensure the failure of the coalition government it created. They provided critical support to those Libyans in the east determined to reject the national government and substitute their own under a military warlord. Russia then made common cause with all those opposed to the so-called 'Islamists' and 'Muslim Brotherhood.' This aligned them internationally with the UAE and the coalition of Gulfi states seeking to prevent democracy or any Islamist-aligned movements from thriving on Libyan soil.

The Russians also took this opportunity to connect their Libya policy to larger regional ambitions with the introduction of sophisticated Russian military aircraft in Libya and a semi-permanent base at Jufra, in Libya's south central region. They also introduced President Putin's personal mercenary army, the Wagner Group, led by his 'chef,' Yevgeny Prigozhin, whom the US later indicted and sanctioned for his role in undertaking active measures against the American elections in 2016.[35] Following Haftar's invasion of Tripoli, the Wagner Group became an important component of the attacks on the ground, as its snipers targeted and killed front-line soldiers resisting Haftar's advance.[36]

Russian support for Haftar, adjacent to that of the Emiratis, the Egyptians, the Jordanians and the Saudis, might have eventually enabled Haftar to enter Tripoli, although probably not to hold it, given the likely level of Libyan resistance. Yet it, in turn, generated the forceful re-entry of Turkey into the militarization of Libya. As of January 2020, Turkey sent in its own drones in response to those of the UAE and its own mercenaries from Syria in response to those of Russia.[37]

The Turkish intervention

Russia's interventionism in Libya threatened not only the installation of Haftar as the country's dictator, but a victory for the UAE and Egypt and a 'loss' for Turkey in terms of long-term political influence in the country as well as economic opportunities. At the time of the 2011 Libyan Uprisings, Turkish construction companies were among the most important foreign businesses operating in the country, and they brought with them tens of thousands of Turkish workers. Indeed, some 25,000 Turks were evacuated during the anti-Qadhafi uprisings,[38] leaving behind some $15 billion worth of construction contracts, along with unfinished projects and abandoned heavy equipment.[39] Most of these contracts had been struck with ODAC—that most paradoxical of Libya's semi-sovereign economic institutions—that Mr Pack describes with penetrating wit in Chapter 4.

Whatever chance Turkey might have of recovering any back-payments depended on it stopping Haftar's advance—and combating the Russian, Emirati, Egyptian and other forces besieging Tripoli and seeking to benefit from their own old contracts with Qadhafian semi-sovereign institutions. Furthermore, rescuing the GNA from Haftar would give Turkey a host of new economic opportunities, which included putative grants of oil and gas rights of dubious legality from the GNA in the waters of the eastern Mediterranean.[40] The 27 November 2019 agreement between GNA Prime Minister Al-Sarraj and Turkish President

Erdoğan illustrated the cascading impact of competing agendas in Libya. Its most immediate impact was to draw a fierce denunciation from Greece, which in turn created an intra-EU row over the EU's overall support of the GNA, amid calls for Turkish withdrawal from the country.[41]

At the start of 2020, Turkey deployed some one hundred Turkish military officers,[42] multiple shiploads of weapons and military equipment, deployed air defences and stationed warships off the Libyan coast to conduct missile strikes against Haftar's forces. It also deployed at least 2,000 Syrian mercenaries to combat the Russian forces in the area around Tripoli. The result was successful—it pushed Haftar's forces and the associated foreign ones back from the city, ultimately causing Haftar to abandon his effort to conquer Tripoli by force.[43] The Turkish intervention led to Libya being once again divided between east and west, with spheres of influence and unstable borders exemplified by Sirte, which Tripoli and Misrata had taken from the Islamic State in 2016, and which Haftar had then occupied in January 2020.

By mid-2020, the Turkish victory in the War for Tripoli had led to two contradictory phenomena. On the one hand, Turkey and Russia were now each taking the lead in trying to negotiate solutions to the Libyan conflict, each representing their opposing Libyan clients. Both sides pushed ahead with these efforts even when their clients, such as Haftar, refused to deal, even after Russian President Putin and Turkish President Erdoğan both pressured him to do so.[44] Conversely, while they sought to negotiate in tandem to prevent the Libya file from being dominated by the UN or the West, these countries continued to lead forces facing off against one another in combat and potential combat.

Hence by the summer of 2020, the Libyan disorder risked leading to a widescale regional conflict involving not only Libyans, but also their sponsors. Rather than containing that disorder, the intervening countries had stimulated it, and expanded it. The risk of a broader conflict did have a salutary impact—it caused those involved to step back from the brink, making it possible for Libyans to move forward with another UN sponsored political process that ultimately resulted in the formation of a new transitional Government of National Unity (GNU) in February 2021 and the promise of national elections set for 24 December 2021. Notably, all of that happened only after the US itself had another round of national elections, resulting in the defeat of Donald Trump and his policies that had been indifferent to restraining the foreign competition fuelling Libyan disorder.

The Trump Administration's Libya failure

The United States played a critical role in achieving Libya's dystopia during the period covered by the GNA, from 2016 through to the end of 2020. Under the disordered presidency of Donald Trump, instead of seeking to counter and contain the Enduring Disorder as the Obama Administration sought to do, the US fanned it. It did so through charting an inconsistent course, which during 2017 and 2018 was largely one of neglect, and which became in 2019 one that was simultaneously feckless, reckless, and fragmented.

During 2017 and 2018, career US diplomats, including Ambassador to Libya Peter Bodde, and military officials at AFRICOM, did their best to continue to implement a policy in which the US backed the efforts of UN SRSG Salamé to broker further political agreements, while the White House remained largely disengaged, other than granting permission to the Defense Department to do its best to work with Libyans to take out terrorists.

But in the meantime, as discussed in this volume's preface, the Emiratis and the Egyptians continued discussions with the

Trump Administration to pave a road to the White House accepting a military dictatorship under Haftar. This culminated sometime in early 2019 when National Security Advisor John Bolton gave what was interpreted by Haftar, and likely his foreign sponsors, as a green light[45] for his effort to conquer Tripoli that he then initiated on 4 April 2019.[46] Trump then telephoned Haftar, sending a public signal of US support for his military campaign. Following the phone call, the White House promptly issued a press release that contained the Orwellian, and ludicrous statement that Trump and Haftar 'discussed a shared vision for Libya's transition to a stable, democratic political system.'[47]

Mr Pack describes this incident in the preface as leading many to mistakenly believe that it reflected a change in official American policy. In fact, it reflected only the actions of a President who disdained policy entirely, and therefore, personally became an element of disorder. In a normal US administration, the US typically seeks to bring disparate foreign governments with competing goals into greater alignment on most issues. By contrast, Trump's ad hoc, casual, and contemptuous approach to foreign policy simply induced chaos. Thus, the Trump-Haftar phone call was merely a continuation of Trump's approach from 2017–19, and as a result eighteen further months of chaos in Libya followed Haftar's invasion. Both were a direct consequence of President Trump's neither understanding nor caring what happened in Libya, and reflected his comfortable embrace of chaos.

In practice, the actions of the UAE and Egypt in securing Trump's and Bolton's acceptance of Haftar's attack on the Libyan government had succeeded in turning Libya into a free-for-all for any country wanting to participate in the conflict. No wonder that in the ensuing months, Libya had the honour of becoming contested territory for military forces from Chad, Egypt, France, Jordan, Russia, Sudan, Turkey, the UAE, with other states such as Saudi Arabia providing weapons or other support. All this was documented by the UN Panel of Experts responsible for monitoring the UN Arms Embargo, and none paying any diplomatic price.

In this period, the Trump Administration blocked a series of proposed UN Resolutions intended to condemn and stop the growing Libyan conflict, while Haftar and his allies proceeded to kill thousands of Libyans and displace hundreds of thousands of others, advancing Russian interests, influence, and power in the process.[48]

Thus, under President Trump, the US helped Russia, as well as Egypt and the UAE, achieve greater influence in Libya at the cost of potential coordinated Western efforts to stabilize the country. This was a reflection of global disorder to be sure. But rather than a consequence of giant tectonic forces which could not be tamed by any government—as Mr Pack seems to suggest in his analysis—the disorder in Libya of 2019 and 2020, was in my perspective, the direct result of Russia's years of effort to secure influence there through its support of Haftar, and Donald Trump's peculiarly casual approach to policymaking.

It is not reasonable to expect order in a country like Libya emerging from civil conflict when it becomes a playground for other countries to systematically violate the rules they have agreed upon. When there is no price for betraying international commitments, they cease having meaning. Instead of becoming instruments of alignment to build order, they become obstacles to recognizing actual facts, allowing states to hide behind the cover of their commitments, while violating them at the same time.

One result therefore of the Putin-Trump relationship was to do further damage to international norms and to the United Nations as an institution. What Mr Pack has described as the Enduring Disorder was heightened by the peculiar disruptive personality of Trump, which enabled and amplified the disruptive actions by Russia and other countries to make Libya a test-case for their experiments to see what they could get away with and how they could weaken order providing institutions like the UN.

Bringing order out of chaos

The first casualty of the foreign interventions and failed policies that led to Haftar's effort to conquer Tripoli was the UN's efforts to broker progress on further Libyan political agreements which were intended to lead to reforms, a new constitution and elections. A year after Haftar undertook his invasion of Tripoli, UN SRSG Salamé resigned, citing physical exhaustion after two and a half years in the position.[49]

His position was filled for the remainder of 2020 by an Acting SRSG, Stephanie Williams, a highly regarded former US foreign service officer who warned the foreign interveners that no military solution was possible, and that their approach risked broader war.

Under Trump's next National Security Advisor Robert O'Brien, the US—increasingly concerned about the impact of the Russian presence in Libya—gradually reverted over the course of 2020 to the policies of the Obama years. It once again gave more than lip service to the UN's efforts to broker a political agreement.[50] Ambassador Williams also made the critical decision to move ahead with Libyan political talks through convening a group of 75 hand-picked Libyans, asking them to approve a transition towards elections without foreigners being present in the room. The exclusion of direct foreign participation in the talks had some positive impact, as Libyan-to-Libyan discussions began over the autumn of 2020 to clarify potential pathways that could provide an alternative to conflict.[51] Meanwhile, the '5+5' Joint Military Commission talks convened by UNSMIL, involving security forces from both the GNA and the LNA, achieved a cease fire in late October and early November 2020 that provided an extended break in military conflict and space for further political discussions.[52] Notably, the agreement included the promise that foreign fighters—the mercenary forces on both sides—would depart Libya no later than 23 January 2021. In late 2020, some observers were cautiously optimistic that the mercenary portion of the foreign intervention problem might actually be at least partially implemented.[53] Yet foreign intervening parties have continued to quietly arm their Libyan clients, despite the ceasefire, and at the end of 2020 there remained some 20,000 mercenaries in place within Libya's national territory. As of the spring of 2021, the foreign force problem remained front-and-centre as an ongoing risk for the country's future, as reflected in yet another UN Security Council resolution calling on all the foreign forces to leave—including those sponsored by at least one of its signatories to the resolution, Russia.[54]

To secure Libya, Libyans will need to be prepared to push out any foreign forces that compete with Libyans maintaining sovereignty over Libyan territory. In addition, countries sitting on the UN Security Council can begin to take actions to insist that the 'order' reflected in UNSC Resolutions, including the arms embargo on Libya, is respected, and that those who violate it suffer consequences. It may be that the consequences are imposed only ad hoc, by individual nation states, especially when the perpetrators, like Russia, are permanent members of the UNSC. Major powers have the opportunity to do this, if they are paying attention and willing to use the tools they have at hand.

Enduring Disorder, or just a mess that needs to be cleaned up?

Libya's disorder over the decade following the 2011 Libyan Uprisings well reflected the competing agendas of foreign states, and was grossly exacerbated by those agendas in a political form of Gresham's Law, in which bad policy drove out good policy.[55] The competing agendas of the foreign intervenors wreaked havoc inside Libya and gave the intervenors undue, and destructive, influence over the county's future, which they repeatedly used to fracture the country.

Inconsistent US engagement under President Obama, and the negligence, inconsistency, and ignorance of President Trump, played roles in the development of Libyan disorder. Focused attention to promote Libyan order during President Obama's second term and in the final year of the Trump Administration by certain career functionaries helped combat the disorder. Many senior officials in the Biden Administration had previously served in the Obama Administration. As I write this in its early months, these officials have demonstrated a focus in seeking to resolve conflicts, rather than perpetuate them. Even those conflicts entered into for a good cause are being unwound, as evidenced in President Biden's decision to withdraw US forces from Afghanistan after 20 years of counter-terrorism efforts there. When it comes to Libya, the US now has a unified interest in stability over disorder, compromise over chaos, the development of national institutions capable of countering threats to the physical safety of Libyans and foreigners alike, and a stable, sustainable economy. The Biden Administration has no interest in seeing France squabble with Italy over influence, Turkey and Egypt at one another's throats, the UAE and Saudi Arabia escalating their differences with Qatar, or Russia building and expanding its military presence in the Mediterranean. A successful transition from the Government of National Unity to an elected government at the end of 2021 is consistent with multiple US goals, including attenuating the risk of Enduring Disorder. To get there, the US must continue trying to convince foreign intervenors to stop what it has called their 'toxic interference' in Libya.

Libya will be lucky if it is able to break free from outside intervention, especially amid the intensifying global competition for power and influence among the United States, Russia and China, alongside the fierce regional competitions that now occupy the MENA region. A decade after the 2011 Libyan Uprisings, and as reflected in the establishment of the transitional Government of National Unity, Libyans can save themselves and achieve a peaceful transition of power by reaching agreements with other Libyans rather than depending on foreign patrons to back their claims to domination.[56]

Mr Pack has aptly noted the absence of a 'captain' and order provider in the international system. But a boat can be sailed safely into harbour by a crew too, so long as they have agreed on a particular course, and are competent enough to make the required adjustments based on the actual weather. In the contemporary world, nation-states do continue to make their own sovereign decisions, and international law remains a matter of standards and norms, rather than actual law. But these standards and norms do provide ordering principles that nation-states can enforce or deliberately shred. The current disorder described by Mr Pack will endure so long as powerful states choose the latter approach and it will be substantially attenuated when they revert to the former.

NOTES

PREFACE: WELCOME TO THE ENDURING DISORDER

1. Plato's analogy of policymaking in a democracy as akin to steering a 'ship of state' appears in book 6 of the Republic (488a–489d). Plato has Socrates compare the population at large to a strong, but near-sighted 'shipowner' whose knowledge of seafaring is lacking. The quarrelling sailors on his vessel represent demagogues, politicians, and common people, while the ship's navigator represents the philosopher (in modern terms, he is the technocrat or 'expert'). The sailors flatter themselves by claiming to know the theories of seafaring better than the navigator, though in reality they know nothing of it. They are constantly vying with one another for the approval of the 'shipowner' so as to captain the ship, going so far as to stupefy the shipowner with drugs and wine. Meanwhile, they dismiss the navigator (the only true, yet modest, expert) as a useless stargazer, though he is the only one with adequate seafaring knowledge to direct the ship's course. Constant reversals and short-sighted decisions ensue. *The Republic of Plato*, trans. Allan Bloom, 3rd ed. (Basic Books, 2016).

2. A 'technical' is a light improvised fighting vehicle, typically an open-backed civilian pickup truck with a machine gun, anti-aircraft gun, or other artillery piece mounted to its back. The term derives from Somalia in the 1990s. Matteo Latorraca, 'Technicals: The Vehicles That Changed the Asymmetric Conflicts', 6 November 2014, geopolitica.info, https://www.geopolitica.info/technicals/

3. Jason Pack and Nate Mason, 'A Trumpian Peace Deal in Libya?', *Foreign Affairs*, 10 January 2017, https://www.foreignaffairs.com/articles/libya/2017–01–10/trumpian-peace-deal-libya. During the transition period in the lead up to his inauguration, President Trump's outer circle confidants and donors had potential reasons to believe that Libya would be an important part of the president's agenda, as it had featured prominently during the campaign as a talking point to attack Hillary Clinton's record as secretary of state. Their logic held that the president would adopt a novel and pragmatic approach to Libya to match the genuine buzz that major Trump donors and confidants gave to the issue. In reality, as time unfolded, Libya was not treated as a top tier issue for the administration. Similarly to Ukraine, Saudi Arabia, and the smaller Gulf countries, Libya remained a foreign policy issue towards which the Trump administration sought to conduct a shadow foreign policy separate from the official institutions of government. For more on the concept of 'shadow policy', consult footnote 18.

4. In the spring of 2020, these adversaries would counsel radically different approaches to the Covid pandemic, with one constantly minimizing the danger, mocking the experts' warnings, and trying to keep the economy open, while the other sought a sober, cautious, technocratic approach to the challenges, no matter how grim the realities or profound the short-term pain might be.

5. Author discussions with Senior Fellow at the Atlantic Council Karim Mezran and anonymous Italian and French Foreign Ministry officials, May 2020.

6. Haftar is a former Qadhafi-era general, who after his capture in Chad in the 1980s and defection to the United States, returned to Libya during the Arab Spring hoping to be appointed commander-in-chief of the rebels' armed forces. When he failed to achieve that distinction, he gradually built up support and launched a series of coup attempts until he forged his own breakaway military grouping that he called 'The Libyan National Army'. For more on Haftar's biography, consult Jason Pack, 'Kingdom of Militias: Libya's Second War of Post-Qadhafi Succession', *ISPI*, March 2019; Barak Barfi, 'Khalifa Haftar: Rebuilding Libya from the Top Down', *Washington Institute*, Research Notes 22, August 2014,

https://www.washingtoninstitute.org/policy-analysis/view/khalifa-
haftar-rebuilding-libya-from-the-top-down

7. Secretary General Guterres did not immediately denounce the attack
   or make any press statement. Rather, after taking cover at a UN-owned
   villa in the Tripoli suburbs, he continued his original plans by flying
   to Benghazi to meet with Haftar the next day. This granted de facto
   legitimacy to Haftar, even as the offensive he launched was still underway. 'UN Chief Says "Deeply Concerned" after Meeting with Libya's
   Haftar', *France 24*, 5 April 2019, https://www.france24.com/en/
   20190405-libya-un-guterres-khalifa-haftar-meeting-tripoli

8. David Kirkpatrick, 'Trump Endorses an Aspiring Libyan Strongman,
   Reversing Policy', *New York Times*, 19 April 2019, https://www.
   nytimes.com/2019/04/19/world/middleeast/trump-libya-khalifa-hifter.
   html; Steve Holland, 'White House Says Trump Spoke to Libyan
   Commander Haftar on Monday', *Reuters*, 19 April 2019, https://www.
   reuters.com/article/us-libya-security-trump/white-house-says-trump-
   spoke-to-libyan-commander-haftar-on-monday-idUSKCN1RV0WW

9. Author discussions with anonymous Trump advisors and outer circle
   confidants, February 2020.

10. Vivian Salama et al., 'Trump Backed Libyan Warlord after Saudi Arabia
    and Egypt Lobbied Him', *Wall Street Journal*, 12 May 2019, https://
    www.wsj.com/articles/trump-backed-libyan-warlord-after-saudi-
    arabia-and-egypt-lobbied-him-11557668581; Eric Schmitt et al., 'On
    Muslim Brotherhood, Trump Weighs Siding with Autocrats and
    Roiling Middle East', *New York Times*, 6 May 2019, https://www.
    nytimes.com/2019/05/06/world/middleeast/muslim-brotherhood-
    trump.html

11. Author discussions with Trump advisors appraised in real time on the
    progress of the meetings, April 2019.

12. David Kirkpatrick, 'The White House Blessed a War in Libya, But
    Russia Won It', *New York Times*, 14 April 2020, https://www.nytimes.
    com/2020/04/14/world/middleeast/libya-russia-john-bolton.html

13. The aforementioned interviews with Trump outer circle officials.

14. Ashish Kumar Sen and Karim Mezran, 'Trump Wades into Libyan
    Crisis, and Why That's Not Good News', *New Atlanticist*, 22 April

2019, https://www.atlanticcouncil.org/blogs/new-atlanticist/trump-libya-haftar/

15. For more on France's unique approach to Libya since 2016, see Farah Rasmi, 'Beyond the War: The History of French–Libyan Relations', *Atlantic Council*, 8 April 2021, https://www.atlanticcouncil.org/in-depth-research-reports/issue-brief/beyond-the-war-the-history-of-french-libyan-relations/; Jalel Harchaoui, 'La politique libyenne de la France et ses antécédents historiques', *Revue internationale et stratégique* 4, no. 116 (2019), pp. 33–43, https://www.cairn.info/revue-internationale-et-strategique-2019-4-page-33.html#; Karim Mezran and Federica Saini Fasanotti, 'France Must Recognize Its Role in Libya's Plight', *New Atlanticist*, 21 July 2020, https://www.atlanticcouncil.org/blogs/new-atlanticist/france-must-recognize-its-role-in-libyas-plight/

16. *Rai'i Al-Youm Libiyya,* كلهم حفتر بالنسبة الينا، و كلهم وقفوا في خندق حلف الناتو و قصفه لليبيا . و مكالمة ترمب قد تكون حسمت طرابلس

20 April 2019, https://www.raialyoum.com/index.php/%E2%80%8F

17. Julian E. Barnes, 'Ex-C.I.A. Asset, Now a Libyan Strongman, Faces Torture Accusations', *New York Times*, 18 February 2020, https://www.nytimes.com/2020/02/18/us/politics/hifter-torture-lawsuit-libya.html

18. I use the term shadow policy to refer to a phenomenon that was quite common during the Trump administration: deliberately conducting the White House's preferred policy towards a given issue through non-official channels, without curbing contradictory actions being conducted simultaneously through official channels that are also subordinate to the executive branch. Jared Kushner's dealings with the Emiratis during the crisis over the blockade of Qatar in 2017 is a well-reported example of an instance of shadow policy undoing and contradicting official State Department policy by Secretary of State Rex Tillerson towards the same issue.

19. *Al Jazeera News*, 'Trump Ally Erik Prince Violated Libya Arms Embargo: UN Report', 20 February 2021, https://www.aljazeera.com/news/2021/2/20/trump-ally-erik-prince-violated-libya-arms-embargo-un-report

20. Phone calls with State Department, AFRICOM, and USAID officials serving on the Libya portfolio at the time.

21. For more on the author's background, please consult https://www.mei.edu/experts/jason-pack; http://www.libya-analysis.com/team/; and http://www.libya-analysis.com/wordpress/wp-content/uploads/2020/08/Jason-Pack_CV_2020.pdf

22. *Al-Monitor Lobbying Tracker*, Libya, 'Update' and '2019 Overview' tabs, https://lobbying.al-monitor.com/pulse/libya#tab1

23. That Libyan leaders attempt to underplay the jihadi problem via their lobbying agenda and overtly sidestep it in their public statements is an issue I will return to at the end of Chapter 2, because it indirectly illustrates a classic example of leadership/coordination failure.

24. Saul Kelly, *Cold War in the Desert: Britain, the United States, and the Italian Colonies, 1945–52* (Palgrave Macmillan, 2000); William Roger Louis, 'Libya: The Creation of a Client State', in William Roger Louis and Prosser Gifford (eds), *Decolonization and African Independence: The Transfers of Power 1960–80* (Yale University Press, 1988); Scott L. Bills, *The Libyan Arena: The United States, Britain and the Council of Foreign Ministers, 1945–1948* (Kent State University Press, 1995); Mikhail Zygar, *All the Kremlin's Men: Inside the Court of Vladimir Putin* (PublicAffairs, 2016).

25. Anonymous DoD officials and Washington-based journalists spoke to the author of Patrick Shanahan's desire to continually, and proactively, appease President Trump to stay in the role. For the Defense Department's biography of Patrick Shanahan, the then-acting secretary of defense, see https://www.defense.gov/Our-Story/Biographies/Biography/Article/1252116/patrick-shanahan/

26. Conversations with former ambassadorial-ranked American State Department officials, June 2020; Steve Benen, *The Impostors: How Republicans Quit Governing and Seized American Politics* (William Morrow, 2020).

27. Mietek Boduszyński and Christopher K. Lamont, 'Trump Changed U.S. Policy toward Libya: This Is Why It Matters', *Washington Post*, Monkey Cage, 3 May 2019, https://www.washingtonpost.com/politics/2019/05/03/trump-changed-us-policy-towards-libya-this-is-why-it-matters/; David Kirkpatrick, 'Trump Endorses an Aspiring Libyan Strongman, Reversing Policy', *New York Times*, 19 April 2019,

https://www.nytimes.com/2019/04/19/world/middleeast/trump-libya-khalifa-hifter.html; Salama et al., 'Trump Backed Libyan Warlord after Saudi Arabia and Egypt Lobbied Him'.

28. Anonymous Libyan author, تعرف على تفاصيل مكالمة هاتفية بين «حفتر» والرئيس الأمريكي «ترامب» *Ain Libya*, 20 April 2019, https://www.eanlibya.com/بين-حفت-تعرف-على-تفاصيل-مكالمة-هاتفية/.

29. Jeremy Diamond, 'Trump, alongside Italian PM, Says No US Role in Libya', *CNN*, 20 April 2017, https://www.cnn.com/2017/04/20/politics/donald-trump-paolo-gentiloni/index.html

30. Benen, *Impostors*, traces how widespread and wrongheaded this common analysis of Trump's foreign policy has become and puts forth a similar case for why it is incorrect.

31. Evan Osnos et al., 'Trump, Putin, and the New Cold War', *New Yorker*, 24 February 2017, https://www.newyorker.com/magazine/2017/03/06/trump-putin-and-the-new-cold-war

32. Brian Whitmore, Senior Fellow and Russia program director at the Center for European Policy Analysis, testimony to the US Helsinki Commission Hearings on 20 November 2019, available at https://www.csce.gov/sites/helsinkicommission.house.gov/files/III.%20D.%20Witness%20Testimonies-%20BW.pdf

33. Paul Stronski, 'Kazakhstan at Twenty-Five: Stable But Tense', *Carnegie Endowment for International Peace*, 2016, https://carnegieendowment.org/files/Stronsky_Kazakhstan.pdf

34. One compelling example of this genre is John Micklethwait and Adrian Wooldridge, *The Wake Up Call: Why the Pandemic Has Exposed the Weakness of the West; And How to Fix It*, (Short Books, 2020), pp. 103–21. John Micklethwait is the editor-in-chief of *Bloomberg* and Adrian Wooldridge is the former political editor of the *Economist*.

35. Mark Episkopos, 'No Return to Normalcy: What Biden's Foreign Policy Speech Means', *National Interest*, 6 February 2021, https://nationalinterest.org/feature/no-return-normalcy-what-bidens-foreign-policy-speech-means-177830

36. Elizabeth Crisp, 'Progressives Not Impressed with Biden's Executive Orders: "3rd Obama Term Is Not Good Enough"', *Newsweek*, 29 January 2021, https://www.newsweek.com/progressives-conservatives-not-impressed-bidens-executive-orders-1565522

37. For the purpose of this volume, 'collective action problems' can be understood as how divergent actors with different interests, ideologies, predilections, and sensitivities work together to transcend conflicts and achieve those outcomes that on the whole benefit the collective while minimizing harm to those members who may suffer losses to their specific interests. The notion of economic or foreign policy issues constituting 'collective action problems' that can be optimally solved could be said to be a natural extension of both a game theorist's and a utilitarian/Benthamite view of the world. For a concise and particularly useful definition that unpacks all the term's connotations, see 'Collective Action Problem', *Encyclopaedia Britannica*, https://www.britannica.com/topic/collective-action-problem-1917157. For further background and scholarship on this important concept, please consult Keith Dowding, *Rational Choice and Political Power* (Bristol University Press, 2019); Katharina Holzinger, *Transnational Common Goods: Strategic Constellations, Collective Action Problems, and Multi-Level Provision* (Palgrave, 2008).

38. Sean McFate, *Goliath: Why the West Isn't Winning. And What We Must Do about It* (Penguin, 2019).

39. John Ikenberry (ed.), *America Unrivaled: The Future of the Balance of Power* (Cornell University Press, 2002).

40. The existence of a crisis in the 'old international order' of the late Cold War and early post-Cold War periods was broadly acknowledged at the time. Yet the main currents in the literature anticipate a rebalancing, Chinese leadership, or a new form of consensus-based Western order, e.g., Richard Haass, *A World in Disarray: American Foreign Policy and the Crisis of the Old Order* (Penguin, 2017). This is a work I will return to often as a strawman of this volume as it is essentially an overview of the establishment thinking on the post-Cold War world order by a prominent centrist and self-acclaimed 'realist' American IR practitioner. For more on his 'realism', consult Amitai Etzioni, 'The Realism of Richard Haass', *National Interest*, 31 May 2013, https://nationalinterest.org/commentary/the-realism-richard-haass-8534

41. William Roger Louis, *The Oxford History of the British Empire* (Oxford University Press, 1999); Jack Gallagher and Ronald Robinson, *Africa*

and the Victorians: The Official Mind of Imperialism (Macmillan, 1961); Sir Christopher Bayly, *The Birth of the Modern World, 1780–1914: Global Connections and Comparisons* (Blackwell, 2004). Author conversations with the late Professor Sir Christopher Bayly, June 2013. He felt that others in the global history movement might contest this point as they see the sphere of the global as beginning with the age of exploration, but for Prof. Bayly (my late supervisor at Cambridge) the emergence of the British Empire was the first moment when all politics and commerce became intrinsically global. However, it is worth noting that most of the academic global history movement is not concerned with the extent of the flow of goods and people, but focuses on ideas and social movements, which are able to be globalized prior to the technological means required for the extensive globalization of people and goods.

42. D.C. Watt, *Succeeding John Bull: America in Britain's Place, 1900–1975; A Study of the Anglo-American Relationship and World Politics in the Context of British and American Foreign-Policy-Making in the Twentieth Century* (Cambridge University Press, 1984).

43. Richard Little, 'Hans J. Morgenthau's *Politics among Nations*', in Richard Little, *The Balance of Power in International Relations: Metaphors, Myths and Models* (Cambridge University Press, 2007), pp. 91–127; Michael Williams, *Realist Tradition and the Limits of International Relations* (Cambridge University Press, 2005).

44. For example, Robert Kaplan, *The Coming Anarchy* (Random House, 2000); Haass, *World in Disarray*; Martin Van Creveld, *The Rise and Decline of the State* (Cambridge University Press, 1999) and Van Creveld, *Pussycats: Why the Rest Keeps Beating the West and What Can Be Done About It* (CreateSpace, 2016); Sean McFate, *Goliath: Why the West Doesn't Win Wars. And What We Must Do about It* (Penguin, 2019); Eliot A. Cohen, 'History and the Hyperpower', *Foreign Affairs*, 1 July 2004, https://www.foreignaffairs.com/articles/united-states/200407–01/history-and-hyperpower. Richard Haass and Robert Kaplan differ from the other scholars by perceiving the world already moving increasingly into disarray from the fall of the Berlin Wall onwards. Others trace the key moment of this drive to disorder as the fallout from the US invasion of Iraq in 2003. This book adopts the latter analysis.

45. 'The Middle East in an Era of Great Power Competition: A Conversation with Barry Posen and Stephen Walt', *Middle East Institute*, 16 April 2020, https://www.mei.edu/events/middle-east-era-great-power-competition-conversation-barry-posen-and-stephen-walt

46. Margaret MacMillan, *The War That Ended Peace: The Road to 1914* (Random House, 2014); Christopher Clark, *The Sleepwalkers: How Europe Went to War in 1914* (Penguin, 2013).

47. Van Creveld, *Rise and Decline of the State*; Cohen, 'History and the Hyperpower', pp. 49–63.

48. A typical example is Jin Kai, *Rising China in a Changing World: Power Transitions and Global Leadership* (Palgrave Macmillan, 2016).

49. Jennifer Rudolph and Michael Szonyi (eds), *The China Questions: Critical Insights into a Rising Power* (Harvard University Press, 2019).

50. For example, Clifford A Kiracofe, 'US Hostility toward China Rooted in Hegemonic Struggle', *Global Times*, 28 July 2020, https://www.globaltimes.cn/content/1195881.shtml

51. This book uses the term 'neo-populism' in its most widely understood contemporary sense to describe a distinctly twenty-first-century political phenomenon, which is sometimes referred to in the popular press and in academia as 'illiberal populism'. The logic for this choice is that 'illiberal populism' has existed throughout history, but the term neo-populism conveys that the political movement or ideology under question 'is distinct from 20th century populism[s] such as Fascism or Marxism or the range of populisms in the colonial and post-colonial developing world in that it radically combines, or perhaps redefines, classically opposed left–right political attitudes and incorporates various new electronic media as a means of popular dissemination'. For the above quote and the broadly understood definition of the term, please consult, Wikipedia, 'Talk: Neo-populism'; Wiktionary, 'Neopopulism', https://en.wiktionary.org/wiki/neopopulism

52. *Economist*, 'How the Pandemic Strengthened the Chinese Communist Party', 24 December 2020, https://www.economist.com/china/2020/12/30/how-the-pandemic-strengthened-the-chinese-communist-party

53. Paul Miller, 'Yes, Blame China for the Virus', *Foreign Policy*, 25 March 2020, https://foreignpolicy.com/2020/03/25/blame-china-and-xi-jinping-for-coronavirus-pandemic/

54. Jasper Becker, *Made in China: Wuhan, Covid and the Quest for Biotech Supremacy* (Hurst, 2021).

55. Frederic Wehrey and Sandy Alkoutami, 'China's Balancing Act in Libya', *Lawfare*, 10 May 2020, https://carnegieendowment.org/2020/05/10/china-s-balancing-act-in-libya-pub-81757

56. Malte Brosig, *The Role of BRICS in Large-Scale Armed Conflict: Building a Multi-Polar World Order* (Palgrave Macmillan, 2019).

57. Francis Fukuyama, *The End of History* (Free Press, 1992); Kenneth Pomerantz, *The Great Divergence: China, Europe, and the Making of the Modern World Economy* (Princeton University Press, 2001).

58. Bruce Jones, 'China and the Return of Great Power Strategic Competition', *Brookings Institution*, February 2020, https://www.brookings.edu/research/china-and-the-return-of-great-power-strategic-competition/

59. Line 8.28 reads 'ἀεὶ Λιβύη φέρει τι καινόν'. Aristotle, *Historia animalium*, trans. D.M. Balme, Cambridge Classical Texts and Commentaries (Cambridge University Press, 2011). For Aristotle, as with all classical Greek and Roman authors, the term Libya refers to all of North Africa west of Egypt, but in Polybius and Aristotle it is mostly used to refer to modern-day Tunisia and Libya.

60. Jason Pack, 'Turkey Doubles Down on Libya', *Middle East Institute*, 10 December 2019, https://www.mei.edu/publications/turkey-doubles-down-libya

61. Jamie Metzl, 'Defunding the WHO Mid-Pandemic Is Lunacy', *Newsweek*, 16 April 2020, https://www.newsweek.com/defunding-who-mid-pandemic-lunacy-opinion-1498369

62. Peter Turchin, *Ultra Society: How 10,000 Years of War Made Humans the Greatest Co-Operators on Earth* (Beresta, 2016).

63. Phone interviews with Syria, Yemen, and climate change experts in the UK and United States.

64. Pack, 'Kingdom of Militias'.

65. Jason Pack and Wolfgang Pusztai, 'Turning the Tide: How Turkey Won the War for Tripoli', *Middle East Institute*, 10 November 2020, https://www.mei.edu/publications/turning-tide-how-turkey-won-war-tripoli

66. Jason Pack, 'The Turkish Victory Dividend in Libya', *Inside Arabia Magazine*, 25 May 2019, https://insidearabia.com/the-turkish-victory-dividend-in-libya/

67. Jason Pack, 'Libya Has a New Prime Minister and His Family Legacy Is as Complex, Shady, and Wealthy as the Country Itself', *Middle East Institute*, 8 February 2021, https://www.mei.edu/blog/monday-briefing-what-exactly-biden-plan-yemen#pack

68. The crux of this argument 'Libya as a harbinger of political outcomes during the Enduring Disorder' has undergirded most of my own writing on Libya since late 2018. A similar argument has also been eloquently and concisely put forward by Walter Russell Mead, 'Libya's Foul Foretaste of the Post-American World', *Wall Street Journal*, 7 July 2020, https://www.wsj.com/articles/libyas-foul-foretaste-of-the-post-american-world-11594228201

INTRODUCTION: THE GREAT UNRAVELLING

1. The Preface explained that 'multipolarity' implies multiple poles of competing order seeking to extend their spheres of influence.

2. The Cold War was a lopsided battle between two poles of competing order. The winner propagated its order the widest and most comprehensively. William C. Wohlforth, 'Realism and the End of the Cold War', *International Security* 19, no. 3 (Winter 1994–5), pp. 91–129.

3. Broadly put, conventional conservatives across the continent are unwilling to capitalize on anti-migrant xenophobia in the way the neo-populist right can. Sasha Polakow-Suransky, *Go Back to Where You Came From: The Backlash against Immigration and the Fate of Western Democracy* (Nation Books, 2017).

4. For a fairly impartial timeline of the fiendishly complex chain of events related to 'emailgate', see Casey Hicks, 'Timeline of Hillary Clinton's Email Scandal', *CNN Politics*, 7 November 2016, https://www.cnn.com/2016/10/28/politics/hillary-clinton-email-timeline/index.html

5. Furthermore, most Americans were not aware that the essence of 'emailgate' was Clinton's handling of classified information about Libya. That aspect of the story was not stressed in the American media.

6. Obviously identifying what constitutes 'utility' when it comes to international geopolitics is difficult, if not impossible. 'Utility' in this context may be loosely understood via a Benthamite paradigm applied to the international arena. It has been argued that Bentham and his non-English disciples intended as such. See David R. Armitage, 'Globalizing Jeremy Bentham', *History of Political Thought* 32, no. 1 (2011), pp. 63–82, https://dash.harvard.edu/bitstream/handle/1/11211544/Armitage_GlobalizingJeremy.pdf?sequence=1

7. Oliver Bullough, *Moneyland: The Inside Story of the Crooks and Kleptocrats Who Rule the World* (St. Martin's Press, 2019); Nicholas Shaxson, 'Tackling Tax Havens', *Finance & Development* 56, no. 3 (September 2019), https://www.imf.org/external/pubs/ft/fandd/2019/09/tackling-global-tax-havens-shaxon.htm

8. John Ikenberry (ed.), *America Unrivaled: The Future of the Balance of Power* (Cornell University Press, 2002).

9. Eugene Rogan, *The Fall of the Ottomans: The Great War in the Middle East, 1914–1920* (Penguin, 2015); David Fromkin, *A Peace to End All Peace: The Fall of the Ottoman Empire and the Creation of the Modern Middle East* (Holt, 2009).

10. Thomas Ricks, *Fiasco* (Penguin, 2007).

11. Haass, *World in Disarray*, chapter 'The Other Order', pp. 56–70; Van Creveld, *Rise and Decline of the State*.

12. Ibid.

13. Fehim Tastekin, 'Can Malta's Diplomacy Tip Balance in Libya toward Turkey?', *Al-Monitor*, 12 August 2020, https://www.al-monitor.com/pulse/originals/2020/08/turkey-egypt-libya-greece-can-malta-support-tip-balance.html#ixzz6VIQQqwL7

14. The UN also has its mechanisms for pooling members' sovereignty. One way is through UNSC resolutions that have moral and legal force against sovereign governments' actions, especially when coherently enforced by the UNSC's permanent five members. Another is through the creation of organizations within the UN structure that carry out transnational governmental functions, such as UNHCR and IAEA. UNHCR resettles refugees and cares for them like a government would until they are resettled. IAEA enforces the nuclear non-

proliferation treaty and highlights violations, which can lead to other actions such as sanctions. UN peacekeeping missions also exhibit the member states' pooled sovereignty once authorized. Thanks to Jonathan Winer for his wisdom on this point.

15. The Global Challenges Foundation exists to promote global governance, which it defines as already underway and being undertaken by the UN; https://globalchallenges.org/global-governance/

16. Darwin, *After Tamerlane* (Bloomsbury, 2009); Niall Ferguson, *Empire: How Britain Made the Modern World* (Penguin, 2017); Halford MacKinder, *The Geographical Pivot of History* (Cosimo Classics, 2020); Carroll Quigley, *The Evolution of Civilizations* (Liberty Fund, 1961).

17. These largely consensus values-based tenets were thought by some liberal thinkers, like Francis Fukuyama, to have become near universal in the years after the collapse of the Soviet Union and according to others on their way to being embedded in enforceable international legal structures. But since the start of the Enduring Disorder and the concomitant end of the post-Cold War period, the limits to transforming supposedly universal values into both legally binding mechanisms and voluntary agreement on policies have become increasingly visible. Thanks to Jonathan Winer for sharing with me his personal experiences of how these limits play out in practice.

18. Stephen Sestanovich, 'The West's Post-Cold War Strategies Worked', *New York Times*, 22 December 2016, https://www.nytimes.com/roomfordebate/2016/12/22/since-the-fall-of-the-soviet-union/the-wests-post-cold-war-strategies-worked

19. William Roger Louis and Roger Owen, *Suez 1956: The Crisis and Its Consequences* (Clarendon, 1989). The Falklands War is not an exception, as even it could not have been won by Britain without American help. Michael Getler, 'U.S. Aid to Britain in Falklands War Is Detailed', *Washington Post*, 7 March 1984, https://www.washingtonpost.com/archive/politics/1984/03/07/us-aid-to-britain-in-falklands-war-is-detailed/6e50e92e-3f4b-4768-97fb-57b5593994e6/

20. A classic example of this phenomenon is the GCC's utter powerlessness to facilitate or formulate a compromise between Qatar and its other members since the conflict broke out between them in 2017. It

was only able to be resolved when the pressure of American action by an incoming Biden administration clarified minds and led to a deal to lift the blockade of Qatar in January 2021. Guney Yildiz, 'GCC Summit: Will Lifting of the Qatar Blockade Reshape the Middle East?', *Forbes*, 4 January 2021,https://www.forbes.com/sites/guneyyildiz/2021/01/04/gcc-summit-will-lifting-of-the-qatar-blockade-reshape-the-middle-east/?sh=27b54b676e1f; for more background, see Kristian Coates Ulrichsen, *Qatar and the Gulf Crisis* (Hurst, 2020).

21. Darwin, *After Tamerlane*; MacKinder, *Geographical Pivot*; Ferguson, *Empire*.

22. Fouad Ajami, *The Foreigner's Gift: The Americans, the Arabs, and the Iraqis in Iraq* (Simon & Schuster, 2006); Ricks, *Fiasco*; Bob Woodward, *Plan of Attack* (Simon & Schuster, 2004).

23. Ajami, *Foreigner's Gift*.

24. Drew Middleton, 'NATO Allies Differ on Vietnam Policies', *New York Times*, 2 March 1964, https://www.nytimes.com/1964/03/02/archives/nato-ailies-differ-on-vietnam-policies.html

25. It is amazing that our new normal during the Enduring Disorder includes sustained and effective Russian, Chinese, Emirati, and Israeli attempts to influence American and British policymaking and elections from the inside. By contrast, the limited examples of the Soviet Union attempting to sway American elections during the Cold War were done in extremely minor and ineffective ways, like holding back hostages, and not through the kinds of mass influence operations that the Mueller Report has made famous.

26. Jeff Desjardins, '2,000 Years of Economic History in One Chart', *Virtual Capitalist*, September 2017, https://www.visualcapitalist.com/2000-years-economic-history-one-chart/

27. Robert Kaplan, 'The Post-Imperial Moment: Vulgar, Populist Anarchy Will Define the Twenty-First Century', *National Interest*, 22 April 2016, https://nationalinterest.org/feature/the-post-imperial-moment-15881

28. Fawaz Gerges, *Obama and the Middle East: The End of America's Moment?* (St. Martin's Griffin, 2013); Jason Pack, 'Obama and the Middle East: The End of America's Moment', *Journal of North African*

Studies 18, no. 2 (2013), pp. 383–5, http://dx.doi.org/10.1080/13629 387.2013.770200

29. Gerges, *Obama and the Middle East.*
30. Mieczysław P. Boduszyński, *US Democracy Promotion in the Arab World: Beyond Interests vs. Ideals* (Lynne Rienner, 2019).
31. Richard Northern and Jason Pack, 'The Role of Outside Actors', in Jason Pack (ed.), *The 2011 Libyan Uprisings and the Struggle for the Post-Qadhafi Future* (Palgrave Macmillan, 2013).
32. Martin van Creveld and Jason Pack, 'Upheaval in Qaddafi's Libya Isn't Just Another Arab Uprising', *Christian Science Monitor*, 23 February 2011, https://www.csmonitor.com/Commentary/Global-Viewpoint/ 2011/0223/Upheaval-in-Qaddafi-s-Libya-isn-t-just-another-Arab-uprising
33. As peaceful protestors were denouncing the human rights abuses of the regime on 17 February, *Qurina* wrote that they had interrupted the 'planned youth activities' of those trying to loyally show their support to Qadhafi—claiming the protestors had marched on central Benghazi 'raising banners with slogans against the authority of the people'. *BBC News Arabic*, ليبيا : دعوات غربية للاستجابة لتطلعات الشعب و الالتزام بضبط النفس February 2011, https://www.bbc.com/arabic/middleeast/2011/02/ 110217_libya_protests
34. In the English press, the term 'rebels' was frequently used, but this was not the way that the anti-Qadhafi protestors and fighters self-identified. They used the term *thuwwar* or revolutionaries, whereas the term *mutamaridiin* (rebels) has a negative connotation in Arabic and was never used as it implies that one is rebelling against a just order and hence causing *fitna* (Islamically sinful dissent).
35. Jason Pack and Barak Barfi, 'In War's Wake: The Struggle for the Post-Qadhafi Future', *Washington Institute for Near East Policy*, February 2012.
36. The words of this famous refrain 'لتطهير ليبيا بيت بيت، شبر شبر، زنقة زنقة' roughly translate as 'We will purify Libya, house by house, street by street, alley by alley.' *France24*, و خطابات القذافي القديمة الحديثة تغزو شبكة الانترنت March 2011. https://www.france24.com/ar/20110303-gaddafi-speech-internet-facebook-libya-africa-youtube-dailymotion

37. A post-facto compilation of all these speeches is available at Mr. Katzz, 'Gaddafi: They Love Me All My People (Noy Alooshe)', *YouTube*, 3 March 2012, https://www.youtube.com/watch?v=K2TqyyeZlrk

38. Noy Alooshe, 'Muammar Gaddafi: Zenga Zenga Song', *YouTube*, 22 February 2011, https://www.youtube.com/watch?v=cBY-0n4esNY

39. Isabel Kershner, 'Qaddafi YouTube Spoof by Israeli Gets Arab Fans', *New York Times*, 27 February 2011, https://www.nytimes.com/2011/02/28/world/middleeast/28youtube.html

40. The campaign that launched the manhunt for Joseph Kony of the Lord's Resistance Army is a classic example of this. For further illustration of this phenomenon, consult David Gauvey Herbert, 'Billions of Dollars Later, Joseph Kony Remains at Large and the First World Has Lost Interest in Bringing Him to Justice', *Quartz*, 27 April 2017, https://qz.com/960220/billions-of-dollars-later-joseph-kony-remains-at-large-and-the-first-world-has-lost-interest-in-bringing-him-to-justice/

41. *United Nations*, 'In Swift, Decisive Action, Security Council Imposes Tough Measures on Libyan Regime, Adopting Resolution 1970 in Wake of Crackdown on Protesters', SC/10187/REV.1, 26 February 2011, https://www.un.org/press/en/2011/sc10187.doc.htm

42. Northern and Pack, 'Role of Outside Actors', pp. 114–15.

43. Pack, *2011 Libyan Uprisings*, p. xiv, Maps 1–4

44. In reality, the Syrian opposition was overtly self-interested—deriving from highly prescient Syrian fears that an Arab decision to support a UN-approved no-fly zone over Libya might later constitute a useful precedent for a foreign military intervention against Syria justified via the Responsibility to Protect principle due to actions it might commit against its own citizens. *Al-Masry Al-Youm*, الجامعة العربية تطالب بفرض حظر و سوريا تتحفظ, 12 March 2011 https://www.almasryalyoum.com/news/details/118623

45. Richard Leiby, 'Arab League's Backing of No-Fly Zone over Libya Ramps Up Pressure on West', *Washington Post*, 12 March 2011, http://www.washingtonpost.com/wp-dyn/content/article/2011/03/12

46. Karin Badt, 'Bernard-Henri Levy and the West's Intervention in Libya: A Discussion with Experts', *Huffington Post*, 11 June 2011, http://

www.huffingtonpost.com/karin-badt/bernard-henri-levy-libya_
b_1575573.html

47. Tara McKelvey, 'Samantha Power's Case for War on Libya', *Daily Beast*,
22 March 2011, http://www.thedailybeast.com/articles/2011/03/23/
libya-war-samantha-power-and-the-case-for-liberal-interventionism.
html

48. Claudia Gazzini, 'Was the Libya Intervention Necessary?', *MERIP* 261,
(Winter 2011), https://merip.org/2011/11/was-the-libya-intervention-
necessary/

49. Geoff Dyer, 'Obama's Messy Foreign Policy Legacy', *Financial Times*,
16 January 2017, https://www.ft.com/content/f08c3476-d7a4-11e6-
944b-e7eb37a6aa8e

50. To grapple with how *sui generis* and destabilizing this new era is, we
should envision possible trajectories. For example, despite the wokeness
and postcolonial guilt that is cresting in the aftermath of George Floyd's
murder in mid-2020, it could still be that in a generation's time if the
Enduring Disorder has not already been superseded by some new
historical age rooted in a stable consensus-driven international order,
new nostalgic political movements of the not-yet-born could rebel
against their parents' generation's wokeness and advocate a return to
the 'simpler era' of the hegemonies of the British and American Empires
and be willing to sweep the injustices of those eras back under the rug.
For more background to this train of thought, consult Andrew Sullivan,
'The Roots of Wokeness', *Weekly Dish*, 2 August 2020, https://
andrewsullivan.substack.com/p/the-roots-of-wokeness

51. Haass spoke against the concept of a no-fly zone—even after the Arab
League's 12 March statement and US participation in the no-fly zone.
Richard Haass, 'Prepared Statement to Committee on Foreign
Relations, United States Senate on Perspectives on the Crisis in Libya',
Senate Foreign Relations Committee, 6 April 2011, https://www.for-
eign.senate.gov/imo/media/doc/Haass%20Testimony.pdf

52. Firstly, what he defines as the paramount principle of the post-Second
World War order: no annexation of territory by force on the European
mainland; and secondly, what he and other theorists have postulated
is the paramount principle of the post-Cold War order: denucleariza-

tion and the maintenance of sovereign and internationally protected buffer-states between Russia and NATO as enshrined in the 1994 Budapest Memorandum. Haass, *World in Disarray*.

53. Jason Pack and Brendan Simms, 'A Weak E.U. Can't Stop Putin', *New York Times*, 27 March 2014, https://www.nytimes.com/2014/03/28/opinion/a-weak-eu-cant-stop-putin.html

54. In Haass's analysis, the failures were based on incorrect strategic assessments and implementation rather than the coordination challenges that this book seeks to highlight. In *A World in Disarray* (p. 160), he states: 'Libya proved to be a textbook case of where the United States and the world got it wrong (and contributed significantly to disorder), first by doing too much, then by doing too little.'

55. Jason Pack, 'Libya Is Too Big to Fail: International Intervention Is the Right Move—and Not Just for Humanitarian Reasons', *Foreign Policy*, 18 March 2011, https://foreignpolicy.com/2011/03/18/libya-is-too-big-to-fail/

56. In a way, Russia, Turkey, and the UAE's rise to the position of dominant patrons of the warring sides in the Second Libyan Civil War (April 2019–June 2020) has amply illustrated this fact by harming Western interests throughout the entire Mediterranean.

57. At the start of the Uprisings, Qadhafi's Libya was the country with the third most small arms per capita, eclipsed by only the US and Yemen. Qadhafi's total stockpiles of small arms were one hundred times those of the British Army. Andrew Feinstein, 'Where Is Gaddafi's Vast Arms Stockpile?', *The Guardian*, 26 October 2011, https://www.theguardian.com/world/2011/oct/26/gadaffis-arms-stockpile

58. Dirk Vandewalle (ed.), *Libya since 1969: Qadhafi's Revolution Revisited* (Palgrave Macmillan, 2008).

59. Jason Pack, 'Engagement in Libya Was and Remains the Right Answer', *Spectator*, 30 January 2013, https://www.spectator.co.uk/article/engagement-in-libya-was-and-remains-the-right-answer

60. Ibid.

61. As bad as the current situation in Libya is circa 2021, the results of Western inaction in 2011 would likely have been worse. I warned in Pack, 'Libya Is Too Big to Fail', that once the domino of a stable, eco-

nomically reforming pro-Western Libya would fall—either to a neo-rogue resurgent Qadhafi regime or to a post-Qadhafi chaos—a chain reaction would ensue, engendering an influx of African migrants, the rise of neo-populism throughout Europe, and a war for regional dominance in the Eastern Mediterranean. And this is what has happened. In one way or another, Russia, Turkey, and the UAE's rise to the position of dominant patrons of the warring sides during the period of the War for Tripoli (April 2019–June 2020) amply illustrates that NATO powers have been displaced as guarantors of the regional order. This trend would have been even more profound in a post-2011 Libya with a neo-rogue Qadhafi regime in place.

62. Author interviews with British diplomats at the UK's UN Mission.

63. Pack, 'Libya Is Too Big to Fail'.

64. Josh Rogin, 'Who Really Said Obama Was "Leading from Behind"?', *Foreign Policy*, 27 October 2011, https://foreignpolicy.com/2011/10/27/who-really-said-obama-was-leading-from-behind/

65. Mikhail Zygar, *All the Kremlin's Men: Inside the Court of Vladimir Putin* (Public Affairs, 2016).

66. Michael McFaul, *Russia's Unfinished Revolution: Political Change from Gorbachev to Putin* (Mariner Books, 2019).

67. Zygar, *All the Kremlin's Men*.

68. Northern and Pack, 'Role of Outside Actors', p. 142.

69. AFP, 'L'intervention Francaise en Libye, un "Investissment sur l'avenir", Assure Juppe', *Le Parisien*, 27 August 2011, https://www.lexpress.fr/actualites/1/politique/l-intervention-francaise-en-libye-un-investissement-sur-l-avenir-assure-juppe_1024446.html

70. Why NATO was given the untraditional role of enforcing a UN resolution is fully explained in Florence Gaub, *The Cauldron* (Hurst, 2018).

71. Matteo Latorraca, 'Technicals: The Vehicles That Changed the Asymmetric Conflicts', *geopolitica.info*, 6 November 2014, https://www.geopolitica.info/technicals/

72. Brian McQuinn, 'After the Fall: Libya's Evolving Armed Groups', *Small Arms Survey*, October 2012, http://www.smallarmssurvey.org/fileadmin/docs/F-Working-papers/SAS-WP12-After-the-Fall-Libya.pdf

73. Kareem Fahim and David D. Kirkpatrick, 'Heavy Fighting Reported

in Tripoli; Rebels Encircle City', *New York Times*, 20 August 2011, https://www.nytimes.com/2011/08/21/world/africa/21libya.html

74. Sam Dagher, Charles Levinson, and Margaret Coker, 'Tiny Kingdom's Huge Role in Libya Draws Concern', *Wall Street Journal*, 17 October 2011; 'Qatar Admits It Had Boots on Ground in Libya', *Agence France-Presse*, 26 October 2011, http://www.dailystar.com.lb/ArticlePrint.aspx?id=152269&mode=print

75. Richard Norton-Taylor and Simon Rogers, 'Arab States Play Limited Role in Battle against Muammar Gaddafi's Regime', *The Guardian*, 23 May 2011; Kareem Shaheen, 'UAE Fighter Jets on the Way to Libya', *The National*, 26 March 2011.

76. Jason Pack, 'The Two Faces of Libya's Rebels', *Foreign Policy*, 5 April 2011.

77. Pack and Barak, 'In War's Wake', pp. 17–18.

78. Jason Pack and Sami Zaptia, 'The Face of the Libyan Arab Spring, Mahmoud Jibril, Felled by COVID-19', *Middle East Institute*, 9 April 2020, https://www.mei.edu/publications/face-libyan-arab-spring-mahmoud-jibril-felled-covid-19

79. Confidential author discussions with American and European diplomats who served in Libya during the Uprisings.

80. Nicholas Confessore and Michael S. Schmidt, 'Clinton Friend's Memos on Libya Draw Scrutiny to Politics and Business', *New York Times*, 18 May 2015, https://www.nytimes.com/2015/05/19/us/politics/clinton-friends-libya-role-blurs-lines-of-politics-and-business.html; WikiLeaks, 'Britain Hid Secret MI6 Plan to Break Up Libya from US, Hillary Clinton Told by Confidante', reposted by *The Daily Telegraph*, https://www.telegraph.co.uk/news/worldnews/hillary-clinton/11616018/Britain-hid-secret-MI6-plan-to-break-up-Libya-from-US-Hillary-Clinton-told-by-confidante.html and http://adam.curry.com/art/1432059461_kLcq3xzA.html; Avi Asher-Schapiro, 'Libyan Oil, Gold, and Qaddafi: The Strange Email Sidney Blumenthal Sent Hillary Clinton in 2011', *Vice News*, 12 January 2016, https://www.vice.com/en_us/article/gy9d49/libyan-oil-gold-and-qaddafi-the-strange-email-sidney-blumenthal-sent-hillary-clinton-in-2011

81. Ibid.

82. Pratap Chatterjee, 'Halliburton Makes a Killing on Iraq War', *CorpWatch*, 20 March 2003, https://corpwatch.org/article/halliburton-makes-killing-iraq-war

83. Please consult the sources in endnotes 4, 5, 80, and 81 for more on the ways in which the Hillary Clinton email scandal provides us with these insights.

84. Lisa Anderson, 'Afterword: Libya a Journey from Extraordinary to Ordinary', in Pack, *2011 Uprisings*.

85. Mark Shaw and Fiona Mangan, 'Illicit Trafficking and Libya's Transition: Profits and Losses', *USIP*, 24 February 2014, https://www.usip.org/publications/2014/02/illicit-trafficking-and-libyas-transition-profits-and-losses

86. Author interviews in Tunis with DFID, USAID, and GIZ personnel as well as with Libyan grantees.

87. *Office of the Director of National Intelligence*, 'Five Eyes Intelligence Oversight and Review Council (FIORC)', https://www.dni.gov/index.php/who-we-are/organizations/enterprise-capacity/chco/chco-related-menus/chco-related-links/recruitment-and-outreach/217-about/organization/icig-pages/2660-icig-fiorc

88. For a full study of the EU's haphazard and poorly coordinated policy towards post-Qadhafi Libya from 2011–2021, consult Stefano Marcuzzi, *The EU, NATO and the Libya Conflict: Anatomy of a Failure.* (Routledge, 2021).

89. Stanley Kurtz, 'I and My Brother against My Cousin', *EPPC*, https://eppc.org/publications/i-and-my-brother-against-my-cousin/

90. The concept of 'segmentary' tribes is intimately connected to Libya, although it was first used by Evans-Pritchard in describing the Nuer tribes of Sudan. 'Segmentary' refers to tribes consisting of kinship units or 'segments' of roughly the same structure and size. Evans-Pritchard believed segmentary structures reached their apogee and natural conclusion in Cyrenaica. E.E. Evans-Pritchard, *The Sanusi of Cyrenaica* (Clarendon, 1949); D. Johnson, 'Evans-Pritchard, the Nuer, and the Sudan Political Service', *African Affairs* 81, no. 323 (1982), pp. 231–46. The theory holds that the overall structure of a 'segmentary' tribe necessitates institutionalized opposition between the 'seg-

ments' and therefore they only 'unite' to form a cohesive unit in relation to the existence of other tribes and various exogenous pressures confronting the kinship segments. Emrys L. Peters, *The Bedouin of Cyrenaica: Studies in Personal and Corporate Power* (Cambridge, 1990), Introduction.

91. Jason Pack and Nate Mason, 'Could Coronavirus Lead to an Arab Spring 2.0?', *Middle East Institute*, 25 March 2020, https://www.mei.edu/publications/could-coronavirus-lead-arab-spring-20

92. Humeyra Pamuk and Andrea Shalal, 'Trump Administration Pushing to Rip Global Supply Chains from China: Officials', *Reuters*, 4 May 2020, https://www.reuters.com/article/us-health-coronavirus-usa-china/trump-administration-pushing-to-rip-global-supply-chains-from-china-officials-idUSKBN22G0BZ

93. Fareed Zakaria, 'On the Domestic Front, Biden Is All Ambition: Why Not on Foreign Policy?', *Washington Post*, 11 February 2021, https://fareedzakaria.com/columns/2021/2/11/on-the-domestic-front-biden-is-all-ambition-why-not-on-foreign-policy

94. For example, at the Vail Symposium and World Denver in 2018 and at the 2020 Model Arab League with a talk entitled, 'From Qadhafi to Chaos: Libya's Centrality in Western Geostrategy', https://www.youtube.com/watch?v=EOn8AQXviZ4&feature=youtu.be

95. For background on Khalifa Haftar, please consult footnote 6 of the Preface.

96. The methodology used to research and write this book has sought at all costs to avoid smug 'retroactive predictions'. To avoid relying on 20/20 hindsight, all of the major conceptual claims relating to causation are only those I put forward speculatively at the time. For example, I wrote in *The National Interest* on 8 October 2015: 'The migrant crisis of 2015 is exposing Europe's inability to formulate a coherent coordinated response. But this time, the US isn't going to smash heads until the Europeans get their act together ... I wonder if Hungary isn't just experiencing in microcosm trends that will take roughly a decade to play out across the continent ... As if by some undiscovered Newtonian law, today's attempts at humanitarian internationalism are sowing the seeds for tomorrow's resurgent anti-globalization nationalisms.' Jason

Pack, 'The Hungary Model: Resurgent Nationalism', *National Interest*, 8 October 2015, https://nationalinterest.org/feature/the-hungary-model-resurgent-nationalism-14025. There, I argued that a study of the salient social, political, cultural, and economic dynamics of Hungary led me to forecast that Orbán was indicative of things to come for Western democracies. I think this point is key for this book's credibility. Furthermore, I strongly believe that forecasting, although not a science, should be done according to a rigorous method. My firm, Libya-Analysis LLC, has as its core business forecasting vectors like oil production, port closures, and terrorist incidents. Such real-time forecasts and much of my other writings on Trump, Brexit, Ukraine, and Libya lend credence to my track-record on making such contextualizations and using the methods described by Philip Tetlock and Dan Gardner, *Superforecasting: The Art & Science of Prediction* (Random House, 2016).

97. If Libya was the first cacophonous Scherzo movement of the Enduring Disorder and Syria its melancholy Andante second movement, then crises relating to Ukraine are the whole symphony's dominant leitmotif—repeating throughout and providing lyrical coherence. As such, I will reference Ukraine as a comparison to Libya quite frequently in this book. In the first weeks after Putin's annexation of Crimea in 2014, I argued that if a unified European response was not shortly forthcoming, the prevailing Western-led, values-based global order would be proven to be completely lacking enforcement mechanisms, further encouraging rogue states like Russia, Iran, and North Korea to violate their treaty commitments. For this line of argumentation, please consult Pack and Simms, 'Weak E.U. Can't Stop Putin'; furthermore, the concept of Ukraine as the central chess square over which the twenty-first-century powers would compete derives from the pre-First World War writings of Halford Mackinder, which appear very prescient when examined in light of the events surrounding the first impeachment trial of Donald Trump. For more on the concept of 'Ukraine as the cockpit of world history' and Trump's unique dereliction of his national security duties, consult Jason Pack, 'When It Comes to Ukraine, Trump's Alleged Misdeeds Go Beyond Quid Pro

Quos', *Washington Post*, 25 November 2019, https://www.washing-tonpost.com/outlook/2019/11/25/when-it-comes-ukraine-trumps-alleged-misdeeds-go-beyond-quid-pro-quos/

98. Jason Pack and Will Raynolds, 'Why Libya Is So Hard to Govern: Inter-Group Squabbling Reigns as the Country Stalls on Drafting Its New Constitution', *The Atlantic*, 8 October 2013, https://www.theatlantic.com/international/archive/2013/10/why-libya-is-so-hard-to-govern/280392/

99. November 2020 email exchange with a former British ambassador to Libya. '[Similarly to you], I would not argue that it [post-Qadhafi Libya] was bound to fail ... The failure of the international community in 2011/12 was a failure [at an institutional level] to understand basic points about the legacy of Qadhafi [and then plan for their implications for Western policymaking. It was widely known] that there was no institutional capacity to govern, no culture of political discourse, a lack of national identity, a lack of leadership and regional/tribal fragmentation. [And yet we did not develop appropriate plans to address these issues. This failure is even more striking as so many of the top diplomatic brass had witnessed the mistakes in Iraq first-hand].' This remarkable admission was echoed by the American and French former ambassadors to Libya that I also interviewed.

100. 'Jonathan Winer, Special Envoy for Libya', *U.S. Department of State*, https://2009-2017.state.gov/r/pa/ei/biog/bureau/240474.htm; Jonathan Winer, *MEI scholar page*, https://www.mei.edu/profile/jonathan-m-winer

1. THE APPEASEMENT TRAP

1. Sabina Henneberg, *Managing Transition: The First Post-Uprising Phase in Tunisia and Libya* (Cambridge University Press, 2020); Jason Pack and Haley Cook, 'The July 2012 Libyan Elections and the Origin of Post-Qaddafi Appeasement', *Middle East Journal* 69, no. 2 (Spring 2015).

2. An interesting contemporary example would be President Trump's overtures to North Korea in which he compromised the United States' and South Korea's deterrence posture without gaining anything con-

crete in return. Christopher R. Hill, 'Trump's Appeasement of North Korea Is Failing', *Japan Times*, 16 September 2019, https://www.japantimes.co.jp/opinion/2019/09/16/commentary/world-commentary/trumps-appeasement-north-korea-failing/

3. Jason Pack, 'Introduction: The Center and Periphery', in Pack, *2011 Libyan Uprisings*.

4. Pack and Barfi, 'In War's Wake'.

5. Pack, 'Introduction'.

6. Evans-Pritchard, *Sanusi of Cyrenaica*; Peters, *Bedouin of Cyrenaica*.

7. Lisa Anderson, *The State and Social Transformation in Tunisia and Libya* (Princeton University Press, 1986).

8. Jason Pack, 'The Antecedents and Implications of the So-Called Anglo-Sanussi War (1915–17)', in T.G. Fraser (ed.), *The First World War and its Aftermath: The Shaping of the Middle East* (Ginkgo Library, 2015).

9. Dirk Vandewalle, *A History of Modern Libya* (Cambridge University Press, 2006); Vandewalle, *Libya since Independence: Oil and State Building* (Cornell University Press, 1998).

10. Haley Cook and Jason Pack, 'Mu'ammur Qadhafi: Power, Personality, and Ideology', in Frank Jacob (ed.), *Dictatorships without Violence? How Dictators Assert Their Power*, Comparative Studies from a Global Perspective 2 (Königshausen & Neumann, 2014).

11. *European Eye on Radicalization*, 26, فين : الدعم التركي و القطري للارهاب في ليبيا التكي-والقطري-تحالف المتطر April, 2019. https://eeradicalization.com/ar/المتطرفينالدعمتحالف/

12. Alkhaleej, قطر وتركيا...تحالف تاريخي لدعم وتمويل الإرهاب, 22 June, 2017. https://www.alkhaleej.ae/الإرهاب-وتمويل-لدعم-تاريخي-تحالف-وتركيا-قطر/لعالم/والسياسي المالي

13. Jonathan Schanzer, تركيا...حرب بالوكالة في ليبيا, translated, *National Center for Research and Opinion Polls*, March 22, 2015. http://ncro.sy/2015/03/22/ في القذافي سقوط بعد البلاد لإسلاميي دعمها

14. *International Crisis Group*, 'Addressing the Rise of Libya's Madkhali-Salafis', 25 April 2019, https://www.crisisgroup.org/middle-east-north-africa/north-africa/libya/addressing-rise-libyas-madkhali-salafis; Layli Foroudi, 'Sufi Cultural Sites Caught in Crossfire of Libya Civil War', *Reuters*, 16 March 2020, https://www.reuters.com/article/libya-

conflict-monuments/feature-sufi-cultural-sites-caught-in-crossfire-of-libya-civil-war-idUSL8N2AH3XR

15. Northern and Pack, 'Role of Outside Actors', pp. 138–43.

16. Pack and Barfi, 'In War's Wake'.

17. Ibid.

18. Pack and Cook, 'July 2012 Libyan Elections'.

19. In this book, I treat the events of 2011 as 'uprisings' rather than a civil war as transpired in 2014–15 and again in 2019–20. The logic behind this nomenclature is that a 'civil war' entails fighting amongst two or more distinct population groups differentiated geographically, religiously, linguistically, ideologically, ethnically, or socially. Conversely, what transpired in Libya in 2011 was a multiplicity of different social groupings fighting against an incumbent regime, which although it continued to draw support from roughly 20 per cent of the Libyan population, did not experience any spontaneously organized popular support for its cause, even from its loyalist social segment. Hence, what transpired in 2011 was akin to disconnected, militarized 'uprisings' against an incumbent government. For more on this logic consult Pack, *The 2011 Libyan Uprisings*, 'Introduction', pp. 1–23.

20. For background on the Gremlins, https://en.wikipedia.org/wiki/Gremlins#Plot

21. Jason Pack, Karim Mezran, and Mohamed Eljarh, 'Libya's Faustian Bargains: Breaking the Appeasement Cycle', *Atlantic Council*, 5 May 2014, https://www.atlanticcouncil.org/wp-content/uploads/2014/05/Libyas_Faustian_Bargains.pdf

22. NB: Most of Libya's internationally held sovereign wealth has remained frozen via the blanket freeze on the Libyan Investment Authority's (LIA) foreign accounts—a freeze that all post-Qadhafi chairmen of the LIA have advocated for the international community to maintain, although they have increasingly lobbied in recent years for the ability to manage the frozen funds. For more on this, consult: Tim Eaton, 'Libya: Investing the Wealth of a Nation', *Chatham House Long-Read*, 2021, https://chathamhouse.shorthandstories.com/libya-investing-wealth-of-nation/

23. This understanding derives from my experience of these events as well

as interviews in 2020 with various Libyan and Western diplomats serving in Tripoli at the time.

24. The excerpt is composed of portions of Parts 1, 2, 3, and 5 of the original think tank report. As with other excerpts in this book, the text has been presented exactly as it was originally published except for being converted to British English and Hurst's style guide concerning capitalization, dates, numbers, and punctuation marks. Removed text is marked with ellipses and added text with *italics* inside [brackets]. The excerpts were selected to give a taste of the complexity of militia, Islamist, Jihadi, Federalist, and tribal group actors which filled the political vacuum in the wake of Qadhafi's ouster rather than to present a comprehensive overview of all relevant players. The specific militias and individuals covered in this excerpt were chosen because they or their successors are referenced elsewhere in this volume.

25. Ironically, this form of local popular governance bore a striking resemblance to the form of direct democracy outlined in Qadhafi's *Green Book* that only existed in puppet forms during Qadhafi's rule. Jason Pack, 'Qaddafi's Legacy', *Foreign Policy*, 20 October 2011, http:// www.foreignpolicy.com/articles/2011/10/20/qaddafi_s_legacy; Pack, 'Post-Gaddafi Libya Should Think Local', *Guardian*, 23 October 2011, http://www.theguardian.com/commentisfree/2011/oct/23/post-gaddafi-libya-local.

26. For an overview of the spontaneous nature of the uprisings and how they formed local and national structures, see Pack, *2011 Libyan Uprisings*, and Pack and Barfi, 'In War's Wake'.

27. For more on the formation of the centre and periphery in Libya, see Pack, 'Introduction'.

28. Fascinatingly, the militias did not immediately demand salaries but rather medical treatment and rehabilitation for their members. As NTC did not deal properly with financing and sending abroad of patients, protests ensued for more money to go to the *thuwwar* (revolutionaries). This opened the door for a system of placating *thuwwar* demands with transfer payments.

29. For more on the Temporary Constitutional Declaration (TCD), see Youssef Sawani and Jason Pack, 'Libyan Constitutionality and

Sovereignty Post-Qadhafi: The Islamist, Regionalist, and Amazigh Challenges', *Journal of North African Studies* 18, no. 4 (2013), pp. 523–43; The text of the TCD is available on the High National Election Commission website: http://www.hnec.ly/uploads/publisher/6_ntc_2011.pdf

30. For example, the reinforcing of pre-existing feuds between the Arab Zwai and Tubu in the South, certain Arab and Amazigh groups against each other in Jabal Nafusa, and local, regional, ethnic and tribal rivalries like those which prevail between Misrata and Tawerga, Zwara and its neighbours, and Warshafanna and Zawiyya. For more on this, see Wolfram Lacher, 'The Rise of Tribal Politics', in Pack, *2011 Libyan Uprisings*; Lacher, 'Libya's Fractious South and Regional Instability', *Small Arms Survey*, dispatch no. 3, February 2014, http://www.smallarmssurvey.org/fileadmin/docs/R-SANA/SANA-Dispatch3-Libya%27s-Fractuous-South.pdf

31. Ibrahim Sharqieh, 'Reconstructing Libya: Stability through National Reconciliation', *Brookings Institution*, 3 December 2013, http://www.brookings.edu/research/papers/2013/12/03-libya-national-reconciliation-sharqieh

32. US Department of Energy, 'February 2014 Monthly Energy Review', Washington, DC: US Energy Information Administration, 24 February 2014, http://www.eia.gov/totalenergy/data/monthly/pdf/mer.pdf

33. Jason Pack and Mohamed Eljarh, 'Talk about Political Dysfunction', *New York Times*, 18 October 2013, http://www.nytimes.com/2013/10/19/opinion/talk-about-political-dysfunction.html?_r=0

34. This phenomenon exists throughout Libya but is most pronounced in the South. For more, see Lacher, 'Libya's Fractious South and Regional Instability'.

35. Karim Mezran of Johns Hopkins, Noman Benotman of the Quilliam Foundation, Alison Pargeter of MENAS Associates, Jason Pack of Cambridge University, Wolfram Lacher of Stiftung Wissenschaft und Politik (SWP), Christopher Chivvis of the RAND Corporation, and Fred Wehrey of the Carnegie Institute have all more or less painted a picture of weak central authorities backing down in the face of armed opposition. See Karim Mezran and Fadel Lamen, 'Security Challenges

to Libya's Quest for Democracy', Atlantic Council, 12 September 2012, http://www.atlanticcouncil.org/publications/issue-briefs/security-challenges-to-libyas-quest-for-democracy; Noman Benotman, Jason Pack, and James Brandon, 'Islamists', in Pack, *2011 Libyan Uprisings*; Alison Pargeter, *Libya: The Rise and Fall of Qaddafi* (Yale University Press, 2012); Wolfram Lacher, 'Fault Lines of the Revolution: Political Actors, Camps and Conflicts in the New Libya', *SWP Research Paper*, May 2013; Lacher, 'Rise of Tribal Politics'; Pack and Barfi, 'In War's Wake', pp. 3–4; Frederic Wehrey, 'The Struggle for Security in Eastern Libya', *Carnegie Endowment for International Peace*, 19 September 2012.

36. Ronald Bruce St John, 'Libyan Election Breaks Arab Spring Pattern', *International Spectator: The Italian Journal of International Affairs* 47, no. 3 (2012), pp. 13–19.

37. There exists a substantial academic literature dealing with 'appeasement' as a government policy option. Much but not all of this literature focuses on British policy in the 1930s. For a broader definition of the concept and how once 'appeasement is consciously or unconsciously adopted as a policy, it promotes further appeasement, please consult, Stephen Rock, *Appeasement in International Politics*, (University Press of Kentucky, 2000) and Martin Gilbert, *The Roots of Appeasement* (Weidenfeld & Nicolson, 1970).

38. Seen in a comparative perspective, the behaviour of the Libyan militias is not so atypical. It is merely an extreme case of the so-called 'honey pot' rent-seeking arrangement. This thesis posits that oil-rich states lacking in institutions generate violent forms of rent-seeking that are likely to take the form of 'greed-based' insurgencies. Paul Collier and Anke Hoeffler, 'Greed and Grievance in Civil War', *Oxford Economic Papers* 56, no. 4 (2004).

39. This assumption is supported by the rhetoric of many different groups in the lead up to the 2012 GNC elections.

40. Pargeter, *Libya*; Benotman, Pack, and Brandon, 'Islamists'. The political isolation law and other anti-government actions have also been supported inside the GNC by the powerful Martyr's bloc which was assembled inside the GNC after the election grouping together many independent candidates and different Islamist-leaning currents.

41. Karim Mezran, Fadel Lamen, and Eric Knecht, 'Post-Revolutionary Politics in Libya: Inside the General National Congress', *Atlantic Council*, May 2013, http://www.atlanticcouncil.org/images/publications/postrevolutionary_politics_libya.pdf; Karim Mezran and Eric Knecht, 'Libya's Fractious New Politics', *Atlantic Council*, 9 January 2013, http://www.atlanticcouncil.org/blogs/menasource/libyas-fractious-new-politics

42. Authors' interviews with Mohammed Sawan and other Islamist leaders in Tripoli throughout 2012–13.

43. The most prominent exponents of this view are Dirk Vandewalle and Sami Zaptia. Dirk Vandewalle, 'After Qadhafi: The Surprising Success of the New Libya', *Foreign Affairs*, November–December 2012; Jonathan Tepperman and Dirk Vandewalle, 'Foreign Affairs Focus: Libya after Qaddafi with Dirk Vandewalle', *Foreign Affairs*, 8 November 2012, http://www.foreignaffairs.com/discussions/audio-video/foreign-affairs-focus-libya-after-qaddafi-with-dirk-vandewalle; Dirk Vandewalle email to author, 8 June 2013; Sami Zaptia, 'No Shame in Seeking Western Help', *Saudi Gazette*, 19 July 2013, http://www.saudigazette.com.sa/index.cfm?method=home.regcon&contentid=20130719174004; author's conversation with Zaptia in Tripoli, 30 August 2013.

44. Nicolas Pelham, 'Losing Libya's Revolution', *New York Review of Books*, 10 October 2013, http://www.nybooks.com/articles/archives/2013/oct/10/losing-libyas-revolution/?pagination=false; Nicholas Pelham, 'The Struggle for the Post-Qadhafi Future: Islamists, Militias and the Role of Britain in Today's Libya', panel discussion, UK House of Commons, 10 September 2013; Pelham, 'Libya in the Shadow of Iraq: The "Old Guard" versus the Thuwwar in the Battle for Stability', *International Peacekeeping* 19, no. 4 (2012), pp. 539–48.

45. 'Libyan Prime Minister Abu Shagur Dismissed', *BBC*, 7 October 2012, http://www.bbc.co.uk/news/world-africa-19864136

46. 'Al-Mu'tamar al-watani al-'amm yuqarirr intikhab al-lajna al-ta'sisiyya al-mukallifa bi-kitaba al-dustur intikhaban mubashiran', *Wikalat al-anba' al-libiyya*, 9 April 2013, http://tinyurl.com/d3zzo29

47. *The National*, 'Libya Loses Assembly Leader to New Law', 28 May 2013.

48. Feras Bosalum and Ulf Laessing, 'Libya's Central Bank Lends $2 Bln for Emergency Budget', *Reuters*, 25 March 2014, http://af.reuters.com/article/libyaNews/idAFL5N0MM48B20140325

49. The public sector currently employs 85 percent of the labour force.

50. Zeidan survived multiple no confidence votes only because his opponents could not agree on who to replace him. See, for example, Pack and Eljarh, 'Talk about Political Dysfunction'.

51. Ahmed Elumami, 'Gun Ownership Law Passed by Congress', *Libya Herald*, 16 December 2013, http://www.libyaherald.com/2013/12/16/gun-ownership-law-passed-by-congress/#axzz2ngTdFC7Y

52. Omar Ashour, 'Libyan Islamists Unpacked: Rise, Transformation, and Future', *Brookings Institution Doha Center*, policy briefing, May 2012, p. 5, http://www.brookings.edu/~/media/research/files/papers/2012/5/02%20libya%20ashour/omar%20ashour%20policy%20briefing%20english.pdf/

53. Ibid., p. 4.

54. Ruth Sherlock, 'Leading Libyan Islamist Met Free Syrian Army Opposition Group', *Daily Telegraph*, 27 November 2011, http://www.telegraph.co.uk/news/worldnews/africaandindianocean/libya/8919057/Leading-Libyan-Islamist-met-Free-Syrian-Army-opposition-group.html

55. Osman Heshri and Nigel Ash, 'SSC Still Necessary: Abdel Raouf Kara', *Libya Herald*, 13 September 2013, http://www.libyaherald.com/2013/09/13/ssc-still-necessary-abdel-raouf-kara/#axzz2oB9OZhfS

56. Benotman, Pack, and Brandon, 'Islamists', pp. 201–10; Joseph Felter and Brian Fishman, 'Al-Qaeda's Foreign Fighters in Iraq: A First Look at the Sinjar Records', West Point: Combating Terrorism Center, 2 January 2007, http://www.ctc.usma.edu/posts/al-qaidas-foreign-fighters-in-iraq-a-first-look-at-the-sinjar-records

57. Rod Nordland and Scott Shane, 'Libyan, Once a Detainee, Is Now a U.S. Ally of Sorts', *New York Times*, 25 April 2011, http://www.nytimes.com/2011/04/25/world/guantanamo-files-libyan-detainee-now-us-ally-of-sorts.html

58. Nancy Youssef, 'Benghazi, Libya, Has Become Training Hub for Islamist Fighters', McClatchy, 12 December 2013, http://www.

mcclatchydc.com/2013/12/12/211488/benghazi-libya-has-become-training.html

59. David Kirkpatrick, 'Suspect in Libya Attack, in Plain Sight, Scoffs at U.S.', *New York Times*, 18 October 2012, p. A1; Kirkpatrick, 'A Deadly Mix in Benghazi', *New York Times*, 28 December 2013, http://www.nytimes.com/projects/2013/benghazi/#/?chapt=0

60. Thomas Joscelyn, 'State Department Designates 3 Ansar al Sharia Organizations, Leaders', Long War Journal, 10 January 2014, http://www.longwarjournal.org/archives/2014/01/state_department_des_2.php

61. Asmaa Elourfi, 'Al-Qaeda Elements Surface in Derna', *Magharebia*, 5 April 2012.

62. *Reuters*, 'Exclusive: The Mysterious Journey of the Libya Oil Tanker', 19 March 2014, http://www.reuters.com/article/2014/03/19/us-libya-tanker-identity-idUSBREA2I19K20140319

63. For more on the possible implications of an international stabilization or peacekeeping force in Libya, see Christopher S. Chivvis and Jeffrey Martini, *Libya after Qaddafi: Lessons and Implications for the Future* (RAND, 2014).

64. Abigail Hauslohner and Karen DeYoung 'U.S. Plan for New, Western-Trained Libyan Force Faces Obstacles', *Atlantic Council*, 5 December 2013, https://www.atlanticcouncil.org/blogs/natosource/us-plan-for-new-western-trained-libyan-force-faces-obstacles/

65. Jason Pack discussion with senior European, Arab, and American diplomatic and military personnel from January to February 2014.

66. *Defense Security Cooperation Agency*, 'Libya: General Purpose Force Training', 22 January 2014, http://www.dsca.mil/major-arms-sales/libya-general-purpose-force-training

67. For more on US Congressional procedure concerning foreign military sales, consult, Richard Grimmett, 'Arms Sales: Congressional Review Process', *Congressional Research Service*, 1 February 2012, http://www.fas.org/sgp/crs/weapons/RL31675.pdf

68. These and other cogent questions have been raised by many experts as the policy of training Libyan recruits has been debated by various Western legislatures and foreign ministries. For an overview of the

issues at stake, consult, Fred Wehrey, 'Senate Foreign Relations Committee Testimony', *Senate Foreign Relations Committee Testimony*, 21 November 2013, http://www.foreign.senate.gov/imo/media/doc/Wehrey_Testimony.pdf

69. *BBC*, 'Libyan Soldiers "Raped Man in Cambridge after Leaving Barracks"', 6 May 2015, https://www.bbc.com/news/uk-england-cambridgeshire-32610470

70. Chris Stephen and Ewen MacAskill, 'Cameron's Plan to Train Libyan Soldiers Had Makings of Disaster from the Start', *Guardian*, 4 November 2014, https://www.theguardian.com/world/2014/nov/04/cameron-plan-train-libyan-soldiers-problems-money

71. Sami Zaptia, 'Audit Bureau Releases Its 2017 Annual Report', *Libya Herald*, 24 May 2018, https://www.libyaherald.com/2018/05/24/audit-bureau-releases-its-2017-annual-report/

72. *Daily Sabah*, 'Libya Loses Over $8 Billion in 7 Months Due to Haftar's Oil Blockade', 12 August 2020, https://www.dailysabah.com/politics/libya-loses-over-8-billion-in-7-months-due-to-haftars-oil-blockade/news

73. This figure is speculative but emerges from my discussions with NOC and Western commodities trading experts.

74. As a point of reference, a trillion and a half US dollars is a large amount of money, even by the standard of major global governments: it is roughly half the annual public spending of the US government in a pre-Coronavirus year or the entire annual economic output of Spain or Russia.

75. Fernando Coronil, *Magical State: Nature, Money, and Modernity in Venezuela* (University of Chicago Press, 1997).

76. Famously, on 18 April 2015, Marleni Olivo threw a mango inscribed with a sharpie bearing a request for a subsidized apartment at the Venezuelan president. After the media uproar the incident created, she received said state-subsidized apartment. One does not need to be a rocket scientist to know that this episode promoted a wave of imitations. Venezuelan leaders are now constantly bombarded (sometimes quite literally) with requests for appeasement. Raul Gallegos, *Crude Nation: How Oil Riches Ruined Venezuela* (Potomac Books, 2019),

pp. 159–85, describes this form of appeasement cycle as 'Mango Management'.

77. Sebastian Edwards, *Left Behind: Latin America and the False Promise of Populism* (University of Chicago Press, 2010).

78. Phone interview with Raul Gallegos, 2021.

79. Gallegos, *Crude Nation*, p. 30.

80. Phone interview with Raul Gallegos, 2021.

81. Gallegos, *Crude Nation*, p. 174.

82. Phone interview with Raul Gallegos, 2021.

83. Various conversations with USAID-funded survey experts. One informed me: 'There is a wealth of survey data illustrating that regular Libyans and Venezuelans do not have ideological views on economic issues nor are they motivated by political goals for which they would want to sacrifice personal, familial, and national improvements in the standard of living.'

84. From which this chapter's excerpt was drawn.

85. The importance of subsidies to the Libyan economy and state structure was briefly introduced in the excerpt but will be expanded on at length in Chapters 4 and 5 of this volume.

86. These themes will also be discussed further in Chapters 4 and 5 of this volume. Jason Pack, 'It's the Economy Stupid: How Libya's Civil War Is Rooted in Its Economic Structures', *IAI* (Rome), 19, 17 September 2019, https://www.iai.it/sites/default/files/iaip1917.pdf

87. Author phone and email conversations with Laura Cretney, March and April 2021. For her overview of the Yemen conflict and the ways in which it serves as a microcosm for the global Enduring Disorder, see *The Bunker Daily*, 'Arabian Vortex; Understanding Yemen's Nightmare', 3 October 2021, https://player.fm/series/the-bunker-2609648/daily-arabian-vortex-understanding-yemens-nightmare

88. Arguably the most relevant comparison to Libya in this regard is post-Soviet Russia, where major structural elements of the Soviet economy were privatized as part of the loans for shares scheme. The oligarchs and oil warlords who were created as a result of this process fostered relationships between state power and private enterprise that are broadly the same as in Libya. Thane Gustafson, *Wheel of Fortune: The Battle*

for Oil and Power in Russia (Belknap Press of Harvard University Press, 2017)

89. Pack, 'Introduction'.
90. The partisan blame game around Benghazi is one of the few events in Libya over the last decade that is genuinely popular knowledge throughout North America and Europe, but for those who want to brush up on the controversy please See Tom Rogan, 'Out of Benghazi's Many Tragedies, the Worst Is Washington's Blame Game', *Guardian*, 16 January 2014, https://www.theguardian.com/commentisfree/2014/jan/16/benghazi-senate-report-washington-blame-game
91. Jason Pack, 'Honoring Chris Stevens', *Foreign Policy*, 14 September 2012, https://foreignpolicy.com/2012/09/14/honoring-chris-stevens/. My particular perspective on the episode comes from private conversations with Ambassador Stevens about three months before his murder, where he made clear to me that he understood the security risks of travel in Libya and that the State Department and intelligence community were relying on him for an assessment of those risks, rather than he relying on them to provide him with security assessments or more security personnel. This inverts much of what the post facto blame game has alleged.
92. David M. Herszenhorn, 'House Benghazi Report Finds No New Evidence of Wrongdoing by Hillary Clinton', *New York Times*, 28 June 2016, https://www.nytimes.com/2016/06/29/us/politics/hillary-clinton-benghazi.html
93. Ethan Chorin, 'What Libya Lost', *New York Times*, 13 September 2012, https://www.nytimes.com/2012/09/14/opinion/what-libya-lost-when-ambassador-stevens-died.html
94. Pack, 'Honoring Chris Stevens'. From my conversations with Chris and knowledge of his value system, he would not have been pleased with the way the Obama administration responded to his murder by abandoning reconstruction in Libya, but he would have been completely crestfallen to know that his decision to go to Benghazi to open a hospital and 'an American corner' contributed to Donald J. Trump's election.
95. These developments are public record, but this analysis of causality is supported by my interviews with former American and British dip-

lomatic personnel who served in Libya at the time. These officials pointed out to me that Ambassador Stevens knew the dangers he faced and also asked his superiors not to engage in an overly securitized policy towards Libya. Some noted that his prior statements and preferences were unlikely to have affected the decision to not deploy American military force in Southern Italy to reconquer the special mission while the ambassador was asphyxiating. Rather, that decision had either to do with bureaucratic coordination failures or with the post-2003 reluctance to use American military force to protect American interests in violation of other nations' sovereignty.

96. Jason Pack and Andrea Khalil, 'Amid Chants of "Free Libya Terrorists Out", a Nation at a Crossroads: After the Attack Came Antimilitant, Pro-U.S. Demonstrations', *Wall Street Journal*, 16 September 2012.

97. Pack, 'Honoring Chris Stevens'.

98. Van Creveld, *Pussycats*.

99. For example, Kaplan, *Coming Anarchy*; Haass, *World in Disarray*; Van Creveld, *Rise and Decline of the State*; McFate, *Goliath*.

100. Author interviews with seven former US, UK, and EU ambassadors to Libya about the period 2011–14, conducted between 2017 and 2020.

101. Pack and Eljarh, 'Talk about Political Dysfunction'.

2. JIHADIS ARE JUST A SYMPTOM

1. Of course, like all historical phenomena, they themselves have antecedents. This volume has proposed many explanations for the increase in ungoverned spaces and global coordination failures over the last decades. Rather than rehashing those here, this chapter seeks to explore how those phenomena engender the growth of jihadi organizations.

2. Hassan Hassan, *ISIS: Inside the Army of Terror* (Regan Arts, 2016); Charles Lister, *The Syrian Jihad: Al-Qaeda, the Islamic State and the Evolution of an Insurgency* (Hurst, 2016).

3. Shi'a jihadi groups like Hezbollah have a long track record of mastering quasi-governance activity and have different theological and structural approaches to the doctrine of *imamah* (discussed in endnote 23 of

this chapter) that facilitate this. Augustus Richard Norton, *Hezbollah: A Short History* (Princeton University Press, 2018). For the related argument that radical Sunni groups, with their 'cult of martyrdom' and focus on a messianic deliverer, invoke elements more readily associated with Shi'a Islam, see Alia Brahimi, 'Ideology and Terrorism: Causes and Motivations', in Erica Chenoweth et al. (eds), *The Oxford Handbook on Terrorism* (Oxford University Press, 2019).

4. J. M. Berger, *Extremism* (MIT Press, 2018).

5. Syria's Alawite Baathist regime under Hafez al-Assad was still able to export al-Qaeda fighters to Iraq post-2003 and Saddam Hussein was trafficking in Palestinian jihadis in the 1990s despite both leaders having to fend off attacks from similar groups at home. In Libya in the early 2000s, Qadhafi faced the threat of an insurgency at the hands of jihadis who trained in Afghanistan, while at the very same time trying to train jihadis in Derna and export them to Iraq (discussed in detail later in this chapter). Fred Lawson, *Demystifying Syria* (Saqi, 2012); John McHugo, *Syria: A Recent History* (Saqi, 2015); Charles Tripp, *A History of Iraq* (Cambridge University Press, 2015); Vandewalle, *History of Modern Libya*.

6. Jason Pack, 'Gaddafi's Right-Hand Man Should Not Be Underestimated', *Guardian*, 24 February 2011, https://www.theguardian.com/commentisfree/2011/feb/24/gaddafi-successor-abdullah-senussi; Ken Silverstein, 'How Kadafi Went from Foe to Ally', *Los Angeles Times*, 4 September 2005, https://www.latimes.com/archives/la-xpm-2005-sep-04-fg-uslibya4-story.html

7. Patrick Seale, *Asad: The Struggle for the Middle East* (University of California Press, 1989).

8. Lister, *Syrian Jihad* and McHugo, *Syria*.

9. Hisham Sharabi, *Neopatriarchy: A Theory of Distorted Change in Arab Society*, (Oxford University Press, 1988). The accusation of 'weak authoritarianism' is in contrast to places like the USSR or Nazi Germany where a significant part of the population appears to have bought into the ruling ideology rather than merely performing its rituals. Lisa Wedeen, *Ambiguities of Domination: Politics, Rhetoric, and Symbols in Contemporary Syria* (University of Chicago, 1999). Conversely, other scholars believed

the Arab republics to be resilient authoritarianisms but were proven to be wrong. They extrapolated from their proven resilience against jihadi insurgencies and assumed that that robustness was also vis-à-vis the population.

10. For strong examples of how Tunisia's constitutional precedents and Egypt's identity and army led to state continuation, please consult, Henneberg, *Managing Transition* and Hazem Kandil, *The Power Triangle: Military, Security, and Politics in Regime Change* (Oxford University Press, 2016)

11. Hanna Batatu, *The Old Social Classes and the Revolutionary Movements of Iraq: A Study of Iraq's Old Landed and Commercial Classes and of Its Communists, Ba'thists and Free Officers* (Saqi, 2012)

12. Philip Khoury, *Syria and the French Mandate: The Politics of Arab Nationalism, 1920–1945* (Princeton University Press, 1989)

13. My thanks go to Joshua Landis for making this point in a March 2021 phone interview. For more on the struggle of 'aggrieved' majorities seeking to displace 'privileged' minorities throughout Eastern Europe and the Middle East over the last century, see Nikolaos Van Dam, *Destroying a Nation: The Civil War in Syria* (I.B. Tauris, 2017) and Timothy Snyder, *Bloodlands*, (Basic Books, 2012)

14. John McHugo, *A Concise History of Sunnis and Shi'is* (Saqi, 2018)

15. They are not, however, the ill-fated spawn of the 1916 Sykes–Picot agreement—as is frequently misstated by both Arab and anti-imperial activists. Sykes–Picot was a secret concord among France, Britain, and tzarist Russia, which was neither legally binding on any of the powers nor ever implemented. Furthermore, the Sykes–Picot agreement called for quite different borders than those that took shape on the ground in the wake of the First World War and were then formalized into international law after diplomacy between Britain, France, and America was codified with the 1920 San Remo Conference and the ensuing League of Nations mandates. This history is frequently misstated at rallies, in newspaper articles, and in jihadi videos that claim to be 'undoing Sykes–Picot' or 'protesting the legacy of Sykes–Picot'.

16. Hanna Batatu, *Syria's Peasantry, the Descendants of Its Lesser Rural Notables, and Their Politics* (Princeton University Press, 1999).

17. More than 90 per cent of Libya's population is of the Malaki Sunni *madhhab* (or legal school), which is generally considered to be less literalist and less tolerant of the Salafi approach to Islam than either the Hanafi and Hanbali *madhahib* (plural of *madhhab*) that prevail in Iraq and Syria.

18. Alison Pargeter, 'Qaddafi and Political Islamic in Libya,' in Vandewalle, *Libya since 1969*, p. 94.

19. Alia Brahimi, 'Islamic Radicalisation in Libya', in George Joffe (ed.), *Islamist Radicalisation in North Africa: Politics and Process* (Routledge, 2011).

20. Benotman, Pack, and Brandon, 'Islamists', pp. 191–228.

21. Ibid.

22. Nathaniel Rosenblatt, 'All Jihad Is Local: What ISIS' Files Tell US about Its Fighters,' *New America Foundation*, July 2016, https://na-production.s3.amazonaws.com/documents/ISIS-Files.pdf

23. *Imama* is the theological principle asserting that believers need to live under an overarching political institution that is Islamically organized and that can uphold the principles of collective Muslim life. *Takfir* is the practice by jihadi organizations of denouncing other Muslims (especially the rulers of states they dislike) as apostates.

24. Rhiannon Smith and Jason Pack, 'Al-Qaida's Strategy in Libya: Keep it Local, Stupid', *Perspectives on Terrorism* 11, no. 6 (2017).

25. Kathryn Dunn Tenpas, 'Tracking Turnover in the Trump Administration', *Brookings Institution*, August 2020 https://www.brookings.edu/research/tracking-turnover-in-the-trump-administration/

26. Randy Borum, 'Psychology of Terrorism', *Mental Health Law & Policy Faculty Publications*, 2004.

27. One example of such an ignorant and racist attitude is available at https://dudeism.com/smf/index.php?topic=113.0

28. Nicolas Pelham, 'Bogged Down in Libya', *New York Review of Books*, 21 March 2011, http://www.politique-actu.com/dossier/bogged-down-libya-nicolas-pelham/266686/

29. Ben Quinn, 'Tommy Robinson Link with Quilliam Foundation Raises Questions', *Guardian*, 12 October 2013, https://www.theguardian.

com/uk-news/2013/oct/12/tommy-robinson-quilliam-foundation-questions-motivation

30. Silverstein, 'How Kadafi Went from Foe to Ally'.

31. All such statements were later expunged from his Twitter feed.

32. Instances of this phenomenon and its implications were illustrated in the excerpt in Chapter 1.

33. 'The Struggle for the Post-Qadhafi Future: Islamists, Militias, and Foreign Powers' a book launch conference featuring Jason Pack, Noman Benotman, and Ambassador Richard Northern, chaired by the late Professor Sir Christopher Bayly at St Catharine's College, Cambridge, 27 June 2013, https://www.youtube.com/watch?v=B5RIBHGIkZE

34. Conversations with journalists who spoke with Noman during this period from English-language publications including *The Economist*, *The Guardian*, and *The Wall Street Journal*.

35. All tweets were subsequently deleted, but as a Twitter follower of Noman's, I witnessed the evolution of his messaging over time.

36. Anonymous conversations with Libyan interlocutors with both Haftar and the GNA.

37. *al-Manassa al-Libeyya*, نعمان بن عثمان...مستشار سياسي أم عميل مخابرات 12 February 2019, https://elmanassa.com/news/view/21232

38. al-Sanusi Biskiri, الازدواجية المقيتة في الحكم على نعمان بن عثمان, al-Arabi 21, 25 May 2019, https://arabi21.com/story/1183338/الازدواجية-المقيتة-في-الحكم-على-نعمان-بن-عثمان

فبتطوافه من خانة أنصار سبتمبر مرورا بعملية الكرامة وصولا إلى مناصري فبراير، أظهر ابن عثمان أن جُل، أو ربما كل، من استجاب لخطابه عقليا ووجدانيا من كل هذه التيارات لا يهمه من هو ابن عثمان، وماذا يمثل، وماذا يريد، وما هي مصادر معلوماته ودرجة صدقية ما يقوله، فما يعنيهم أنه في صفهم (سبتمبر، كرامة، فبراير) ويدعم موقفهم ويشفي غليلهم ممن خالفهم.

(In the original Arabic presented above, the commentator uses the Arabic terms 'September' to mean supporting the Qadhafi regime, 'Dignity' for supporting the LNA and Haftar, and 'February' for supporting those who proclaim themselves die-hard revolutionaries even in the current post-Qadhafi context.)

39. Mehdi Hasan and Dina Sayedahmed, 'Blowback: How Israel Went from Helping Create Hamas to Bombing It,' *The Intercept*, 19 February 2018, https://theintercept.com/2018/02/19/hamas-israel-palestine-conflict/

40. Phone and email conversations with Laura Cretney, March and April 2021. For her overview of the Yemen conflict and the ways in which it serves as a microcosm for the global Enduring Disorder, see *The Bunker Daily*, 'Arabian Vortex; Understanding Yemen's Nightmare', 3 October 2021, https://player.fm/series/the-bunker-2609648/daily-arabian-vortex-understanding-yemens-nightmare

41. Michael J. Willis, *Power and Politics in the Maghreb: Algeria, Tunisia and Morocco from Independence to the Arab Spring* (Hurst, 2012).

42. The excerpt is comprised of portions of the 'Findings' and Sections IV, V, VI, VII, and VIII of the original think tank report. Removed text is marked with ellipses and newly added text is marked with *italics* inside [brackets].

43. Haim Malka and Margo Balboni, 'Libya: Tunisia's Jihadist Nightmare', CSIS, June 2016, http://foreignfighters.csis.org/tunisia/libya.html

44. 'ISIS in Action', Eye on ISIS, 19 January 2016, http://eyeonisisinlibya.com/isis-in-action/action-jan-19-2016/

45. Jack Moore, '5,000 Foreign Fighters Flock to Libya as ISIS Call for Jihadists', *Newsweek*, 3 March 2015, http://www.newsweek.com/5000-foreign-fighters-flock-libya-isis-call-jihadists-310948

46. Emily Estelle and Sarah Lossing, 'U.S. Counter-ISIS Air Campaign Expands to Sirte', *Critical Threats*, 4 August 2016, http://www.criticalthreats.org/libya/estelle-lossing-us-counter-isis-air-campaign-expands-to-sirte-august-4-2016

47. Aaron Y. Zelin, 'Islamic State's First Colony in Libya', *Washington Institute for Near East Policy*, 10 October 2014, http://www.washingtoninstitute.org/policy-analysis/view/the-islamic-states-first-colony-in-libya

48. Rhiannon Smith, 'A House Divided: Jihadis Battle for Derna', *Tony Blair Faith Foundation*, 10 July 2015 http://tonyblairfaithfoundation.org/religion-geopolitics/commentaries/opinion/house-divided-jihadis-battle-derna

49. Maggie Michael, 'How a Libyan City Joined the Islamic State Group', *Associated Press*, 9 November 2014, http://bigstory.ap.org/article/195a7ffb0090444785eb814a5bda28c7/how-libyan-city-joined-islamic-state-group

50. *Institute for the Study of War*, 'ISIS Loses Libyan Stronghold', 24 June 2015, http://www.understandingwar.org/backgrounder/isis-loses-libyan-stronghold

51. First author phone conversations with Aaron Zelin, December 2014.

52. *Libyan Institute for Advanced Studies*, 'Beheadings, Car Bombings, and the Islamic State's expansion in Libya', June 2015, https://www.scribd.com/document/267533356/LIAS-Terrorism-in-Libya-020615

53. Jomana Karadsheh, 'Alleged Al-Qaeda Operative Abu Anas Al-Libi Dies in a U.S. Hospital, Family Says', *CNN*, 3 January 2015, http://www.cnn.com/2015/01/03/us/us-libya-al-libi/

54. Chris Stephen, 'Ten Killed as Gunmen Storm Luxury Hotel in Libyan Capital', *Guardian*, 27 January 2015, https://www.theguardian.com/world/2015/jan/27/libya-gunmen-kill-guards-take-hostages-luxuy-hotel-tripoli

55. 'ISIS in Action', *Eye on ISIS in Libya*, 28 December 2014, http://eyeonisisinlibya.com/isis-in-action/action-28-december-2014/; 'ISIS in Action', *Eye on ISIS in Libya*, 19 January 2015, http://eyeonisisinlibya.com/isis-in-action/action-19-january-2015/

56. 'ISIS in Action', *Eye on ISIS in Libya*, 16 February 2015, http://eyeonisisinlibya.com/isis-in-action/action-16-february-2015/

57. Salem Ali, 'Eight Guards Die as IS Attacks Fourth Oilfield: Two Foreigners Reported Abducted', *Libya Herald*, 6 March 2015, https://www.libyaherald.com/2015/03/06/eight-guards-die-as-is-militants-attack-a-fourth-oilfield/

58. 'ISIS in Action', *Eye on ISIS in Libya*, 3 November 2014, http://eyeonisisinlibya.com/isis-in-action/action-3-november-2014/; the DMSC is a conglomeration of extremist militias that have confronted both Haftar's anti-Islamist forces and ISIS in Derna. It may have cooperated with Haftar briefly to expel ISIS in 2015.

59. Nathaniel Barr, 'The Islamic State's Uneven Trajectory in Libya', *Terrorism Monitor* 13, no. 19 (17 September 2015), http://www.jamestown.org/programs/tm/single/?tx_ttnews%5Btt_news%5D=44385&cHash=13680742087e383966454520362fc1d8#.V9LsVJMrLsk

60. Ibid.

61. Leo Dobbs, 'Displaced Libyans Return to Rebuild Gaddafi's Hometown;

Face Needs', *UNHCR*, 16 April 2012, http://www.unhcr.org/news/stories/2012/4/4f8c2e7b6/displaced-libyans-return-rebuild-gaddafis-hometown-face-needs.html

62. Aref Nayed, 'Extremism, Trauma, and Therapy', in *Radical Engagements: Essays on Religion, Extremism, Politics, and Libya* (Kalam Research and Media, 2017), pp. 73–84.

63. *Tamimi*, 'Milishiat Ansar al-Sharia Tashtabak ma'a Jeishna al-Watani' (Arabic), 28 April 2013, http://tamimi.own0.com/t130071-topic

64. *Wakalat Al-Anbaa al-Islamiya*, 'Istishaad Amr Ansar al-Sharia b-Sirte wa Qaid Katibat al-Farouq Misrata a'ala yid Katibat min al-Jaysh a-Libi'i Tadum Muwaleen al-Qaddafi' (Arabic), 4 August 2013, https://dawaalhaq.com/post/5206

65. 'Anti-ISIS Coalition', *Eye on ISIS in Libya*, 14 December 2014, http://eyeonisisinlibya.com/the-anti-isis-coalition/anti-14-december-2014/

66. Skype and email discussions with Suliman Ali Zway of *The New York Times*, March and November 2016.

67. *Al-Wasat*, Salem al-Abeydi, 'Insihab Latibat Shuhada al-Zaqiya min Sirt ba'ad ta'Urudha li-Hajum Muslih' (Arabic), 12 March 2014, http://alwasat.ly/ar/news/libya/8365/%D8%A7%D9%86%D8%B3%D8%AD%D8%A7%D8%A8-%D9%83%D8%AA%D9%8A%D8%A8%D8%A9-%D8%B4%D9%87%D8%AF%D8%A7%D8%A1-%D8%A7%D9%84%D8%B2%D8%A7%D9%88%D9%8A%D8%A9-%D9%85%D9%86-%D8%B3%D8%B1%D8%AA-%D8%A8%D8%B9%D8%AF-%D8%AA%D8%B9%D8%B1%D8%B6%D9%87%D8%A7-%D9%84%D9%87%D8%AC%D9%88%D9%85-%D9%85%D9%8F%D8%B3%D9%84%D8%AD.htm

68. Skype and email discussions with Suliman Ali Zway of *The New York Times*, March and November 2016.

69. James Roslington and Jason Pack, 'Who Pays for ISIS in Libya?', *Hate Speech International*, 24 August 2016, https://www.hate-speech.org/who-pays-for-isis-in-libya/

70. *International Organization on Migration Displacement Tracking Matrix*, 'Sirte Displacement: Top Ten Host Communities', Round 4, 20 July 2016, http://reliefweb.int/sites/reliefweb.int/files/resources/Sirte%20displacement%20map_20July2016_En.pdf. The exact statistics are

unknowable. It is possible that fewer people were displaced than the IOM estimate.

71. Tamer El-Ghobashy and Hassan Morajea, 'Islamic State Tightens Grip on Libyan Stronghold of Sirte', *Wall Street Journal*, 29 November 2015, http://www.wsj.com/articles/islamic-state-entrenches-in-sirte-libya-1448798153

72. Mahmoud Al-Salouha, 'The Assassination of Salafist Sheikh Khalid Furjani in Sirte' (Arabic), *Al-Wasat*, 11 August 2015, http://www.alwasat.ly/ar/news/libya/85303/

73. *Spokesman for the UN High Commissioner for Human Rights*, 'Press Briefing Notes on Libya, Syria, and Yemen', 18 August 2015, http://www.ohchr.org/EN/NewsEvents/Pages/DisplayNews.aspx?NewsID=16329&LangID=E; Jared Malsin, 'ISIS Re-Establish Their Stronghold on Qaddafi's Home Town after Crushing a Rebellion', *Time*, 19 August 2015, http://time.com/4003049/isis-sirte-rebellion/

74. *UN Security Council*, 'Report of the Secretary-General on the United National Support Mission in Libya', 25 February 2016, https://unsmil.unmissions.org/Portals/unsmil/Documents/N1604043.pdf

75. The phrase derives from a Quranic passage. The term is poetic, and its meaning is frequently translated into English as 'solid structure' or 'steadfast wall'.

76. Study of the anti-ISIS coalition posts and timeline highlights this dynamic; see 'The Anti-ISIS Coalition', Eye on ISIS in Libya, http://eyeonisisinlibya.com/category/the-anti-isis-coalition/

77. 'Freedom of the Press 2015: Libya', *Freedom House*, 2015, https://freedomhouse.org/report/freedom-press/2015/libya

78. Joachim Dagenborg and Lamine Chikhi, 'Algeria's In Amenas Gas Plant Returning to Normal after Attack', *Reuters*, 1 September 2014, http://www.reuters.com/article/us-statoil-bp-algeria-idUSK-BN0GW2N820140901

79. Sudarsan Raghavan, 'Inside the Brutal But Bizarrely Bureaucratic World of the Islamic State in Libya', *Washington Post*, 23 August 2016, https://www.washingtonpost.com/world/murders-taxes-and-a-dmv-how-isis-ruled-its-libyan-stronghold/2016/08/22/2ce3b8f4–5e60–11e6–84c1–6d27287896b5_story.html

80. Aaron Y. Zelin, 'The Islamic State's Burgeoning Capital in Sirte, Libya', *Washington Institute for Near East Policy*, 6 August 2015, http://www.washingtoninstitute.org/policy-analysis/view/the-islamic-states-burgeoning-capital-in-sirte-libya

81. Ibid. For more on ISIS's finances and administrative model, see the below section, 'The Financial Dimension of ISIS in Libya'.

82. Rod Nordland and Nour Youssef, 'Libya: Unified against ISIS, Fragmented After', *New York Times*, 3 September 2016, http://www.nytimes.com/2016/09/04/world/middleeast/libya-unified-against-isis-fragmented-after.html

83. *International Crisis Group*, 'The Libyan Political Agreement: Time for a Reset', Crisis Group Middle East and North Africa Report, no. 170, 4 November 2016, p. 7.

84. This section and other areas treating finances derive from a modified version of the argument, including some extended quotes, from Roslington and Pack, 'Who Pays for ISIS in Libya?'

85. First author discussion with the anonymous Libyan sources relied upon in the Eye on ISIS project.

86. *Akhbar Libya*, 'Tanzim al-Dawla fi Libiya' (Arabic), 25 August 2015, cited in Geoffrey Porter, 'How Realistic Is Libya as an Islamic State "Fallback"?', *CTC Sentinel*, 17 March 2016; 'Establishing a New Social Contract for Sirte', *Eye on ISIS in Libya*, 15 December 2015, http://eyeonisisinlibya.com/isis-in-action/action-15-dec-2015/

87. For more on the propaganda surrounding ISIS's supposedly sharia-compliant ways of raising money, consult 'ISIS in Action', *Eye on ISIS in Libya*, 2 March 2016, http://eyeonisisinlibya.com/isis-in-action/action-2-march-2016/

88. Personal communication with an UNSMIL official, 4 February 2016, cited in Porter, 'How Realistic Is Libya as an Islamic State "fallback"?'

89. The international community's push for early elections was understood to be too soon by many observers and participants. For more, see Pack and Cook, 'July 2012 Libyan Elections', pp. 171–98.

90. Jason Pack and Mohamed Eljarh, 'Localizing Power in Libya', Atlantic Council, 26 November 2013, http://www.atlanticcouncil.org/publications/articles/localizing-power-in-libya; 'The Can Do City',

Economist, 3 October 2013, http://www.economist.com/news/business/21587264-entrepreneurs-libyas-commercial-hub-are-undeterred-post-war-chaos-can-do-city/

91. *International Crisis Group*, 'The Libyan Political Agreement: Time for a Reset', 4 November 2016, https://www.crisisgroup.org/middle-east-north-africa/north-africa/libya/libyan-political-agreement-time-reset

92. *International Republican Institute*, 'Libya Poll: High Confidence in Legitimacy of Local Councils, Despite Poor Outreach by Local Governments', 9 November 2016, http://www.iri.org/resource/libya-poll-high-confidence-legitimacy-local-councils-despite-poor-outreach-local

93. Ahmed Elumami and Aidan Lewis, 'U.S. Air Strike Hits Islamic State in Libya, 43 Dead', *Reuters*, 19 February 2016, http://www.reuters.com/article/libya-security-idUSKCN0VS1A5

94. 'Western Response', *Eye on ISIS in Libya*, 30 May 2016, http://eyeonisisinlibya.com/western-response/western-30-may-2016/

95. Chris Stephen, 'Three French Special Forces Soldiers Die in Libya', *Guardian*, 20 July 2016, https://www.theguardian.com/world/2016/jul/20/three-french-special-forces-soldiers-die-in-libya-helicopter-crash

96. Jacopo Barigazzi, 'Diplomatic Divide over Libya Threatens EU Unity on Defense', *Politico*, 11 October 2016, http://www.politico.eu/article/accusations-of-french-ambiguity-in-libya-show-difficult-eu-security-integration/; 'Libyan Renegade General Hails Support of Egyptian Leadership', *Middle East Eye*, 21 September 2016, http://www.middleeasteye.net/news/renegade-general-haftar-admits-receiving-support-egyptian-leadership-662681585

97. Jason Pack and Wolfgang Pusztai, 'Turning the Tide: How Turkey Won the War for Tripoli', *Middle East Institute*, 10 November 2020, https://www.mei.edu/publications/turning-tide-how-turkey-won-war-tripoli

98. *Reuters*, 'Militants Stage Attacks between Libyan Stronghold of Sirte and Coastal Misrata', 5 May 2016, http://www.reuters.com/article/us-libya-security-idUSKCN0XW1SN

99. Jason Pack, 'Don't Believe Libya's Race to Sirte Rhetoric', *Middle East Eye*, 10 May 2016, http://www.middleeasteye.net/columns/dont-

believe-libyas-race-sirte-rhetoric-690524639; *Economist*, 'The Scramble for Sirte', 14 May 2016, http://www.economist.com/news/middle-east-and-africa/21698671-libyas-armed-groups-take-aim-jihadists-and-each-other-scramble

100. 'Anti-ISIS Coalition', *Eye on ISIS in Libya*, 30 May 2016, http://eyeonisisinlibya.com/the-anti-isis-coalition/anti-30-may-2016/

101. 'ISIS in Action', *Eye on ISIS in Libya*, 13 June 2016, http://eyeonisisinlibya.com/isis-in-action/action-13-june-2016/

102. 'ISIS in Action', *Eye on ISIS in Libya*, 27 June 2016, http://eyeonisisinlibya.com/isis-in-action/action-27-june-2016/

103. Jason Pack, 'After Sirte, What's Next for ISIS in Libya?', *Tony Blair Faith Foundation*, 17 August 2016, http://tonyblairfaithfoundation.org/religion-geopolitics/commentaries/opinion/after-sirte-whats-next-isis-libya

104. Adam Entous and Missy Ryan, 'In Libya, United States Lays Plans to Hunt Down Escaped Islamic State Fighters', *Washington Post*, 11 November 2016, https://www.washingtonpost.com/world/national-security/in-libya-united-states-lays-plans-to-hunt-down-escaped-islamic-state-fighters/2016/11/11/97098090-a755-11e6-8fc0-7be8f848c492_story.html

105. '*U.S. Africa Command Press Release*, 'U.S. Airstrikes in Support of the GNA, October 13', 14 October 2016, http://www.africom.mil/NewsByCategory/pressrelease/28445/u-s-airstrikes-in-support-of-gna-oct-13

106. 'Western Response', *Eye on ISIS in Libya*, 4 July 2016, http://eyeonisisinlibya.com/western-response/western-4-july-2016/

107. 'ISIS in Action', *Eye on ISIS in Libya*, 15 August 2016, http://eyeonisisinlibya.com/isis-in-action/action-15-august-2016/

108. Hani Amari, 'Libyan Forces Reduce Islamic State's Grip in Sirte to Final Few Blocks', *Reuters*, 4 October 2016, http://www.reuters.com/article/us-libya-security-idUSKCN1241MJ

109. 'Isis in Action', *Eye on ISIS in Libya*, 6 December 2016, http://eyeonisisinlibya.com/isis-in-action/action-6-dec-16/

110. 'ISIS in Action', *Eye on ISIS in Libya*, 13 December 2016, http://

eyeonisisinlibya.com/isis-in-action/bm-forces-sweep-sirte-for-isis-fighters-mines/

111. 'ISIS in Action', *Eye on ISIS in Libya*, 29 August 2016, http://eyeonisisinlibya.com/isis-in-action/action-29-august-2016/

112. 'ISIS in Action', *Eye on ISIS in Libya*, 20 September 2016, http://eyeonisisinlibya.com/isis-in-action/action-20-sept-16/

113. 'ISIS in Action', *Eye on ISIS in Libya*, 3 January 2017, http://eyeonisisinlibya.com/isis-in-action/reports-of-isis-presence-in-southern-libya/

114. 'US Conducts Airstrikes on Daesh Camps in Libya', *AFRICOM*, 19 January 2017, http://www.africom.mil/media-room/pressrelease/28594/us-conducts-air-strikes-on-daesh-camps-in-libya.

115. Eric Schmitt, 'Warnings of a "Powder Keg" in Libya as ISIS Regroups', *New York Times*, 21 March 2017, https://www.nytimes.com/2017/03/21/world/africa/libya-isis.html?_r=0. I do not give credence to this estimate, as there is no scientific way to quantify the existing number of ISIS fighters post-Sirte (even for the US Department of Defense).

116. 'ISIS in Action', *Eye on ISIS in Libya*, 28 March 2017, http://eyeonisisinlibya.com/isis-in-action/22-28-mar-us-will-maintain-force-in-libya-to-counter-isis/

117. Ibid.

118. Hassan Hassan, 'What ISIL Really Wants from the Battle for Mosul', *National*, 30 October 2016, http://www.thenational.ae/opinion/comment/what-isil-really-wants-from-the-battle-for-mosul

119. Scott Peterson, 'Reclaiming Mosul: Concerns Run High about the Politics of the "Day After"', *Christian Science Monitor*, 28 October 2016, http://www.csmonitor.com/World/Middle-East/2016/1028/Reclaiming-Mosul-concerns-run-high-about-the-politics-of-the-day-after

120. Jason Pack and Rhiannon Smith, 'Defeating the Islamic State? Lessons from Libya', *Hate Speech International*, 4 November 2016, https://www.hate-speech.org/defeating-the-islamic-state-lessons-from-libya/

121. This larger behaviour pattern of statesmen avoiding complex, yet

important issues has been amply illustrated for a non-specialist audience via which aspects of the Brexit negotiations the press and the Johnson government presented as make or break issues. Concrete, easy to address, easy to understand, and fundamentally economically unimportant issues like fishing rights featured prominently in negotiations and press statements, while issues relating to complex regulations of financial services and freedom of movement for skilled human labour were largely ignored despite their orders of magnitude greater economic and geostrategic importance. For a coherent overview of why relatively unimportant issues from a strategic or economic standpoint are frequently elevated in the public consciousness by neo-populist leaders, consult the *Remainiacs* podcast series, especially episodes focusing on the fisheries issue, such as, https://www.stitcher.com/show/remainiacs/episode/dealcast-the-fake-escape-80463698

122. Roslington and Pack, 'Who Pays for ISIS in Libya?'
123. Consult Aaron Zelin's collection of jihadi recruitment videos at https://jihadology.net/
124. *Economist*, 'Fighting Islamic State in Libya', 17 June 2016, http://www.economist.com/news/middle-east-and-africa/21700723-battle-sirte-fighting-islamic-state-libya
125. The prediction from which much of the section below derives is available here: Jason Pack, 'ISIS Loss in Sirte May Deepen Libyan Rifts', in 'After Sirte, What's Next for ISIS in Libya?', *Tony Blair Faith Foundation*, 17 August 2016, https://institute.global/policy/after-sirte-whats-next-isis-libya. For the outcome, see Lachlan Wilson and Jason Pack, 'The Islamic State's Revitalization in Libya and Its Post-2016 War of Attrition', *CTC Sentinel*, March 2019, https://ctc.usma.edu/islamic-states-revitalization-libya-post-2016-war-attrition/
126. *The Economist*, 'The Scramble for Sirte', 12 May 2016, https://www.economist.com/middle-east-and-africa/2016/05/12/the-scramble-for-sirte; Pack, 'Don't Believe Libya's "Race to Sirte" Rhetoric'.
127. Jason Pack, 'US Policy on Libya Comes Up Short', *Arab Weekly*, 16 October 2016, http://www.thearabweekly.com/Opinion/6751/US-policy-on-Libya-comes-up-short

128. Deutsche Welle, 'حكومة السراج تطلب دعم و اشنطن لطرد 'داعش' من ليبيا', trans-
lated, 1 August 2016, https://www.dw.com/ar/%D8%AD%D9%83%
D9%88%D9%85%D8%A9-%D8%A7%D9%84%D8%B3%D8%
B1%D8%A7%D8%AC-%D8%AA%D8%B7%D9%84%D8%A8-
%D8%AF%D8%B9%D9%85-%D9%88%D8%A7%D8%B4%D
9%86%D8%B7%D9%86-%D9%84%D8%B7%D8%B1%
D8%AF-%D8%AF%D8%A7%D8%B9%D8%B4-%D9%85%
D9%86-%D9%84%D9%8A%D8%A8%D9%8A%D8%A
7/a-19442695

129. C.J. Arlotta, 'As Obama Bombs ISIS in Libya, Are We Backing the
Right Regime?', *Fiscal Times*, 3 August 2016, http://www.thefiscal-
times.com/2016/08/03/Obama-Bombs-ISIS-Libya-Are-We-Backing-
Right-Regime

130. Jason Pack and Rhiannon Smith, 'Libya: Unity First, Military
Victories Second', *Arab Weekly*, 11 September 2016, https://thear-
abweekly.com/libya-unity-first-military-victories-second

131. Author conversations with USAID-funded Libyan civil society organizations and residents of Libya at the time.

132. Jason Pack and Rhiannon Smith, '"Coup" Attempt Could Complicate
Libya's Fight against ISIS', *Tony Blair Faith Foundation*, 24 October
2016, https://institute.global/policy/coup-attempt-could-complicate-
libyas-fight-against-isis

133. See also Alia Brahimi and Jason Pack, 'Strategic Lessons from the
Ejection of ISIS from Sirte', *Atlantic Council*, 16 May 2017, https://
www.atlanticcouncil.org/blogs/menasource/strategic-lessons-from-
the-ejection-of-isis-from-sirte/

134. Smith and Pack, 'Al-Qaida's Strategy in Libya'.

135. For more information on the demographic composition of ISIS fighters in Libya, see Wilson and Pack, 'Islamic State's Revitalization in
Libya. Footnotes 51 to 58 and the corresponding text treat this issue
and the ways in which we ascertained what is knowable about it.

136. Jason Pack, 'The Hifter Effect on the Battle for Libya's Sirte',
Al-Monitor, 14 October 2016, http://www.al-monitor.com/pulse/
originals/2016/10/libya-battle-sirte-isis-general-hifter.html#ixzz
4NB7IYgzT

137. Omar Mukhtar was the leader of the military wing of the Sanussi Sufi

order's movement to end the Italian occupation in the 1920s and early '30s. He was executed after being captured in 1932. To this day, he remains Libya's only truly national hero—revered equally in Cyrenaica, his birthplace, as in Tripolitania or Fezzan. His legacy was an important source of legitimacy in the kingdom period: used in public discourse to tie the Sanussiyya to the anti-Italian struggle in the popular imagination. In the Qadhafi period, his image was printed on Libyan money as Qadhafi tried to ground his legitimacy via anti-imperial messaging. This 'Qadhafian appropriation of Mukhtar' is remarkable, because one of the main symbolic aspects of the Qadhafi regime was the demolition of Sanussi shrines and attempts to write the Sanussi out of Libyan history. Post-Qadhafi, Mukhtar is still invoked by politicians, civil society groups, and even militia brigades (some of which bear his name and likeness). There have been Islamist-leaning militias calling themselves the Omar Mukhtar Brigade, while conversely the LNA formed an Omar Mukhtar Operations Room assigned to 'liberate' Derna from the Islamist jihadis in 2017–18.

138. Lydia Sizer and Jason Pack, 'ISIS Fuels Discord in Libya: Using Oil to Weaken the Unity Government', *Foreign Affairs*, 17 May 2016, https://www.foreignaffairs.com/articles/libya/2016–05–17/isis-fuels-discord-libya

139. Thomas Friedman, 'Obama on the World', *New York Times*, 8 August 2014, https://www.nytimes.com/2014/08/09/opinion/president-obama-thomas-l-friedman-iraq-and-world-affairs.html

140. Ben Hubbard et al., 'Abandoned by U.S. in Syria, Kurds Find New Ally in American Foe', *New York Times*, 23 October 2019, https://www.nytimes.com/2019/10/13/world/middleeast/syria-turkey-invasion-isis.html

141. According to one former senior British official serving in Libya in 2016–17, the 'main problem with Daesh after their defeat in Sirte was that they dispersed all over the country. The problem for foreign intelligence agencies [like the CIA and MI6] was that they had no local partner to work with in trying to identify terrorist cells. This allowed the jihadis to operate in crucial theatres like Tripoli without hindrance ...' Similarly, according to a former American intelligence operative who was previously active on the Libya file, 'after the fall

of Sirte, Libya was unique among major jihadi hotspots in that the US did not maintain active undercover agents inside the country for the purpose of counterterrorism'.

142. Author conversations with USAID and DFID staff who served during the period.

143. Stefano Marcuzzi and Jason Pack, 'Terrorist and Armed Groups in the Fezzan-Sahel Region: Recruitment and Communication Tactics', *NATO Strategic Communications*, Centre of Excellence, December 2020, https://www.stratcomcoe.org/terrorist-and-armed-groups-fezzan-sahel-region-recruitment-and-communication-tactics? fbclid= IwAR3KNHFZpe9Jg8Qog2yIhcqau OB6FT a6NfYYZMgi Q0U7Y yEXbA07DfVliiA

144. Niall Ferguson, *Empire: The Rise and Demise of the British World Order and the Lessons for Global Power* (Basic, 2004).

145. Correlation is not the same as causation, of course. Most of the anonymous interviews with policymakers that I cite in this book indirectly suggest this causal analysis, but of course none can ever conclusively prove a direct cause and effect linkage.

146. Consult Aaron Zelin's collection of jihadi recruitment videos at https://jihadology.net/

147. This positive feedback loop dynamic is particularly noticeable in Libya's under-governed southern underbelly. Marcuzzi and Pack, 'Terrorist and Armed Groups in the Fezzan-Sahel Region'.

148. Phone interview with Joshua Landis, March 2021.

149. Hisham Sharabi, *Neopatriarchy*.

150. The above anecdote was originally told in my obituary of Jibril. See Jason Pack and Sami Zaptia, 'The Face of the Libyan Arab Spring, Mahmoud Jibril, Felled by COVID-19', *Middle East Institute*, 9 April 2020, https://www.mei.edu/publications/face-libyan-arab-spring-mahmoud-jibril-felled-covid-19

151. Karim Mezran, Elissa Miller, and Emelie Chace-Donahue, للخروج من ازمتها : امل ليبيا اللامركزية, translation, *Atlantic Council*, 27 June 2017, http://www.acharircenter.org/the-potential-for-decentralization-in-libya-ar/

152. Understanding these institutions, their evolution, and their connec-

tion to the Enduring Disorder is the subject of Chapter 4. An overview of the meaning of this term is defined in endnote 10 of Chapter 4.

3. UNREGULATED CYBERSPACE LEADS TO NEO-POPULISM

1. *Stanford Internet Observatory*, 'Analysis of April 2020 Twitter Takedowns Linked to Saudi Arabia, the UAE, Egypt, Honduras, Serbia, and Indonesia', 2 April 2020, https://cyber.fsi.stanford.edu/io/news/april-2020-twitter-takedown

2. Shelby Grossman, Khadeja Ramali, and Renee DiResta, 'Blurring the Lines of Media Authenticity: Prigozhin-Linked Group Funding Libyan Broadcast Media', *Stanford Internet Observatory*, 20 March 2020, https://cyber.fsi.stanford.edu/io/news/libya-prigozhin

3. Peter Pomerantsev, *This Is Not Propaganda*: *Adventures in the War against Reality* (Public Affairs, 2019).

4. Amal Obeidi, *Political Culture in Libya* (Routledge, 2001).

5. Disinformation is information that is false and deliberately created by propagandists to harm their opponents and help their allies. It is often state-linked, although attribution may be difficult. By contrast misinformation is information that is false but was not necessarily created with malign intent. Its creators may be naïve or themselves deceived.

6. *EBU press release*, 'Trusted News Initiative Announces Plans to Tackle Harmful Coronavirus Disinformation', 27 March 2020, https://www.ebu.ch/news/2020/03/trusted-news-initiative-announces-plans-to-tackle-harmful-coronavirus-disinformation; James Pamment, 'EU Code of Practice on Disinformation: Briefing Note for the New European Commission', *Carnegie Endowment*, 3 March 2020, https://carnegieendowment.org/2020/03/03/eu-code-of-practice-on-disinformation-briefing-note-for-new-european-commission-pub-81187

7. Josh Loeb, 'World Walled Web: The National Firewalls Shutting Out the Internet', *E&T*, 19 February 2018, https://eandt.theiet.org/content/articles/2018/02/world-walled-web-the-national-firewalls-shutting-out-the-internet/

8. For those put off by this narrative, the myth of the revolutionary fighter and 'independent community' reigning supreme is substituted.

9. Carl Miller, *Death of the Gods: The New Global Power Grab* (William Heinemann, 2018).

10. Jason Pack, 'Kingdom of Militias: Libya's Second War of Post-Qadhafi Succession', *ISPI*, 31 May 2019, https://www.ispionline.it/en/pubblicazione/kingdom-militias-libyas-second-war-post-qadhafi-succession-23121

11. Jason Pack, 'Khalifa Haftar's Miscalculated Attack on Tripoli ...', *Foreign Policy*, 10 April 2019, https://foreignpolicy.com/2019/04/10/khalifa-haftars-miscalculated-attack-on-tripoli-will-cost-him-and-libya-dearly-un-benghazi-gna-lna/ For more on Haftar's motivations, consult the quote from Former US Special Envoy to Libya Jonathan Winer.

12. Ali Abdurraouf, المقدس إلى المدنس: تصوراتفيالصورة الذهنية والبصرية لميدان التحرير, *Midan Masr*, 11 May 2013, http://www.midanmasr.com/article.aspx?ArticleID=248.

13. Amal al-Helali, ناشطات ليبيات: خرجنا ضد القذافي لكن الإسلاميين أسوأ منه, *Radio Sawa*, 29 August 2014. https://www.radiosawa.com/archive/2014/08/29/ناشطات-ليبيات-خرجنا-ضد-القذافي-الإسلامين-أسوأ-منه.

14. Fred Wehrey, *Burning Shores of Tripoli* (Penguin 2018); Wolfram Lacher, *Libya's Fragmentation: Structure and Process in Violent Conflict* (I.B. Tauris, 2020).

15. Youssef Mohammad Sawani, 'Gaddafi's Legacy, Institutional Development, and National Reconciliation in Libya', *Contemporary Arab Affairs* 13, no. 1 (2020), pp. 46–68, https://doi.org/10.1525/caa.2020.13.1.46

16. Pack, 'Introduction', pp. 1–23.

17. Ibid.

18. *Al-Watan Voice*, مئات الآلاف من أهالي بنغازي يهتفون برحيل القذافي ويعلنون تحررهم, 25 February 2011, https://www.alwatanvoice.com/arabic/content/print/169845.html. A representative source from the first days of the protests stated that 'Hundreds of thousands of demonstrators opposing Qadhafi's government in the city of Benghazi chanted slogans condemning the Libyan leader and demanding his departure, such as "The people want to collapse the regime," and "Libya is free when Qadhafi's leaves."'

19. Pack and Cook, 'July 2012 Libyan Elections', pp. 171–98.

20. Rachel Simon, *Libya between Ottomanism and Nationalism: The*

Ottoman Involvement in Libya during the War with Italy (1911–1919) (K. Schwarz, 1987).

21. Ali Abdullatif Ahmida, *The Making of Modern Libya: State Formation, Colonization and Resistance*, 1830–1932 (Albany, 1994).
22. Simon, *Libya between Ottomanism and Nationalism.*
23. Anna Baldinetti, *The Origins of the Libyan Nation: Colonial Legacy, Exile and the Emergence of a New Nation-State* (Abingdon, 2010).
24. Vandewalle, *History of Libya.*
25. Lisa Anderson, 'The Development of Nationalist Sentiment in Libya, 1908–1922', in Rashid Khalidi (ed.), *The Origins of Arab Nationalism* (Columbia University Press, 1991), pp. 225–42; Anderson, *State and Social Transformation.*
26. Paul D. Kenny, 'The Origins of Patronage Politics: State Building, Centrifugalism, and Decolonization', *British Journal of Political Science* 45, no. 1 (January 2015), pp. 141–71, https://www.cambridge.org/core/journals/british-journal-of-political-science/article/origins-of-patronage-politics-state-building-centrifugalism-and-decolonization/B26E9093D687C33463F6A53E80097BAD
27. Susan Stokes et al., *Brokers, Voters, and Clientelism: The Puzzle of Distributive Politics* (Cambridge University Press, 2013).
28. Pack, Mezran, and Eljarh, 'Libya's Faustian Bargains'.
29. Author conversations at the time with Prime Minister-elect Mustafa Abushagur and State Department officials who were serving in Tripoli.
30. Naji Barakat, من اسقط حكومة أبو شاقور 'Ain Libya, 8 October 2012, https://www.eanlibya.com/من-اسقط-حكومة-ابوشاقور/.
31. Khaled al-Maheer, 'أبو شاقور' الصراعات وأدت حكومة مصطفى, *al-Jazeera*, 8 October 2012, https://www.aljazeera.net/news/reportsandinterviews/2012/10/8/الحكوميتين اللتين عرضهما
32. The 2014–15 First Libyan Civil war pitted Libya Dawn (led by Misratan militiamen) against Libya Dignity (led by Haftar and his LNA). It was not really a battle between Islamists and anti-Islamists as has frequently been claimed. Although neither of the sides were cohesive, the primary logic behind the evolving alliance structures could be conceptualized as those who opposed lustration (removal from all positions of public trust of Qadhafi-era officials) and those who demanded it. This dynamic

of exploring the war is presented in, Jason Pack, 'Libya: Situation Report', *Tony Blair Faith Foundation*, First published: 10 November 2014, updated: 4 March 2015, http://www.libya-analysis.com/wordpress/wp-content/uploads/Tony-Blair-Faith-Foundation-Pack-Libya-Sit-Rep-March-2015-Ver.pdf

33. Jason Pack, 'Libya Has a New Prime Minister and His Family Legacy Is as Complex, Shady, and Wealthy as the Country Itself', *Middle East Institute*, 8 February 2021, https://www.mei.edu/blog/monday-briefing-what-exactly-biden-plan-yemen#pack

34. Sami Zaptia, 'The HoR's Reunified Sirte Session: Second Day Roundup; Questioning PM Designate Al-Dabaiba', *Libya Herald*, 10 March 2021, https://www.libyaherald.com/2021/03/10/the-hors-reunified-sirte-session-second-day-roundup-questioning-pm-designate-aldabaiba/

35. Tarek Megerisi, 'Libya Crisis: The Unity Government's Success Hides Serious Dangers Ahead', *Middle East Eye*, 13 April 2021, https://www.middleeasteye.net/opinion/libya-new-unity-government-dangers-ahead; *International Crisis Group*, 'Libya Turns the Page', 21 May 2021, https://www.crisisgroup.org/middle-east-north-africa/north-africa/libya/222-libya-turns-page

36. Note that the appointment of Najla Mangoush as Libya's first female foreign minister in March 2021 was not an exception to this rule. She achieved prominence by becoming an official at a US think tank and then a professor at an American University. She could not have risen to prominence in this way had she stayed in Libya. This point repeatedly emerged from the interviews conducted for this book. But special thanks go to former British Ambassador to Libya Peter Millett for clarifying how he believes this plays out in practice.

37. Henneberg, *Managing Transition*.

38. 'Israel's Diplomatic Giant Eban Dies', *BBC*, 8 November 2002, http://news.bbc.co.uk/2/hi/middle_east/2486473.stm

39. Grossman, Ramali, and DiResta, 'Blurring the Lines'.

40. *Ukrayinska Pravda*, 'Путин надеется, что Германия поддержит его стремления' (Putin hopes Germany will support his ambitions), 18 March 2014, https://www.pravda.com.ua/rus/news/2014/03/18/7019425/; Andrew Wilson, *Ukraine Crisis: What It Means for the West*

(Yale University Press, 2014), p. 35, explains the origins of the 'Russian World' concept.

41. *Novoye Vremya*, 'Путин надеется на возвращение Украины в так называемый "русский мир"—Полторак' (Putin hopes for Ukraine's return to the so-called 'Russian world'—Poltorak), 5 April 2018, https://nv.ua/ukraine/politics/putin-nadeetsja-na-vozvrashchenie-ukrainy-v-tak-nazyvaemyj-russkij-mir-poltorak-2462329.html

42. See Wilson, *Ukraine Crisis*, p. 23 for the full-length and highly prescient quotes from Sergey Markov and Gleb Pavlovsky.

43. Benedict Anderson, *Imagined Communities: Reflections on the Origin and Spread of Nationalism* (Verso, 2016).

44. *Altai Consulting*, 'Libya Media Assessment: One Year Later; An Assessment of the Media Landscape and Consumption Patterns', May 2013, pp. 71–3, http://www.altaiconsulting.com/wp-content/uploads/2016/03/Altai-Consulting-Libyan-Media-One-Year-Later.pdf

45. For more on Dar al-Farajani's history, especially how it survived the Qadhafi period, see Salem Abuzahir, نشر الكتاب الورقي .... واقعه و مستقبله, *Libya al-Mustaqbal*, 30 June 2016, http://www.libya-al-mostakbal. org/top/1307/نشرالكتاب-الورقي-الليبي-واقعه-ومستقبله-استطلاع-سالم-أبوظهير.html

46. This is an extremely low figure in comparison to Libya's neighbours, Tunisia, Algeria, and Egypt, where the figures appear to be hundreds-fold higher. Discussions with Dar Farjani. Furthermore, in *Altai Consulting*, 'Libya Media Assessment' books are not discussed while all other print media are. Presumably, this is because they are an insignificant part of the media consumption landscape in Libya.

47. Author interviews with Al Jazeera Media Institute experts June 2020.

48. Professional social media analytics data and *Altai Consulting*, 'Libya Media Assessment'.

49. *Yes Libya*, ماذا يفضل الليبيون من مواقع التواصل الاجتماعي, 26 October 2020, https://yeslibya.ly/2020/10/26/ ماذا-يفضل-الليبيون-من-مواقع-التواصل-ال.

50. I established Libya-Analysis in 2011. We are a small consulting firm specializing in producing evidence-based analysis, forecasting, and research on Libya. For more on our history, mission, products, or team, please consult http://www.libya-analysis.com/our-story/. The Media Mapping study referenced here was conducted by my consult-

ing firm Libya-Analysis with the help of MiCT in Germany. For more on it, see http://www.libya-analysis.com/media-mapping/

51. Libya-Analysis LLC's Media Mapping work remains confidential. However, a big-picture overview of what it entails is available at, http://www.libya-analysis.com/media-mapping/

52. There are not any accurate published comprehensive overviews in English or Arabic of the current state of the Libyan media. However, a useful, but partial, resource in Arabic is available from the Libyan Center for Freedom of Press; see https://lcfp.org.ly/wp-content/uploads/2017/06/New-report-on-hate-speech-and-incitement-March.pdf

53. The term cultural imaginary is a social science term used to refer to the 'notion of the nation as a community that gives culture ... that is socially constructed through narratives, myths of origins, symbols, rituals, and collective memory ... imagined by people who see themselves as part of that group ...' 'The Cultural Imaginary', *Wikiversity*, https://en.wikiversity.org/wiki/Cultural_imaginary

54. Author interviews with Al Jazeera Media Institute experts, June 2020.

55. Elie Podeh, *Rethinking Nasserism: Revolution and Historical Memory in Modern Egypt*, (University Press of Florida, 2004).

56. For a good example of Libya's top oil official using YouTube to appeal to the citizenry, see https://www.youtube.com/watch?v=-4xakvBfGlA &t=17s

57. The excerpt consists of sections of Part I, III, IV, and V of the original think tank report. Removed sections are represented by ellipses and additions in [brackets and *italics*].

58. Pack, 'Introduction', pp. 1–23.

59. Jason Pack, 'Libya Situation Report', *Tony Blair Faith Foundation*, 12 June 2015.

60. In this paper, we treat the events of 2011 as 'uprisings' rather than a civil war. For more on this choice consult Jason Pack, 'Introduction: The Center and the Periphery', in Jason Pack (ed.), *The 2011 Libyan Uprisings and the Struggle for the Post-Qaddafi Future* (Palgrave Macmillan, 2013), pp. 1–23.

61. Camille Tawil, 'Operation Dignity: General Haftar's Latest Battle May Decide Libya's Future', *Jamestown Foundation*, 30 May 2014, https://

jamestown.org/program/operation-dignity-general-haftars-latest-battle-may-decide-libyas-future/

62. Mohamed Eljarh, 'A Coup Attempt in Tripoli', *Foreign Policy*, 19 May 2014, https://foreignpolicy.com/2014/05/19/a-coup-attempt-in-tripoli/

63. Borzou Daragahi, 'Hero of Libya's Revolution Wages War on Government', *Financial Times*, 25 August 2014, https://www.ft.com/content/b07f2b56-2467-11e4-be8e-00144feabdc0

64. Nicola Missaglia, 'Chaos in Libya: A Background', *Italian Institute for International Political Studies(ISPI)*, 2 February 2017, https://www.ispionline.it/it/pubblicazione/chaos-libya-background-17108

65. Emily Estelle, 'A Strategy for Success', *American Enterprise Institute*, November 2017.

66. It is worth noting that the LNA's General Command, while in theory coordinating with the eastern-based government's Ministry of Interior, attempts to assert control over all the paramilitary and internal security agencies in eastern, central, and southern Libya, including those that are not actually parts of the LNA, such as the PFG, local security directorates, internal security, criminal investigation departments, and others.

67. Floor El Kamouni-Janssen, Hamzeh Shadeedi, and Nancy Ezzeddine, 'Local Security Governance in Libya: Perceptions of Security and Protection in a Fragmented Country', *Clingendael* (Netherlands Institute of Foreign Relations), October 2018, https://www.clingendael.org/sites/default/files/2018–10/diversity_security_Libya.pdf

68. Nadine Dahan, 'Haftar Forces Launch Fresh Attack on Besieged Libyan city of Derna', *Middle East Eye*, 16 May 2018, https://www.middleeasteye.net/news/haftar-forces-launch-fresh-attack-besieged-libyan-city-derna

69. *BBC Arabic*, 'Libya "War Crimes" Videos Shared on Social Media', 1 May 2019, https://www.bbc.com/news/av/world-africa-48105968/libya-war-crimes-videos-shared-on-social-media

70. Al-Zubayr Salem, 'The War in Derna', *Cadmus—European University Institute*, September 2018, http://cadmus.eui.eu/bitstream/handle/1814/56084/PolicyBrief_2018_09(EN).pdf?sequence=1

71. Analysts Oded Berkowitz and Arnaud Delalande, among others, fol-

lowed and documented these deployments during the course of the siege. See https://twitter.com/Oded121351/status/996071419179098112

72. *Alwasat*, 'LNA Spox: Military Operations in Derna Are Complete, We Are Asking the Population to Cooperate with the Security Services', 14 February 2019, http://en.alwasat.ly/news/libya/235972

73. For more on the origins of Madkhali Salafism and the role it plays in Libya's various armed groups, see *International Crisis Group*, 'Addressing the Rise of Libya's Madkhali-Salafis', Middle East and North Africa Report no. 200, 25 April 2019, https://d2071andvip0wj.cloudfront. net/200-libyas-madkhali-salafis.pdf

74. Walid Abdullah, 'Pro-Haftar Forces Launch Military Operation in S. Libya', *Anadolu Agency*, 15 January 2019, https://www.aa.com.tr/ en/africa/pro-haftar-forces-launch-military-operation-in-s-libya/ 1365259

75. Sami Zapita, 'Hafter Launches Murzuq Basin Military Campaign in South', *Libya Herald*, 24 October 2018, https://www.libyaherald. com/2018/10/24/hafter-launches-murzuq-basin-military-campaign- in-south/

76. *Middle East Eye*, '"We Do Not Have Freedom": Haftar's Forces Accused of War Crimes in Libya's South', 26 February 2019, https://www. middleeasteye.net/news/we-do-not-have-freedom-haftars-forces- accused-war-crimes-libyas-south

77. Sami Zapita, 'LNA Claims Control of Ghat and Awainat', *Libya Herald*, 3 March 2019, https://www.libyaherald.com/2019/03/03/lna-claims- control-of-ghat-and-awainat/

78. Ahmed Gatnash and Nadine Dahan, 'In Libya, Traditional and Social Media Are Used to Fuel War', *Arab Tyrant Manual*, 14 April 2019, https://arabtyrantmanual.com/articles/in-libya-traditional-and-social- media-are-used-to-fuel-war/; *AFP*, 'Fake News War: In Libya, Battles Also Rage on Social Media', 18 April 2019, https://www.france24. com/en/20190418-fake-news-war-libya-battles-also-rage-social-media

79. Pack, 'Khalifa Haftar's Miscalculated Attack'. See especially the quote from former US special envoy to Libya Jonathan Winer.

80. Jared Malsin and Summer Said, 'Saudi Arabia Promised Support to Libyan Warlord in Push to Seize Tripoli: As Some Nations Looked to

Khalifa Haftar for Stability in Libya, Others Backed His Army', *Wall Street Journal*, 12 April 2019, https://www.wsj.com/articles/saudi-arabia-promised-support-to-libyan-warlord-in-push-to-seize-tripoli-11555077600

81. Nathan Vest, 'Is an Escalation Imminent in Western Libya?', *RAND*, 27 March 2019, https://www.rand.org/blog/2019/03/is-an-escalation-imminent-in-western-libya.html

82. Anonymous interviews with on the ground sources.

83. For more on Libya-Analysis's comprehensive mapping of Libya's tradition (i.e. non-social) media, please consult http://www.libya-analysis.com/media-mapping/

84. Pack, 'Antecedents and Implications of the So-Called Anglo-Sanussi War'.

85. Cook and Pack, 'Mu'ammur Qadhafi'.

86. For a classic example of this phenomenon, see Peter Baker, 'The White House Called a News Conference: Trump Turned It into a Meandering Monologue', *New York Times*, 14 July 2020, https://www.nytimes.com/2020/07/14/us/politics/trump-news-conference.html

87. Libya-Analysis LLC confidential weekly politics and conflict reports 2014–16.

88. Jason Pack, 'Tragedy and Farce in Libya', *Middle East Institute*, 4 May 2020, https://www.mei.edu/blog/tragedy-and-farce-libya

89. For an example of a story that encapsulates how Haftar and his allies were able to manipulate the media's coverage of the conflict, see *Reuters*, 'UAE Says Egypt Initiative for Libya Boosts Peace Track', 8 June 2020, https://www.reuters.com/article/us-libya-security-emirates/uae-says-egypt-initiative-for-libya-boosts-peace-track-idUSKBN23F0SX

90. I expand on the relation between conquering territory and the media optics it provides at the start of Chapter 5's excerpt.

91. For more on Trump's highly unfortunate use of this terminology, see Jamie McIntyre, '"Dominate the Battlespace": Pentagon Advises Warlike Strategy to Defeat and Deter Violent Protesters', *Washington Examiner*, 2 June 2020, https://www.washingtonexaminer.com/policy/defense-national-security/dominate-the-battlespace-pentagon-advises-warlike-strategy-to-defeat-and-deter-violent-protesters; Thomas Gibbons-Neff et al., 'Former Commanders Fault Trump's Use of Troops

against Protesters', *New York Times*, 2 June 2020, https://www.nytimes.com/2020/06/02/us/politics/military-national-guard-trump-protests.html

92. John Connelly, *From Peoples into Nations: A History of Eastern Europe* (Princeton University Press, 2019) critiques the dominant theories of nationalism of Eric Hobsbawm, Ernest Gellner, and Benedict Anderson by downplaying the capitalist or Marxist components and stressing the victimization and narrative aspect of all nationalisms, and as such seems a useful paradigm for understanding neo-populist nationalism during the Enduring Disorder.

93. Ernest Nolte, *Three Faces of Fascism: Action Française, Italian Fascism, National Socialism* (Henry Holt, 1966).

94. Luke Darby, 'How the "White Replacement" Conspiracy Theory Spread around the Globe', *GQ*, 21 June 2019, https://www.gq.com/story/white-replacement-conspiracy-theory

95. Cristóbal Rovira Kaltwasser et al. (eds), *The Oxford Handbook of Populism* (Oxford University Press, 2020)

96. Libya-Analysis LLC Proprietary 2020 Social Media Mapping and Monitoring project. The original Arabic terms are أمير المخنثين المعتوه, literally 'the retarded prince of gays'. This usage employees a derogatory term for homosexuals, primarily in reference to Erdoğan but also the supporters of the GNA; and قردوغان (Qerdogan), which is a portmanteau word blending 'monkey' (*qard* in Arabic) and Erdoğan. It is employed to dehumanize and ridicule those with non-Arab, i.e. partially Turkish or Amazigh blood, as monkeys linked to Erdoğan.

97. Pomerantsev, *This Is Not Propaganda*.

98. Miller, *Death of the Gods*.

99. Alexander Hamilton, 'Objections and Answers Respecting the Administration of the Government', 18 August 1792, available at https://founders.archives.gov/documents/Hamilton/01-12-02-0184-0002#ARHN-01-12-02-0184-0002-fn-0005

4. LIBYA VERSUS THE GLOBAL ECONOMY

1. As alluded to in Chapters 1 and 3, the issues of subsidies, appeasement, semi-sovereign institutions, indirect rentierism, foreign exchange con-

trols, the war economy, and ideological rather than technocratic dominance over economic decision-making appear to make Venezuela and Libya fraternal twins. This illustrative comparison has been obscured by the discipline of area studies lumping together neighbouring countries while generally ignoring comparisons with countries with another language, religion, or in another hemisphere.

2. Arguably the most famous instances of this genre are: See Noria Research, 'Predatory Economies in Eastern Libya', *Global Initiative*, June 2019, https://globalinitiative.net/wp-content/uploads/2019/06/GITOC-Predatory-Economies-Eastern-Libya-WEB.pdf; Suliman Zway, 'Libya's Shadow Economy', *Mercy Corps*, 20 April 2017, https://www.mercycorps.org/sites/default/files/Mercy%20Corps_Libya%20Shadow%20Economy.pdf (no longer accessible); *Global Witness*, 'Discredited: How Libya's Multibillion-Dollar Trade Finance Scheme Risks Defrauding the Country via London Banks', 19 February 2021, https://www.globalwitness.org/en/campaigns/natural-resource-governance/discredited/; *International Crisis Group*, 'Of Tanks and Banks: Stopping a Dangerous Escalation in Libya', May 2019, https://www.crisisgroup.org/middle-east-north-africa/north-africa/libya/201-tanks-and-banks-stopping-dangerous-escalation-libya; and Mediapart, *Sarkozy–Kadhafi: Des billets et des bombes* (Delcourt, 2019).

3. Tim Eaton, 'Libya's War Economy: Predation, Profiteering and State Weakness', Research Paper, *Chatham House*, 2018, https://www.chathamhouse.org/publication/libyas-war-economy-predationprofiteering-and-state-weakness; Eaton, 'Libya: Rich in Oil, Leaking Fuel', *Chatham House*, 2019, https://chathamhouse.shorthandstories.com/libya-rich-in-oil-leaking-fuel/index.html; Eaton et al., 'Conflict Economies in the Middle East and North Africa', *Chatham House*, Royal Institute of International Affairs, 2019, https://www.chathamhouse.org/publication/conflict-economiesmiddle-east-and-north-africa; Eaton, 'Libya: Investing the Wealth of a Nation', *Chatham House*, 2021, https://chathamhouse.shorthandstories.com/libya-investing-wealth-of-nation/

4. The definitive academic works about the economic reforms of the late Qadhafi period are: Vandewalle, *Libya since 1969*; and Waniss A. Otman

and Erling Karlberg, *The Libyan Economy: Economic Diversification and International Repositioning* (Springer, 2007). Furthermore, many studies of its oil sector have been published from 1970 to 2009, but strangely none of those scholars updated their findings to take into consideration the evolution of the post-Qadhafi period. Of course, in the general think tank, policy blog, and op-ed space prior to 2017, there were some lone voices trying to call attention to the economic drivers of conflict and reframe the errors in the received wisdom about Libya's post-Qadhafi economy. For such a piece of precocious scholarship consult, Lydia Sizer, 'The Myth of Libya's Wealth', *Atlantic Council*, 3 February 2015, https://www.atlanticcouncil.org/blogs/menasource/the-myth-of-libya-s-wealth/

5. According to an American government official who served at the US embassy in Libya during the détente period: 'This "globalization" myth applied mostly to political officers and various American political appointees. This view was not widely held by actual economists and economic policymakers. Back in 2006 USTR, Commerce, and some State Econ officers all believed the point of encouraging an economic opening was to hasten the fall of the regime. Economic policy types tended to believe the Cuban regime exists purely because of sanctions. The assumption was that lifting sanctions on Qadhafi would cause his regime to eventually collapse. The hope in those days was that as we were working on reforming economic structures of the 2005–2010 period they would create something to build on when the Qadhafi regime would crumble. But the goal was always to cause it to crumble. That said, nobody believed the regime was as brittle as it turned out to be, so it collapsed much faster than anyone anticipated.'

6. For a presentation of how the globalization myth functioned, please consult Pack, 'Engagement in Libya Was and Remains the Right Answer'.

7. Judith Gurney, *Libya: The Political Economy of Oil* (Oxford University Press, 1996).

8. The personalization of Libyan institutions is described in detail in George Joffé and Emmanuella Paoletti, 'The Foreign Policy Process in Libya', *Journal of North African Studies* 16, no. 2 (2011), pp. 183–213. They argue that as a result of 'personalization' that the Libyan semi-

sovereigns were not 'real institutions'. My perspective as illustrated in this chapter is quite different.

9. The concepts of Libya's 'statelessness' and 'institution-lessness' are a defining feature of the scholarship. Dirk Vandewalle, Moncef Dzairi, and Lisa Anderson have demonstrated how a peculiarly Libyan form of 'statelessness' and reliance on tribal structures was a defining characteristic of the Qadhafian period. Anderson posits that Libyan statelessness is an ongoing legacy of the Italian period. Vandewalle, however, largely attributes statelessness to Qadhafian ideology rather than colonialism. George Joffé, on the other hand, believes that Libyan 'statelessness' was an ideology that Qadhafi attempted to impose on Libyan society, but that it never reflected the reality on the ground, and he dismisses the claim that Libya has a unique Ottoman, Italian, or British legacy of statelessness. Alia Brahimi, John Davis, Omar Fathali and Monte Palmer, John Wright, and Joffé all show that Idriss al-Sanussi's state-building, particularly in the wake of the discovery of oil, was suffused with tribalism, Cyrenaican bias, and anachronistic, anti-bureaucratic tendencies.

10. This chapter deals primarily with Libya's economic structures, the most unique of which are its 'semi-sovereign institutions'—a term I first coined in the IAI paper that is this chapter's excerpt. Defining what constitutes a semi-sovereign institution is quite challenging, but the excerpt fleshes out the definition, stressing that they are separate entities initially established by government to conduct an economic or governmental function—like banking, foreign currency exchange, construction, telecoms, oil production, etc.—and then given a legal monopoly, a pot of money, and/or privileged access to help them conduct that function. Next, drawing on these special privileges, the entities in question have over time developed powers that government can no longer restrain. In the archetypal Libyan case, institutions that were initially only semi-independent when established in the Qadhafi period, have progressively in the early post-Qadhafi period gained complete independence. Then as governance bifurcated and collapsed over the course of 2014–15, they were forced to acquire a modicum of sovereignty separate from the state, which was then enshrined in the Skhirat

Agreement. This has happened because the post-revolutionary situation has meant that these entities have had no genuine domestic oversight and no effective way for government to control or even monitor their actions, let alone replace their institutional heads.

11. Jason Pack, 'The UN Deliberately (Albeit Mistakenly) Accorded Sovereignty to Post-Qadhafi Libya's Economic Institutions', *Middle East Institute*, 26 September 2019, https://www.mei.edu/publications/un-deliberately-albeit-mistakenly-accorded-sovereignty-post-gadhafi-libyas-economic

12. Jason Pack, 'How Libya's Economic Structures Enrich the Militias', *Middle East Institute*, 23 September 2019, https://www.mei.edu/publications/how-libyas-economic-structures-enrich-militias

13. The excerpt is composed of sections 1, 2, 3, and 4 of the original think tank report with removed text noted by ellipses and additions in [brackets and *italics*]. Policy recommendations have mostly been removed (as they are dealt with in the next chapter's excerpt), while all segments focusing on explaining the structures of the Libyan economy and their origins retained.

14. Vandewalle, *History of Modern Libya*; Anderson, *State and Social Transformation*; John Wright, *A History of Libya* (Hurst, 2010); Pack, 'Introduction', pp. 1–22.

15. Anderson, *State and Social Transformation*; Simon, *Libya between Ottomanism and Nationalism*.

16. Claudio G. Segrè, *Fourth Shore: The Italian Colonization of Libya* (University of Chicago Press, 1974); Federico Cresti, *Oasi di italianità: La Libia della colonizzazione agraria tra fascismo, guerra e indipendenza (1935–1956)* (Società editrice internazionale, 1996). Vandewalle, *History of Modern Libya*; Wright, *History of Libya*.

17. Shukri Ghanem, 'The Libyan Economy before Independence', in E.G.H. Joffé and K.S. McLachlan (eds), *Social & Economic Development of Libya* (Middle East & North African Studies Press, 1982), pp. 141–59; Saul Kelly, *War & Politics in the Desert: Britain and Libya during the Second World War* (Silphium Press, 2010); E.A.V. De Candole, *The Life and Times of King Idriss of Libya* (privately published by Mustafa ben Ghalbon, 1990); William Roger Louis, 'Libya: The Creation of a Client State', in Prosser Gifford and William Roger Louis (eds),

Decolonization and African Independence: The Transfers of Power, 1960–1980 (Yale University Press, 1988), pp. 503–28.

18. Vandewalle, *Libya since Independence*; Vandewalle, *Libya since 1969*; Dana Moss and Jason Pack, 'Libya since 1969: Qadhafi's Revolution Revisited', *Journal of North African Studies* 16, no. 2 (2011), pp. 299–310.

19. The system was brought into being by the publication and implementation of Qadhafi's *Green Book*.

20. Hanspeter Mattes, 'Formal and Informal Authority in Libya since 1969', in Vandewalle, *Libya since 1969*, pp. 55–81.

21. Pinset Masons, 'ODAC Removed from List of Libyan Entities Subject to Financial Sanctions', *Out-Law News*, 25 January 2013, https://www.pinsentmasons.com/out-law/news/odac-removed-from-list-of-libyan-entities-subject-to-financial-sanctions

22. Stefano Ugolini, *The Evolution of Central Banking: Theory and History* (Palgrave Macmillan, 2017); Stefano Battilossi, Youssef Cassis, and Kazuhiko Yago, *Handbook of the History of Money and Currency* (Springer Nature, 2018).

23. *Central Bank of Libya* website: 'History', https://cbl.gov.ly/en/history

24. *National Oil Corporation* website: 'NOC in Brief', https://noc.ly/index.php/en/about-us-2

25. Deena Dajani, 'Libya's Sovereign Wealth Scandal: Taxpayers' Billions Squandered through Nepotism, Incompetence and Wild Gambling', *New Arab*, 30 November 2017, https://www.alaraby.co.uk/english/indepth/2017/11/30/libyas-sovereign-wealth-scandal-taxpayers-billions-squandered-through-incompetence

26. Author interviews with former US and UK embassy officials who served in Tripoli from 2008 to 2010.

27. Author discussions with senior Libyan officials, Tripoli, October 2008.

28. Michael E. Porter, 'Libyan Economic Development Board Blueprint', *Monitor Company Group*, 2007, https://www.hbs.edu/faculty/Pages/item.aspx?num=46472

29. The oversight institutions were themselves so complex that Libyan institutions lacked the requisite competencies to administer them. As such, AECOM had the management contract for all of HIB's construc-

tion, which required oversight by the PPA. After that contract fell void after the revolution, they sought another management contract to clarify the existing contracts issued by the HIB and ODAC, but even that discrete project was never implemented as Libyan decision-makers preferred ad-hoc solutions, none of which were acceptable to international creditors. See 'AECOM Wins $209m Housing Contract', Libya-Business News, 6 December 2013, https://wp.me/p77Sqt-4PV

30. I was one such outside consultant, indirectly hired by a Western consulting firm to first study and then advise the Libyan authorities on the nature of the Qadhafian economic structures.

31. For more on how the political class and the militia leaders have used Libya's pre-existing Qadhafian economic structures to enrich themselves, please consult: Pack, 'How Libya's Economic Structures Enrich the Militias'.

32. Pack, 'Engagement in Libya Was and Remains The Right Answer'

33. Mohsin Khan and Karim Mezran, 'The Libyan Economy after the Revolution: Still No Clear Vision', Atlantic Council, Issue Briefs, 28 August 2013, https://www.atlanticcouncil.org/publications/issue-briefs/the-libyan-economy-after-the-revolution-still-no-clear-vision

34. Pack and Cook, 'July 2012 Libyan Election', pp. 171–98.

35. Pack, Mezran, and Eljarh, 'Libya's Faustian Bargains'.

36. Fascinatingly, for a country with one of the world's highest rates of corruption per capita, Qadhafi's Libya had no fewer than six semi-independent financial oversight bodies. See UNODC, 'Libya Anti-Corruption related Authorities', http://193.138.94.211/LegalLibrary/LegalResources/Libya/Authorities/Libya-Anti-Corruption-related Authorities.pdf

37. The most significant change since 2011 has been the transparent publication of the AB reports. Yet legally the reports should be submitted to the legislative branch which then should issue them, but in practice the Audit Bureau simply drops them on its website.

38. According to a former Libyan employee of AECOM, the new Audit Bureau has not prevented the outflow of the Libya's billions, in fact it can be argued that the old People's Oversight Committee (Raqaba) was much more effective in doing so during the Qadhafi regime.

39. According to an ambassador of a major Western nation active in Libya during the time period in question: 'The question of the constitutional legitimacy of the GNA was moot. All major Western powers dealt with them using 2259 as the legal basis. But the HOR and many Libyan legal experts rejected the GNA because it was not endorsed by the HOR and there was no constitutional amendment.'

40. According to the same former ambassador as of April 2021: 'The GNU now has HOR endorsement but the constitutionality issue is still open for the reasons you state.'

41. UNSCR 2259 drafted by the UK 'welcomes' its signing and endorses it as the basis of future international engagement—essentially making it a part of international law. See UN Security Council, 'Resolution 2259 (2015)', 23 December 2015, https://undocs.org/S/RES/2259(2015)

42. This is a crucial under-appreciated point that I address in: Jason Pack, 'The UN Deliberately (Albeit Mistakenly) Accorded Sovereignty to Post-Gadhafi Libya's Economic Institutions', *MEI Policy Analysis*, 26 September 2019, https://www.mei.edu/publications/un-deliberately-albeit-mistakenly-accorded-sovereignty-post-gadhafi-libyas-economic

43. For the text of the Skhirat Agreement, see UNSMIL, 'Libyan Political Agreement: As Signed on 17 December 2015', https://unsmil.unmissions.org/sites/default/files/Libyan%20Political%20Agreement%20-%20ENG%20.pdf

44. Technical presentation given by GECOL to the author, May 2017.

45. The transition from the Soviet Union to Putin's Russia provides a deep appreciation of this fact.

46. Gustafson, *Wheel of Fortune*.

47. This is an example of a collective action failure and an outcome that the conditions of the Enduring Disorder makes more likely in the wake of new regime changes.

48. In Arabic, institutions or things referred to as an 'entity' (*jihaz or kiyaan*) as opposed to institution (*mu'assa'ssa*) usually have a sinister bent to them—Israel was traditionally referred to in the Arabic media as 'The Zionist Entity' (*al-kiyana al-sihyawniyya*).

49. Biographical details of Ali Dubaiba come from Libya-Analysis LLC proprietary research.

50. Militant Nasserism was common among many high school teachers trained in Libya by Egyptian teachers in the 1950s and 60s. Vandewalle, *History of Libya*, *op cit*.

51. Author interviews with Libyans living in Misrata at the time.

52. ODAC was established by 'General People's Committee Resolution No. 371 of 1989G in Respect of the Establishment of the Office for the Development of Administrative Centers'. And Dubaiba was its first head.

53. March 2021 interview with a leading Libyan businessman.

54. Qadhafian officials did several quick stints in jail to chastise them for corruption. In Russia, many of the country's leading billionaires have gone to jail briefly or had part of their assets seized, only later to re-emerge as key Putin allies. For more, see Gustafson, *Wheel of Fortune*.

55. Ibid.

56. Al-Marsad, المرصد تغوص في امبراطورية ال ادبيبة, 10 June 2016, https://almarsad. co/2016/06/10/%d8%a8%d8%a7%d9%84%d9%85%d8%b3%d8% aa%d9%86%d8%af%d8%a7%d8%aa%d8%b9%d8%b4%d8%b1% d8%a7%d8%aa-%d8%a7%d9%84%d8%b4%d8%b1%d9%83%d8 %a7%d8%aa-%d9%88-%d8%a7%d9%84%d8%b9%d9%82%d8% a7%d8%b1%d8%a7%d8%aa-%d9%88/. Although al-Marsad is generally a suspect source, this article is clearly well informed. However, the author is not in a position to judge the accuracy of all of the statements and documents it presents.

57. This process was discussed in section 1.3 of this chapter's excerpt entitled 'Attempts to Modernize Libya's Economy Only Made Things Worse'.

58. Al-Marsad, علي الدبيبة : يعلن موقفه من الاحداث في طرابلس و يكشف حقيقة نبأ تواصله مع الجيش, 23 April 2019, https://almarsad.co/2019/04/23/%d8%b9% d9%84%d9%8a-%d8%a7%d9%84%d8%af%d8%a8%d9%8a%d8 %a8%d8%a9-%d9%8a%d8%b9%d9%84%d9%86-%d9%85% d9%88%d9%82%d9%81%d9%87-%d9%85%d9%86-%d8%a7%d

9%84%d8%a3%d8%ad%d8%af%d8%a7%d8%ab%d9%81%d9%8a-%d8%b7%d8%b1/

59. Al-Marsad, المرصد تغوص في تغوص في إمبراطورية ال ادبيبة عشرات الشركات والعقارات والمنتجعات الفاخرة

60. Mediapart, Sarkozy–Kadhafi.

61. Ali Dubaiba and Abdul-Hamid Dabaiba are paternal first cousins, in that they share a paternal grandfather; additionally, they are brothers-in-law, as Ali Dubaiba's wife is Abdul-Hamid Dabaiba's sister. This is a type of familial relationship that is encouraged in certain Muslim societies and is thought to be the strongest possible non-nuclear family tie. For more on this complex relationship and its political implications, see *Afrigate News*, 7 معلومات اكتشف الدبيبة السيد عبد من, 5 February 2021, https://www.afrigatenews.net/article/%D8%A7%D9%83%D8%AA%D8%B4%D9%81-8-%D9%85%D8%B9%D9%84%D9%88%D9%85%D8%A7%D8%AA-%D8%B9%D9%86-%D8%B9%D8%A8%D8%AF-%D8%A7%D9%84%D8%AD%D9%85%D9%8A%D8%AF-%D8%A7%D9%84%D8%AF%D8%A8%D9%8A%D8%A8%D8%A9/

62. The correct IJMES transliteration of both their surnames should be Dubaiba, but since the current prime minister of the GNU uses the spelling Dabaiba in his 2021 press releases, I am using that spelling to refer to him while retaining the Dubaiba spelling for his brother-in-law as this is the spelling which ODAC documents from the Qadhafi period tended to employ for him. This will also help readers keep the two figures separate in their minds.

63. Pack, 'Libya Has a New Prime Minister'.

64. *Dar al-Hayah*, اتهامات صادمة بتورط رئيس الحكومة الليبية في قضايا فساد, 9 March 2021, https://darhaya.com/news/2021/03/09/26609/-فساد-قضايا-في-الليبية
اتهامات-صادمة-بتورط-رئيس-الحكومة

65. *Al-Sa'a24*, علي الدبيبة : متهم ببناء امبراطوريته المالية من جيوب الليبيين و البحث عن حصانتها برشاوي الحوار, 16 November 2020, https://www.alsaaa24.com/2020/11/16/
علي-الدبيبة-متهم-ببناء-إمبراطوريته-ال.

66. Letter dated 8 March 2021 from the Panel of Experts on Libya established pursuant to Resolution 1973 (2011) addressed to the president of the Security Council (S/2021/229), http://undocs.org/S/2021/229

67. *Afrigate News*, لماذا تخشى أطراف عدة من خروج حَفَظَة أسرار القذافي إلى النور؟ 20,
February 2018, https://www.afrigatenews.net/article/-النور-إلى-القذافي ار
‏/.لماذا-تخشى-أطراف-عدة-من-خروج-حَفَظَة-أسرار-.

68. Egor Vinogradov, 'Олигархи в России работают, как полицейские под
прикрытием', *Deutsche Welle*, 14 September 2010, https://www.dw.
com/ru/%D0%BE%D0%BB%D0%B8%D0%B3%D0%B0%D1%
80%D1%85%D0%B8-%D0%B2-%D1%80%D0%BE%D1%
81%D1%81%D0%B8%D0%B8-%D1%80%D0%B0%D0%B1%D
0%BE%D1%82%D0%B0%D1%8E%D1%82-%D0%BA%
D0%B0%D0%BA-%D0%BF%D0%BE%D0%BB%D0%B8%D1
%86%D0%B5%D0%B9%D1%81%D0%BA%D0%B8%D0%B5-
%D0%BF%D0%BE%D0%B4-%D0%BF%D1%80%D0%B8%D
0%BA%D1%80%D1%8B%D1%82%D0%B8%D0%B5%D0%B
C/a-6004062

69. Of course, the literature on Ukraine does not use my terminology.
Pseudo-privatized parts of the former Soviet economic institutions in
Ukraine are usually called 'state companies', and the entities that issue
tenders (playing the role of ODAC) are sometimes referred to as parastatal entities. I would argue both are semi-sovereign institutions.
Alternatively, the shell companies used in procurement scams in Ukraine
tend to be referred to as ghost companies, padding firms, or *firmy-prokla-
dky*. These are not semi-sovereigns but their counterparties.

70. *BBC*, 'Ukraine Crisis: Yanukovych and the Tycoons', 11 December
2013, https://www.bbc.com/news/world-europe-25323964

71. *Ukrayinska Pravda*, 'Україна щорічно "дарує" Росії 5 мільярдів
доларів—Азаров' (Ukraine annually 'donates' $ 5 billion to Russia—
Azarov), 16 October 2012, https://www.epravda.com.ua/news/2012/
10/16/339797/

72. Stephen Grey et al., 'Special Report: Putin's Allies Channelled Billions
to Ukraine Oligarch', *Reuters*, 16 November 2014, https://www.reuters.
com/article/russia-capitalism-gas-special-report-pix-idUSL3N0T-
F4QD20141126

73. *International Monetary Fund*, 'Press Release: IMF Executive Board
Concludes 2013 Article IV Consultation, First Post-Program
Monitoring, and Ex Post Evaluation of Exceptional Access with

Ukraine', 19 December 2013, https://www.imf.org/en/News/Articles/2015/09/14/01/49/pr13531

74. For an excellent overview of this incredibly complex process, see Wilson, *Ukraine Crisis*, pp. 45–60.

75. Ibid.

76. *New York Times*, 'U.S. Sanctions Key Ukrainian Oligarch', *New York Times*, 5 March 2021, https://www.nytimes.com/2021/03/05/world/europe/ukraine-sanctions-oligarch-kolomoisky.html

77. According to my interviews in early 2021 with a handful of Libya's most knowledgeable businessmen, the new head of ODAC, the current mayor of Misrata, and certain notable post-Qadhafi actors in Misratan and Tripolitan business circles have all achieved their positions thanks to the Dubaiba clan, and hence, stand ready to help Abdul Hamid during his premiership.

78. Hazem Kandil, *Soldiers, Spies, and Statesmen: Egypt's Road to Revolt* (Verso, 2012).

79. *Reuters Investigates*, 'From War Room to Boardroom: Military Firms Flourish in Sisi's Egypt', 16 May 2018, https://www.reuters.com/investigates/special-report/egypt-economy-military/

80. David Kirkpatrick, 'Named Egypt's Winner, Islamist Makes History', *New York Times*, 25 June 2012, https://www.nytimes.com/2012/06/25/world/middleeast/mohamed-morsi-of-muslim-brotherhood-declared-as-egypts-president.html

81. Muhammed Abdullah, بوفاة مبارك... هل يرث السيسي الدولة العسكرية والعميقة, *al-Jazeera*, 26 February 2020, https://www.aljazeera.net/news/politics/2020/2/26/وفاة-بعد-العميقة-الدولة-السيسي-يرث-هل

82. Nina Schick, *Deep Fakes and the Infocalypse: What You Urgently Need to Know* (Monoray, 2020).

83. March 2021 discussions with New York-based hedge fund owner specializing in Eastern European and Asian markets.

84. Tom Burgis, *The Looting Machine* (Public Affairs, 2015).

85. For an example of this in Guinea, see ibid., pp. 103–30.

86. Rachel Maddow, *Blowout: Corrupted Democracy, Rogue State Russia, and the Richest, Most Destructive Industry on Earth* (Crown, 2019), is one such example.

87. Esteban Ortiz-Ospina and Diana Beltekian, 'Trade and Globalization', *Our World in Data*, 2018, https://ourworldindata.org/trade-and-globalization

88. Obviously, there are a few exceptions, mostly in sub-Saharan Africa where kleptocratic behaviour has become a part of the social contract—so expected by the populace that it can be done in the open without eliciting significant push back. Burgis, *Looting Machine*.

89. I am supposedly one of the few world experts on these cases, and yet after years of well paid and rigorous due diligence work, I do not truly understand all the relevant intricacies. That said, if the reader has a layman's interest in these cases, I suggest consulting, Chris Wright, 'Libyan Plot Thickens for Goldman with Palladyne "Money-Laundering" Suit', *EuroMoney*, 28 March 2014, https://www.euromoney.com/article/b12kjy0qznf4qq/libyan-plot-thickens-for-goldman-with-palladyne-money-laundering-suit; Mirza Manraj, 'Cayman Court Provides Valuable Guidance on Dealing with Frozen Assets under Libyan Sanctions', *Harneys*, 17 May 2019, https://www.harneys.com/insights/cayman-court-provides-valuable-guidance-on-dealing-with-frozen-assets-under-libyan-sanctions; Kit Chellel and Matthew Campbell, 'Goldman Sachs Wins Suit Over $1.2 Billion Libyan Fund Losses', *Bloomberg*, 14 October 2016, https://www.bloomberg.com/news/articles/2016-10-14/goldman-sachs-wins-libya-investment-funds-1-2-billion-lawsuit

90. Not much about this episode is present in the public domain, but some interesting summaries can be found on the Bulgarian investigative charity website www.Bivol.bg, such as, *Bivol*, 'Greece Annuls Apostille for Tanker *Badr*'s Fake Mortgage', 11 December 2019, https://bivol.bg/en/greece-annuls-apostille-for-tanker-badrs-fake-mortgage.html

91. Ahmed Sanussi, فلوسنا (Our money), episode 22, *Al Wasat TV*, 1 June 2020, https://www.youtube.com/watch?v=IxtQoODLlnI. Mr Ahmed Sanussi, a prominent Libyan TV host, interviewed the general manager of Libya's semi-sovereign shipping company, the General National Maritime Transport Company (GNMTC), Mr Khalid Al Tawati; Mr Mohamed Al Ahrash, the head of the insurance and compensation unit within GNMTC; and Mr Mohamed Al Dani, head of the

legal unit at the GNMTC. They discussed many of the possible theories of the BADR case and the possibility of complicity among GNTMC, other parts of the Libyan parastatal system, and various European commercial and criminal entities.

92. Bullough, *Moneyland*.
93. For insights into how corruption, patronage, and the resource industries work in the Congo and Angola as well as how dysfunctional economic arrangements pervert third parties who interact with them, see Burgis, *Looting Machine*, especially pp. 74–5.
94. If you are wondering, why dictators' toddlers have *actually* been known to ask their parents' friends for more BVI shell companies and not chocolate cake, puppies, gold bars, or even Swiss bank accounts, there are many quite rational reasons. Some of them are explained here: Noah Friedman and Alana Kakoyiannis, 'How the Super-Wealthy Hide Billions Using Tax Havens and Shell Companies', *Business Insider*, 17 September 2019, https://www.businessinsider.com/jake-bernstein-panama-papers-offshore-banking-shell-companies-2018–2; Stephanie Baker, 'Sun, Sand, and the $1.5 Trillion Offshore Economy', *Bloomberg Businessweek*, 10 July 2019, https://www.bloomberg.com/news/features/2019-07-03/the-bvi-s-struggle-to-protect-its-offshore-economy; Bullough, *Moneyland*.
95. Vandewalle, *Libya since Independence*; Vandewalle, *Libya since 1969*.
96. If you want to see a few of the buildings ODAC has commissioned and how it promoted itself, see https://www.odac.ly/%d9%85%d8%b4%d8%a7%d8%b1%d9%8a%d8%b9-%d8%aa%d9%85-%d8%aa%d9%86%d9%81%d9%8a%d8%b0%d9%87%d8%a7/#
97. Thanks to Tim Eaton for sharing this observation about how the macroeconomically sound provisions of Qadhafian Libyan law necessitated these structures' existence as officially outside the state's formal remit for such massive spending campaigns to be enacted off the state's official books, hence avoiding the strict debt-to-GDP ratio provisions enacted by the Qadhafi regime.
98. See 'Austria–Libya BIT', *Juris Legal Information*, June 2002, https://arbitrationlaw.com/library/austria-libya-bit
99. Legal cases where the semi-sovereigns and the Libyan state, which was

acting on their behalf, have been exonerated include Way2B vs ODAC, Oztach Turkish Company vs LIA, Before Trading Offshore vs State of Libya. For more on this phenomenon, see *Menas Associates*, 'Libya's Commercial Arbitration Winning Streak', 10 June 2018, https://www.menas.co.uk/blog/libya-wins-two-commercial-arbitration/

100. Rather than being perplexed over their behaviour, there is an argument that most of the international companies with back payment issues in Libya have acted rationally. According to a May 2020 interview with a former US Commerce Department official who oversaw the North Africa portfolio: 'The average Western construction company spent a few years after the revolution spending small amounts of money seeking to get the Libyan state to pay them large amounts of money. Then after the Libyan civil war broke out in 2014, they gave up and left. Hence, when the dust settled, all of the arbitration cases which broke out after 2015. Yet, some construction and project management companies (including American ones) have not sued and still dream of restarting their projects, because the initial contracts are so lucrative that even if the companies have racked up tens of millions of dollars of loses over the last decade, those can all be recouped if the projects are ever restarted on the terms initially contracted.'

101. On the eve of the First World War, many major British and French investment houses were loath for the allies to invade the Ottoman Empire, even after it declared war on the Triple Entente. They lobbied strongly against the invasion as they were simply owned too much Ottoman debt and did not want to run the risk that they might never get their money back in a post-Ottoman world.

102. For a clinical definition consult, Ana Gotter, 'Battered Woman Syndrome,' *Healthline*, 6 May 2021, https://www.healthline.com/health/battered-woman-syndrome. Fundamentally, the phenomenon has to do with psychological entrapment by an incumbent power holder.

103. Ben Bartenstein et al., 'One Country, Nine Defaults: Argentina Is Caught in a Vicious Cycle', *Bloomberg*, 24 May 2020, https://www.

bloomberg.com/news/photo-essays/2019–09–11/one-country-eight-defaults-the-argentine-debacles

104. One could even assert that there is an interagency conspiracy to defraud foreign companies who are owed back payments, and the 2014 and 2015 Libyan Audit Bureau reports establish and document 'motive' and 'intent' on behalf of HIB and ODAC to not pay outstanding debts and to find a rationale for other institutions of the Libyan government to deny payment or deny the existence of legitimate debt. For a telling example in English, see 2014 Libyan AB report, sections 51–9, http://audit.gov.ly/home/pdf/EN-LABR-2014.pdf

105. Pack and Pusztai, 'Turning the Tide'.

106. Ibid.

107. Maddow, *Blowout*.

108. Zygar, *All the Kremlin's Men*.

109. Wilson, *Ukraine Crisis*.

110. When I was first sent to Libya in 2008 to work for a consulting company trying to help in overseeing the reform of the Libyan economy, my direct boss was an Oxford-educated American who was a fluent Russian-speaker that had worked in Moscow in the 1990s trying to help the Russian government with privatization, while his boss's boss was a former Harvard economist who had worked in Kiev and Moscow on similar issues.

111. Nadav Safran, *Saudi Arabia: The Ceaseless Quest for Security* (Cornell University Press, 1998).

112. Pack, 'How Libya's Economic Structures Enrich the Militias'.

113. Burgis, *Looting Machine, op cit*.

114. Brian Klaas, *Corruptible* (Simon & Schuster, forthcoming), https://www.simonandschuster.com/authors/Brian-Klaas/172306477

115. John Darwin, *The Empire Project: The Rise and Fall of the British World-System, 1830–1970* (Cambridge University Press, 2009); K. Mantena, *Alibis of Empire: Henry Maine and the Ends of Liberal Imperialism* (Princeton University Press, 2010).

116. 'Trade in Goods with Russia', US Census Bureau, https://www.census.gov/foreign-trade/balance/c4621.html and https://www.census.gov/foreign-trade/balance/c4610.html

117. 'Trade in Goods with United Arab Emirates', US Census Bureau, https://www.census.gov/foreign-trade/balance/c5200.html#1985

118. For more on the salience of those investments, see UAE Embassy in the USA, 'UAE–US Economic Relationship', n.d., https://www.uae-embassy.org/uae-us-relations/key-areas-bilateral-cooperation/uae-us-economic-relationship

119. Although it is less frequently discussed, the research surrounding the Mueller Report suggested that Emirati influence may have had an even larger impact than any other foreign actor excluding Russia. Jon Gambrell, 'Powerful Emirati Crown Prince Entangled by Mueller Report', *AP*, 19 April 2019, https://www.bloomberg.com/news/articles/mueller-report-uae-crown-prince

120. Joseph Schumpeter, *Capitalism, Socialism, and Democracy* (Sublime Books, 2015); Schumpeter, *Essays: On Entrepreneurs, Innovations, Business Cycles and the Evolution of Capitalism* (Routledge, 2017).

121. Robert Reich, *Saving Capitalism: For the Many, Not the Few* (Vintage, 2016); Reich, *The System: Who Rigged It, How We Fix It* (Knopf, 2020).

5. THE US–LIBYA (ANTI-)BUSINESS ASSOCIATION

1. Pack, 'Engagement in Libya Was and Remains the Right Answer'.

2. For an excellent overview of the Libyan pipeline grid, and the work that is needed to upgrade it to twenty-first-century standards, please consult Hassan S. Hassan and Christopher Kendall, 'History and Future of the Petroleum Industry in Libya', *SEPM Strata*, 2008, http://www.sepmstrata.org/page.aspx?pageid=152; as of 2021, the rusting of infrastructure and damages caused by stopping and starting due to blockades means that tens of billions of dollars more work is actually needed than Hassan and Kendall describe.

3. Gurney, *Libya*; Frank C. Waddams, *The Libyan Oil Industry* (Croom Helm, 1980).

4. Relative to 2010, more than a million guest worker jobs have already been lost due to Libya's implosion. If we also count new Libyan jobs and those who produce the goods or services for importation into the

Libyan market, the number of jobs that a booming Libyan economy would create is more than three million—quite impressive for a country with under six million citizens. This phenomenon is carried to its greatest extreme in Qatar—a country of roughly 300,000 citizens—that creates over two million jobs inside Qatar and over five million jobs globally.

5. Ghassan Salamé, 'Libya and the New Global Disorder: A Conversation with Ghassan Salamé', *Carnegie Endowment Webinar*, 15 October 2020, https://carnegieendowment.org/2020/10/15/libya-and-new-global-disorder-conversation-with-ghassan-salam-event-7439

6. Ibid.

7. Morgan Downey, *Oil 101* (Wooden Table, 2019); Daniel Yergin, *The Prize: The Epic Quest for Oil, Money & Power* (Free Press, 1991).

8. See the USLBA website at www.us-lba.org

9. Although USLBA advocated only for American businesses, most of these corporate behemoths had London offices as well and could represent themselves as British businesses when it was advantageous for them to do so.

10. That is an era in which incumbent powerholders sought to block the kind of coherent collective action that they perceived as threatening their inherited privileges.

11. It was a contract between me and a third party, the National Foreign Trade Council, to be offered employment by that third party and then be seconded to USLBA through an arrangement that violated USLBA's own bylaws.

12. David Montero, *Kickback: Exposing the Global Corporate Bribery Network* (Viking, 2018).

13. Alexandra Stevenson, 'Och-Ziff to Pay Over $400 Million in Bribery Settlement', *New York Times*, 29 September 2016, https://www.nytimes.com/2016/09/30/business/dealbook/och-ziff-bribery-settlement.html

14. Montero, *Kickback*.

15. Ronald Bruce St John, *Libya and the United States: Two Centuries of Strife* (University of Pennsylvania Press, 2002).

16. Polybius, *The Histories*, trans. Robin Waterfield (Oxford University Press, 2010).

17. Nearly all ancient historians were actually participants in the events they sought to describe. Their contemporaries would have considered them lacking in credibility if they were not. Thucydides, most frequently thought of as the father of history, was an active participant at the leadership level in the Peloponnesian Wars, about which he writes. However, he does not bring a psychological or institutional perspective to his investigation of causation nor does he focus on trying to understand 'the world system' the way that Polybius does. It is also well established that Polybius self-consciously draws upon themes from both Herodotus and Thucydides, seeking to synthesize and systematize their specific techniques into a comprehensive historical method. As such, Polybius himself claims to be the first global historian. Christopher Smith and Liv Mariah Yarrow (eds), *Imperialism, Cultural Politics, & Polybius*, (Oxford University Press, 2012).

18. Sadly, there are too many examples one could mention here, but the death of my fellow PhD candidate in the Cambridge History Department Giulio Regeni in Egypt at the hands of regime thugs is a famous example of a grad student being accused of being a spy who was clearly not. Over the years, the Iranians have held scores of journalists (famously Jason Reziaian, Nicolas Pelham, and Nazanin Zaghari-Ratcliffe), accusing them of spying even though in most cases it was obvious that they were not. The regimes and militias seemingly engage in this behaviour to cow those who might write unfavourable portrayals of them, something they are not afraid business executives or lobbyists will do.

19. This is not a common practice at comparable trade associations, but it is certainly within the board's legal purview, just as under American or British law it is legally allowed for any kind of member's club to allow current members to 'blackball' prospective members, so long as they do not do so on grounds like race, sexual orientation, or religion.

20. Jason Pack, 'Donald Trump: Welfare Queen of the Casino Economy', *Al Jazeera English*, 5 November 2016, https://www.aljazeera.com/indepth/opinion/2016/11/donald-trump-casino-business-161103115701497.html

21. Slight changes in optics have a way of snowballing in a fluid environment like Libya. Knowing this, USLBA was initially set up to get the ball rolling in ways that would provide key pushes when needed to get the American and Libyan governments to overcome their reluctance to engage with each other. In the first stages of the détente period with the Qadhafi regime (2005–8), that involved drumming up interest in Congress for getting Libya off the terrorism list. Then after that was achieved, it morphed to helping Libyan officials create public events and government meetings in Washington, as they largely lacked the capacity to do that themselves. In the post-Qadhafi period, when the Libyan embassy was already a respected player in Washington and mostly capable of arranging its own public events, Congressional outreach, and US government meetings, USLBA's primary value add for the US–Libya relationship should have been trade missions and ensuing B2G matchmaking.

22. Brian M. Pollins, 'Does Trade Still Follow the Flag?', *American Political Science Review* 83, no. 2 (June 1989), pp. 465–80, https://www.cambridge.org/core/journals/american-political-science-review/article/does-trade-still-follow-the-flag/8F689BC164FD2639715AA2D4651F09D9

23. Jack Gallagher and Ronald Robinson, *Africa and the Victorians: The Official Mind of Imperialism* (Macmillan, 1961); 'The Imperialism of Free Trade', *Economic History Review* 6, no. 1 (1953); Wm. Roger Louis and Ronald Robinson, *Imperialism: The Robinson and Gallagher Controversy* (New Viewpoints, 1976).

24. I have put 'exports' in quotes as pertains to the potential trade mission, as most USLBA member companies did not plan to make traditional exports to Libya. Usually, they either produced oil there or had previously managed projects for the Libyans or provided security services for other Western firms. Actual exports to Libya were the preserve of more normal firms that created physical things. Even the member companies who did manufacture were generally not concerned with directly selling them to the Libyans. They were concerned with collecting on back payments they were previously owed. Hence, when meeting with US government officials, I chose not to mention that (1) the only money

that would directly change hands as a result of the trade mission would be back payments, and (2) it is nearly impossible to conceive collecting a back payment for a service partially rendered a decade ago as promoting US exports.

25. See the 'About Events' sections of the LBBC website: https://lbbc.org.uk/about-events/

26. Bringing Qadhafi in from the cold after he paid off the Lockerbie families so that US sanctions could be lifted and the big American oil companies could return to their consortia and concessions.

27. Paul Barker, 'The Development of Libyan Industry', in John Anthony Allan (ed.), *Libya since Independence: Economic and Political Development* (Croom Helm, 1982), pp. 56–69; Ronald Bruce St John, 'The Libyan Economy in Transition: Opportunities and Challenges', in Vandewalle, *Libya since 1969*; Marie-Louise Gumuchian, 'Security Concerns Worsen for Oil Firms in Libya', *Reuters*, 20 September 2012 http://in.reuters.com/article/2012/09/20/libya-oil-attack-idINL5E8KJID220120920; Marie-Louise Gumuchian and Ali Shuaib, 'Libya Sees Return to Pre-War Oil Output in October', *Reuters*, 26 July 2012, http://www.reuters.com/article/2012/07/26/ozabs-libya-oil-idAFJOE86P03H20120726; *Reuters*, 'Shell Abandons Oil Exploration on Two Libya Blocks', 29 May 2012, http://www.reuters.com/article/2012/05/29/libya-oil-shell-exploration-idAFL5E8GTA7720120529

28. Lin Noueihed, 'Exxon to Cut Back Libya Presence as Security Crumbles', *Reuters*, 17 September 2013, https://www.reuters.com/article/libya-exxonmobil/exxon-to-cut-back-libya-presence-as-security-crumbles-idUSL5N0HD1UM20130917

29. In March 2018, Marathon Petroleum sold their 2/11ths share in the Waha Consortium to French supermajor TOTAL for $450 million. Commodities experts have told me that 1.3 billion euros would have been a fairer price, but none of the other supermajors had the desire or political backing to go into Libya, so TOTAL was able to benefit from a buyer's market. Independent of the price, America's long-term geostrategic and commercial position in North Africa was meaningfully weakened. Olivia Pulsinelli, 'Marathon Oil Exits Libya with $450M Divestiture', *Houston Business Journal*, 2 March 2018, https://

www.bizjournals.com/houston/news/2018/03/02/marathon-oil-exits-libya-with-450m-divestiture.html; James Cockayne, 'Waha: Total Says Done & Dusted, Libya Thinks Otherwise', *MEES* 61, no. 17 (27 April 2018), https://www.mees.com/2018/4/27/oil-gas/waha-total-says-done-dusted-libya-thinks-otherwise/6a570f00-4a2c-11e8-a8d7-c3457fd81613

30. Or even to push Washington to marry commercial strategies with the guidelines of national interest. Fascinatingly, the two biggest oil deals of the last decade done by ExxonMobil, the world's largest oil company, in both Russia and the KRG, can be said to have undermined US diplomatic positions. This lack of coordination is part and parcel of the Enduring Disorder.

31. Throughout his business career, Trump has shown himself to be the very epitome of a zero-sum thinker, who wishes to protect privileged access, extract rents, and screw potential partners. Jason Pack, 'Donald Trump: Welfare queen of the casino economy,' *Al Jazeera English*, 5 Novemver 2016, https://www.aljazeera.com/indepth/opinion/2016/11/donald-trump-casino-business-161103115701497.html

32. Samantha Gross, "Why there's no bringing coal back," *Brookings Institution*, 16 January 2019, https://www.brookings.edu/blog/planetpolicy/2019/01/16/why-theres-no-bringing-coal-back/

33. *White House Statement*, 'President Biden to Sign Executive Order Strengthening Buy American Provisions, Ensuring Future of America Is Made in America by All of America's Workers', 25 January 2021, https://www.whitehouse.gov/briefing-room/statements-releases/2021/01/25/president-biden-to-sign-executive-order-strengthening-buy-american-provisions-ensuring-future-of-america-is-made-in-america-by-all-of-americas-workers/

34. Coca-Cola, Walmart, Hallmark, Amazon, Airbnb, Disney, and Mastercard are just a few examples of corporate titans who stopped donating to certain Republicans in response to the Capitol Hill riot. Gareth Hutchens, 'Corporate Donors Flee Republican Party following Capitol Hill Riot, and It's Only the Beginning', *Australian Broadcasting Corporation*, 15 January 2021, https://www.abc.net.au/news/2021–01–16/us-political-donations-dry-up-after-capitol-insurrection/13062376

35. Kevin Stankiewicz and Emma Newburger, 'U.S. Companies Face Boycott Threats, Mounting Pressure to Take Sides in America's Voting Rights Battle', *CNBC*, 3 April 2021, https://www.cnbc.com/2021/04/03/georgia-texas-gop-election-laws-us-companies-face-pressure-to-oppose.html

36. Robert Kuttner, *Can Democracy Survive Global Capitalism?* (W.W. Norton, 2019).

37. Gustafson, *Wheel of Fortune*; Maddow, *Blowout*; Zygar, *All the Kremlin's Men*.

38. How to conduct audits and to promote transparency in Libya is dealt with in the 'What the International Community Can Do' and 'Conclusions and the Way Forward' sections of Pack, 'It's the Economy Stupid'.

39. As mentioned in Pack, 'It's the Economy Stupid', this step can be done prior to the convening of the convention if achieving requisite buy-in from stakeholders proves impossible.

40. Eaton, 'Libya'.

41. Pack, 'Introduction'.

42. Pack, 'It's the Economy Stupid'.

43. Pack, 'UN Deliberately (Albeit Mistakenly) Accorded Sovereignty to Post-Qadhafi Libya's Economic Institutions'.

44. Jason Pack, 'How to End Libya's War', *New York Times*, 21 January 2015, https://www.nytimes.com/2015/01/22/opinion/how-to-end-libyas-war.html

45. Christopher M. Blanchard, 'Libya: Transition and U.S. Policy', *Congressional Research Service*, 2 May 2018, https://fas.org/sgp/crs/row/RL33142.pdf

46. Pack, 'UN Deliberately (Albeit Mistakenly) Accorded Sovereignty to Post-Qadhafi Libya's Economic Institutions'.

47. S.L. Bills, *The Libyan Arena: The United States, Britain and the Council of Foreign Ministers, 1945–1948* (Kent State University Press, 1995); Adrian Pelt, *Libyan Independence and the United Nations: A Case of Planned Decolonization* (Yale University Press, 1970).

48. Mediapart, *Sarkozy–Kadhafi*.

49. Tim Eaton, 'Libya Needs an Economic Commission to Exit From Violence', Chatham House Expert Comment, 20 November 2019,

https://www.chathamhouse.org/expert/comment/libya-needs-economic-commission-exit-violence
50. Ibid.

CONCLUSION: QUO VADIS?

1. The reader is also free to consider disorder as a positive or to argue the controversial position that global disorder is beneficial for incumbent powers, in specific, and all of humanity, in general, as it destroys inefficient regimes and promotes innovation. The latter argument has been put forward by the former American military officer, Ralph Peters, who wrote in 2001 that 'Historically, instability abroad has been to America's advantage...' despite the irony that 'the consistent, pervasive goal of Washington's foreign policy [had been] stability'. This volume strongly disagrees with Ralph Peters' argument: that instability abroad somehow benefits American and Western long-term interests. I do however agree with Peters that a kind of status quo paralysis and incumbent psychology has gripped many American diplomats since the end of the Cold War. We both see this paralysis as not beneficial to securing American interests as its practitioners assume that current conditions can be made to last indefinitely. Ralph Peters, 'Stability, America's Enemy', *The US Army War College Quarterly: Parameters*, Volume 31, Number 4, 2001.

2. John Micklethwait and Adrian Wooldridge, *The Wake Up Call: Why the Pandemic Has Exposed the Weakness of the West; And How to Fix It* (Short Books, 2020), pp. 103–21.

3. Brad Roberts (ed.), *Order and Disorder after the Cold War* (MIT Press, 1995); see also McFate, *Goliath*, pp. 247–8. Roberts's concept of 'durable disorder' is slightly different from this book's version of Enduring Disorder but highly relevant to this discussion.

4. Roland Bleiker, 'Order and Disorder in World Politics', in Alex J. Bellamy (ed.), *International Society and Its Critics* (Oxford University Press, 2004).

5. For Hegel, history, despite apparent set-backs, is a continual process of humanity achieving ever greater levels of self-consciousness, which Hegel understood as freedom.

6. Giambattista Vico was an eighteenth-century Italian philologist and pro-

lific author. He is widely thought to be the founder of the discipline of the philosophy of history. He believed that each historical era was defined by its own patterns of thought or unique psychology which affected the decision-makers operating in that era. For Vico, such mindsets inherently bring about counterreactions. Hence, historical periods evolve cyclically and dialectically cause their opposites. Hence in a Viconian sense, the psychology underpinning the Enduring Disorder could suddenly come to an end because it has caused its opposite due to the cyclical nature of history and sociology. That 'incumbent psychology', which is at the very root of the Enduring Disorder, may eventually give rise to an opposite way of thinking. G.W. Trompf, 'Vico's Universe: La Provvedenza and la Poesia in the New Science of Giambattista Vico', *British Journal for the History of Philosophy*, 2, no. 1 (1994), pp. 55–86.

7. For an excellent overview of the Extinction Rebellion movement and the ways it touched on themes of global collective action, see Cameron Joshi and Boden Franklin, 'Extinction Rebellion: In or Out?', *New Internationalist*, 5 December 2018, https://newint.org/features/2018/12/05/extinction-rebellion-%E2%80%93-or-out

8. For a similar approach to the Black Lives Matter protests in the wake of the killing of George Floyd, consult, *Association of Psychological Science*, 'Collective Action and Black Lives Matter', 11 June 2020, https://www.psychologicalscience.org/publications/observer/obsonline/collective-action-and-black-lives-matter.html

9. It is rooted on track records, intuition, and trend analysis. See David Staley, *Alternative Universities: Speculative Design for Innovation in Higher Education* (Johns Hopkins University Press, 2019); Tetlock and Gardner, *Superforecasting*.

10. Deepfakes are digital forgeries of videos or voice recordings. They can be used to make a given politician or leader appear to say something that she/he never said. Schick, *Deep Fakes*.

11. Thanks to Ambassador Peter Millett for an interesting discussion on this point in November 2020.

12. Haass, *World in Disarray*; McFate, *Goliath*; Van Creveld, *Rise and Decline of the State*; Yuval Harari, *Homo Deus: A Brief History of Tomorrow* (HarperCollins, 2018).

13. Schumpeter correctly argued that such a claim would naturally be the myth of incumbent powerhouses. Schumpeter, *Capitalism, Socialism, and Democracy*; Schumpeter, *Essays*.

14. Karl Polanyi, *The Great Transformation* (Penguin, 2001).

15. Reich, *Saving Capitalism*; Reich, *System*.

16. Jason Pack, 'The Hungary Model: Resurgent Nationalism', *National Interest*, 8 October 2015, https://nationalinterest.org/feature/the-hungary-model-resurgent-nationalism-14025

17. This observation has been echoed by Emile Simpson, *War from the Ground Up: Twenty-First Century Combat as Politics* (Hurst, 2018); McFate, *Goliath*.

18. This view is in line with the provocative argument in René Girard, *Battling to the End* (Michigan State University Press, 2009). Thanks to Dr Karl Karim Zakhour for this thought-provoking observation.

19. Haass, *World in Disarray*.

20. For more on why the Chinese take this approach, please see pages xlvi–liv of the Preface.

21. 'Timeline of WHO's Response to COVID-19', WHO, https://www.who.int/news-room/detail/29-06-2020-covidtimeline

22. Ikenberry, *America Unrivaled*.

23. For a magisterial overview of the concept of the 'balance of power' in guiding British foreign policy formation as well as the psychological underpinnings of the concept, see T.G. Otte, *The Foreign Office Mind: The Making of British Foreign Policy, 1865–1914* (Cambridge University Press, 2011).

24. Michael Sheehan, *Balance of Power* (Routledge, 1996).

25. Not all IR theories/frameworks (e.g. constructivism) view states or the people ruling them as rational actors. However, in general, realist IR theory treat states as 'rational actors' that attempt to maximize their interests, just as traditional economists view individuals as rational actors who try to maximize their utility.

26. Richard H. Thaler, *Misbehaving: The Making of Behavioral Economics* (W.W. Norton, 2016).

27. Michelle Baddeley, *Behavioural Economics: A Very Short Introduction* (Oxford University Press, 2017).

28. Some have embraced the new way of thinking; others have fought rear-guard actions to cling on to the established ways.

29. See McFate, *Goliath*, p. 246.

30. Yemen's, Syria's, and Libya's post-Arab Spring conflicts simply couldn't have played out as slow-moving state implosions decades ago. The Americans and Soviets might have back opposing sides in those conflicts, but they would have forbidden medium powers from occupying the position of dominant intervenors and would have stepped in to fill vacuums of authority.

31. Ceslav Ciobanu, *Frozen and Forgotten Conflicts in the Post-Soviet States: Genesis, Political Economy, and Prospects for Solution* (Columbia University Press, 2010).

32. That is to say, they are nowhere near China, and the world is no longer divided into two overarching alliances.

33. Thomas A. Schwartz, *Henry Kissinger and American Power: A Political Biography* (Hill and Wang, 2020); Niall Ferguson, *Colossus: The Rise and Fall of the American Empire* (Penguin, 2004).

34. In the future, other coalitions of states (e.g. a coalition of India, Australia, Japan, and the NATO countries designed to constrain China) may play a similar role, but there is as of yet no successful precedent in the modern period.

35. Commentators have postulated that the meeting in Alaska between National Security Advisor Jake Sullivan and Secretary of State Antony Blinken and their Chinese counterparts represents the high-water mark of tensions between China and the USA since the Nixon administration. Nahal Toosi, 'China and U.S. Open Alaska Meeting with Undiplomatic War of Words', *Politico*, 18 March 2021, https://www.politico.com/news/2021/03/18/china-us-alaska-meeting-undiplomatic-477118

36. Lawrence Wright, 'Crossroads: A Scholar of the Plague Thinks That Pandemics Wreak Havoc—and Open Minds', *New Yorker*, 20 July 2020.

37. Haass, *World in Disarray*, pp. 56–70.

38. He happens to have gotten Spanish Influenza at the Versailles conference and then never recovered his former capacity or will to coordinate the international system. For more on this fascinating episode, see

Laura Spinney, *Pale Rider: The Spanish Flu of 1918 and How It Changed the World* (Public Affairs, 2017).

39. Ikenberry, *America Unrivaled*.

40. Tetlock and Gardner, *Superforecasting*.

AFTERWORD

1. Jonathan M. Winer served as the former US Special Envoy for Libya, 2014–2017. He is a Non-Resident Scholar at the Middle East Institute.

2. Paolo Pizzolo, 'The Greed versus Grievance Theory and the 2011 Libyan Civil War: Why grievance offers a wider perspective for understanding the conflict outbreak,' *Small Wars Journal*, 28 October 2020, https://smallwarsjournal.com/jrnl/art/greed-versus-grievance-theory-and-2011-libyan-civil-war-why-grievance-offers-wider. Pizzolo argues that greed played little part in the Uprisings, that the main motivators were various forms of legitimate grievance, including over lack of political rights, nepotism, and corruption, as well as economics. That finding does not suggest, however, that greed has not played an increasingly significant role in the post-Qadhafi period. In 2019–2021, getting established interest groups to give up the revenue streams they had accumulated during the transition remained a major obstacle to progress on political reform.

3. International sanctions imposed on Libya mainly hit its poorer citizens and widened the gap between rich and poor there, Alison Parteger, *Libya: The Rise and Fall of Qaddafi*, (Yale, 2012), pp. 172–3.

4. *Middle East Monitor*, 'UAE and the Muslim Brotherhood: A Story of Rivalry and Hatred,' 14 June 2017, https://www.middleeastmonitor.com/20170615-uae-and-the-muslim-brotherhood-a-story-of-rivalry-and-hatred/

5. On the competition between Saudi Arabia and Iran for power and legitimacy in and around the Gulf see for example Fozia Lubna Abid Ali, 'Iran-Saudi Relations: From Rivalry to Nowhere,' *Global Social Sciences Review*, October 2018, https://pdfs.semanticscholar.org/1888/7888ef35 2162f8df2a2af0e731daf2fc266a.pdf; Luíza Gimenez Cerioli, 'Roles and International Behaviour: Saudi–Iranian Rivalry in Bahrain's and Yemen's

Arab Spring,' *Contexto Internacional*, vol. 40(2), May/Aug 2018, https://www.scielo.br/pdf/cint/v40n2/0102-8529-cint-2018400200295.pdf

6. Erin Cunningham and Heba Habib, 'Video shows purported beheading of Egyptian Christians in Libya,' *The Washington Post*, 15 February 2015, https://www.washingtonpost.com/world/middle_east/video-shows-purported-beheading-of-egyptian-christians-in-libya/2015/02/15/b8d0f092-b548-11e4-bc30-a4e75503948a_story.html

7. Anas Gomati, 'Haftar's Rebranded Coups,' *Carnegie Endowment*, 30 July 2019, https://carnegieendowment.org/sada/79579 discusses how Haftar built a patronage system modelled in part on Qadhafi's approach.

8. For a detailed, early account of the Qatari role in Libya, see Sam Dagher, Charles Levinson, and Margaret Coker 'Tiny Kingdom's Huge Role in Libya Draws Concern,' 17 October 2011, *The Wall Street Journal*, https://www.wsj.com/articles/SB100014240529702040023045766270 0922764650. For an assessment of how its Libyan operations fit into the broader goals of Qatari foreign policy see Lina Khatib, 'Qatar's foreign policy: the limits of pragmatism,' *International Affairs*, 89:2, 2013, https://academic.oup.com/ia/article/89/2/417/2535108. Ms. Khatib's article also examines multiple possible motivations for Qatar's involvement in Libya, including: its goal of appealing to and exercising leverage on the international community; sustaining its leading regional position as a mediator among competing Islamist groups; providing support as a form of outreach and engagement that can prevent enmities through cooptation; sustaining its leading role with Muslim Brotherhood-related groups in the MENA region; maintaining its influence with related rebel groups in Syria; as well as demonstrating its strength and independence from Saudi Arabia. Notably, none of these objectives focused on what might be in the best long-term interests of Libya, and whether the continued provision of arms was consistent with those interests.

9. David B. Roberts, 'Reflecting on Qatar's "Islamist" Soft Power,' *Brookings Institution*, April 2019, https://www.brookings.edu/wp-content/uploads/2019/04/FP_20190408_qatar_roberts.pdf

10. David Kirkpatrick, 'Recordings Suggest Emirates and Egyptian Military Pushed Ousting of Morsi,' *The New York Times*, 1 March 2015, https://

www.nytimes.com/2015/03/02/world/middleeast/recordings-suggest-emirates-and-egyptian-military-pushed-ousting-of-morsi.html

11. Chris Stephen, 'Libya accuses Khartoum of flying weapons to Islamist rebels in Tripoli,' *The Guardian*, 7 September 2014, https://www.theguardian.com/world/2014/sep/07/libya-khartoum-weapons-islamist-rebels and 'Final report of the Panel of Experts on Libya regarding the implementation of the measures related to the arms embargo, the assets freeze and the travel ban,' pursuant to resolution 1973 (2011), S/2015/128, 23 February 2015 https://www.securitycouncilreport.org/atf/cf/%7B65BFCF9B-6D27-4E9C-8CD3-CF6E4FF96FF9%7D/s_2015_128.pdf

12. *Deutsche Welle*, 'Libya Prime Minister Abdullah al-Thinni survives assassination attempt,' 26 May 2015, https://www.dw.com/en/libya-prime-minister-abdullah-al-thinni-survives-assassination-attempt/a-18477700; see also Jonathan M. Winer, 'Origins Of The Libyan Conflict and Options For Its Resolution,' *Middle East Institute*, Policy Paper 2019–12, May 2019, pp. 12–13, https://www.mei.edu/sites/default/files/2019–05/Libya_Winer_May%202019%20update_0.pdf

13. Missy Ryan and Hassan Morajea, 'In Libya, trying to make one government out of two,' *The Washington Post*, 18 September 2015, https://www.washingtonpost.com/world/national-security/in-libya-trying-to-make-one-government-out-of-two/2015/09/18/4c50627e-5d6b-11e5-9757-e49273f05f65_story.html

14. Issandr El Amran, 'How Much of Libya Does the Islamic State Control?,' i, 18 February 2016, https://foreignpolicy.com/2016/02/18/how-much-of-libya-does-the-islamic-state-control/

15. See e.g. Julian Hattem, 'Benghazi panel criticizes Clinton's actions in new 800-page report,' *The Hill*, 28 June 2016, https://thehill.com/policy/national-security/285126-benghazi-committee-releases-800-page-report-bringing-close-to-long and Dan Merica, 'Another GOP congressman says Benghazi panel meant to hurt Clinton,' *CNN*, 14 October 2015, https://www.cnn.com/2015/10/14/politics/hillary-clinton-benghazi-committee/index.html

16. See e.g., *The Economist*, 'Libya's government and the militias—Is the tide turning? The defeat of an Islamist militia raises hope that law and

order may return,' 15 June 2013, https://www.economist.com/middle-east-and-africa/2013/06/15/is-the-tide-turning

17. Alison Pargeter, 'Haftar, Tribal Power, And The Battle For Libya,' *War on the Rocks*, 15 May 2020, https://warontherocks.com/2020/05/haftar-tribal-power-and-the-battle-for-libya/

18. Amanda Kadlec, 'Dignity Battles The Dawn: The Complex Web Of Libya's Civil War,' *War on the Rocks*, 14 August 2014, https://warontherocks.com/2014/08/dignity-battles-the-dawn-the-complex-web-of-libyas-civil-war/

19. 'President Obama: Libya aftermath "worst mistake" of presidency,' 11 April 2016, BBC, https://www.bbc.com/news/world-us-canada-36013703, citing his statement to Mike Wallace on FOX News.

20. See e.g. Allen J. Kuperman, 'Obama's Libya Debacle, How a Well-Meaning Intervention Ended in Failure,' *Foreign Affairs*, March/April 2015, https://www.foreignaffairs.com/articles/libya/2019–02–18/obamas-libya-debacle, Dominic Tierney, 'The Legacy of Obama's "Worst Mistake," There's a problem with the American way of war,' *The Atlantic*, 15 April 2016, https://www.theatlantic.com/international/archive/2016/04/obamas-worst-mistake-libya/478461/ and Bill Powell, 'What Obama's Military Intervention in Libya Left Behind for the Next Sitting President,' *Newsweek*, 30 June 2016, https://www.newsweek.com/2016/07/08/obama-libya-smart-power-qaddafi-476093.html

21. See William Wechsler, 'US Withdrawal from the Middle East: Perceptions and Reality,' *Atlantic Council*, October 2019, https://www.atlanticcouncil.org/wp-content/uploads/2019/10/MENA-Chapter-one.pdf, noting 'recent history has led local leaders to question the American will to lead. That question is now prominent enough that it has driven a growing perception of American withdrawal. And that perception has driven actions that have predictably undermined longstanding US interests by threatening energy security and regional stability, and by welcoming in the United States' global peer competitors.'

22. See e.g. Stephen Blackwell, 'Saving the King: Anglo-American Strategy and British Counter-Subversion Operations in Libya, 1953–59,' *Middle Eastern Studies*, Vol. 39, No. 1 (Jan., 2003), pp. 1–18, https://www.jstor.org/stable/4284275?seq=1 and

23. Yehudit Ronen, 'Britain's Return to Libya: From the Battle of al-Ala-mein in the Western Libyan Desert to the Military Intervention in the "Arab Spring" Upheaval,' *Middle Eastern Studies*, 49:5, 2013, pp. 675–695, DOI: 10.1080/00263206.2013.811651, https://www.tandfonline.com/doi/full/10.1080/00263206.2013.811651?needAccess=true

24. 'Little Britain: The country is running down its armed forces and its diplomatic resources, to the despair of allies,' *The Economist*, April 4, 2015, https://www.economist.com/britain/2015/04/04/little-britain

25. See for example Cyril Bensimon, Madjid Zerrouky et Frédéric Bobin, 'Trois membres de la DGSE morts en Libye, le gouvernement libyen proteste,' *Le Monde*, July 20, 2016, https://www.lemonde.fr/international/article/2016/07/20/trois-militaires-francais-tues-en-libye_4972142_3210.html

26. Maggie Michael, 'Backed by Italy, Libya enlists militias to stop migrants,' *Associated Press*, 29 August 2017. https://apnews.com/articl e/9e808574a4d04eb38fa8c688d110a23d

27. *The White House*, 'U.S.-Gulf Cooperation Council Camp David Joint Statement,' 14 May 2015, https://obamawhitehouse.archives.gov/the-press-office/2015/05/14/us-gulf-cooperation-council-camp-david-joint-statement

28. Libyan Political Agreement, signed 17 December 2015, https://unsmil.unmissions.org/sites/default/files/Libyan%20Political%20Agreement%20-%20ENG%20.pdf

29. When faced with the reality that a majority of the HoR was ready to endorse the GNA's geographically-balanced cabinet, Aquilah and his similarly minded colleagues locked the doors of the HoR and turned off the electricity. One of the participants in this denial of democracy proudly told me he personally participated in the lockdown to ensure no vote would take place.

30. See Rinat Sagdiev, Aidan Lewis, 'Supplies of banknotes from Russia to east Libya accelerated this year-data,' *Reuters*, 9 October 2019 https://www.reuters.com/article/libya-economy/update-1-exclusive-supplies-of-banknotes-from-russia-to-east-libya-accelerated-this-year-data-idUKL8N27E3HN and *RWR Data*, 'Russia's Currency Printing Company, with ties to Venezuela and Syria, Looks to Reduce External

Dependency After Allegations of Printing Counterfeit Banknotes for Libya,' 4 June 2020, https://www.rwradvisory.com/russias-currency-printing-company-with-ties-to-venezuela-and-syria-looks-to-reduce-external-dependency-after-allegations-of-printing-counterfeit-banknotes-for-libya/

31. For the early development of this relationship in 2015, see 'Russia and Libya: A brief history of an on-again-off-again friendship,' Federica Saini Fasanotti, *Brookings Institution*, 1 September 2016, https://www.brookings.edu/blog/order-from-chaos/2016/09/01/russia-and-libya-a-brief-history-of-an-on-again-off-again-friendship/. For the relationship between Russia and the eastern branch of Libya's Central Bank under Ali al-Hibri, see 'Russia discloses amount of banknotes sent to Libyan Central Bank in Al-Bayda,' *TV 218*, 30 October 2019 https://en.218tv.net/2019/10/30/russia-discloses-amount-of-banknotes-sent-to-libyan-central-bank-in-al-bayda/. For the forced loans from banks in Libya's east see the analysis of Tim Eaton, 'As Conflict Escalates In Libya, The Economy Veers Toward Crisis, 19 May 2020, *War on the Rocks*, https://warontherocks.com/2020/05/as-conflict-escalates-in-libya-the-economy-veers-toward-crisis/

32. For the evolution of Russian military support for Haftar see 'Russia seeks influence in Libya: Moscow last week hosted Libyan warlord Khalifa Haftar, who has requested military aid and political support. What are Russia's political and economic interests in the Libyan conflict?,' Deutsche Welle Online (DW), 6 December 2016, https://www.dw.com/en/russia-seeks-influence-in-libya/a-36663867. For the Russian-Emirati-Egypt-Haftar connection see Point Blank Investigative Unit, 'Egypt, Russia and UAE sent arms to Libya's Haftar,' *Al Jazeera*, 13 November 2019, https://www.aljazeera.com/news/2019/11/13/point-blank-egypt-russia-and-uae-sent-arms-to-libyas-haftar and Awad Mustafa, 'Russia and UAE Discuss Terrorism in Libya and Intelligence Ties,' in *Defense News*, 4 February 2016, https://www.defensenews.com/global/mideast-africa/2016/02/04/russia-and-uae-discuss-terrorism-in-libya-and-intelligence-ties/ both suggest that the UAE and Russia began work inside Libya on behalf of Haftar in early

February 2016, just weeks after the UAE and Russia had agreed to support the GNA.

33. *BBC News*, 'Libya crisis: UN warns attacks on civilians may amount to war crimes,' 9 April 2019, https://www.bbc.com/news/world-africa-47868691

34. Patrick Wintour, 'UN postpones Libya national conference amid fighting in Tripoli: Decision comes as a blow to those hoping it would smooth path to democratic elections,' *The Guardian*, 9 April 2019, https://www.theguardian.com/world/2019/apr/09/un-postpones-libya-national-conference-amid-fighting-tripoli

35. *BBC News*, 'Powerful "Putin's chef" Prigozhin cooks up murky deals,' 4 November 2019, https://www.bbc.com/news/world-europe-50264747; Michelle Nichols, 'Up to 1,200 deployed in Libya by Russian military group: U.N. report,' *Reuters*, 6 May 2020, https://www.reuters.com/article/us-libya-security-sanctions/up-to-1200-deployed-in-libya-by-russian-military-group-u-n-report-idUSKBN22I2XW

36. David Kirkpatrick, 'Russian Snipers, Missiles and Warplanes Try to Tilt Libyan War: Moscow is plunging deeper into a war of armed drones in a strategic hot spot rich with oil, teeming with migrants and riddled with militants,' *The New York Times*, 5 November 2019. https://www.nytimes.com/2019/11/05/world/middleeast/russia-libya-mercenaries.html

37. Jason Pack, 'Turning the Tide: How Turkey Won The War For Tripoli,' *Middle East Institute*, November 2020, https://www.mei.edu/sites/default/files/2020–11/Turning%20the%20Tide%20-%20How%20Turkey%20Won%20the%20War%20for%20Tripoli.pdf

38. Daren Butler, 'World governments send planes, ships for Libya evacuation,' *Reuters*, 23 February 2001, https://www.reuters.com/article/us-libya-protests-evacuation/world-governments-send-planes-ships-for-libya-evacuation-idUSTRE71M3PQ20110223

39. *Reuters*, 'Libya may compensate Turkish firms over frozen projects,' 20 February 2013 https://www.reuters.com/article/turkey-libya-construction/libya-may-compensate-turkish-firms-over-frozen-projects-idUSL6N0BKF5020130220

40. See Jason Pack's detailed analysis of the economic benefits for Turkey

in 'Turkey doubles down on Libya,' *Middle East Institute*, 10 December 2019, https://www.mei.edu/publications/turkey-doubles-down-libya

41. *Deutsche Welle*, 'Turkey-Libya maritime deal triggers Mediterranean tensions, Turkey has boosted military aid to allies in Libya, but the maritime deal that comes with it has inflamed Mediterranean geopolitics. Greece and Egypt were among those to voice vehement objections,' 29 November 2019, https://www.dw.com/en/turkey-libya-maritime-deal-triggers-mediterranean-tensions/a-51477783

42. Metin Gurcan, 'Will Libya become Turkey's next Syria?' *Al-Monitor*, 16 December 2019, https://www.al-monitor.com/pulse/originals/2019/12/turkey-is-libya-becoming-ankaras-second-syria.html

43. The International Crisis Group (ICG) summarized the scope of the Turkish intervention, the reasons for it, and its pluses and minuses for regional security in an extensive article entitled 'Turkey Wades into Libya's Troubled Waters.' The reports subtitle also summarizes its analysis: 'Turkish intervention in Libya's war stopped the besieged Tripoli government from collapsing. But fighting with Field Marshal Khalifa Haftar's forces has since escalated, threatening a protracted conflict. Both Ankara and Haftar's regional backers should urge their allies toward a return to negotiations and a ceasefire,' ICG Report No 257, April 30, 2020. https://www.crisisgroup.org/europe-central-asia/western-europemediterranean/turkey/257-turkey-wades-libyas-troubled-waters

44. David M. Herszenhorn, 'As EU stumbles, Putin and Erdoğan take charge in Libya: Russia and Turkey exert newfound influence as West confronts fallout of Trump's chaos, *Politico*, 8 January 2020. https://www.politico.eu/article/as-eu-stumbles-vladimir-putin-and-recep-tayyip-erdogan-take-charge-in-libya/

45. Former UN Special Envoys to Libya refer to the Bolton call as 'green lighting' the attack in, Stephanie Williams and Ghassan Salamé, 'Why There's Hope for Libya,' *NewLines Magazine*, 22 April 2021, https://newlinesmag.com/argument/why-theres-hope-for-libya/

46. Samer Al-Atrush, Jennifer Jacobs, and Margaret Talev, "Trump Backed Libyan Strongman's Attack on Tripoli, U.S. Officials Say," *Bloomberg*,

April 24, 2019, https://www.bloomberg.com/news/articles/2019-04-24/ trump-libya-haftar-tripoli

47. *The New York Times* quoted Libya expert Frederick Wehrey as saying the Trump actions and statement were 'nuts' even by the standards of the Trump Administration. David Kirkpatrick, 'Trump Endorses an Aspiring Libyan Strongman, Reversing Policy,' *The New York Times*, 19 April 2019, at https://www.nytimes.com/2019/04/19/world/middleeast/trump-libya-khalifa-hifter.html

48. See David Kirkpatrick, 'The White House Blessed a War in Libya, but Russia Won It,' *The New York Times*, 15 April 2020. https://www.nytimes.com/2020/04/14/world/middleeast/libya-russia-john-bolton.html The article was published on the one-year anniversary of the Trump/Haftar phone call. The Times summarized its reporting with the apt subheading, 'Russia wanted more leverage over an aspiring Libyan strongman. The White House provided it by assenting to a disastrous civil war.'

49. *BBC*, 'Libya conflict: "Stressed" Ghassan Salamé resigns as UN envoy,' 2 March 2020, https://www.bbc.com/news/world-africa-51713683

50. One such statement which shows the difference in tone of the Trump Administration in 2020 reads, 'The United States is deeply troubled by the escalating conflict in Libya. We strongly oppose foreign military involvement, including the use of mercenaries and private military contractors, by all sides. The ongoing efforts of foreign powers to exploit the conflict—for example, by establishing an enduring military presence or exerting control over resources that belong to the Libyan people—pose grave threats to regional stability and global commerce. Furthermore, these efforts undermine the collective security interests of the United States and our allies and partners in the Mediterranean region. Escalation will only deepen and prolong the conflict... As an active, but neutral, actor, the United States is pursuing a 360-degree diplomatic engagement with Libyan and external stakeholders across the conflict to find a solution that supports Libyan sovereignty and protects the shared interests of the United States, our allies, and partners. To that end, we call on all parties—both those responsible for the current escalation and those working to end it—to enable the

National Oil Corporation to resume its vital work, with full transparency, and to implement a demilitarized solution for Sirte and al-Jufra, respect the UN arms embargo, and finalize a ceasefire under the UN-led 5+5 military talks,' Statement from National Security Adviser Robert C. O'Brien Regarding Libya, 4 August 2020 https://www.whitehouse. gov/briefings-statements/statement-national-security-adviser-robert-c-obrien-regarding-libya/. The Libya policy articulated in this statement is essentially identical to that which I pursued in the second term of the Obama Administration.

51. *UN News*, 'Libyans charting way to secure and prosperous future, but challenges lie ahead,' 19 November 2020, summarizing a presentation by Acting SRSG Williams, https://news.un.org/en/story/2020/11/1078102

52. 'Libyan sides agree plan on implementing ceasefire deal,' 4 November 2020, https://news.un.org/en/story/2020/11/1076852

53. *International Crisis Group*, 'Fleshing Out the Libya Ceasefire Agreement.' 4 November 2020, https://www.crisisgroup.org/middle-east-north-africa/north-africa/libya/b80-fleshing-out-libya-ceasefire-agreement

54. *UN News*, 'Libya: Security Council backs ceasefire mechanism, calls for withdrawal of foreign forces and mercenaries,' 16 April 2021, https://news.un.org/en/story/2021/04/1089992

55. 'Gresham's Law,' https://www.investopedia.com/terms/g/greshams-law.asp

56. *Arab Weekly*, 'Libya's GNA hands power to Government of National Unity,' 16 March 2021, https://thearabweekly.com/libyas-gna-hands-power-government-national-unity

BIBLIOGRAPHY

Books and book chapters about Libya

Ahmida, Ali Abdullatif, *The Making of Modern Libya: State Formation, Colonization and Resistance, 1830–1932* (Albany University Press, 1994).

Anderson, Lisa, *The State and Social Transformation in Tunisia and Libya* (Princeton University Press, 1986).

——— 'The Development of Nationalist Sentiment in Libya, 1908–1922', in Rashid Khalidi (ed.), *The Origins of Arab Nationalism* (Columbia University Press, 1991), pp. 225–42.

Anthony, John Allan (ed.), *Libya since Independence: Economic and Political Development*, (Croom Helm, 1982).

Baldinetti, Anna, *The Origins of the Libyan Nation: Colonial Legacy, Exile and the Emergence of a New Nation-State* (Routledge, 2010).

Benotman, Noman, Jason Pack, and James Brandon, 'Islamists', in Jason Pack (ed.), *The 2011 Libyan Uprisings and the Struggle for the Post-Qaddafi Future* (Palgrave, 2013), pp. 191–228.

Bills, Scott, *The Libyan Arena: The United States, Britain and the Council of Foreign Ministers, 1945–1948* (Kent State University Press, 1995).

Brahimi, Alia, 'Islamic Radicalisation in Libya', in George Joffé (ed), *Islamist Radicalisation in North Africa: Politics and Process* (Routledge, 2011).

Cook, Haley and Jason Pack, 'Mu'ammur Qadhafi: Power, Personality, and Ideology', in Frank Jacob (ed.), *Dictatorships without Violence? How*

BIBLIOGRAPHY

Dictators Assert Their Power, Comparative Studies from a Global Perspective 2 (Königshausen & Neumann, 2014).

De Candole, E.A.V., *The Life and Times of King Idriss of Libya* (privately published by Mustafa ben Ghalbon, 1990).

Evans-Pritchard, E.E., *The Sanusi of Cyrenaica* (Oxford University Press, 1949).

Gifford, Prosser and Wm. Roger Louis (eds), *Decolonization and African Independence: The Transfers of Power, 1960–1980* (Yale University Press, 1988).

Gurney, Judith, *Libya: The Political Economy of Oil* (Oxford University Press, 1996).

Henneberg, Sabina, *Managing Transition in Tunisia and Libya: The Role of the Democratic Governments* (Cambridge University Press, 2020).

Joffé, George and Keith Stanley McLachlan (eds.), *Social & Economic Development of Libya* (Middle East & North African Studies Press, 1982).

Kelly, Saul, *Cold War in the Desert: Britain, the United States, and the Italian Colonies, 1945–52* (Palgrave, 2000).

———— *War & Politics in the Desert: Britain and Libya during the Second World War* (Silphium Press, 2010).

Lacher, Wolfram, *Libya's Fragmentation: Structure and Process in Violent Conflict* (I.B. Tauris, 2020).

Libyan Institute for Advanced Studies, 'Beheadings, Car Bombings, and the Islamic State's Expansion in Libya', June 2015.

Louis, Wm. Roger, 'Libya: The Creation of a Client State', in Wm. Roger Louis and Prosser Gifford (eds.), *Decolonization and African Independence: The Transfers of Power 1960–80* (Yale University Press, 1988).

Marcuzzi, Stefano, *The EU, NATO and the Libya Conflict: Anatomy of a Failure.* (Routledge, 2021).

Mattes, Hanspeter, 'Formal and Informal Authority in Libya since 1969', in Dirk Vandewalle (ed.), *Libya since 1969: Qadhafi's Revolution Revisited* (Palgrave, 2008)

Nayed, Aref, 'Extremism, Trauma, and Therapy', in *Radical Engagement: Essays on Religion, Extremism, Politics, and Libya* (Kalam Research and Media, 2017).

BIBLIOGRAPHY

Obeidi, Amal, *Political Culture in Libya* (Routledge, 2001).

Otman, Waniss A. and Erling Karlberg, *The Libyan Economy: Economic Diversification and International Repositioning* (Springer, 2007).

Pack, Jason (ed.), *The 2011 Libyan Uprisings and the Struggle for the Post-Qadhafi Future* (Palgrave, 2013).

——— 'The Antecedents and Implications of the So-Called Anglo-Sanussi War (1915–17)', T.G. Fraser (ed.), *The First World War and Its Aftermath: The Shaping of the Middle East* (Ginkgo Library, 2015).

Pargeter, Alison, *Libya: The Rise and Fall of Qaddafi* (Yale University Press, 2012).

Pelt, Adrian, *Libyan Independence and the United Nations: A Case of Planned Decolonization* (Yale University Press, 1970).

Peters, Emerys, *The Bedouin of Cyrenaica: Studies in Personal and Corporate Power* (Cambridge University Press, 1990).

Simon, Rachel, *Libya between Ottomanism and Nationalism: The Ottoman Involvement in Libya during the War with Italy (1911–1919)* (Schwarz, 1987).

St John, Ronald Bruce, *Libya and the United States: Two Centuries of Strife* (University of Pennsylvania Press, 2002).

Vandewalle, Dirk, *Libya since Independence: Oil and State Building* (Cornell University Press, 1998).

——— *A History of Modern Libya* (Cambridge University Press, 2006).

——— (ed.), *Libya since 1969: Qadhafi's Revolution Revisited* (Palgrave, 2008).

Waddams, Frank C., *The Libyan Oil Industry* (Croom Helm, 1980).

Wehrey, Fred, *Burning Shores of Tripoli* (Penguin, 2018).

Wright, John, *A History of Libya* (Hurst, 2010).

Journal articles, commentary, and think tank scholarship on Libya

Ashour, Omar, 'Libyan Islamists Unpacked: Rise, Transformation, and Future', *Brookings Institution*, May 2012.

Barr, Nathaniel, 'The Islamic State's Uneven Trajectory in Libya', *Terrorism Monitor*, 13, no. 19, (17 September 2015).

Blanchard, Christopher, 'Libya: Transition and U.S. Policy', *Congressional Research Service*, 2 May 2018.

BIBLIOGRAPHY

Boduszyński, Mietek and Christopher K. Lamont, 'Trump Changed U.S. Policy toward Libya: This Is Why It Matters', *Washington Post Monkey Cage*, 3 May 2019.

Brahimi, Alia and Jason Pack, 'Strategic Lessons from the Ejection of ISIS from Sirte', *Atlantic Council*, 16 May 2017.

Chorin, Ethan, 'What Libya Lost', *New York Times*, 13 September 2012.

Dajani, Deena, 'Libya's Sovereign Wealth Scandal: Taxpayers' Billions Squandered through Nepotism, Incompetence and Wild Gambling', *New Arab*, 30 November 2017.

Eaton, Tim, 'Libya: Rich in Oil, Leaking Fuel', *Chatham House*, October 2019.

——— 'Libya Needs an Economic Commission to Exit from Violence', *Chatham House*, 20 November 2019.

——— 'As Conflict Escalates in Libya, the Economy Veers Toward Crisis', *War on the Rocks*, 19 May 2020.

——— 'Libya: Investing the Wealth of a Nation', *Chatham House*, February 2021.

Eaton, Tim et al., 'Conflict Economies in the Middle East and North Africa', *Chatham House*, June 2019.

El Amran, Issandr, 'How Much of Libya Does the Islamic State Control?', *Foreign Policy*, 18 February 2016.

El Kamouni-Janssen, Floor et al., 'Local Security Governance in Libya', *Clingendael* (Netherlands Institute of Foreign Relations), October 2018.

Eljarh, Mohamed, 'A Coup Attempt in Tripoli', *Foreign Policy*, 19 May 2014.

Fasanotti, Federica Saini, 'Russia and Libya: A Brief History of an On-Again-off-Again Friendship', *Brookings Institution*, 1 September 2016.

Gatnash, Ahmed and Nadine Dahan, 'In Libya, Traditional and Social Media Are Used to Fuel War', *Arab Tyrant Manual*, 14 April 2019.

Gazzini, Claudia, 'Was the Libya Intervention Necessary?', *MERIP*, 261 (Winter 2011).

Global Witness: 'Discredited: How Libya's Multibillion-Dollar Trade Finance Scheme Risks Defrauding the Country via London Banks', 19 February 2021.

BIBLIOGRAPHY

Gomati, Anas, 'Haftar's Rebranded Coups', *Carnegie Endowment*, 30 July 2019.

Grossman, Shelby, Khadeja Ramali, and Renee DiResta, 'Blurring the Lines of Media Authenticity: Prigozhin-Linked Group Funding Libyan Broadcast Media', *Stanford Internet Observatory*, 20 March 2020.

Hassan, Hassan and Christopher Kendall, 'History and Future of the Petroleum Industry in Libya', *SEPM Strata*, 2008.

Hauslohner, Abigail and Karen DeYoung, 'U.S. Plan for New, Western-Trained Libyan Force Faces Obstacles', *Atlantic Council*, 5 December 2013.

Joffé, George and Emmanuella Paoletti, 'The Foreign Policy Process in Libya', *Journal of North African Studies* 16, no. 2 (2011).

Kadlec, Amanda, 'Dignity Battles the Dawn: The Complex Web of Libya's Civil War', *War on the Rocks*, 14 August 2014.

Khan, Mohsin and Karim Mezran, 'The Libyan Economy after the Revolution: Still No Clear Vision', *Atlantic Council*, 28 August 2013.

Kuperman, Allen J., 'Obama's Libya Debacle, How a Well-Meaning Intervention Ended in Failure', *Foreign Affairs*, March/April 2015.

Lacher, Wolfram, 'Fault Lines of the Revolution: Political Actors, Camps and Conflicts in the New Libya', *SWP*, May 2013.

Malka, Haim and Margo Balboni, 'Libya: Tunisia's Jihadist Nightmare', *CSIS*, June 2016.

Marcuzzi, Stefano and Jason Pack, 'Terrorist and Armed Groups in the Fezzan-Sahel Region: Recruitment and Communication Tactics', *NATO Strategic Communications Centre of Excellence*, December 2020.

McQuinn, Brian, 'After the Fall: Libya's Evolving Armed Groups', *Small Arms Survey*, October 2012.

Megerisi, Tarek, 'Libya Crisis: The Unity Government's Success Hides Serious Dangers Ahead', *Middle East Eye*, 13 April 2021, https://www.middleeasteye.net/opinion/libya-new-unity-government-dangers-ahead

Mezran, Karim and Eric Knecht, 'Libya's Fractious New Politics', *Atlantic Council*, 9 January 2013.

Mezran, Karim, Fadel Lamen, and Eric Knecht, 'Post-Revolutionary Politics in Libya: Inside the General National Congress', *Atlantic Council*, May 2013.

BIBLIOGRAPHY

Moss, Dana and Jason Pack, 'Libya since 1969: Qadhafi's Revolution Revisited', *Journal of North African Studies*, 16, no. 2 (2011).

Pack, Jason, 'Gaddafi's Right-Hand Man Should Not Be Underestimated', *Guardian*, 24 February 2011.

———— 'Libya Is Too Big to Fail', *Foreign Policy*, 18 March 2011.

———— 'The Two Faces of Libya's Rebels', *Foreign Policy*, 5 April 2011.

———— 'Qaddafi's Legacy', *Foreign Policy*, 20 October 2011.

———— 'Post-Gaddafi Libya Should Think Local', *Guardian*, 23 October 2011.

———— 'Honoring Chris Stevens', *Foreign Policy*, 14 September 2012.

———— 'Engagement in Libya Was and Remains the Right Answer', *Spectator*, 31 January 2013.

———— 'How to End Libya's War', *New York Times*, 21 January 2015.

———— 'ISIS Loss in Sirte May Deepen Libyan Rifts', *Tony Blair Faith Foundation*, 17 August 2016.

———— 'The Hifter Effect on the Battle for Libya's Sirte', *Al-Monitor*, 14 October 2016.

———— 'Khalifa Haftar's Miscalculated Attack on Tripoli ...', *Foreign Policy*, 10 April 2019.

———— 'Kingdom of Militias: Libya's Second War of Post-Qadhafi Succession', *ISPI*, 31 May 2019 [Chapter 3's extract].

———— 'It's the Economy Stupid: How Libya's Civil War Is Rooted in Its Economic Structures', *IAI* (Rome), 17 September 2019 [Chapter 4's extract].

———— 'How Libya's Economic Structures Enrich the Militias', *Middle East Institute*, 23 September 2019.

———— 'The UN Deliberately (Albeit Mistakenly) Accorded Sovereignty to Post-Gadhafi Libya's Economic Institutions', *Middle East Institute*, 26 September 2019.

———— 'Turkey Doubles Down on Libya', Middle East Institute, 10 December 2019.

———— 'An International Financial Commission Is Libya's Last Hope', *Middle East Institute*, September 2020 [Chapter 5's extract].

———— 'Libya Has a New Prime Minister and His Family Legacy Is as Complex, Shady, and Wealthy as the Country Itself', *Middle East Institute*, 8 February 2021.

BIBLIOGRAPHY

Pack, Jason and Barak Barfi, 'In War's Wake: The Struggle for Post-Qadhafi Libya', *Washington Institute for Near East Policy*, February 2012.

Pack, Jason and Haley Cook, 'The July 2012 Libyan Elections and the Origin of Post-Qaddafi Appeasement', *Middle East Journal* 69, no. 2 (Spring 2015).

Pack, Jason, Karim Mezran, and Mohamed Eljarh, 'Libya's Faustian Bargains: Breaking the Appeasement Cycle', *Atlantic Council*, 5 May 2014 [Chapter 1's excerpt].

Pack, Jason and Mohamed Eljarh, 'Talk about Political Dysfunction', *New York Times*, 18 October 2013.

———— 'Localizing Power in Libya', *Atlantic Council*, 26 November 2013.

Pack, Jason and Nate Mason, 'A Trumpian Peace Deal in Libya?', *Foreign Affairs*, 10 January 2017

Pack, Jason and Will Raynolds, 'Why Libya Is So Hard to Govern: Inter-Group Squabbling Reigns as the Country Stalls on Drafting Its New Constitution', *The Atlantic*, October 2013.

Pack, Jason and Rhiannon Smith, 'Libya: Unity First, Military Victories Second', *Arab Weekly*, 11 September 2016.

———— 'Defeating the Islamic State? Lessons from Libya?', *Hate Speech International*, 4 November 2016.

Pack, Jason, Rhiannon Smith, and Karim Mezran, 'The Origins and Evolution of ISIS in Libya', *Atlantic Council*, 20 June 2017 [Chapter 2's extract].

Pack, Jason and Wolfgang Pusztai, 'Turning the Tide: How Turkey Won the War for Tripoli', *Middle East Institute*, 10 November 2020.

Pack, Jason and Youseef Sawani, 'Libyan Constitutionality and Sovereignty Post-Qadhafi: the Islamist, Regionalist, and Amazigh Challenges', *Journal of North African Studies*, 18, no. 4 (2013).

Pack, Jason and Sami Zaptia, 'The Face of the Libyan Arab Spring, Mahmoud Jibril, Felled by COVID-19', *Middle East Institute*, 9 April 2020.

Parteger, Alison, 'Haftar, Tribal Power, and the Battle for Libya', *War on the Rocks*, 15 May 2020.

Pelham, Nicolas, 'Bogged Down in Libya', *New York Review of Books*, 21 March 2011.

BIBLIOGRAPHY

———— 'Libya in the Shadow of Iraq: The "Old Guard" versus the Thuwwar in the Battle for Stability', *International Peacekeeping* 19, no. 4 (2012).

———— 'Losing Libya's Revolution', *New York Review of Books*, 10 October 2013.

Pizzolo, Paolo, 'The Greed versus Grievance Theory and the 2011 Libyan Civil War: Why Grievance Offers a Wider Perspective for Understanding the Conflict Outbreak', *Small Wars Journal*, 28 October 2020.

Porter, Geoffrey, 'How Realistic Is Libya as an Islamic State "Fallback"?', *CTC Sentinel*, March 2016.

Porter, Michael E., *Libyan Economic Development Board Blueprint* (Monitor Company Group, 2007).

Rasmi, Farah, 'Beyond the War: The History of French–Libyan Relations', *Atlantic Council*, 8 April 2021.

Roslington, James and Jason Pack, 'Who Pays for ISIS in Libya', *Hate Speech International*, August 2016.

Russel Mead, Walter, 'Libya's Foul Foretaste of the Post-American World', *Wall Street Journal*, 7 July 2020.

Salamé, Ghassan, 'Libya and the New Global Disorder: A Conversation with Ghassan Salamé', *Carnegie Endowment Webinar*, 15 October 2020.

Sawani, Youssef Mohammad, 'Gaddafi's Legacy, Institutional Development, and National Reconciliation in Libya', *Contemporary Arab Affairs* 13, no. 1 (2020), pp. 46–68.

Segrè, Claudio G., *Fourth Shore: The Italian Colonization of Libya* (University of Chicago Press, 1974).

Sen, Ashish Kumar and Karim Mezran, 'Trump Wades into Libyan Crisis, and Why That's Not Good News," *New Atlanticist*, 22 April 2019.

Sharqieh, Ibrahim, 'Reconstructing Libya: Stability through National Reconciliation', *Brookings Institution*, 3 December 2013.

Shaw, Mark and Fiona Mangan, 'Illicit Trafficking and Libya's Transition: Profits and Losses', *USIP*, 24 February 2014.

Sizer, Lydia, 'The Myth of Libya's Wealth', *Atlantic Council*, 3 February 2015.

Smith, Rhiannon, 'A House Divided: Jihadis Battle for Derna', *Tony Blair Faith Foundation*, 10 July 2015.

BIBLIOGRAPHY

Smith, Rhiannon and Jason Pack, 'Al-Qaida's Strategy in Libya: Keep it Local, Stupid', *Perspectives on Terrorism* 11, no. 6 (2017).

St John, Ronald Bruce, 'Libyan Election Breaks Arab Spring Pattern', *International Spectator: The Italian Journal of International Affairs* 47, no. 3 (2012).

Tierney, Dominic, 'The Legacy of Obama's "Worst Mistake": There's a Problem with the American Way of War', *The Atlantic*, 15 April 2016.

Van Creveld, Martin and Jason Pack, 'Upheaval in Qaddafi's Libya Isn't Just Another Arab Uprising', *Christian Science Monitor*, 23 February 2011.

Vandewalle, Dirk and Sami Zaptia, 'After Qadhafi: The Surprising Success of The New Libya', *Foreign Affairs*, November/December 2012.

Vest, Nathan, 'Is an Escalation Imminent in Western Libya?', RAND, 27 March 2019.

Wehrey, Frederic, 'The Struggle for Security in Eastern Libya', Carnegie Endowment for International Peace, 19 September 2012.

Wilson, Lachlan and Jason Pack, 'The Islamic State's Revitalization in Libya and Its Post-2016 War of Attrition', *CTC Sentinel*, March 2019.

Winer, Jonathan, 'Origins of the Libyan Conflict and Options for Its Resolution', *Middle East Institute*, May 2019.

Zelin, Aaron Y., 'Islamic State's First Colony in Libya', *Washington Institute for Near East Policy*, 10 October 2014.

——— 'The Islamic State's Burgeoning Capital in Sirte, Libya', *Washington Institute for Near East Policy*, 6 August 2015.

Foreign language sources on Libya, Russia, and Ukraine

Abdullah, Muhammed, بوفاة مبارك. هل يرث السيسي الدولة العسكرية والعميقة, *al-Jazeera*, 26 February 2020.

Abdurraouf, Ali, من المقدس إلى المدنس: تصورات في الصورة الذهنية والبصرية لميدان التحرير, *Midan Masr*, 11 May 2013.

Abuzahir, Salem, نشر الكتاب الورقي الليبي... واقعه ومستقبله, *Libya al-Mustaqbal*, 30 June 2016.

AFP, 'L'Intervention Francaise en Libye, un "Investissment sur l'avenir", Assure Juppe', *Le Parisien*, 27 August 2011.

BIBLIOGRAPHY

Ain Libya, تعرف على تفاصيل مكالمة هاتفية بين حفتر والرئيس الأمريكي ترامب, 20 April 2019.

Afrigate News, اكتشف 7 معلومات عن عبد الحميد الدبيبة, 5 February 2021.

—— لماذا تخشى أطراف عدة من خروج حَفَظَة أسرار القذافي إلى النور؟, 20 February 2018.

al-Abeydi, Salem, 'Insihab Latibat Shuhada al-Zaqiya min Sirt ba'ad ta'Urudha li-Hajum Muslih' (Arabic), *Al-Wasat*, 12 March 2014.

al-Helali, Amal, ناشطات ليبيات: خرجنا ضد القذافي لكن الإسلاميين أسوأ منه, *Radio Sawa*, 29 August 2014.

Al-Khaleej, قطر وتركيا... تحالف تاريخي لدعم وتمويل الإرهاب, 22 June 2017.

al-Maheer, Khaled, الصراعات وأدت حكومة مصطفى أبو شاقور, *al-Jazeera*, 8 October 2012.

al-Manassa al-Libeyya, نعمان بن عثمان... مستشار سياسي أم عميل مخابرات, 12 February 2019.

Al-Marsad, عشرات الشركات والعقارات والمنتجعات الفاخرة المرصد تغوص في إمبراطورية آل ادبية, 10 June 2016.

—— علي الدبيبة يعلن موقفه من الأحداث في طرابلس ويكشف حقيقة نبأ تواصله مع الجيش, 23 April 2019.

Al-Sa'a24, علي الدبيبة. متهم ببناء إمبراطوريته المالية من جيوب الليبيين والبحث عن حصانتها رشاوى الحوار السياسي 16 November 2020.

Al-Salouha, Mahmoud, 'The assassination of salafist Sheikh Khalid Furjani in Sirte' (Arabic), *Al-Wasat*, 11 August 2015.

al-Sennousi, Bskeeri, الازدواجية المقيتة في الحكم على نعمان بن عثمان, *al-Arabi*, 25 May 2019.

al-Watan Voice, مئات الآلاف من أهالي بنغازي يهتفون برحيل القذافي ويعلنون تحررهم, 25 February 2011.

Barakat, Naji, من اسقط حكومة أبو شاقور, '*Ain Libya*, 8 October 2012.

Cresti, Federico, *Oasi di italianità: La Libia della colonizzazione agraria tra fascismo, guerra e indipendenza (1935–1956)* (Società editrice internazionale, 1996).

Dar al-Hayah, اتهامات صادمة بتورط رئيس الحكومة الليبية في قضايا فساد, 9 March 2021.

Harchaoui, Jalel, 'La politique libyenne de la France et ses antécédents historiques', *Revue internationale et stratégique*, 4, no. 116 (2019), pp. 33–43.

Mediapart, *Sarkozy–Kadhafi: Des billets et des bombes* (Delcourt, 2019).

Novoye Vremya, 'Путин надеется на возвращение Украины в так называемый "русский мир"—Полторак' Putin hopes for Ukraine's return to the so-called 'Russian world'—Poltorak), 5 April 2018.

BIBLIOGRAPHY

Rai'i Al-Youm Libiyya, ... كلهم حفتر بالنسبة الينا, و كلهم وقفوا في خندق حلف الناتو و قصفه كلهم حفتر بالنسبة الينا, و كلهم وقفوا في خندق حلف الناتو و قصفه, ليبيا . و مكالمة ترمب قد تكون حسمت طرابلس 20 April 2019.

Sanussi, Ahmed, فلوسنا, *Al Wasat TV*, Episode 22, 1 June 2020.

Tamimi, 'Milishiat Ansar al-Sharia Tashtabak ma'a Jeishna al-Watani' (Arabic), 28 April 2013.

Ukrayinska Pravda, 'Україна щорічно "дарує" Росії 5 мільярдів доларів— Азаров' (Ukraine annually 'donates' $5 billion to Russia—Azarov), 16 October 2012.

—— 'Путин надеется, что Германия поддержит его стремления' (Putin hopes Germany will support his ambitions), 18 March 2014.

Vinogradov, Egor, 'Олигархи в России работают, как полицейские под прикрытием' (Oligarchs in Russia operate like undercover enforcers), *Deutsche Welle*, 14 September 2010.

Wakalat Al-Anbaa al-Islamiya, 'Istishaad Amr Ansar al-Sharia b-Sirte wa Qaid Katibat al-Farouq Misrata a'ala yid Katibat min al-Jaysh a-Libi'i Tadum Muwaleen al-Qadhafi' (Arabic), 4 August 2013.

Yes Libya, ماذا يفضل الليبيون من مواقع التواصل الاجتماعي 26 October 2020.

History, economics, area studies, and global politics scholarship

Ajami, Fouad, *The Foreigner's Gift: The Americans, the Arabs, and the Iraqis in Iraq* (Simon & Schuster, 2006).

Anderson, Benedict, *Imagined Communities: Reflections on the Origin and Spread of Nationalism* (Verso, 2016).

Baddeley, Michelle, *Behavioural Economics: A Very Short Introduction* (Oxford University Press, 2017).

Batatu, Hanna, *Syria's Peasantry, the Descendants of Its Lesser Rural Notables, and Their Politics* (Princeton University Press, 1999).

——— *The Old Social Classes and the Revolutionary Movements of Iraq: A Study of Iraq's Old Landed and Commercial Classes and of Its Communists, Ba'thists and Free Officers* (Saqi, 2012).

Bayly, Christopher, *The Birth of the Modern World, 1780–1914: Global Connections and Comparisons* (Oxford University Press, 2004).

Becker, Jasper, *Made in China: Wuhan, Covid and the Quest for Biotech Supremacy* (Hurst, 2021).

BIBLIOGRAPHY

Bellamy, Alex J. (ed.), *International Society and Its Critics* (Oxford University Press, 2004).

Benen, Steve, *The Impostors: How Republicans Quit Governing and Seized American Politics*, (William Morrow, 2020).

Berger, J. M., *Extremism* (MIT Press, 2018).

Boduszyński, Mieczysław P., *US Democracy Promotion in the Arab World: Beyond Interests vs. Ideals* (Lynne Rienner, 2019).

Borum, Randy, 'Psychology of Terrorism', *Mental Health Law & Policy Faculty Publications*, 2004.

Brahimi, Alia, 'Ideology and Terrorism: Causes and Motivations', in Erica Chenoweth, Richard English, Andreas Gofas, and Stathis Kalyvas (eds), *The Oxford Handbook on Terrorism* (Oxford University Press, 2019).

Bullough, Oliver, *Moneyland: The Inside Story of the Crooks and Kleptocrats Who Rule the World* (St. Martin's Press, 2019).

Burgis, Tom, *The Looting Machine* (Public Affairs, 2015).

Ciobanu, Ceslav, *Frozen and Forgotten Conflicts in the Post-Soviet States: Genesis, Political Economy, and Prospects for Solution* (Columbia University Press, 2010).

Clark, Christopher, *The Sleepwalkers: How Europe Went to War in 1914* (Penguin, 2013).

Cohen, Eliot A, 'History and the Hyperpower', *Foreign Affairs*, 1 July 2004, pp. 49–63.

Collier, Paul and Anke Hoeffler, 'Greed and Grievance in Civil War', *Oxford Economic Papers* 56, no. 4 (2004).

Connelly, John, *From Peoples into Nations: A History of Eastern Europe* (Princeton University Press, 2019).

Coronil, Fernando, *Magical State: Nature, Money, and Modernity in Venezuela* (University of Chicago Press, 1997).

Cristóbal, Rovira Kaltwasser et al. (eds), *The Oxford Handbook of Populism* (Oxford University Press, 2020)

Darwin, John, *After Tamerlane* (Bloomsbury, 2009).

Dowding, Keith, *Rational Choice and Political Power* (Policy Press, 2019).

Downey, Morgan, *Oil 101* (Wooden Table, 2019).

Edwards, Sebastian, *Left Behind: Latin America and the False Promise of Populism* (University of Chicago Press, 2010).

BIBLIOGRAPHY

Etzioni, Amitai, 'The Realism of Richard Haass', *National Interest*, 31 May 2013.

Fawaz, Gerges, *Obama and the Middle East: The End of America's Moment?* (St. Martin's Griffin, 2013)

Felter, Joseph and Brian Fishman, 'Al-Qaeda's Foreign Fighters in Iraq: A First Look at the Sinjar Records', *CTC at West Point*, 2 January 2007.

Ferguson, Niall, *Empire: The Rise and Demise of the British World Order and the Lessons for Global Power* (Basic Books, 2004).

—— *Colossus: The Rise and Fall of the American Empire* (Penguin, 2004).

Fromkin, David, *A Peace to End All Peace: The Fall of the Ottoman Empire and the Creation of the Modern Middle East* (Holt, 2009).

Gallagher, Jack and Ronald Robinson, *Africa and the Victorians: The Official Mind of Imperialism* (Macmillan, 1961).

Gallegos, Raúl, *Crude Nation: How Oil Riches Ruined Venezuela* (Potomac Books, 2019).

Gilbert, Martin, *The Roots of Appeasement* (Weidenfeld & Nicolson, 1970).

Grey, Stephen, Tom Bergin, Sevgil Musaieva and Roman Anin, 'Special Report: Putin's Allies Channelled Billions to Ukraine Oligarch', *Reuters*, 16 November 2014.

Gustafson, Thane, *Wheel of Fortune: The Battle for Oil and Power in Russia* (Belknap Press of the University of Harvard Press, 2017).

Haass, Richard, *A World in Disarray: American Foreign Policy and the Crisis of the Old Order* (Penguin, 2017).

Harari, Yuval, *Homo Deus: A Brief History of Tomorrow* (HarperCollins, 2018).

Hassan, Hassan, *ISIS: Inside the Army of Terror* (Regan Arts, 2016).

Holzinger, Katharina, *Transnational Common Goods: Strategic Constellations, Collective Action Problems, and Multi-Level Provision* (Palgrave, 2008).

Ikenberry, John (ed.), *America Unrivaled: The Future of the Balance of Power* (Cornell University Press, 2002).

Joffé, George (ed.), *Islamist Radicalisation in North Africa: Politics and Process* (Routledge, 2011).

Kai, Jin, *Rising China in a Changing World: Power Transitions and Global Leadership* (Palgrave, 2016).

Kandil, Hazem, *Soldiers, Spies, and Statesmen: Egypt's Road to Revolt* (Verso, 2012).

Kaplan, Robert, 'The Post-Imperial Moment: Vulgar, Populist Anarchy Will Define the Twenty-First Century', *National Interest*, 22 April 2016.

Khoury, Philip, *Syria and the French Mandate: The Politics of Arab Nationalism, 1920–1945* (Princeton University Press, 1989).

Klaas, Brian, *Corruptible* (Simon & Schuster, 2021).

Kuttner, Robert, *Can Democracy Survive Global Capitalism?* (W.W. Norton, 2019).

Lawson, Fred, *Demystifying Syria* (Saqi, 2012).

Lister, Charles, *The Syrian Jihad: Al-Qaeda, the Islamic State and the Evolution of an Insurgency* (Hurst, 2016).

Little, Richard, *The Balance of Power in International Relations: Metaphors, Myths and Models* (Cambridge University Press, 2007).

Louis, William Roger, *The Oxford History of the British Empire* (Oxford University Press, 1999).

Louis, William Roger and Roger Owen, *Suez 1956: The Crisis and Its Consequences* (Oxford University Press, 1989).

Louis, William Roger and Ronald Robinson, *Imperialism: The Robinson and Gallagher Controversy* (New York, 1976).

MacKinder, Halford, *The Geographical Pivot of History* (Cosimo Classics, 2020).

MacMillan, Margaret, *The War That Ended Peace: The Road to 1914* (Random House, 2014).

Maddow, Rachel, *Blowout: Corrupted Democracy, Rogue State Russia, and the Richest, Most Destructive Industry on Earth* (Crown, 2019).

McFate, Sean, *Goliath: Why the West Isn't winning; And What We Must Do about It* (Penguin, 2019).

McFaul, Michael, *Russia's Unfinished Revolution: Political Change from Gorbachev to Putin* (Mariner Books, 2019).

McHugo, John, *Syria: A Recent History* (Saqi, 2015).

——— *A Concise History of Sunnis and Shi'is* (Saqi, 2018).

Micklethwait, John and Adrian Wooldridge, *The Wake Up Call: Why the Pandemic Has Exposed the Weakness of the West—and How to Fix It* (Short Books, 2020).

BIBLIOGRAPHY

Miller, Carl, *Death of the Gods: The New Global Power Grab* (William Heinemann, 2018).

Montero, David, *Kickback: Exposing the Global Corporate Bribery Network* (Viking, 2018).

Nolte, Ernest, *Three Faces of Fascism: Action Française, Italian Fascism, National Socialism* (Henry Holt, 1966).

Norton, Augustus Richard, *Hezbollah: A Short History* (Princeton University Press, 2018).

Otte, T.G., *The Foreign Office Mind: The Making of British Foreign Policy, 1865–1914*, (Cambridge, 2011).

Pack, Jason, 'The Hungary Model: Resurgent Nationalism', *National Interest*, 8 October 2015.

———— 'Donald Trump: Welfare Queen of the Casino Economy', Al Jazeera English, 5 November 2016.

———— 'When It Comes to Ukraine, Trump's Alleged Misdeeds Go Beyond Quid Pro Quos', *Washington Post*, 25 November 2019.

Pack, Jason and Brendan Simms, 'A Weak E.U. Can't Stop Putin', *New York Times*, 27 March 2014.

Peters, Ralph, 'Stability, America's Enemy', The US Army War College Quarterly: *Parameters*, 31, 4, 2001.

Podeh, Elie, *Rethinking Nasserism: Revolution and Historical Memory in Modern Egypt* (University Press of Florida, 2004).

Polakow-Suransky, Sasha, *Go Back to Where You Came From: The Backlash against Immigration and the Fate of Western Democracy* (Bold Type Books, 2017).

Pollins, Brian M., 'Does Trade Still Follow the Flag?', *American Political Science Review*, 83, no. 2 (June 1989).

Polanyi, Karl, *The Great Transformation* (Penguin, 2001).

Pomerantsev, Peter, *This Is Not Propaganda: Adventures in the War against Reality* (Public Affairs, 2019).

Quigley, Carroll, *The Evolution of Civilizations* (Liberty Fund, 1961).

Reich, Robert, *Saving Capitalism: For the Many, Not the Few* (Vintage, 2016).

———— *The System: Who Rigged It, How We Fix It* (Knopf, 2020).

Ricks, Thomas, *Fiasco* (Penguin, 2007).

Roberts, Brad (ed), *Order and Disorder after the Cold War* (MIT Press, 1995).

Rock, Stephen, *Appeasement in International Politics* (University Press of Kentucky, 2000).

Rogan, Eugene, *The Fall of the Ottomans: The Great War in the Middle East, 1914–1920* (Penguin, 2015).

Rudolph, Jennifer and Michael Szonyi (eds), *The China Questions: Critical Insights into a Rising Power* (Harvard University Press, 2019).

Schick, Nina, *Deep Fakes and the Infocalypse: What You Urgently Need to Know* (Monoray, 2020).

Schumpeter, Joseph, *Capitalism, Socialism, and Democracy,* (Sublime Books, 2015).

——— *Essays: On Entrepreneurs, Innovations, Business Cycles and the Evolution of Capitalism* (Routledge, 2017).

Seale, Patrick, *Asad: The Struggle for the Middle East* (University of California Press, 1989).

Sharabi, Hisham, *Neopatriarchy: A Theory of Distorted Change in Arab Society* (Oxford University Press, 1988).

Shaxson, Nicholas, 'Tackling Tax Havens', *Finance & Development* 56, no. 3 (September 2019).

Sheehan, Michael, *Balance of Power* (Routledge, 1996).

Simpson, Emile, *War from the Ground Up: Twenty-First Century Combat as Politics* (Hurst, 2018).

Snyder, Timothy, *Bloodlands* (Basic Books, 2012).

Spinney, Laura, *Pale Rider: The Spanish Flu of 1918 and How It Changed the World* (Public Affairs, 2017).

Smith, Christopher and Liv Mariah Yarrow (eds), *Imperialism, Cultural Politics, & Polybius,* (Oxford University Press, 2012).

Tetlock, Philip and Dan Gardner, *Superforecasting: The Art & Science of Prediction* (Random House, 2016).

Thaler, Richard H., *Misbehaving: The Making of Behavioral Economics* (W.W. Norton, 2016).

Tripp, Charles, *A History of Iraq* (Cambridge University Press, 2015).

Turchin, Peter, *Ultra Society: How 10,000 Years of War Made Humans the Greatest Co-Operators on Earth* (Beresta, 2016).

BIBLIOGRAPHY

Ugolini, Stefano, *The Evolution of Central Banking: Theory and History* (Palgrave, 2017).

Van Creveld, Martin, *The Rise and Decline of the State* (Cambridge University Press, 1999).

———— *Pussycats: Why the Rest Keeps Beating the West, and What Can Be Done about It* (CreateSpace, 2016).

Van Dam, Nikolaos, *Destroying a Nation: The Civil War in Syria* (I.B. Tauris, 2017).

Watt, D.C., *Succeeding John Bull: America in Britain's Place, 1900–1975; A Study of the Anglo-American Relationship and World Politics in the Context of British and American Foreign-Policy-Making in the Twentieth Century* (Cambridge University Press, 1984).

Wedeen, Lisa, *Ambiguities of Domination: Politics, Rhetoric, and Symbols in Contemporary Syria* (University of Chicago Press, 1999)

Williams, Michael, *Realist Tradition and the Limits of International Relations* (Cambridge University Press, 2005).

Willis, Michael J., *Power and Politics in the Maghreb: Algeria, Tunisia and Morocco from Independence to the Arab Spring* (Hurst, 2012).

Wilson, Andrew, *Ukraine Crisis: What It Means for the West* (Yale University Press, 2014).

Wohlforth, William C., 'Realism and the End of the Cold War', *International Security* 19, no. 3 (Winter 1994–5).

Woodward, Bob, *Plan of Attack* (Simon & Schuster, 2004).

Wright, Lawrence, 'Crossroads: A Scholar of the Plague Thinks That Pandemics Wreak Havoc—and Open Minds', *New Yorker*, 20 July 2020.

Yergin, Daniel, *The Prize: The Epic Quest for Oil, Money & Power* (Free Press, 1991).

Zygar, Mikhail, *All the Kremlin's Men: Inside the Court of Vladimir Putin* (Public Affairs, 2016).

Primary and ancient sources

Aristotle, *Historia animalium*, trans. D.M. Balme (Cambridge University Press, 2011).

Haass, Richard, 'Prepared Statement to Committee on Foreign Relations', *United States Senate on Perspectives on the Crisis in Libya*, 6 April 2011.

BIBLIOGRAPHY

Hamilton, Alexander, 'Objections and Answers Respecting the Administration of the Government', Enclosure 5, *Hamilton Papers*, Library of Congress, 18 August 1792.

International Organization on Migration, 'Sirte Displacement: Top Ten Host Communities', Displacement Tracking Matrix, 20 July 2016.

International Republican Institute, 'Libya Poll: High Confidence in Legitimacy of Local Councils, Despite Poor Outreach by Local Governments', 9 November 2016.

Plato, *The Republic of Plato*, trans. Allan Bloom (Basic Books, 2016).

Polybius, *The Histories*, trans. Robin Waterfield (Oxford University Press, 2010).

United Nations, 'Final Report of the Panel of Experts on Libya regarding the Implementation of the Measures Related to the Arms Embargo, the Assets Freeze and the Travel Ban, Pursuant to resolution 1973 (2011), S/2015/128', 23 February 2015.

——— 'Libyan Political Agreement: As Signed on 17 December 2015'.

——— 'Letter Dated 8 March 2021 from the Panel of Experts on Libya Established Pursuant to Resolution 1973 (2011) Addressed to the President of the Security Council (S/2021/229)'.

UN Security Council, 'Report of the Secretary-General on the United National Support Mission in Libya,' 25 February 2016.

——— 'Resolution 2259 (2015)', 23 December 2015.

INDEX

INDEX

INDEX

INDEX

INDEX

Iraq War (2003–11) and US
  relations with, 12, 14
Islamic State, conflict with, 146
Italy, relations with, 53
Libyan Uprisings (2011), 20,
  21, 28, 29, 30, 31, 32, 33,
  34, 38
security forces, training of
  Libyans, 91, 96
Suez Crisis (1956), 9
free markets, 243, 245, 254,
  262–3, 268, 271, 283, 304–5,
  337, 339
free speech, 168–71
Freud, Sigmund, 308
Furjan tribe, 136, 138–9

G20, 344
G7, 4
G8, 97
Gallegos, Raul, 102, 231
game theory, 39, 79, 341
Gaub, Florence, 61
General Electricity Company of
  Libya (GECOL), 218, 220,
  221, 222, 286, 320, 323
General National Congress
  (GNC), 29, 59, 60, 67, 69–70,
  73, 74–9, 96, 172
appeasement by, 74–9
constitutional committee, rela-
  tions with, 60, 67, 78–9, 87
election (2012) of, 59, 67, 69,
  74, 78, 85, 178, 179
Islamic State and, 138

patronage politics and, 175–6
Political Isolation Law (2013)
  passed by, 60, 74, 78–9, 112,
  361
General People's Congress (GPC)
  under Qadhafi, 218
General Purpose Force (GPF),
  95–7
genocide, 18, 20
Gentiloni, Paolo, xxii, xxxv
Germany, xliii, xlvi, 12, 32, 313,
  330
Gharghour incident (2013), 71
al-Ghariyani, Sadiq, 184
Gharyan, 196
ghost ship metaphor, 332, 344
GIZ, 35
global financial crisis (2008), xliv,
  356
global governance, 6
globalism, xl, 3, 52, 103, 339,
  349–50
globalization, xl, xlix, 3, 13, 49,
  113, 122, 160, 224, 261, 265,
  339
Covid pandemic and, 40, 41
hacking of, 246
money flows and, 260
myths about, 211–12, 214, 256,
  261
neo-populism and, 8, 122
social media and, 260
Goldman Sachs Affair, 247
Gómez, Juan Vicente, 100
Gorka, Sebastian, 124

506

INDEX

INDEX

INDEX

INDEX

INDEX

INDEX

INDEX

National Security Council (US),
11
national sovereignty, 6–8, 340
National Transitional Council
(NTC), 18, 20, 30–32, 172,
225, 362
    appeasement and, 59, 64, 65–7,
        70, 72, 73, 74, 77–8, 80, 82
    eastern region and, 86
    economic model of, 225
    patronage politics and, 175
nationalism, 181–2, 334, 339
    Arab nationalism, 57, 116, 169,
        173, 174
natural gas, 82, 193, 239–40
Navy SEALs, 90, 121
Nawasi Brigade, 85
Nawfaliya, 139
negative unity, 173
neo-colonialism, 39, 326
neo-liberalism, 211, 213–14,
    256–7, 261–2, 268–9
neo-mercantilism, 46, 105, 262,
    269, 280, 284, 295, 309, 328,
    329, 331, 332, 333
neo-populism, *see* populism
Netanyahu, Benjamin, 126, 204
New York City, New York, 261,
    309
Newtonian correction, to
    international system, 342, 347
Nigeria, 137, 154, 161, 245, 284
no-fly zones, 19, 20, *22*, 26, 27,
    28, 35, 64–5
non-governmental organizations
    (NGOs), 210

North Atlantic Treaty
    Organization (NATO), xxxix,
    6, 10, 28–9, 39, 64, 345, 347,
    362, 365
North Korea, xxxviii, l, 26, 90,
    222
Northern Ireland, 97
Northern, Richard, 28

O'Brien, Robert, 376
Obama, Barack, xxx, xlv, 14–16,
    21–8, 53, 96, 109, 149, 150,
    156, 364, 366–7, 369, 376, 378
Obiang, Teodoro, 307
Occidental, 301
Och-Ziff, 276
oil, 17, 20, 32, 40, 44, 57–8, 69,
    104, 172, 209, 267, 270,
    300–301
    blockades, 79, 99, 193–194,
        289, 300
    foreign investment, 224
    glut (2020) of, 99
    Islamic State and, 134, 138,
        142, 158
    Morning Glory incident (2014),
        90–91
    National Oil Corporation
        (NOC), 219, 221, 230, 274,
        286, 314, 318
    Petroleum Facilities Guard, 83,
        89, 148
    Qadhafi era (1969–2011),
        79–80, 356, 357
    rent seeking, 299, 303

516

INDEX

INDEX

INDEX

INDEX

INDEX

INDEX

INDEX

INDEX

INDEX